Car-free
Los Angeles
& Southern
California

CAR-FREE

LOS ANGELES
& SOUTHERN CALIFORNIA

Nathan Landau

 WILDERNESS PRESS . . . *on the trail since 1967*

Car-free Los Angeles & Southern California

1st EDITION 2011

Front cover photo copyright © by Hemis/Alamy; back cover photo copyright © by Richard Broadwell/Alamy
Interior photos, except where noted, by Nathan Landau
Maps: Lohnes+Wright
Cover design: Scott McGrew
Interior design and layout: Annie Long
Editor: Amber Kaye Henderson

ISBN 978-0-89997-656-3

Manufactured in the United States of America

Published by: **Wilderness Press**
c/o Keen Communications
PO Box 43673
Birmingham, AL 35243
(800) 443-7227
info@wildernesspress.com
www.wildernesspress.com

Visit our website for a complete listing of our books and for ordering information.
Distributed by Publishers Group West

Frontispiece: Amtrak's Pacific Surfliner; *front cover:* Third Street Promenade, Santa Monica; *back cover:* Angels Flight funicular

Disclaimer
We remind you to maintain awareness and practice caution in all of the destinations described in this book just as you would when venturing to any unfamiliar location. Please also note that prices, hours, and public transportation routes can fluctuate over time, and that information often changes under the impact of many factors that influence the travel industry. We therefore suggest that you write or call ahead for confirmation when making your travel plans. Every effort has been made to ensure the accuracy of information throughout this book, and the contents of this publication are believed to be correct at the time of printing. Nevertheless, the publisher cannot accept responsibility for errors or omissions, for changes in details given in this guide, or for the consequences of relying on information provided by the same. Assessments of sites are based on the author's own experience; therefore, descriptions given in this guide necessarily contain an element of subjective opinion, which may not reflect the publisher's opinion or dictate a reader's own experience on another occasion.

■ contents

■ list of maps

i. introduction

■ 1 Traveling Car-free in Southern California

I FIRST EXPLORED LOS ANGELES AS A CAR-FREE TRAVELER. Somehow I hadn't gotten the memo that you could *not* visit Los Angeles on transit. It was 1984, and Los Angeles County voters had recently passed Proposition A, increasing funding for transit. No rail lines existed yet, but buses were plentiful and cheap. I stayed at a residential hotel in Beverly Hills and took the Santa Monica and Wilshire Boulevard buses to the Mark Taper theater and to Santa Monica beach. I found a café in Beverly Hills that would let me nurse a coffee for hours. I read Rodney Steiner's *Los Angeles: The Centrifugal City,* which explained and mapped how Los Angeles had grown.

It was a great trip and I was smitten. I had gained an unshakable belief that LA is a great, fascinating—and transit-accessible—city.

What This Book Is About

This book is designed to be a complete guide to a car-free vacation in Southern California, from the time you arrive here until the time you leave. *Car-free Los Angeles and Southern California* tells you how to get from the airport—or the train or bus station—into town. If you already live in Los Angeles or elsewhere in Southern California, this book tells you how to plug into the transit network and start traveling car-free to the fun places.

I also list good places to stay that are transit accessible and tell you about the terrific things to see in Southern California and how to get there. Whether your sightseeing tastes run to beaches or museums or shopping—or something else altogether—this book will get you there. It guides you to good places to eat or places to buy groceries. Southern California neighborhoods have so many good restaurants and cafés that this book can only give you a sampling of them. And when it's time to leave, you can look back at the directions to the airport.

The difference between this guidebook and other guidebooks is that it doesn't assume you need to have tons of personal steel—a car—with you to travel. This book assumes that you're curious enough and savvy enough, and maybe green enough, to travel by train, by bus, on foot, and by bike. Most of the time it's not even that hard. (You may not wish to reveal this, so you can retain more street cred from your "incredibly arduous" Southern California transit trip.)

I've made sure that the car-free trips in this book are possible by taking them myself. Since that first trip, I've continued to travel car-free in Southern California, long before I planned to write a book about it. I've gone car-free to every community in the book and traveled between them. I've taken the buses and trains morning, noon, and night. I don't recommend that you take a trip unless I'm willing to take it myself. You too can head out without a car in the world.

I Want Feedback from You

Feedback from you can make this a better book in the future. Tell me about your car-free trip in Southern California—how it worked, when it went well, and when it didn't. Tell me about other car-free places you discovered, or tell me if my description missed the mark. E-mail your comments and thoughts to **landorf1@gmail.com.**

Car-free Travel Can Be Done

The most important thing to know about car-free travel in Southern California is that, yes, it can be done. Many visitors travel car-free in SoCal every day, many of them saying that the transit they encounter

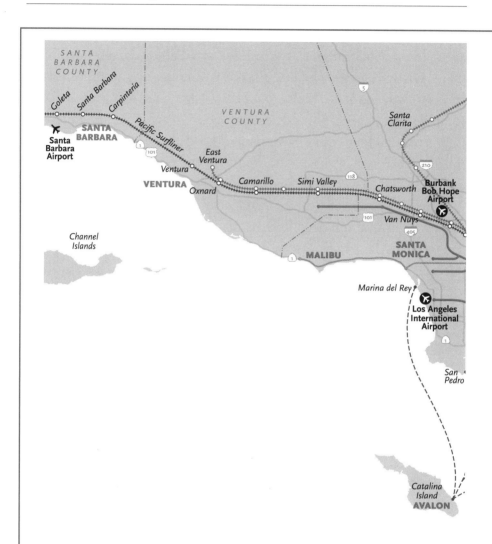

Pacific Ocean

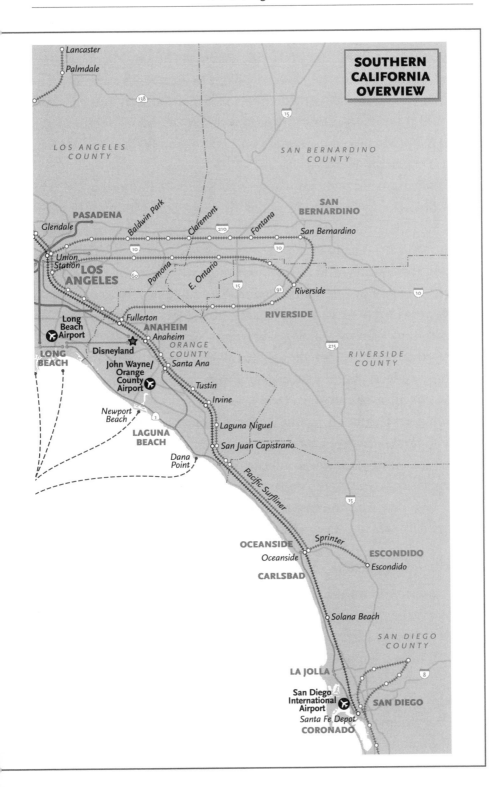

in Los Angeles is as good as or better than elsewhere in the United States. (Visitors from American cities such as Detroit, Miami, Dallas, Houston, and Phoenix are especially likely to notice LA's superior transit.) You can stroll the scented streets of Santa Barbara. You can take light rail through the beautiful Arroyo Seco to Pasadena. You can zip out to Santa Monica on an express bus. You can walk the streets of San Diego's buzzing downtown.

Public transportation networks cross Southern California. You can go to SoCal's big destinations—Los Angeles, Santa Monica, Disneyland, San Diego, and Santa Barbara. You can travel between these cities on Amtrak's Pacific Surfliner—the second-busiest intercity train route in the country. You can get around locally once you get to these places. To some people's amazement, Los Angeles has a subway—a subway that happens to be very useful to visitors. Santa Barbara has electric shuttle buses. Ferries take you to Catalina. Buses are everywhere. You can go to beaches, theme parks, great streets, museums, theaters, concert halls, historic buildings, hundreds of hotels, and thousands of restaurants.

Southern California was in fact first built on railroads. Steam railroads allowed farmers, factory workers, and Midwesterners fleeing their winters to move in. Electric interurban railways made it possible for hundreds of thousands of people to buy homes along the routes. Hundreds of trolley cars converged on Downtown LA daily. Before it was swarmed by cars, LA was on track.

Travel Cheaper, Calmer, and Cleaner

So it's possible to travel car-free in Southern California. Still, why do it? Why buck the conventional wisdom?

Car-free travel is cheaper, less stressful, and better environmentally, and it provides you with more opportunities to exercise as you walk to and from bus stops and train stations. (I've long thought that using transit helps you get you more exercise, and now researchers have proved it with a group of people who switched to using light rail in Charlotte, North Carolina.)

CAR-FREE IS CHEAPER

A car-free traveler can get around Los Angeles for the cost of a $5 Metro day pass. Driving can easily cost 10 times that. When people think of the cost of driving on vacation, they usually think about the cost of car rental and parking. But that's only the beginning of it. Hotels have parking fees; most hotels in main visitor-oriented areas charge $10–$40 per day to park (not to mention tips to the valet). In many popular neighborhoods, the only reasonably accessible parking spaces, even at night, are pay spaces.

Many foreign visitors must get an additional insurance policy for driving in the United States. People younger than 21 find it very difficult to rent a car, and people younger than 25 pay a substantial premium. When you add it all up, driving can get very expensive. For a middle-aged American staying in a mid-range hotel in Los Angeles, typical auto costs might easily be $30 per day for car rental, $20 for hotel parking, $5 for gas, and $5 for other parking, or $60 total per day. That's 12 times the cost of a Metro day pass.

CAR-FREE IS CALMER

Someone else is doing the driving, and you don't have to stress. As a driver, you'd face Los Angeles's traffic jams, rated worst in the United States. Traffic jams here aren't just limited to rush hour but can stretch on through most of the day on various freeways and even on surface (non-freeway) streets. I've been on LA streets where I was able to walk faster than traffic for blocks at a time. It's not an enjoyable visitor experience. When the street isn't congested, too many Angelenos drive unnervingly—speeding, jamming on the brakes at the light, or turning without an inch to spare. Britons, Australians, and New Zealanders can find it particularly difficult to adjust to driving in America because they are used to driving on the other side of the road. A car-free traveler can just sit back and sightsee.

CAR-FREE IS CLEANER

Buses in Southern California run on clean-burning compressed natural gas. The subway and light rail are electrically powered. There's no debate that driving an auto emits greenhouse gases and air pollutants.

The Port of Los Angeles and industry contribute to LA air pollution, but motor vehicles—cars and light trucks—are the major culprit. Despite the huge effort to clean up Southern California's air, it remains stubbornly smoggy and occasionally dangerous. No individual can solve this, of course, but car-free travelers are at least not contributing to it.

Practicalities of Coming to Southern California

Note: *The information in this book, such as prices and transit service, is accurate as of publication. But things change, especially prices and transit timetables. You should always check transit routes and schedules with current information.*

CLIMATE

Coastal Southern California has the much-prized Mediterranean climate. Winters are cool and relatively wet, while summers are warm-hot and dry. Typical winter temperatures range 40°F–70°F (5°C–20°C, respectively), while typical summer temperatures range 55°F–85°F (13°C–30°C, respectively). The weather gets gradually warmer as you go south. However, the biggest climatic difference is between the cooler, foggy coast and warmer inland areas. Inland Los Angeles will typically be hotter than more southerly coast-side San Diego. In July the difference between Santa Monica and Downtown Los Angeles, a mere 15 miles away, is likely to be some 10°F.

Most of Southern California is semiarid or, in the desert, fully arid. Los Angeles typically receives only 13 inches (32 centimeters) of rain per year. Visitors will almost never encounter rain in the summer. In the winter rain is a possibility but not likely on most days. Snow is only found in the mountains in the winter and spring. In California, the snow doesn't fall where most people live; we go to the snow.

ACCEPTABLE DRESS

Southern California is known for casual dress, but people do dress up more for evening activities than they do for daytime recreation. Locals don't routinely wear just bathing suits off the beach, except sometimes in less urban areas right next to the beach. Suits and men's jackets are generally reserved for work, though you wouldn't feel out of place wearing a jacket to the symphony or larger-scale theater. If you go to a higher-quality restaurant, men usually won't need to wear a suit (though you could if you wanted), but don't wear torn shorts either. Sunglasses are very common and are actually useful, not just ornamental, in the strong sunlight of Southern California summer.

Hotels and Motels in Southern California

There's not a sharp distinction between hotels and motels in Southern California. You'll find them listed and discussed together. Motor inns—essentially better-grade motels with more facilities—particularly blur the line. Hotels tend to be larger and have more facilities, though motor inns may have, for example, a restaurant on-site. But it may be worth your while, especially in Los Angeles, to pick your way across the parking lot of a well-located motel in order to save serious dollars.

Bed-and-breakfasts (B&Bs) are a form of lodging adapted from the English B&B, though more upscale. American B&Bs are usually homes modified for use as small hotels, typically with 2–10 guest rooms. Breakfast, served either communally or individually, is part of the B&B rate. While many hotel breakfasts are pretty minimal, some B&Bs pride themselves on their hot, hearty, tasty fare.

Southern California does not have as many B&Bs as, say, New England does. But B&Bs are often located in neighborhoods with few or no hotels, such as Silver Lake in Los Angeles, so they provide a chance to stay in otherwise inaccessible locations. Many, though not all, B&Bs are located on historic properties.

B&Bs generally require reservations, many of which require long notice (for example, 7 days) to cancel. Many B&Bs discourage stays by families with children (outright prohibiting children is generally illegal) and typically provide only one bed per room. Guests often enjoy B&Bs for their interaction with the innkeepers and other guests.

For specific hotel listings, please see the chapters on each city and neighborhood.

HOTEL RESERVATIONS

In general, it's best to have hotel reservations for the length of your trip when you arrive. Otherwise, you run the risk of having no place to stay or having to accept seriously inferior, or expensive lodgings, especially during summer high season or busy times. The risk of booking something you can't use is low—most reservations can be cancelled until close to their effective date, on the date itself, or 24–48 hours ahead. If you're hoping for a better deal, check hotel and other websites every week or so and see if a better deal materializes; it just might.

Some reservations can't be canceled without penalty—these include hotel reservations at special, nonrefundable, advance purchase rates. Reservations made through bidding services such as Hotwire or Priceline also can't be canceled without a penalty. I'm personally reluctant to make nonrefundable reservations, but go ahead and do it if you're very sure of your plans, or if you're willing to pay extra for trip insurance (in which case, are you still saving money?).

HOTEL RATES

Except when hotels are offering special promotions (for example, in winter in San Diego), only motels will charge less than $100 per night. Mid-range three-star hotels in Los Angeles will generally fall somewhere between $100 and $200. In some cases, the lowest rates may only be available to members of specific groups (for example, AARP or AAA). Check websites of the hotel, hotel chains, and hotel discounters (such as Expedia), and/or call the hotels for potential discounts.

In this book, hotels are categorized by price as follows. This is based on the hotel's pre-tax room rate, exclusive of any special add-on charges.

$	Less than $100/night
$$	$100–$149/night
$$$	$150–199/night
$$$$	$200–$299/night
$$$$$	$300 and more/night

HOTEL AMENITIES

■ *Exercise Rooms*

Most hotels will have a fitness center with a few exercise machines, and sometimes more extensive facilities. Some hotels have access to nearby health clubs at reduced rates, so ask the hotel if you're interested.

■ *Business Centers*

Most hotels will have a business center or at least a computer with Internet access and a printer. You're more likely to be charged for use of a business center in an upscale hotel than a moderate or budget motel. Even if there's no business center, virtually any hotel or motel will print out an airline boarding pass for free if you need them to.

■ *Food*

Larger hotels will almost always have a restaurant, sometimes more than one, or sometimes a restaurant and separate bar. Many motels that don't have a restaurant serve a continental breakfast, but often these are pretty minimal. Room service is confined to the more upscale hotels, though some hotels and motels have delivery arrangements with nearby restaurants. Hotel restaurants are usually, though not always, more expensive than other restaurants; room service is always pricey. In the past, people believed that hotel restaurants served inferior food to captive audiences, but now many hotel eateries are top-notch and cater to the city as a whole as well as to the hotel guests.

■ *Swimming Pools*

Usable swimming pools in hotels are less common than exercise rooms. Trendy hotels will often have pools, though they're typically designed more for lounging than swimming. Some motels also have little decorative pools. Pools seem somewhat more common in San Diego, which is overall warmer than Los Angeles. Almost all Southern California hotel pools are outdoors, with rare exceptions (for example, the Biltmore and the Los Angeles Athletic Club in Downtown Los Angeles). For an indoor lap swimming pool, head to a YMCA. Spas are becoming increasingly common in the fancier hotels, though you will pay dearly to use them.

■ *Pets*

Hotels' policies on pets are quite varied, from full inclusion to full exclusion. Size limits and fees to bring pets are fairly common. Some even offer pet turndown service with pet treats in the evening. Always check with the hotel if you're planning to bring a pet.

■ *Smoking*

Virtually all hotels will have nonsmoking rooms; nonsmoking floors are also very common. Some hotels are completely nonsmoking. Check the hotel's website if you're looking for that. At this point in California, smokers more than nonsmokers need to check a hotel's smoking policy.

■ *Laundry*

While you're here, you have several possible methods for doing laundry. Washing clothes in your room is the cheapest option, and some hotels put a retractable clothesline above the bathtub to facilitate this. Some budget-to-moderate hotels and motels, as well as extended stay hotels, have laundry machines in the building. You will rarely see them in other upscale hotels. Self-serve Laundromats are located near many urban hotels and motels. Many Laundromats or dry cleaners will wash laundry and return it in about a day. It's more expensive than a Laundromat, but you don't have to spend your vacation time sitting around a Laundromat, and it's a lot cheaper than using the hotel. Upscale hotels will typically pick up clothes for a cleaning for very high fees, often several dollars per item, so you probably don't want to do this for most of your clothing.

■ *Other Amenities*

In-room safes are pretty standard in all but very bottom-end properties.

One less common but useful feature for car-free travelers is free town car service, where the hotel will drive you to nearby destinations. This might be available in a specified area. For example, the Omni Hotel in Downtown LA will take patrons to destinations within 3 miles.

Car-free Travel with Children

People sometimes wonder if they can travel car-free with a child or children. Of course you can. You'll see lots of children on the buses and trains in Southern California. Some children will enjoy the adventure of traveling on a train or bus. Children also might appreciate being able to talk to a parent when he or she doesn't have to concentrate on driving.

If you have a child in a stroller, it's best to bring a fold-up stroller rather than a full-size one, which could be awkward on crowded buses or trains. Some rides may be long from a child's perspective, so bring along whatever you use to distract your children—small toys, books, and so on—and you're good to go.

Disabled and Mobility-impaired Access

By law, Southern California transit systems are completely wheelchair accessible. Subway stations have elevators, light rail stations have ramps, and buses have ramps or lifts. Older buses "kneel" to get closer to the ground, while newer buses are low floor (close to the ground) and easily boarded. As you'll see, the system is widely used by disabled and mobility-impaired people.

Medical Care

For Americans traveling to Southern California, it's a good idea to check up on the provisions that your health insurance makes for out-of-area health care. Foreigners are advised to buy travelers' health insurance. American health care fees are often shocking to people from elsewhere in the world. Despite the recent passage of the health care reform bill, no comprehensive system of health care exists in the United States, so you could be presented with a bill for hundreds or thousands of dollars.

Reasons to Go to Southern California

The various Southern California destinations offer different attractions and amenities.

Go to **central Los Angeles** for almost everything: for the big city, the real city, the epicenter of pop culture (Hollywood), the epicenter of conspicuous consumption (Beverly Hills), a resurgent downtown, a historic pueblo (El Pueblo de Los Angeles), a theme park (Universal Studios), trendy shopping streets, studio tours, special film programs, live theater, TV tapings, music (popular, jazz, and classical), ethnic neighborhoods, trendy neighborhoods, gay neighborhoods, great restaurants of almost every nationality and description, foodie temples of varietal coffee, cool bars and hot clubs, surprisingly walkable neighborhoods, lovely historic districts, unusual contemporary architecture, great art museums, cutting-edge art galleries, science museums, and a funicular (Angels Flight). This city is much more than people think it is.

Visit the **Westside of Los Angeles** for the LA you see in those glamorous movies, the hip city, and life in the dream factory—for beaches and beachside walks; for special films, live theater, art museums and a museum of culture (UCLA Fowler), and an art park (Bergamot Station); for restaurants—fine dining and otherwise (some with celebrity sightings)—and groovy bars; for a pedestrian street (Third Street Promenade) and a fine walking downtown around it; for an amusement pier; for the shopping and much more shopping; and for the golden city of the silver screen.

Go to **Long Beach** for a different slice of Southern California: for a historic ship (the *Queen Mary*), a large aquarium, and a close-up view of one of the world's biggest harbors.

You know why to go to **Disneyland**—your inner child (or your outer children) demands it!

Visit **Laguna Beach,** a jewel box little town on the coast, for beaches, a lovely little downtown, an art scene, some gay life, good restaurants, and a vision of the sweet life.

Go to **Catalina Island** for a unique locale in SoCal, a place you reach by ferry, not on a road; for island relaxation (almost totally car-free), a huge swath of protected nature, a cute little town, and a brand-new, wicked set of zip lines.

Travel to **San Diego** for a city with a calmer pace than Los Angeles—for beaches, the zoo, a marine mammal theme park (SeaWorld), a lively big city downtown, a Major League Baseball stadium, and actual ships as museums set on a working waterfront; for art, history, and culture museums in City Beautiful Balboa Park; and for a town dating back two centuries, a burgeoning restaurant scene, nationally renowned craft beer, and canyons to hike and bike right in the city.

Travel to **Santa Barbara** for as fine a resort city as you will find anywhere (billed as "America's most beautiful downtown"), a whole city of Mission-style buildings, a mission, beaches, wineries in town and not far away, restaurants (and taquerias) revived by local millionaires, a great little natural history museum, and a charming little zoo.

Getting to Los Angeles

If you come to Los Angeles without a car, your main choices are flying via Los Angeles International (LAX) or Bob Hope Burbank airports, taking an Amtrak train, or taking a Greyhound bus.

WHICH AIRPORT SHOULD I USE?

Many travelers won't have a choice—almost all international and transcontinental flights go into LAX. But if you're coming from the western United States, especially from the West Coast, you may have more options. You can choose based on where in Los Angeles you are initially headed to and leaving from.

LAX has good or reasonably good transit to and from all of the major visitor areas described in this book, except Hollywood. For the Westside—Santa Monica, Venice, and Westwood—nearby LAX is clearly the airport of choice.

Burbank Airport is more convenient for Hollywood, with a direct bus connection. It is also not bad for getting to Downtown Los Angeles, especially on weekdays. If you're going to Pasadena, LAX is somewhat easier, but Burbank is possible; for West Hollywood LAX is also preferred, but Burbank can be reasonable.

INTO LOS ANGELES FROM LOS ANGELES INTERNATIONAL AIRPORT

Los Angeles International Airport, universally referred to as LAX, its airport code, is old and crowded. But it is Southern California's only major international airport, with flights converging from all over the world, including the United States and California. LAX is 15 miles southwest of Downtown LA and 10 miles southeast of Santa Monica, in southwestern Los Angeles adjacent to the Pacific Ocean.

■ *To Downtown LA*

The best transit from LAX to Downtown LA is the **FlyAway bus (lawa. org)** to Union Station. They are bigger and more plush than city buses. After picking up at each airport terminal, the buses run nonstop on the freeway to Union Station, about a 40-minute trip, depending on traffic. They run every 30 minutes during most of the day; run 24 hours a day, 7 days a week; and cost $7. At Union Station, you can catch the Red Line subway and take it two stops to Pershing Square or three stops to 7th St./Metro Center station—most Downtown hotels are near those stations. Union Station also has connections to the Gold Line light rail and numerous bus routes.

■ *To Hollywood*

It's much easier to get to Hollywood from Burbank Airport (see page 19). But if you need to go from LAX, take the FlyAway to Union Station and catch the Red Line subway. Most Hollywood hotels are near the Hollywood Boulevard/Highland Avenue station; some are near the Hollywood Boulevard/Vine Street station. The Red Line ride will cost you an additional $1.50, for a total of $8.50.

■ *To Downtown Santa Monica*

Take the Lot C Shuttle from the terminal to the City Transit Center. There board Big Blue Bus 3. Bus 3 heads up Lincoln Boulevard, and then stops along Fourth Street, toward the eastern side of downtown Santa Monica. Midday it takes about 40 minutes. On weekdays before 10 a.m. and 3–8 p.m., take Big Blue Bus rapid 3, which is a bit faster. The fare is only 75 cents, or you can buy a $2.50 Big Blue Bus day pass.

■ *To Westwood*

FlyAway Westwood goes from the LAX terminals nonstop to 11075 Kinross Ave. in Westwood Village, conveniently located in front of a University of California, Los Angeles (UCLA) parking structure but also near the Wilshire Boulevard/Westwood Avenue transit hub. The FlyAway bus runs every hour on the hour from the airport, 6 a.m.–11 p.m. The fare is $10, payable on the bus with exact change, and travel time generally takes 25–45 minutes. You can also take Culver City Bus 6 (Sepulveda Boulevard) from the City Transit Center to Westwood Village, scheduled to take about 50 minutes at a fare of $1.

■ *To Eastern Santa Monica*

Follow the directions to downtown Santa Monica, and then at Santa Monica Boulevard, take rapid bus 704 Santa Monica Boulevard to your motel.

■ *To Long Beach*

Take the shuttle from the terminal to the Green Line (Aviation) light rail station. Take the Green Line east to Imperial Highway/Wilmington Avenue, about a 15-minute ride. Then transfer to the Blue Line southbound to the Long Beach Transit Mall, about a 30-minute ride. Bus 232 from the LAX transit center (accessed by the Lot C Shuttle) goes directly to Long Beach, but it takes a mind-numbing 1 hour and 40 minutes. I would do the extra transfer instead.

■ *To Disneyland*

John Wayne Orange County Airport is closer to Disneyland, but LAX has flights from a greater number of cities. Disneyland Express also operates from LAX to Disneyland hourly 7:30–10:30 a.m., with service offered every 30 minutes 10:30 a.m.–4:30 p.m. The fare is $20 one-way or $30 round-trip. A traffic-free trip takes about 45 minutes.

You can use regular transit from LAX to Disneyland, but it's a long ride. Take the G Shuttle (free) from the airport terminal to the Aviation Green Line station. Take the Green Line east to Norwalk, and then transfer to Metro 460 bus south to Disneyland. The time is about 2 hours and 15 minutes, and the fare is $2.50.

■ *To Santa Barbara*

From LAX, you can take the Santa Barbara Airbus—a comfortable over-the-road-style coach. It's about a 2.5-hour trip and the fare is $44. One problem is that the bus drops off in Santa Barbara at the Hyatt (the former Hotel Mar Monte), about 10 blocks east of the downtown core. During the day, the Waterfront shuttle will take you to the West Beach area.

■ *Other Transit from LAX*

The FlyAway buses also go to Van Nuys in the San Fernando Valley and Irvine in southern Orange County. Other LAX buses don't operate directly to the terminals—they go to the City Transit Center at the edge of the airport. You have to take the Lot C Shuttle to get there. From there, you can catch a bus to Torrance, Redondo Beach, and South Los Angeles.

INTO LOS ANGELES FROM BURBANK AIRPORT

Los Angeles is served not only by LAX but also by the Bob Hope Burbank Airport. (While away some time by deciding which actor LAX should be named after.) Burbank, a mere fraction of the size of LAX, has direct service to only a dozen cities. It's located some 15 miles northwest of Downtown Los Angeles in the San Fernando Valley. All cities with nonstop flights to Burbank, except New York and Dallas, are in the western or southwestern United States. But if you're coming from a West Coast or southwestern city, Burbank can be a good alternative.

■ *Ground Transport from Burbank*

Burbank Airport has a new, free service. They've contracted with Super-Shuttle to offer free rides from the airport to the North Hollywood Red Line station and the Downtown Burbank Metrolink station. Contact SuperShuttle at the shuttle island in front of the terminal for on-demand service from the airport, call (818) 558-3179 for pickup at both stations to reach the airport, or call (800) 224-7767 to make reservations. Information about regular transit service to North Hollywood is below.

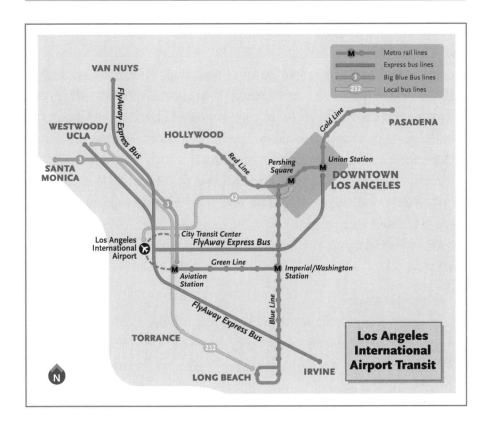

■ *To Hollywood*

Burbank is the most convenient airport if Hollywood is your destination. Catch a direct local bus (line 222) just outside the airport on Empire Way, about a 5-minute walk from the terminal. The bus takes about 30 minutes, though it only runs every 40 minutes.

During weekday morning and afternoon commute hours, Burbank Bus runs to the North Hollywood Red Line Metro station. From there you can easily go to Hollywood; it's just two or three stops on the subway.

■ *To Downtown LA*

On weekdays, getting from Burbank Airport to Downtown LA is reasonably convenient. Metrolink commuter rail and Amtrak service to Downtown LA are literally just outside the airport fence—you can walk from the terminal to the station in about 5 minutes. But the train schedule is very sporadic. Two trains could come within 20 minutes, but hours can go by with no service.

On weekdays, Metro rapid bus 794 now stops on Empire Avenue as well, but it takes about an hour to reach Downtown LA. Local bus 94 runs to Downtown LA on weekdays and weekends and takes about 1 hour and 10 minutes. I don't recommend taking the bus unless there's no Amtrak or Metrolink service and you can't easily reach North Hollywood station.

Again, during peak hours you can use the Burbank Bus to get to North Hollywood station, and then take the Red Line subway to Downtown LA, about a 30-minute ride.

On weekends, only the five Amtrak trains run; there's no Metrolink service.

■ To the Westside

Travel times from Burbank Airport to Santa Monica start at 97 minutes and go up from there, so avoid using Burbank Airport to or from the Westside. However, if you do this, take Metrolink or Amtrak from the Burbank Airport station to Union Station in Downtown Los Angeles, and then Big Blue Bus express 10 to Santa Monica (see page 24).

■ To Santa Barbara

Pacific Surfliner trains stop literally across the street from Burbank Airport. You can walk over from the airport terminal and catch one. It's about a 2-hour ride from Burbank Airport to Santa Barbara.

(NOT) FROM OTHER LOS ANGELES AREA AIRPORTS

The LA area has other airports, but you probably won't want to use them. A very small airport, mostly served by JetBlue, is located at Long Beach. It's useful primarily if you're heading straight to Long Beach (see Chapter 16). A larger airport east of the city at Ontario has no convenient transit into central Los Angeles. John Wayne Orange County Airport is most useful for reaching Disneyland and Orange County destinations, though scheduled bus service runs from LAX to Disneyland. There's no reason to use Orange County to reach Los Angeles destinations, and no convenient way to do that on transit.

Santa Barbara has a small commercial airport, with nonstop flights from eight cities: Denver, Los Angeles, Phoenix, Salt Lake City, Sacramento, San Francisco, San Jose, and Seattle. Theoretically, this ought to be a good quick way of reaching Santa Barbara, but fares even from Los Angeles are high, often hundreds of dollars. So flying there doesn't seem practical for most people. A better option is to fly through Burbank or LAX (see page 20 and page 18, respectively), and travel to Santa Barbara on the ground.

■ Transit from Long Beach Airport to Downtown Long Beach

Direct service from Long Beach Airport to downtown Long Beach is limited. There's only one bus route, Long Beach Transit 111, which runs every 30–40 minutes on weekdays, every 60 minutes on Saturday, and slightly less often on Sunday. There's also service from the airport to Willow station on the Blue Line light rail roughly every 30 minutes on weekdays. From there it's a quick ride on the Blue Line into downtown Long Beach.

■ Transit from John Wayne Orange County Airport to Disneyland

The fastest and easiest transit is on the Disneyland Express, direct from the airport to Disneyland. The service runs hourly, daily, 7–11 a.m., with service offered every 30 minutes 11 a.m.–3 p.m. It's about a 15- to 20-minute trip at times when it is not congested. The fare is $15 one-way or $25 round-trip. You can do this trip much more cheaply, but slowly, on the Orange County Transportation Authority's (OCTA) regular transit buses. Bus 76 serves the airport once an hour; take it to MacArthur Place and Harbor Boulevard in Fountain Valley. There, transfer to northbound bus 43 to Disneyland. The ride on bus 76 is about 30 minutes; the ride on bus 43 is about 40 minutes. The cost is $3 (two $1.50 fares), or you could spring for a $4 day pass.

LINDBERGH FIELD IN SAN DIEGO

If you're coming directly to San Diego from outside Southern California, you're probably flying into Lindbergh Field. If you're traveling within the U.S., you're probably flying to this airport directly. At least a smattering of flights comes from every major U.S. city, more from Northern California and the Pacific Northwest. You won't find flights from Burbank, Santa Barbara, or any other SoCal airport besides LAX. If you're coming from outside the U.S., and especially from outside North America, you may well be flying to another airport and then taking a connecting flight here.

Flying from Los Angeles to San Diego is not a reasonable option, even though there are some flights. The airlines charge hundreds of dollars for the 120-mile, 30-minute hop. You also lose a lot of time going out to LAX or another LA area airport. Take the train instead.

The airport is astonishingly close—3 miles—to downtown San Diego. Landing planes regularly seem to buzz downtown towers and Balboa Park. The good side is that it's an easy trip into the city. The bad news is that the airport is overcrowded and undersized for a metropolitan area of more than 3 million people. There have been efforts for decades to find a new location for an airport, with ideas as far-fetched as putting the airport in the middle of San Diego Bay.

■ *To Downtown San Diego*

San Diego essentially offers one public bus from the airport. Bus 992 zips into downtown via Harbor Drive and Broadway, ending at Horton Plaza (Fourth Street and Broadway), a roughly 15-minute trip. The bus runs approximately 5 a.m.–11 p.m., every 15 minutes on weekdays until 7 p.m., and then every 30 minutes. It's been cut back to every 30 minutes on Saturday and Sunday. The fare is $2.25, but if you expect to use the bus or trolley that day, buy a $5 day pass, which you can do on the bus.

If your destination is outside downtown, you can connect to other transit at Fourth Street and Broadway. You can take bus 30 to Pacific Beach in about 30 minutes or to La Jolla, which takes almost an hour. You can catch bus 901 to Coronado. The Blue Line Trolley will take you on a quick, four-stop run to Old Town.

TIJUANA AIRPORT TO SAN DIEGO

Almost all flights from within Mexico land at Tijuana rather than San Diego airport. Volaris Airlines offers hourly shuttle service from Tijuana

Airport to the downtown San Diego Greyhound station for its own customers. Aeromexico, the other main airline serving Tijuana Airport, also provides transport into San Diego.

INTO SOUTHERN CALIFORNIA VIA AMTRAK TRAINS

Amtrak can bring you to LA from San Francisco, Sacramento, San Jose, Santa Barbara, or San Diego, though some locations also require a bus connection. Los Angeles's main train service is the Pacific Surfliner with service from San Luis Obispo (2 trains a day each way) through Santa Barbara (5 trains a day) and Los Angeles to San Diego (12 trains a day). The five daily San Joaquin trains connect Oakland (with connections to San Francisco) and Fresno with Bakersfield; some trips start in Sacramento.

One train a day—the Coast Starlight—comes all the way down the West Coast from Seattle and Portland through the mountains and Sacramento, past Oakland and San Jose down to Santa Barbara and Los Angeles. It's a scenic route, but the trip from the Bay Area takes about 12 hours, far longer than the San Joaquin route (or Greyhound).

Amtrak also has a train a day from Los Angeles to Albuquerque, Kansas City, and Chicago—sort of the Route 66 run. Three times a week the Sunset Limited goes to Palm Springs, Phoenix, San Antonio, Houston, and New Orleans.

TRANSIT FROM UNION STATION

Because Union Station is a main transit hub (referred to often in this book) located on the northeastern edge of Downtown LA, it's easy to get from there to other parts of LA and Southern California.

■ *To Downtown LA*

To Downtown hotels, take the Red Line subway two or three stops—a very short ride—to Pershing Square or 7th St./Metro Center station. It's possible to do this by walking, but it's more than 1 mile and requires crossing a freeway on an overpass. It's much easier to take the train or a cab.

■ *To Hollywood*

To Hollywood hotels, take the Red Line subway farther to the Hollywood Boulevard/Highland Avenue station. A few hotels are near the station before—Hollywood Boulevard/Vine Street.

■ *To Santa Monica*

Take Big Blue Bus express 10, which makes the trip in just about an hour, longer in rush hour. It's important to know that you don't catch bus 10 at Patsaouras Transit Plaza, where most Union Station buses are, but behind it, on Cesar Chavez Avenue and Vignes Street. The fare is $1.75; a Big Blue Bus day pass including this express is $3.50.

The last trip to Santa Monica on bus 10 leaves about 8:40 p.m., so if you have an on-time 9 p.m. arrival on the Coast Starlight, you'll have to take the Venice Boulevard rapid bus 733 (board it at Patsaouras Transit Plaza). The rapid is scheduled to also take about an hour in the later evenings.

■ *To Westwood*

This is a case where you'll save a good deal of time by transferring. Take a Purple Line train (in the subway marked Red Line) to Wilshire Boulevard and Western Avenue, the end of the line. Transfer to rapid bus 720 Wilshire Boulevard heading west, and you should make it in about 55 minutes.

■ *To Eastern Santa Monica*

Take Big Blue Bus express 10 from Cesar Chavez Avenue and Vignes Street, and get off at Yale Street or 20th Street along Santa Monica Boulevard.

■ *To Disneyland*

Take the Pacific Surfliner Amtrak to Fullerton, a better connecting point than Anaheim. Then take Orange County Transit Authority (OCTA) bus 43 down Harbor Boulevard to Disneyland.

■ *To Laguna Beach*

From Los Angeles take the Pacific Surfliner or Metrolink from Union Station to Santa Ana station. From there, take OCTA bus 83 to the

Laguna Hills Transit Center, the end of the line (it's at the back of a shopping center). At Laguna Hills, take OCTA bus 89 to the Laguna Beach bus station, the end of that line. From Union Station, it's approximately a 2.5-hour trip.

From San Diego take the Amtrak Surfliner to San Juan Capistrano station, near the Mission. From there, take OCTA bus 91 a short ride to Pacific Coast Highway and Del Obispo Street. On PCH, transfer to the northbound OCTA bus 1. Bus 1 makes multiple stops along PCH in Laguna Beach, so you can get off at the stop closest to your hotel.

■ *To San Diego*

The Pacific Surfliner trains come down from Santa Barbara with more trips starting at Los Angeles Union Station and stopping at Anaheim and Santa Ana and other Orange County stations. From LA to San Diego the service is almost hourly. The Surfliners are comfortable, not really speedy, and have good views of the ocean, especially between San Juan Capistrano station and Solana Beach station. A snack bar sells many foods with lots of petrochemicals (you only get real dining cars on long-distance trains such as the Coast Starlight). Amtrak's current Los Angeles to San Diego one-way base fare is $36.

The trains arrive at Santa Fe Depot, at Broadway and Kettner Boulevard, near the western edge of downtown San Diego. You can easily walk to the downtown core hotels, though the Gaslamp Quarter and East Village hotels start to be a bit far with luggage. A Blue Line Trolley stop is literally on the platform—if you're staying in Little Italy, you can take it one stop toward Old Town and shorten your walk. The Orange Line stops across the street at America Plaza. Take it toward 12th Street and Imperial Highway and get off at your waterfront hotel. Downtown San Diego buses stop on Broadway, though not all routes go all the way west to Kettner.

■ *To Santa Barbara*

The most comfortable way to get from Los Angeles to Santa Barbara is on Amtrak's Pacific Surfliner trains, with five round-trips a day from Los Angeles Union Station. Four of those trips start in San Diego, so you can ride directly from San Diego or the Disneyland area. All of the trains stop in the San Fernando Valley at Glendale, Burbank Airport, Van Nuys, and Chatsworth.

It's about a 2.5-hour train trip from Los Angeles to Santa Barbara. Between Ventura and Carpinteria lies a pretty stretch of track along undeveloped coastline, closer to the beach than the highway. The Santa Barbara Amtrak station at 209 State St. is well-located two blocks from the beach and a few blocks from the core of downtown Santa Barbara. The one-way non-discounted fare from Los Angeles is $23.

TRAINS FROM OTHER AREAS OF CALIFORNIA

■ *To San Diego*
From San Bernardino and Riverside you can take an Inland Empire–Orange County Metrolink train, and connect to the Surfliner at Santa Ana. The trains arrive at Santa Fe Depot, at Broadway and Kettner Boulevard, near the western edge of downtown San Diego. You can easily walk to the downtown core hotels, though the Gaslamp Quarter and East Village hotels start to be a bit far with luggage. A Blue Line Trolley stop is literally on the platform—if you're staying in Little Italy, you can take it one stop toward Old Town and shorten your walk. The Orange Line stops across the street at America Plaza. Take it toward 12th Street and Imperial Highway and get off at your waterfront hotel. Downtown San Diego buses stop on Broadway, though not all routes go all the way west to Kettner.

■ *To Santa Barbara*
The Coast Starlight is a once-a-day train from San Jose, Oakland, Sacramento, and points north all the way to Portland and Seattle (San Francisco requires a connection) that stops in Santa Barbara. Amtrak has also stitched together other itineraries from Sacramento, Oakland, and San Jose using a combination of trains in the Bay Area, Thruway buses, and Pacific Surfliners. You'll need to make a reservation for the trip, and current fares vary $48–$70 from the Bay Area.

INTO SOUTHERN CALIFORNIA VIA GREYHOUND BUS STATIONS

You might use a Greyhound bus to get to Southern California because it serves more places than Amtrak. Like Amtrak, Greyhound has fairly frequent service to and from San Francisco, Sacramento, Santa Barbara, and San Diego. Greyhound has numerous buses to Las Vegas, where no passenger rail service exists. The Greyhound trips from San Diego actually originate in Tijuana, where you can connect to buses from various parts of Mexico.

Greyhound buses have well-padded seats and restrooms in the back, but obviously don't give you much chance to move around. On long trips they do make occasional rest stops, usually at fast food outlets. Some people dislike Greyhound's patrons, but I haven't experienced any problems. Travel times are usually comparable to the train, and fares are generally lower.

■ *From the Los Angeles Station to Downtown and Hollywood*

Greyhound's spartan main Los Angeles station is inconveniently located on the southeastern industrial edge of Downtown LA. It's at 1716 E. Seventh St., a couple of blocks east of Alameda Street. The neighborhood isn't unsafe, but it is on the far side of Skid Row from the Downtown Core, so you probably won't want to walk. Greyhound is a good 1.5 miles east of the Downtown Core.

Metro bus 60 stops right by the station and goes Downtown. Rapid bus 760 stops at Seventh and Alameda streets and also heads Downtown. You can connect at Seventh and Hope streets to the Red Line subway to Hollywood at 7th St./Metro Center station and to other Downtown transit routes.

■ *From the Hollywood Station*

Greyhound also has a small station conveniently located for Hollywood at 1715 N. Cahuenga Blvd., just north of Hollywood Boulevard. Some, but not all, of the buses to Santa Barbara, San Francisco, and other destinations to the north stop at Hollywood. Southbound buses to San Diego don't come here. If you take Greyhound to Hollywood, use this station if you can.

■ From the Los Angeles Station to the Westside

Use the (Downtown) Los Angeles Greyhound station because none of the other stations have any connections to the Westside. The one-time Santa Monica Greyhound station is many years gone and has been turned into a Fred Segal clothing store.

From Greyhound, the directions are the same for Beverly Hills, Westwood, or Santa Monica. Head west out of Greyhound on Seventh Street, crossing Alameda Street. Turn right on Central Avenue and walk up to Sixth Street, which is actually a couple of blocks. This is primarily industrial terrain, but I'd feel OK about this 10-minute walk in the daytime, not so good at night. Then catch rapid bus 720 Wilshire Boulevard westward for a trip of about 45 minutes to Beverly Hills, but easily 85 minutes to downtown Santa Monica.

At night, don't do that walk—take bus 60 across from the terminal to Fifth and Figueroa streets in the financial district. Then walk back two blocks along Fifth Street to the rapid bus 720 stop between Grand Avenue and Flower Street. Or you could take a cab at least to this point. I would recommend spending your first night in Downtown LA instead of trying to make your way all the way across the city on your first night.

■ From the Los Angeles Station or Tijuana Station to San Diego

Greyhound runs 19 buses to San Diego over the course of the day, maintaining hourly service for much of it. Greyhound stops at fewer intermediate points than Amtrak, but each bus itinerary is slightly different. Some trips stop at Compton, a number stop at Long Beach, some at Anaheim and Santa Ana, many at Oceanside, and so on.

Greyhound's San Diego station is well located in the heart of downtown, at First Avenue and Broadway, behind the Sofia Hotel. Greyhound's standard Los Angeles to San Diego fare is $29.

Much travel within Mexico is by intercity bus. In Tijuana the buses converge on the Tijuana Central Bus Station. From there you can take a Greyhound/Crucero bus to downtown San Diego. Another option is a cab ride from the bus terminal to the U.S. border, crossing the border on foot, and then getting on the Blue Line Trolley.

■ *From the Los Angeles Station to Santa Barbara*

Greyhound runs four buses a day from Los Angeles to Santa Barbara, although the schedule is a bit awkward. Greyhound stops in Hollywood and North Hollywood, making the trip easier from those areas. Travel times from Downtown LA Greyhound are similar to Amtrak. Fares range from $12 (with advance purchase) to $20.

■ *From Other Areas of California to Santa Barbara*

Greyhound buses head up US 101/El Camino Real corridor to Salinas— the connection for Monterey, Santa Cruz (a locale with no train service), San Jose, Oakland, and San Francisco. Fares to Oakland (for comparison purposes) range $35–$47.

If you're starting for Santa Barbara from anywhere else in the country or the world, get yourself to Los Angeles, and connect to Santa Barbara.

■ *Other Greyhound Stations*

On the Los Angeles–San Diego route, some buses stop at Long Beach or Compton. Some northbound buses also stop at North Hollywood (conveniently next to the Red Line subway and transit hub) and Glendale.

■ 2 Introduction to Los Angeles

LOS ANGELES IS ONE OF THE WORLD'S GREAT CITIES. For better or for worse, no other place in the world has been more important culturally for the last 60 years. Los Angeles has constantly reinvented itself, moving from frontier outpost to seaside playground to industrial giant to suburban garden to urban, cosmopolitan city. Everyone knows about the movie business here, but Los Angeles is also the nation's largest port, one of its largest manufacturing centers, and home to the largest concentration of government employees west of Washington, D.C. More than 36% of LA County's residents are foreign-born, coming not only from Mexico and El Salvador but also Taiwan, India, and even Africa, making Los Angeles one of the most cosmopolitan places in America. The variety within Los Angeles is hard to overstate.

How to See Los Angeles

Los Angeles, as you might have heard, is a big place. The city of Los Angeles alone is big geographically—more than 470 square miles (more than 1,200 square kilometers). It's big in population, with some 3.8 million residents. Dozens of other cities in greater Los Angeles add millions more to the population and hundreds more square miles.

When people in Los Angeles talk about "Los Angeles" or "LA," they usually mean something different from the city (or county) of Los Angeles, different from the vast Los Angeles metropolitan area. People's

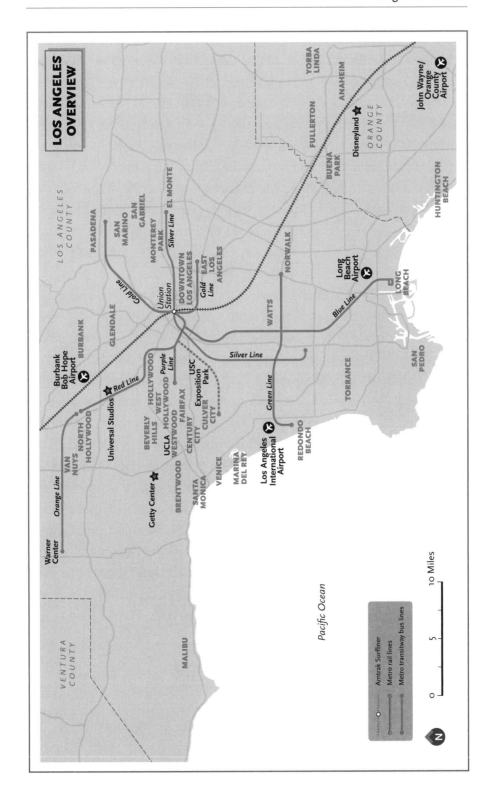

views may differ, but typically Los Angeles includes roughly the area from the Pacific Ocean inland to the San Gabriel River east of Pasadena, from the San Fernando Valley on the north to about the 91 freeway on the south. This includes most, but not all, of the city of Los Angeles, and it includes a number of separate cities as well—such as Santa Monica, Beverly Hills, West Hollywood, Pasadena, Monterey Park, and others.

But more important to travelers, the part of Los Angeles with visitor destinations is very large too. The main area of what I call the "visitors' city" is some 15 miles (25 kilometers) long, stretching from Downtown Los Angeles by the Los Angeles River to Santa Monica by the Pacific Ocean. In New York, the similar zone is about 7 miles long, and in San Francisco it's no more than 5 miles.

In most American cities a visitor can stay downtown and expect to find most sights fairly close at hand. Not in Los Angeles. The most popular sights in LA include the cultural palaces of Downtown, the stars (on the sidewalk) in Hollywood, the store displays of Beverly Hills, and the waves on the beach, all widely separated. Top museums are found anywhere from Pasadena to Brentwood, leading live theaters from Downtown to Venice, and top shopping opportunities from Pasadena to Santa Monica. You could spend a whole enjoyable visit just in Downtown, Pasadena, or Santa Monica, but you'd only see a fraction of what the city has to offer.

So your touring strategy as a visitor, especially as a car-free visitor, needs to be different than it would be in other cities. In many cities, walking is the main method of transportation between different sights. Not in Los Angeles. Within neighborhoods you usually can and should walk, but walking doesn't work very well between neighborhoods. Even "nearby" areas can easily be 3 or 4 miles apart, and the miles in between can be dull on foot. To see a broad swath of the city, you will have to rely on the transit system.

Most Interesting Los Angeles Communities for Visitors

Fortunately, destinations are not spread randomly throughout this big zone. Three particularly important communities are simultaneously visitor destinations, places to stay, and transit hubs. Five additional communities contain a large share of LA's other destinations. Add two key corridors and you've captured even more of LA's destinations.

THE BIG THREE

Downtown Los Angeles, Hollywood, and Santa Monica are special places for any LA visitor but are particularly special for a car-free visitor. They have the most hotels and hotel rooms (except for the grim airport area). Many of the city's great museums, theaters, clubs, and shopping areas are within them. They are top transit hubs—with Downtown Los Angeles being the most important transit hub. Within these communities you can do many, if not all, of your trips by walking. Think of them as your three big anchor points in visitors' Los Angeles.

■ *Downtown Los Angeles*

Downtown LA is toward the eastern end of visitors' LA, though very much in the middle of the metropolitan area as a whole. Downtown was once left for dead but is now the center of new sports stadiums, entertainment venues, restaurants, museums, and even a cathedral—not to mention thousands of new residents. Downtown hotels are mostly business-oriented, but an increasing number of leisure travelers stay there as well. Downtown is served by dozens of transit, mostly bus, lines. Its top transit corridors are the Red and Purple lines subway, the Gold Line light rail, the Blue Line light rail (Long Beach Boulevard corridor), rapid bus 720 Wilshire Boulevard, bus 2 Sunset Boulevard, and bus 16 Third Street.

■ *Hollywood*

Hollywood the industry is spread widely throughout the region, but Hollywood the neighborhood, which is within the city of Los Angeles, is some 7 miles northwest of Downtown at the base of the Hollywood Hills. Hollywood has come roaring back as the city's entertainment district with movies, live theaters, bars, clubs, and more. Hollywood hotels are usually more affordable than Downtown's or Santa Monica's. Hollywood's key transit corridors are the Red Line subway and bus routes on

Hollywood Boulevard (bus 180/181 and rapid bus 780), Sunset Boulevard (bus 2), and Fairfax Avenue (bus 217 and rapid bus 780).

■ *Santa Monica*

Where the city meets the ocean, 15 miles west of Downtown, Santa Monica is a separate city bordered by the city of Los Angeles. The area is known for a pedestrian-only shopping street, a throwback amusement pier, fine dining, the region's best air quality, and pro-tenant politics. Santa Monica has numerous hotels catering to both leisure and business travelers. Its key transit corridors are Santa Monica Boulevard with Metro rapid bus 704 and Santa Monica Big Blue Bus 1, Wilshire Boulevard with Metro rapid bus 720 and Big Blue Bus 2, and Pico Boulevard with Big Blue Bus 7.

FIVE MORE GREAT COMMUNITIES FOR VISITORS

■ *Pasadena*

Northeast of the main visitors' LA, 11 miles northeast of Downtown LA, Pasadena is very much its own place. It is a historic city with much interesting architecture, its own rebuilt and revitalized downtown, and some of the region's leading museums. Pasadena's key transit corridors are the Gold Line light rail (Arroyo Seco corridor to Downtown LA), rapid bus 780, and bus 180/181 Colorado Boulevard to Glendale and Hollywood.

■ *West Hollywood*

West Hollywood has only been an incorporated city since 1984, but under relaxed county governance, it was previously a playland for both gay and straight Angelenos for decades. The center of West Hollywood is about 3 miles west of the center of Hollywood, and on the west the city touches tony Beverly Hills. Boys Town on Santa Monica Boulevard remains a major gay bar zone, while the Sunset Strip has rock redoubts. Santa Monica Boulevard with bus 4 and rapid bus 704 is the transit spine. Sunset Boulevard is served by bus 2.

■ *Westwood*

This neighborhood on the Westside of Los Angeles is located around the University of California at Los Angeles (UCLA), though only the commercial Westwood Village feels much like a college town. West-wood is 3 miles west of Beverly Hills and 5 miles east of Santa Monica. Westwood has some small, fine museums connected to UCLA, noodle joints and Persian restaurants, and live theaters. Westwood's key tran-sit corridors are Wilshire Boulevard with Metro rapid bus 720 in both directions and Big Blue Bus 2 to the west, Sunset Boulevard with Metro bus 2, and Westwood Boulevard with Big Blue Bus 8 and 12.

■ Venice

Where "Funkytown" meets the ocean, just south of Santa Monica, is Ven-ice. Once an independent city, Venice is known for weight lifting on the beach, an oceanfront walk lined with vendors, and one of LA's hottest restaurant rows. Venice's main transit routes are Venice Boulevard, where buses 33 and 733 run, and Main Street, where Big Blue Bus 2 runs.

■ Long Beach

Some people wouldn't consider Long Beach, 25 miles south of Down-town Los Angeles, to be part of LA at all. But this sometimes gritty Los Angeles County city has an eclectic collection of attractions, including the *Queen Mary,* the Aquarium of the Pacific, and a historic downtown. It's also a secondary center for conventions, behind Los Angeles and Anaheim. The main transit routes are the Blue Line light rail—which connects Long Beach with Downtown Los Angeles—and the visitor-oriented free Passport buses, all of which converge at the Long Beach Transit Mall.

CORRIDORS

To get oriented to LA you need to think in terms of corridors. Many neighborhoods and communities in Los Angeles are connected by long, straight boulevards, which can stretch on for 20 miles or more. In the early and mid-20th century, these boulevards were the key connective spines for Los Angeles, just as trolleys had been before them and free-ways would be later. To comprehend the visitors' city, two corridors are critical—Wilshire and Sunset boulevards. Both are featured as rides in Chapter 10.

■ *Wilshire Boulevard*

Wilshire Boulevard stretches for 15 miles across Los Angeles's mid-section, from Downtown Los Angeles to the palisades over the Pacific Ocean in downtown Santa Monica. The most heavily built-up long street, Wilshire has often been called a linear downtown. You could easily have a complete vacation on and near Wilshire Boulevard. You'd have access to a beach, museums, shopping, live theaters, special cinemas, restaurants, bars, and hotels.

West of downtown, the street runs right through the MacArthur Park green space, Koreatown, Museum Row, Beverly Hills, Westwood, and Santa Monica. Landmarks along Wilshire include the one-time site of Bullocks Wilshire (LA's first "suburban," non-downtown department store) the Los Angeles County Museum of Art, the La Brea Tar Pits, and the Beverly Wilshire Hotel. Wilshire has the most frequent bus service in the city, with rapid buses running as frequently as every 3 minutes in rush hour.

■ *Sunset Boulevard*

Sunset Boulevard twists across 25 miles from Downtown Los Angeles to Pacific Coast Highway along the base of the Hollywood Hills and Santa Monica Mountains. (East of downtown the street continues as Cesar Chavez Avenue.) Sunset has traditionally been the boulevard of glamour and entertainment, including the famed Sunset Strip, the portion of Sunset Boulevard in West Hollywood. Sunset is the main street for the groovy Echo Park and Silver Lake districts. It heads through Hollywood and West Hollywood and out into high-priced Westside suburbs, ending in Pacific Palisades. Landmarks along Sunset include the Directors Guild of America (sometimes known as the "film can" building), the Chateau Marmont hotel, the Beverly Hills Hotel, and the north campus of UCLA. Santa Monica Boulevard forks off Sunset after Silver Lake and continues as a major street across the city.

OTHER NOTABLE AREAS

Attractions are also clustered in two of LA's parks—Exposition Park and Griffith Park. Exposition Park is a small, carefully ordered park with several museums, the Coliseum sports arena, and a rose garden, located near the University of Southern California a couple of miles south of Downtown (see page 89 for more information). Griffith Park is a large hillside, largely wildland park midway between Downtown LA and Hollywood. It has the zoo, the Autry (a Western museum), a carousel, and an observatory.

RESTAURANT AREAS

A great many of the city's eateries—fine and funky—are in the eight communities and two corridors listed earlier. But some additional areas also have high concentrations of great food. Monterey Park and San Gabriel in the San Gabriel Valley east of Downtown LA (and south of Pasadena) are Chinese food central for Los Angeles. See Chapter 4. Koreatown is partially covered under Wilshire Boulevard, but the main eating streets are Olympic Boulevard and Vermont Avenue, a north-south street. See Chapter 4. Out west, the Sawtelle Boulevard commercial district is a major area for Japanese restaurants. See Chapter 13.

What to See in Los Angeles

See what you're interested in—almost every form of human activity is represented here. For some folks, LA is famous or infamous as a field

★ LOS ANGELES VISITOR CENTERS ★

DOWNTOWN: 685 S. Figueroa St. at Seventh St.
Monday–Friday, 8:30 a.m. –5 p.m.

HOLLYWOOD: Hollywood & Highland Center, 6801 Hollywood Blvd.
Monday–Saturday, 10 a.m.–10 p.m., and Sunday, 10 a.m.–7 p.m.

LITTLE TOKYO: 307 E. First St. at Judge John Aliso St. Daily, 9 a.m.–6 p.m.

LONG BEACH: 130 E. First St., Long Beach Transit Mall.
Monday–Thursday, 7 a.m.–6 p.m.; Friday–Sunday, 9 a.m.–7 p.m.

PASADENA: 300 E. Green St., Pasadena Civic Auditorium.
Monday–Friday, 8 a.m.–5 p.m., and Saturday, 10 a.m.–4 p.m.

WEST HOLLYWOOD: 8687 Melrose Ave., Ste. M-38, Pacific Design Center.
Monday–Friday, 8:30 a.m.–6 p.m.

★ **LOS ANGELES: GLITZY CITY** ★

1. The Grove shopping center, Fairfax Avenue

2. Hollywood Walk of Fame

3. LA Live (entertainment complex), Downtown Los Angeles

4. Melrose Avenue (shopping street)

5. Rodeo Drive/Beverly Hills Business Triangle

6. Sunset/Hyperion shopping area, Silver Lake

7. Sunset Strip, West Hollywood

8. Third Street Promenade (pedestrian shopping street), Santa Monica

9. Universal Studios (theme park)

10. Views of Hollywood sign

of glitz. The city features the stars in the sidewalk on Hollywood Boulevard, the "billboard" stores of Beverly Hills, the Hollywood sign, and restaurants where celebrities might appear. To others, it's a cultural wonderland with top museums, theaters, and special movie programs. To others still, it fascinates as a city, as a real place on the ground that the world has rushed into. It's hard to say what the top, must-see, or most important attractions are.

Much of the rest of this book is about what to see in Los Angeles. But to give you a start, I've provided not one but three top ten lists for a visit to Los Angeles—one for the glitzy city, one for the city of culture, and one for the city on the ground. They are all listed in alphabetical order.

Eating in Los Angeles

Finding good food is one of the best reasons to travel, and Los Angeles is one of the world's great eating cities today. Jonathan Gold, *LA Weekly*'s food critic—and the only food critic to ever win a Pulitzer Prize—argues that LA is the best food city in America. Be that as it may, good food is usually somewhere close by.

★ LOS ANGELES: CITY OF CULTURE ★

1. **Chung King Road art galleries, Chinatown**

2. **Disney Hall, Downtown Los Angeles**

3. **Egyptian Theatre/American Cinematheque, Hollywood**

4. **J. Paul Getty Museum, Brentwood**

5. **Hollywood Bowl**

6. **Los Angeles County Museum of Art, Wilshire Boulevard**

7. **Museum of Contemporary Art, Downtown Los Angeles**

8. **Pasadena Civic Center**

9. **Tom Bradley wing of Los Angeles Central Library, Downtown Los Angeles**

10. **Watts Towers, South Los Angeles**

Los Angeles restaurants don't merely serve different kinds of food at different price points. They're organized in wholly different ways. At industry watering holes, you will pay through the nose for the privilege of a bad seat in a theoretically celebrity-frequented restaurant. (Meanwhile the celebrities have probably moved on to the next new thing.) There are the temples of celebrity chefs. At holes in the wall, especially in lower-income neighborhoods, food—good, bad, or transcendent—is dished up with no ceremony and less atmosphere. And lots of places are in between—ethnic restaurants that provide a pleasant dining atmosphere and casual fine-dining restaurants where the emphasis is more on the food than the dress or decor.

Unscientifically, LA restaurant prices seem to be higher than San Francisco but lower than New York. Most cuisines are not restricted to one neighborhood in LA but can be found in various areas across the city. But if you want to go to the source, consider some key locales:

JAPANESE FOOD: Little Tokyo section of Downtown LA (see Chapter 4) or Sawtelle district, West Los Angeles (see Chapter 13)

KOREAN FOOD: Koreatown (see Chapter 4)

★ LOS ANGELES: CITY ON THE GROUND ★

1. **Boys Town area (Santa Monica Boulevard), West Hollywood**

2. **Broadway, Downtown Los Angeles**

3. **Cathedral of Our Lady of the Angels**

4. **Farmers Market, Fairfax Avenue**

5. **Koreatown Plaza (shopping center)**

6. **MacArthur Park (the park), Wilshire Boulevard**

7. **Paseo Colorado, Pasadena**

8. **El Pueblo de Los Angeles State Historic Park, Downtown Los Angeles**

9. **Santa Monica Pier (amusement pier)**

10. **Venice Beach and Boardwalk**

CHINESE FOOD: Monterey Park or San Gabriel (see Chapter 4) These are a significant ride away. LA's Chinatown, near Downtown, is small.

In terms of restaurant prices, this guide classifies restaurant prices by the average (pretax) price of the entrée/main item at dinner (or at lunch if the restaurant doesn't serve dinner). Prices at breakfast and lunch will generally be cheaper, if the restaurant serves those meals. Tapas places aren't classified because people will consume different numbers of dishes.

The categories are:

$	Less than $10
$$	$10–$15
$$$	$15–$20
$$$$	$20–$25
$$$$$	$25 and above

EVENING EATING: GETTING TO DINNER

It's easy to reach great food in LA on foot or by transit—most of the time. Lots of good restaurants are in the top visitor neighborhoods of Downtown LA, Hollywood, and Santa Monica. During the day—breakfast and lunchtime—the main restaurant areas have frequent transit. But in the evening, especially after 8 p.m., most lines get less frequent. Unless you eat particularly late, you probably won't be affected much going to dinner, but you may well be affected coming back from dinner, especially if you linger. Though it's a problem citywide, it can particularly be a problem along and around Melrose Avenue and Beverly Center, where dining options abound but transit service is relatively weak. What to do? Here are some strategies for getting to and from dinner.

1. Eat dinner in the area you're staying and walk back.
2. Eat dinner along a line that has relatively frequent evening service. Good candidates include the Gold Line light rail, Red Line subway, rapid bus 720 Wilshire Boulevard, and bus 4 Santa Monica Boulevard.
3. Be very aware of when your bus comes back. Perhaps even let the restaurant know when you need to leave to catch it.
4. Take the bus there, and take a cab back.

Sleeping in Los Angeles: Hotels

The three key visitor communities—Downtown, Hollywood, and Santa Monica—have large clusters of hotels. The section below describes each major hotel area with its pluses and minuses for car-free travelers. The important thing to remember is that Los Angeles is physically huge. It's worth thinking about whether the places you want to see are clustered geographically and whether you can stay closer to them.

WHERE TO STAY IN LA

If you're staying in LA for 4 or more days, think seriously about staying in two different places. Spend 2 or 3 (or more) days in central Los Angeles, Downtown, or Hollywood. Then spend at least a couple of days on the Westside, in Santa Monica, or perhaps in Westwood. That way you can spend the first couple of days going to places that are closer to Downtown—destinations as far west as Beverly Hills. You can then spend the later days on Westside places closer to Santa Monica, such as Venice and Westwood. With this strategy, you'll cut down on your time in transit considerably, avoiding trips of an hour or more between central Los Angeles and the Westside. To me, it's worth the time you'll spend changing hotels.

The different types of lodging in Los Angeles include modern corporate hotels, modern entertainment-oriented hotels, ocean resort-style hotels, motels (basic and upgraded), and upscale renovated historic hotels. You'll see examples of these hotel types in each neighborhood's listings of hotels, though you won't find each type in each area. You also won't find many of the higher-quality older budget hotels that are so helpful to the budget traveler in San Francisco and other cities. Nor will you find many apartment hotels. There weren't as many apartment hotels to begin with, but in Los Angeles the type of buildings that became budget tourist hotels elsewhere have until recently been demolished or have become residential hotels.

LA's leading budget lodging type is motels on the edges of central areas. For Downtown, consider motels in Chinatown (I would not recommend motels just west of the Harbor Freeway). A number of budget hotels and motels are situated along the Red and Purple lines between Hollywood and Downtown. In Pasadena, Colorado Boulevard east of Downtown provides options. On the Westside, inland motels in Santa Monica are far cheaper than their oceanfront counterparts. These highway strips aren't as nice as the central areas, which is the trade-off for their cheaper rates.

BEACH HOTELS

If you're looking for a hotel at the beach, look for hotels in Santa Monica or Venice, or take an extreme transit trip down to beautiful Laguna Beach. (Long Beach, though an interesting place, doesn't really have much of a beach anymore.) Beach hotels, even beach motels, are not cheap, especially in the summer. Santa Monica and Venice are good locations for seeing the coastal area and the Westside but are a long ride from many other parts of the city.

WHERE TO STAY IN DOWNTOWN LOS ANGELES

Downtown's hotels are generally found south of First Street, north of 11th Street, west of Broadway, and east of the 110 Harbor Freeway. The hotels are spread across this roughly square mile area, so Downtown LA doesn't really have a hotel section. LA's Pershing Square is not comparable to New York's Times Square or San Francisco's Union Square. Additional hotels are also in Little Tokyo to the northeast of Downtown, and some budget motels are located in Chinatown near Union Station, north of the main part of Downtown.

Downtown is convenient because it is the single biggest hub of the LA transit network. It has faster transit than Hollywood or Santa Monica to central city areas such as Echo Park, Exposition Park, and Pasadena.

The area also offers the largest supply and largest choice of hotel rooms in a single neighborhood. Lodging in Downtown tends to be multistory, internal corridor hotels, though a few motels are on the edges. It is still a heavily business-oriented location, so on the weekends rooms are often offered at a substantial discount. At the same time, Downtown is growing livelier on the weekend, so it will no longer feel like a ghost town if you stay there, though discounts may also erode. On the downside of staying Downtown, you're well east of many visitor attractions in West Hollywood, Beverly Hills, and areas farther west. Even as Downtown improves, the Bunker Hill/Financial District area is still pretty quiet and a bit eerie on the weekends. See Downtown hotel listings beginning on page 96.

WHERE TO STAY IN HOLLYWOOD

If you want to stay in one place for your whole trip to Los Angeles, Hollywood should be that place for most visitors. It is the most central major hotel area for Los Angeles's main visitor attractions. And Hollywood is a uniquely Los Angeles neighborhood. You won't find any place like it in your hometown.

Hollywood has a couple dozen hotels and motels, most within a few blocks of the Hollywood Boulevard/Highland Avenue or Hollywood Boulevard/Vine Street Red Line subway stations. Many of Hollywood's hostelries are cheap motels (including a Motel 6), some a little too cheap for most visitors. Hollywood features a couple of big, trendy modern hotels and one trendy historic one (the Roosevelt).

As Downtown overcomes its emptiness, so Hollywood overcomes its sleaze. If nightlife is your priority, stay in Hollywood, the hottest neighborhood in town. Hollywood is also the single most active theater neighborhood, though Hollywood's Theater Row is about 0.8 mile south of Hollywood Boulevard.

Hollywood doesn't have nearly as many transit routes as Downtown, but it does have the Red Line subway and other key connections along Hollywood Boulevard, Sunset Boulevard, and Fairfax Avenue. Hollywood has shorter transit rides than Downtown or Santa Monica to Universal Studios—just one subway stop away. Hollywood also has shorter bus rides to West Hollywood, the Fairfax District, Beverly Hills, and Thai Town. See Hollywood hotel listings beginning on page 126.

Caution: Many motels with Hollywood in their name can be as much as 2 or 3 miles east of central Hollywood, often decent places to stay but not in the walkable zone of core Hollywood.

BUDGET HOTELS AND MOTELS ON THE RED AND PURPLE LINES

Motels along the Red and Purple lines subways between Downtown and Hollywood can provide fairly cheap lodgings in central, transit-served locations. These locations also have frequent east-west and north-south bus service. None of the neighborhoods with these motels are fancy, or even particularly visitor-oriented, but they all should be fine for city-savvy travelers. These motels are also listed in Chapter 7.

WHERE TO STAY IN PASADENA

Pasadena is a genuinely charming city, one of the most pleasant and historic in the LA region. Unfortunately, it's not a good base for a car-free SoCal traveler. Pasadena isn't really close to other major visitor areas, as it's more than 10 miles from the closest—Downtown LA. Downtown is at least 30 minutes away, and transit travel times to other places are longer, well over an hour to anywhere west of Hollywood. Pasadena is also a more attractive place to stay during cooler months. In the summer it can get significantly hotter and smoggier than the Westside or even Downtown.

But if you want to spend 1 or 2 days exploring the museums and architecture of Pasadena, or maybe go to a game at the Rose Bowl, then stay here. (Prices soar around the New Year's Day Rose Parade and Rose Bowl college football game, so that's not necessarily a good time to stay here.) Stay here to visit Pasadena, not LA. See Pasadena hotel listings beginning on page 109.

WHERE TO STAY IN THE FAIRFAX DISTRICT

The corner of Wilshire Boulevard and Fairfax Avenue is central to visitors' Los Angeles. Two major transit corridors cross there. Museum Row—encompassing the Los Angeles County Museum of Art and several smaller museums—is there. The only tourist-grade hotel within easy walking distance of Wilshire and Fairfax is the charming Wilshire Crest Hotel (6301 Orange St.; **wilshirecresthotel.com**), about a 5-minute walk away on a quiet residential street. It's a pleasant, moderately priced hotel (no elevator) whose minimal continental breakfast is kosher. The hotel is a short walk from lots of eating and shopping opportunities along Fairfax Avenue and Third Street.

WHERE TO STAY IN WEST HOLLYWOOD

West Hollywood is not the ideal base for a car-free traveler but could make sense if you have particular reasons to be there. Along and immediately off the Sunset Strip is a major location for glamorous, typically expensive, entertainment industry–oriented hotels (where else are you going to stay when you play the Roxy or the Whisky?). A few hotels are down the hill near Santa Monica Boulevard. Transit—bus only, no rail—is pretty good during the day on weekdays, but it is much poorer at night and on weekends. The falloff here is worse than in other places. Hollywood is a better bet for most car-free travelers, unless you want to walk to venues on Sunset or Santa Monica boulevards.

WHERE TO STAY ON THE WESTSIDE

Westside has more total hotel rooms than Downtown LA has; however, it does not have as many in any single area of the Westside. The Westside is known for high hotel rates, but if you can pick your times and places, you can often get reasonable rates. Beach hotels will typically be priciest on weekends, especially holiday weekends. Budget travel on the Westside is not an oxymoron, but it requires thinking about trade-offs between location, amenities, and cost.

To repeat an important suggestion, split your time if you're staying in the Los Angeles area 4 nights or more. Spend some nights in central Los Angeles—in Downtown or Hollywood—and spend a few nights on the Westside. You'll cut down everyday transit travel time greatly, and you'll get to see two parts of town in more detail.

■ *Where to Stay in Santa Monica*

Downtown Santa Monica, also known as the Bayside District, is the Westside location of choice for car-free travelers. The area is attractive, sitting on a cliff, or palisade, overlooking the Pacific Ocean. The pedestrian-only Third Street Promenade is here, providing a nonstop high-energy people-watching experience. Many restaurants, both fast food on the Promenade and fine dining, are also nearby. In addition, it's a major transit hub, with direct service to Venice, Westwood, Beverly Hills, and Downtown LA.

About 20 hotels and motels are within a 1-mile radius of the intersection of Ocean Avenue and Santa Monica Boulevard. Many are pricey, quoting rates upward of $200 per night, at least in summer. Some winter rates are lower. Unlike in Downtown LA, weekends are a popular time here, so rates won't go down then. At least as a car-free visitor you'll save these hotels' parking fees, which can be more than $30 per night.

■ *Eastern Santa Monica Budget Motels*

In central Los Angeles, you can save money by staying along the Red Line between Downtown LA and Hollywood. On the Westside, the most similar area (though it doesn't have rail transit) is eastern Santa Monica along Santa Monica and Wilshire boulevards. It's not the most intrinsically appealing area, but there's nothing really wrong with it, and motels there are a lot cheaper here than they are by the ocean.

■ Where to Stay in Venice

Take me down to "Funkytown," or at least the memory of "Funkytown," and we'll stay at one of the handful of tourist hotels on or near the beachfront in Venice. It's good for hangin' at the beach, but it's a long bus ride to just about anywhere else.

■ Where to Stay in Westwood

Westwood, the area adjacent to the University of California, Los Angeles (UCLA), has a few hotels. It's about 5 miles east of downtown Santa Monica. Westwood is central to many visitor destinations. It's also a major bus hub, as lines converge to serve the campus. Westwood Village, the retail area next to campus, has plenty of places to eat, though it's stronger on cheaper eateries and coffeehouses than fine dining.

Westwood's key east-west transit corridors are Wilshire and Sunset boulevards, and north-south it's Westwood Boulevard. Unfortunately, because there's no express bus except during commute hours, it takes longer to get to Downtown LA from Westwood than it does from Santa Monica, even though Santa Monica is farther away.

Westwood has just a sprinkling of hotels. Hotel bargains should be available when UCLA is not in session, in mid- to late December, in mid- to late March, and from mid-June to mid-September.

■ Where to Stay in Beverly Hills

Some first-rate hotels nestle here, but by and large they are quite expensive; almost everything in town is $200 and up. Beverly Hills is centrally located for visitors, some 3 miles east of Westwood and 8 miles west of Downtown LA. It's served by two of LA's best bus lines on Wilshire and Santa Monica boulevards. But transit to anywhere off these streets requires a transfer and can get lengthy. These two streets, along with Beverly Drive, form the city's famed Golden Triangle or Business Triangle, which also encompasses Rodeo Drive.

WHERE TO STAY IN SAN DIEGO

Tourism is lifeblood for San Diego, and so it has hundreds of hotels and motels, almost as many as the much larger Los Angeles. San Diego has downtown hotels, hotels near beaches, hotels in outlying centers, and roadside motels. San Diego hotels are generally fairly new; a spate of hotel building took place in the early 2000s building boom. There are some historic hotels, especially in and near the downtown. Some hotel areas work well for transit-based visitors, while others do not.

From La Jolla on the north to San Ysidro on the south, there are no fewer than nine major clusters or strips along a roadway of hotels and motels. From north to south, these are University Town Center/Sorrento Valley, La Jolla Village, Pacific Beach, Hotel Circle, Point Loma/Shelter Island, Old Town, Downtown, Coronado, and Chula Vista. Scatters of motels are also along the roadway or around recreational areas such as Mission Bay Park.

I have listed the following areas in roughly the order of preference for car-free travelers.

Downtown, the largest hotel area, is the most convenient for transit-using travelers. It has the most transit service, most restaurants in the area, and numerous attractions. Indeed, hotels break down into subareas of downtown—Little Italy, Downtown Core, Gaslamp Quarter, and Convention Center. Downtown is definitely the preferred car-free location. For specific downtown hotels, see page 333.

Pacific Beach is the beach community with the best bus transit to other parts of San Diego. It's the easiest place to stay if you want to be at the beach but also want to get to other parts of the city. Pacific Beach has hotels ranging from the quite cheap to the very expensive. See page 344 for more information about Pacific Beach hotels.

La Jolla Village and **Coronado** are attractive areas, but they can be hard to reach, especially at night and on weekends. La Jolla in particular has a number of attractions in addition to the beach. I wouldn't use either as a base to explore the city, but you might stay there if you want to spend a few days at the beach. Hotels in Coronado and La Jolla are noted on page 345 and page 348, respectively.

Old Town also works as a hotel locale for transit-using travelers, though much more goes on downtown. Old Town Transit Center is a major trolley and bus transfer point, with the trolley to downtown and buses to beach areas and SeaWorld. About a half-dozen motels are grouped around Old Town. See page 358 for more specifics.

Chula Vista is a working-class city in the southern part of San Diego. A cluster of low-cost motels (though a scarcity of restaurants) is within walking distance of the E Street trolley station. The enormous Naval Station San Diego (the Navy's largest West Coast base) is a short trolley ride from here, so you might stay here if you're going there. It's not the prettiest part of town, but it could work as an affordable locale.

WHERE NOT TO STAY

■ Century City

Though some of LA's fanciest hotels are here, it's not really a good place for car-free travelers. The walking environment is dominated by huge buildings in huge plazas on wide, fast streets. There are decent bus lines located along east-west streets here, but there's almost no north-south service.

■ Los Angeles International Airport (LAX) Area

The area surrounding LAX is grim and unfriendly to pedestrians, and many hotels do not have good transit connections because transit goes to the airport itself. People sometimes want to stay here to save money, but you're really better off at budget motels in eastern Santa Monica, along the Red Line, or in Chinatown. It's not a bargain if it ruins your vacation.

■ Long Beach, Disneyland, and Laguna Beach

These areas are too far away to serve as bases for seeing Los Angeles. But you might want to stay in one of these places when visiting them because among the three, only Long Beach is easy for a day trip from central Los Angeles. See their respective chapters.

■ *Marina del Rey*

Marina del Rey, an unincorporated area south of Venice with motels and modern high-rises, has neither transit nor good walking conditions. If you're looking for a lower rate on the Westside, try eastern Santa Monica.

■ *University Town Center and Sorrento Valley, San Diego*

This is an area of business parks and shopping centers that is sometimes called La Jolla but is fully 5 miles from La Jolla Village. The walking environment isn't great, and it's a long bus ride to anywhere.

■ *Hotel Circle, San Diego*

It is hardly a good walking environment, and there is not much here except dozens of hotels and the occasional Denny's along this road. It's actually a set of roads—Hotel Circle North, Hotel Circle, and Hotel Circle Place. Bus service along Hotel Circle is only once every 30 minutes, with none on Sundays. You can get bargains here, but it just doesn't work very well if you're not driving.

■ *Point Loma and Shelter Island, San Diego*

This low-key, Navy-oriented area is southwest of the airport, with the lovely Cabrillo National Monument at the southern tip and views of the water. It's a pleasant area and wouldn't be a bad place to stay. Unfortunately, there's only one bus line, which runs every 30 minutes Monday–Saturday and every 60 minutes on Sunday.

HOSTELS

Hostels are the cheapest places to stay, usually offering a bed in a dorm of six to eight people. Some folks seem to go to hostels to party rather than sleep, so be aware. Private rooms typically have shared bathrooms. Hostels get used hard and can run down quickly, so I offer no promises here about the condition of these properties. See hostel listings in each neighborhood's chapter.

ii. los angeles

■ 3 Transit and Getting around in Los Angeles

JARRETT WALKER, A TRANSIT CONSULTANT WHO WORKS around the world, says that when he wants to surprise and inspire clients about transit in North America, he tells them about Los Angeles. Los Angeles is first among the 14 largest U.S. metropolitan areas in bus service per square mile, third in bus service per capita, and seventh in rail transit track miles per capita.

Los Angeles's transit gives you comprehensive coverage and frequent service, especially during the daytime. Almost all the places that visitors want to go are easy to reach on transit. The bad news is that a big system is by definition complicated, and more than one agency runs transit service in LA. You may find that your problem is choosing among a number of transit choices, rather than not having transit choices.

This chapter will answer the following questions: What is the transit system in LA, and what service can I use, and how do I plan and take a trip on transit in LA? This chapter will also briefly touch on bicycling—a still edgy but definitely growing transportation method in Los Angeles—and on using taxis. As noted before, walking is a good way to get around within neighborhoods but rarely between neighborhoods.

The LA Transit System

The central LA transit system has three main parts—Metro Rail, Metro Bus, and DASH.

METRO RAIL

Metro Rail refers to the rail transit lines operated by Metro (the Metropolitan Transit Authority), the main transit agency. Rapid transit lines—both rail and bus—are designated by colors. Three Metro Rail lines serve Downtown LA, with a fourth line opening early 2012. The fifth light rail line is the Green Line, which does not serve Downtown Los Angeles.

1. The Red Line subway from Union Station and Downtown LA to North Hollywood via Hollywood (with a short Purple Line branch from Wilshire Boulevard/Vermont Avenue to Wilshire Boulevard/Western Avenue)

2. The Gold Line light rail from East Los Angeles to Pasadena via Union Station

3. The Blue Line light rail from Downtown Los Angeles to Long Beach via Watts

4. The Expo Line, scheduled to open in early 2012, from Downtown Los Angeles to Culver City

5. The Green Line light rail from Norwalk to Redondo Beach (does not serve Downtown)

The Red/Purple Line runs between Union Station, Downtown LA, Koreatown, Thai Town, Hollywood, Universal Studios, and North Hollywood. The Gold Line runs between East Los Angeles, Little Tokyo, Union Station (connection for Downtown LA), Highland Park, South Pasadena, and Pasadena. The Blue Line runs between Downtown Los Angeles, Staples Center/Convention Center, South Los Angeles, Watts, and Long Beach. The first phase of the Expo Line will run south and west from Downtown Los Angeles to the University of South California (USC) and Exposition Park along Exposition Boulevard to Culver City.

Metro Rail is not to be confused with Metrolink, the commuter rail system connecting Downtown LA (Union Station) with the suburbs. Metrolink runs from Downtown LA to Burbank Airport and to Fullerton, the best connection point for Disneyland.

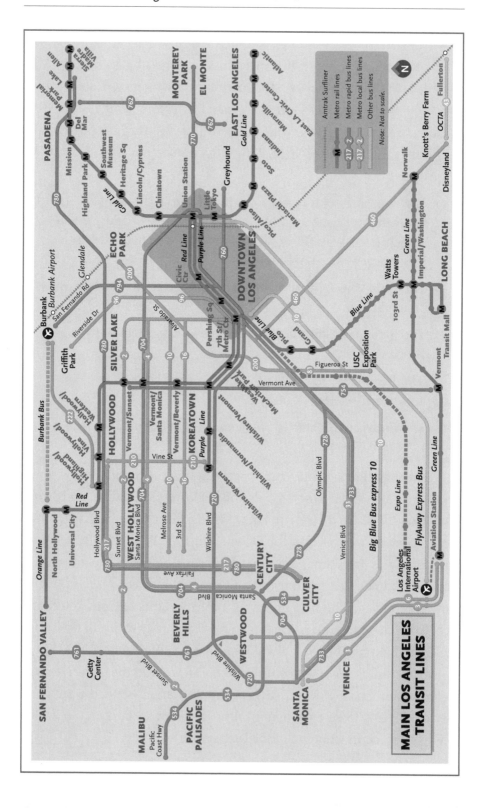

MAIN LOS ANGELES TRANSIT LINES

The bottom line on Metro Rail is that it goes some of the places visitors want to go but not all of them. You need Metro Bus.

METRO BUS

The buses are the backbone of LA's transit system. See the transit map on the facing page. Metro runs some 200 bus routes, blanketing the central neighborhoods of LA, including the visitors' city. Metro Bus routes are designated by number. Metro Bus is divided between Metro rapid, with red buses, and Metro local, which uses orange buses. The red rapid buses are faster because they only stop at major streets and because traffic signals automatically give them priority. Local buses stop at all stops. About two dozen rapid bus lines are in LA, and Metro keeps expanding the network. If you can use a rapid bus instead of a local bus, you should get there faster, though you may have to walk farther to and from the bus stop.

In central and western Los Angeles—in the main visitors' city—most buses run on a single street and stay on that street (except at the end of the route when they turn around). Metro's Wilshire Boulevard buses stay on Wilshire, the Vermont Avenue buses stay on Vermont, and so on. This may sound trivial, but it's not the case in all cities.

■ *The Grid of Bus Routes*

Think of the bus routes as forming a giant, basically perpendicular, grid or matrix of routes, all the way west from Downtown LA to Santa Monica. The grid includes both Metro routes and many Santa Monica Big Blue Bus routes, but not DASH routes, which tend to bend and zigzag through neighborhoods. Because of this grid, you can make most trips either on a single bus or with just one transfer. A few streets—most important, Santa Monica Boulevard—cut diagonally across the grid.

With the grid, a lot of trips can take you in two different ways (in some cases more). For example, if you're at Sunset Boulevard and Alvarado Street in Echo Park and you want to go to Museum Row at Wilshire Boulevard and Fairfax Avenue, you could first go south of Alvarado on bus 200, then west on Wilshire (rapid bus 720). Or you could go west on Sunset (bus 2) and south on Fairfax (bus 217 or rapid bus 780). The two routes aren't necessarily equal; buses on one may be faster or more frequent. In this example, Alvarado to Wilshire would probably be a faster trip, but Sunset to Fairfax would be better for browsing stores.

■ *Three Key Metro Bus Corridors*

Among the hundreds of bus lines serving Los Angeles, three corridors stand out for visitors:

1. WILSHIRE BOULEVARD: Served by **Metro rapid bus 720, Metro bus 20, Big Blue Bus 2** between Westwood Village and Santa Monica city, and the **Purple Line** subway as far west as Western Avenue, Wilshire crosses Los Angeles east to west from Downtown LA to Santa Monica. It is the single most important street in Los Angeles and is often described as a linear downtown. The areas near Wilshire Boulevard are also among the city's busiest.

Rapid bus 720 connects East Los Angeles and Downtown Los Angeles with MacArthur Park, Koreatown, the Fairfax District and LA County Museum, Beverly Hills, Westwood (UCLA), and Santa Monica. Service is very frequent on Wilshire, especially east of Westwood. Bus 720, unlike most rapids, runs seven days a week and in the evening. The rapid stops at major streets, roughly a mile apart (outside of downtown areas), most of which are transfer points for crossing bus lines. Bus 20 serves all stops.

2. SUNSET/SANTA MONICA BOULEVARDS: **Buses 2, 4,** and **rapid bus 704** serve these streets. Sunset Boulevard crosses the city east to west from Downtown LA to Pacific Palisades, going through Echo Park, Silver Lake, Hollywood, West Hollywood, and Westwood. Sunset is the long, connecting street of Entertainment City LA. Santa Monica Boulevard branches off Sunset in Silver Lake and runs through West Hollywood and Beverly Hills to Santa Monica. Sunset and Santa Monica boulevards are roughly parallel to Wilshire, though Santa Monica Boulevard crosses Wilshire in downtown Beverly Hills.

Santa Monica Boulevard has the more frequent bus routes—rapid bus 704 and bus 4. **Big Blue Bus** runs its line 1 on Santa Monica Boulevard between Westwood Village and Santa Monica city. Rapid bus 704

■ THE (NOT-SO-SECRET) ■ LA METRO CODE REVEALED

The Metro bus route number tells you what kind of service the bus provides. The key categories with numerous routes are listed in bold. Any street that has a rapid will also have a local. Usually the local bus number will be similar to the rapid. For example, on Wilshire Boulevard the rapid is bus 720 and the local is 20.

0–99	**Local bus service to and from Downtown LA**
100–199	**East-west local routes beyond Downtown**
200–299	**North-south local routes beyond Downtown**
300–399	Limited stop service (many of these are being converted to rapids)
400–499	Express bus service to and from Downtown Los Angeles
500–599	Express bus service in areas other than Downtown (three routes)
600–699	Shuttles and circulators; neighborhood-level service
700–799	**Rapid buses**
800–899	Rail lines (typically referred to by color)
900–999	Metro Transitway such as the Wilshire Boulevard express

runs daily, but only from roughly 6 a.m.–8 p.m. On weekdays, it runs every 10–20 minutes or more frequently between Union Station and Westwood Boulevard, but only about every 40 minutes from Westwood Boulevard to Santa Monica. On weekends both segments are served roughly every 20 minutes.

3. FAIRFAX AVENUE–HOLLYWOOD BOULEVARD–COLORADO BOULEVARD: Buses **180/181, 217,** and **rapid bus 780** serve this area. This long cross-city route connects Culver City, the Fairfax District, Hollywood, Thai Town, Los Feliz, Glendale, Eagle Rock, and Pasadena. It's served by an overlapping group of local and rapid buses, which do not go through Downtown Los Angeles. Rapid bus 780 operates weekdays only; the local buses also operate on weekends and evenings.

Lively neighborhoods and eating opportunities abound along this route. See the Food Bus 780 route described on page 200. The route uses Fairfax Avenue in the Fairfax District and surrounding areas, Hollywood Boulevard in Hollywood and Thai Town, and Colorado Boulevard in Glendale, Eagle Rock, and Pasadena, as well as connecting streets. Bus 217 covers Fairfax Avenue and about a mile of Hollywood Boulevard east to Hollywood Boulevard/Vine Street station. Bus 180/181 serve the segments from Hollywood Boulevard/Vine Street east through Pasadena.

DASH

DASH routes are local neighborhood bus routes operated by the city of Los Angeles. They have routes in many parts of the city, but the most extensive network of routes is in Downtown Los Angeles. DASH routes run only during the day, and most run Monday–Friday or Monday–Saturday. The fare is 35 cents.

★ KEY DOWNTOWN DASH ROUTES ★

DASH A: Bunker Hill—Civic Center—Little Tokyo—Arts District (weekdays only)

DASH E: 7th St./Metro Center—Historic Core—Fashion District (daily)

DASH F: Bunker Hill—Convention Center—USC—Exposition Park (daily)

OTHER TRANSIT SERVICES

There are also buses from other local transit agencies. You're most likely to use the Santa Monica Municipal Bus Lines, known as Big Blue Bus, especially if you spend time in Santa Monica, Westwood, or Venice. See Chapter 12.

Long Beach (see Chapter 16) and Orange County (see Chapters 17 and 18) each have their own transit system. Long Beach is also served by the Metro Blue Line light rail.

Key Things to Know about Metro Service

FREQUENCY OF SERVICE

The frequency of different bus routes varies, but you usually won't have to wait too long. Almost 60 bus and rail corridors in Los Angeles have service every 15 minutes or more frequently during weekday daytimes. Metro has a map (**tinyurl.com/15minmap**) that shows these lines. Most of the key lines for visitors run frequent service. After about 8 p.m., frequencies are significantly reduced, though specific schedules vary from line to line. Santa Monica Boulevard and Wilshire Boulevard have frequent evening service; the rail lines have trains every 20 minutes in the later evening.

Visitors will make most trips on this 15-minute network. Main routes into Pasadena, Downtown, Hollywood, West Hollywood, Beverly Hills, and Santa Monica have 15-minute service. Destinations that can only be reached with less frequent service are Malibu beach, the Getty Museum, and Huntington Library.

SHORT TURNS

Not every trip necessarily runs the whole length of a bus route. Some routes have short turns, where buses turn around after they've served the busier parts of the route. On bus 2 Sunset Boulevard, for example, some buses go as far west as Fairfax Avenue, some as far as Westwood Village, and others all the way to Pacific Coast Highway. Other routes with short turns include bus 10 on Melrose Avenue, bus 14 on Beverly Boulevard, bus 16 on Third Street, rapid bus 704 on Santa Monica Boulevard, and rapid bus 720 on Wilshire.

Check the bus's head sign or ask the driver so you know how far the bus is going. If a bus is short turning before your destination, it usually makes sense to take it anyway, rather than wait for a bus that's going through. You might be able to catch a different bus line or walk to complete the trip. At worst, you'll have to wait for the next bus at the short turn point.

24-HOUR SERVICE

Many local (not rapid) Metro bus lines operate 24 hours a day. The rail lines shut down for a few hours in the middle of the night, but about 30 bus corridors run 24/7. Most buses run every 30–60 minutes in the post-midnight "owl" hours; some run more frequently. There is 24-hour service on Hollywood Boulevard, Sunset Boulevard (east of Vermont Avenue), Santa Monica Boulevard, Beverly Boulevard, Wilshire Boulevard, Venice Boulevard, Vermont Avenue, and Fairfax Avenue. Look for a complete list of 24-hour bus routes on the Metro website (**metro.net/around/ timetables/24-hour**). Except for FlyAways from Union Station to LAX, other LA transit agencies do not run 24-hour service.

METRO SERVICE WEEKDAYS AND WEEKENDS

Most Metro local lines run on Saturday and Sunday, usually a little less frequently than on weekdays. The rail lines all run on Saturdays and Sundays, as do most of the local bus lines. A number of bus lines that run every 12 minutes on weekdays run every 15 minutes on the weekend. Some rapid bus lines don't run on the weekend, or run only on Saturday but not Sunday. Some rapid bus lines run a shorter route on weekends. Check the Metro website or the system map. If a rapid bus line isn't operating on Saturday or Sunday, a local bus will be covering that route.

COMING SOON

Even as you read this, the Metro system is expanding. Some key changes are underway now.

■ The next phase of the Expo Line will extend the line from Culver City to Westside Pavilion and Santa Monica, which will be a very big improvement, bringing rail transit to the Westside. It's projected to open in 2015.

■ The Orange Line busway in the San Fernando Valley is being extended north from Warner Center to the Chatsworth Amtrak/ Metrolink station. This isn't a main visitor area, but people taking the train from Santa Barbara will be able to use the Orange Line to reach various Valley destinations.

Planning and Taking a Trip on Transit

First, learn what buses or trains you need to take. There are six basic ways to get information about what transit to take to get from point A to point B. These methods are, of course, not mutually exclusive.

1. DIRECTIONS IN THIS GUIDEBOOK

Destinations in this book have transit directions from key transit hubs—typically at least from Downtown Los Angeles, Hollywood, and Santa Monica.

2. TRIP PLANNER ON THE METRO WEBSITE OR ON GOOGLE TRANSIT

The Metro Trip Planner (**mta.net**) will give you transit information for your specific trip—from your starting point to your destination at the time of day and on the day of the week you want to go. The Trip Planner is particularly helpful if you have to transfer as part of your trip because there are often multiple options for which buses to take. The best routing at 10 a.m. may not be the best at 3 p.m. or 9 p.m.

Type in your starting point, your ending point, and what time and day you want to leave (or arrive). The Trip Planner will ask you to confirm in which city your starting point and ending point are. Then voilà, you'll get one or more routes telling you the fastest way to go, listing the bus(es) or train(s) you need to take, and telling you to transfer (if you need to). If you ask for the Advanced Trip Planner, you'll get a few more options, such as how far you're willing to walk to the bus stop.

The Trip Planner is good but not perfect. On some long trips, it's faster to transfer than to take one bus, or occasionally to transfer twice rather than once. The Trip Planner generally won't give you that routing because it tries to minimize

TIP *Trip Planner contains lots of hidden features. If you click on the start or the end point listed in the itinerary, you'll get a map of the area, which can be zoomed out. If you click on the name of the bus route (such as Metro bus 121), you'll get a list of all the stops on that route.*

transfers. Also, in the city of Los Angeles, sometimes two intersections have the same street names (for example, Seventh Street and Grand Avenue in both Downtown LA and San Pedro). In that case, you'll have to distinguish between the two by their zip code.

Google Transit, at **google.com/transit,** also provides an online transit trip planning function. Google Transit's biggest advantage is that it's built off Google Maps. Google Transit is therefore set up in the same way for cities across the nation, and even internationally, so it might look and feel more familiar to you. Its main drawback is that it doesn't cover all transit agencies, so there can be trips that aren't properly addressed. In Los Angeles, Google Transit covers most of the main agencies of interest to visitors—Metro, Big Blue Bus, Long Beach Transit, Burbank Bus, Metrolink commuter rail, and the Orange County Transportation Authority (OCTA) in Orange County. It does not cover the DASH neighborhood buses in Los Angeles, which are particularly important for moving around Downtown LA. Google Transit also misses the FlyAway buses to the airport (LAX) and Culver City Bus.

Google Transit is very similar to the Metro Trip Planner. It asks when you want to leave, or arrive, with a convenient "leave now" choice. It asks for your starting point and ending point. In Google, you can enter these as an address, an intersection, or a business (for example, Los Angeles Athletic Club), another helpful feature. With Google, you're starting on a page that could give directions anywhere in the country, so it speeds things up to type in the city for your starting point and your destination. Google Transit will show you which buses or trains to take, generating a map highlighting your transfer points, if any.

Google Transit and Metro's Trip Planner should usually give you same the routing, but sometimes they don't. The Metro Trip Planner defaults to the trip with the fewest transfers, even if takes slightly longer. Google defaults to the shortest trip, even if it requires an extra transfer. Google's "Show Options" button allows you to ask for "fewest transfers" if that's your priority. There's a link within Google Transit back to the transit agency.

3. TELEPHONE INFORMATION AT (323) GO-METRO

You can get timetable information and routes, in English and Spanish, from this service. Its hours are Monday–Friday, 6:30 a.m.–7 p.m.; Saturday–Sunday, 8 a.m.–4:30 p.m. They will want to know much the same information as the Trip Planner—where you're starting, where you're going, and what time you want to travel.

4. MAP AND TIMETABLE INFORMATION

You can plan your trip using the Metro system map and bus and rail timetables. They're all available online. Paper copies are available in some places, most notably the transit service center at Union Station. A transit service center is located on the corner of Wilshire and La Brea boulevards in the Mid-Wilshire district, and other locations are in East Los Angeles and Baldwin Hills. Each route has a separate timetable, and even routes serving the same street (for example, bus 20 Wilshire Boulevard and rapid bus 720 Wilshire Boulevard) have separate ones.

Request hard-copy maps, timetables, and other brochures via U.S. mail in advance of your trip by submitting a form on the Metro website (**metro.net**). You could ask for a system map, a map of routes that run every 15 minutes or less, and key timetables, such as the Gold Line light rail, Red Line subway, and rapid bus 720.

5. METRO ON YOUR MOBILE DEVICE

Metro now provides extensive transit information for Internet-enabled smartphone users. Versions of the Trip Planner, map and timetable information, and real-time arrival information for rapid buses are available.

6. OTHER SOURCES OF TRANSIT INFORMATION

There are other sources of information about traveling car-free in LA. Most destinations' websites don't have transit information, but some museums and cultural organizations do. It's always worth checking the parking or driving directions section of a website—some places bury their transit information there.

The Experience LA website (**experiencela.com**) has some overall transit information and has built-in links to the Metro Trip Planner for dozens of destinations. Experience LA provides information on recreational destinations such as parks, museums, shopping areas, and so on. Metro's blog, **The Source,** also lists notable weekend events with transit information.

■ **Now that you know which bus to catch, you need to find it on the street.** The Trip Planner will tell you the exact corner where the bus is (for example, Wilshire Boulevard and Fairfax Avenue NE Corner). When you go to the corner, look for the Metro flag or sign that lists the bus routes that stop there and what their destinations are. In some cases, you may be able to zoom in on a view of the stop using Google Earth or Google Maps.

■ **Now it's time to get on and pay your fare.** Metro Rail and Metro Bus cost $1.50 exact change for each trip in each bus or train (there are no transfers). It's usually cheaper to buy a day pass, which gives you unlimited rides on just about all Metro Rail and Metro Bus lines for $5 per day—if you take four or more rides in a day, you save money. Without a pass, you'll need exact change for the bus, or a ticket from a ticket machine for the train. On the rail lines, you must buy a ticket or pass before you board; you can't pay on the train.

Day passes can be bought on the bus, at train stations, or at the Metro pass outlets. If you buy a day pass on the bus, the pass, loaded onto a plastic TAP smart card, will cost you $6. If you already have the TAP card, you can load the pass onto the card for $5. So if you're buying a day pass on more than 1 day, hang onto the TAP card to save $1 per day on the second and subsequent days. You can also buy a paper day pass from ticket vending machines at Metro Rail stations for $5, or find businesses and locations that sell TAP cards on the TAP website—**taptogo.com/ locator.** Nearby TAP outlets are listed for the start and end points of itineraries you put into the Trip Planner.

A 7-day pass is $20, loaded onto a TAP card, and can be bought to cover any 7 consecutive days. So you break even after 3–4 days, and it's more convenient than buying passes daily. Metro has more than 600 pass sales outlets, including its customer service centers, Ralph's grocery stores, and some other markets. A list of sales outlets can be found at **tinyurl.com/daypasslocations.** DASH buses aren't covered by the day pass but only cost 35 cents, so go for it, big spender.

▪ **Now you're on the bus or train, and you need to know when to get off.** On Metro Rail trains each station will be announced. On almost all the buses too, the stops are automatically announced. You can ask the bus driver when you get on to tell you when the bus gets to a certain spot. On some buses, the Transit TV screen will show you where the bus is.

▪ **Be safe.** Riding transit in LA is a safe activity. You should always be aware of your surroundings, of course, but incidents are rare and LA's crime rate has been steadily dropping. A total of 1.4 million trips are taken on Metro every weekday, so a lot of people are usually around. If a bus stop doesn't feel safe to you, walk to the next one. Look for bus stops in front of open businesses at night—statistics show that they are safer. Problems are rare, but they're more likely to happen at a bus stop than on the bus itself. If there's a real problem on the vehicle, you're allowed to change seats, or even get off the bus if needed. It's good to be polite, but it's more important to do what you need to do to feel safe.

LA Transit Tips

TRANSIT CULTURE: HOW PEOPLE ACT

People who don't take transit much sometimes worry about what it will be like on a train or a bus. Worry not—LA transit culture is usually calm, quiet, and reserved. People take more than 1.4 million trips on transit per weekday in LA, so it's not an exotic activity. People talk mostly to their friends and family members, and sometimes, although much less, to fellow passengers (regular passengers may have made friends with other regular passengers).

You'll see lots of mothers and some fathers with young children and plenty of grandmothers too. It's always OK to ask for directions or to ask when to get off the bus. You may see teenagers being what, in my day, we called "loud and wrong." This is almost always just a harmless, if annoying, form of teenagers showing off.

RUSH HOUR

If you can avoid riding Metro at rush hour, do so. Metro can get very crowded at rush hour, especially on main lines such as rapid bus 720 Wilshire Boulevard. Bus travel also gets slowed down at rush hour because of road congestion.

REAL-TIME INFORMATION AT BUS STOPS

Many rapid stops, especially on Wilshire Boulevard, have electronic LED real-time information signs, which give you an estimate, usually pretty accurate, of when the bus is coming. The signs are fairly small, so look for them.

BICYCLES ON METRO

All of Metro's buses have bike racks in front that hold two bikes. You can also bring bikes onto Metro rail lines at any time. Visit **metro.net/around/ bikes/bikes-metro** for rules about bicycles on the Metro.

It used to be a rarity, but bikes on Metro trains and buses are becoming increasingly common. You don't need a bike to make connections in central areas—the transit is pretty good. But as you move farther out, particularly west of Fairfax Avenue, where fewer north-south routes exist, a bike becomes more helpful. (For more information, see below).

SURFBOARDS

Unlike some SoCal transit agencies, Metro does not appear to have any limitations on surfboards, though one does not typically see them on Metro buses. The really avant-garde move would be to go surfing on the LA River.

Getting Around LA: Bikes and Taxis

BICYCLING

You might think that Los Angeles would be a good city for biking. The weather is often mild and it rarely rains. The most populated areas of the city are flat or gently sloping. Grids of long, straight streets cross large sections of the city—potentially ideal for biking separate from traffic on major streets. Physical fitness is practically a religion for many Angelenos, and you see them driving to the gym all the time. And the LA region desperately needs its residents to travel by environmentally clean methods.

But LA is not (now) a great city for biking. A cyclist can travel any street, except a freeway. But because only a few streets are designated for biking, most are not well set up for it. For example, secondary streets may or may not have traffic signals to help a cyclist get across a major street. Some cyclists prefer to ride more direct routes on major streets; you should be prepared for traffic that is both heavy and (many times) fast. The city of Los Angeles is now marking "sharrows," which combine an arrow with an outline of a bike, on some bike routes to help cyclists ride safely and to notify motorists to expect and respect bicyclists.

Metro has published a countywide bike map on its website (**tinyurl.com/labikemap**). You can presumably get a paper copy at transit information centers such as Union Station or Wilshire Boulevard and La Brea Avenue. The city of Los Angeles has just adopted a new plan calling for a major expansion of the bikeway network, so ideally, in the longer term, conditions will improve. Anecdotally, it seems as though more people are biking, and more bikes are showing up on transit. I won't advise you against biking in LA, but certainly be aware that it's a tough environment.

Los Angeles has no public bike-sharing program, but bike rental is widely available.

Meanwhile the League of American Bicyclists has designated Long Beach and Santa Monica as bike-friendly communities. So you should have an easier time within those two cities, which have more developed bikeway networks and flatter landscapes than other Southland cities.

To help cyclists get repairs, information, and in some cases bike rentals, bike stores are listed by neighborhood but not evaluated in this book.

TAXIS

Taxis are not particularly seen as a luxury service in LA, but rather (except for trips to the airport) as serving those obviously benighted souls who either a) don't own cars, b) are too drunk to drive one, or c) still think they're living in New York.

TIP *You are probably generating less pollution by taking a taxi. Most emissions happen when a car has a cold start, when it starts up after a long break. Because the taxis are constantly moving, they have fewer cold starts.*

Nevertheless, taxis can be a supplement to transit in Los Angeles, but they don't work as well as basic transportation. They're useful late at night when some bus lines stop running and other lines run infrequently. You can also use a taxi at night to cross a stretch about which you feel a little nervous, or to get back to a rail station or a main bus line. The basic fare is $2.85 for the first 0.11 mile (at flag drop) plus $2.70 per mile, as well as delay charges. So a 5-mile trip, which is not that far by Los Angeles standards, should be $16.05, plus whatever tip you want to give. If you take more than one cab trip a day, you're probably spending pretty close to what a rental car would cost.

It's also difficult to hail a cab in the city of Los Angeles. It's not illegal, as many people think, but it is illegal for the cab to stop in a red zone, a bus zone, or a no parking zone. That set of rules doesn't leave the cab many legal options, only the occasional parking space or parking lot that's not occupied. You can also take a taxi from a taxi stand or call one. Some city council members would like to liberalize the taxi pickup rules, so this may improve.

■ 4 Downtown Los Angeles

ONCE LEFT FOR DEAD, DOWNTOWN LA HAS EMERGED as Southern California's newest economic center, as well as its oldest one. Until the end of World War I, Downtown was *the* center of Los Angeles, and historic buildings dating back to the 1830s remain to this day. In the latter 20th century, Angelenos above the poverty line refused to live in Downtown LA, but now it is the new hot zone, celebrated even in *Los Angeles Magazine.* Top-notch restaurants were few and far between, but now some are flooded with customers. Trendy bars have popped up. Development has of course slacked off during the Great Recession but seems poised to resume if the national economy improves.

Downtown LA is a good place for car-free visitors to stay, at least for part of the time in Los Angeles. Direct bus and rail transit leads to almost all parts of the city. Ideally you'd stay some of your time in Downtown LA and some on the Westside, in Santa Monica or perhaps Westwood.

Billions of dollars in public and private investment seem to finally be generating business activity and neighborhood life. Metro built the Red Line subway and the Gold Line light rail, refurbished Union Station, and built its own grand tower. Redevelopment dollars built the Convention Center, sports arena Staples Center, and much more. But earlier on they also demolished the Victorian rooming houses of Bunker Hill, one of LA's great urban renewal traumas (the other biggie being the clearing

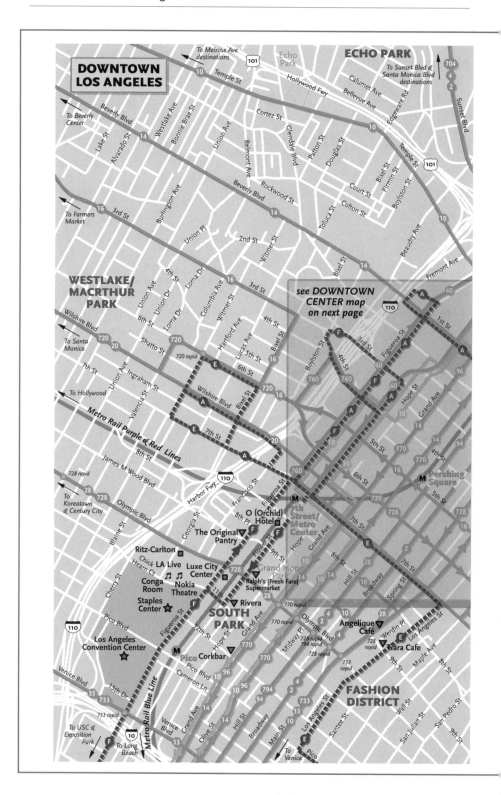

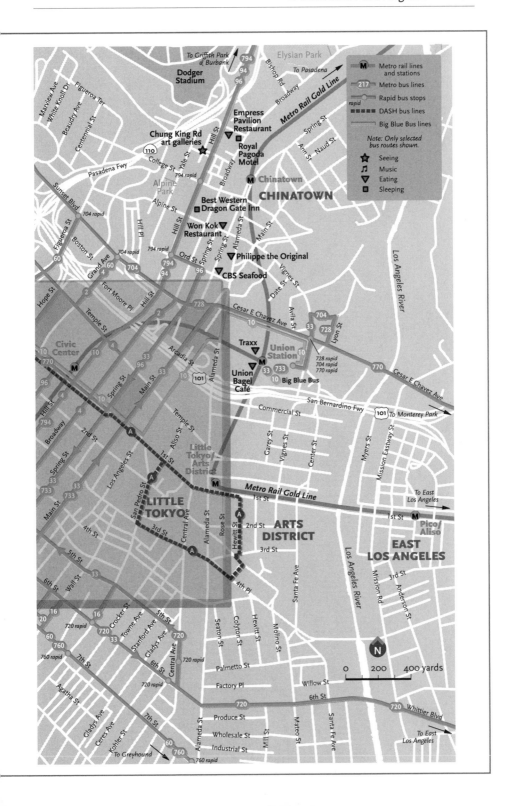

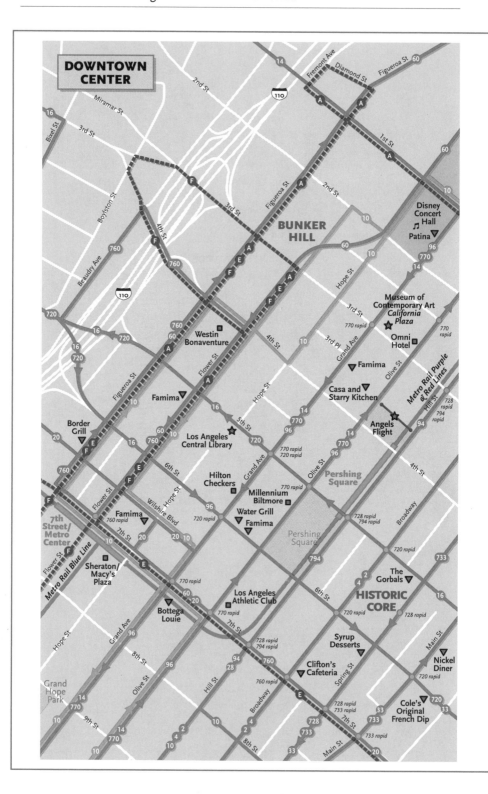

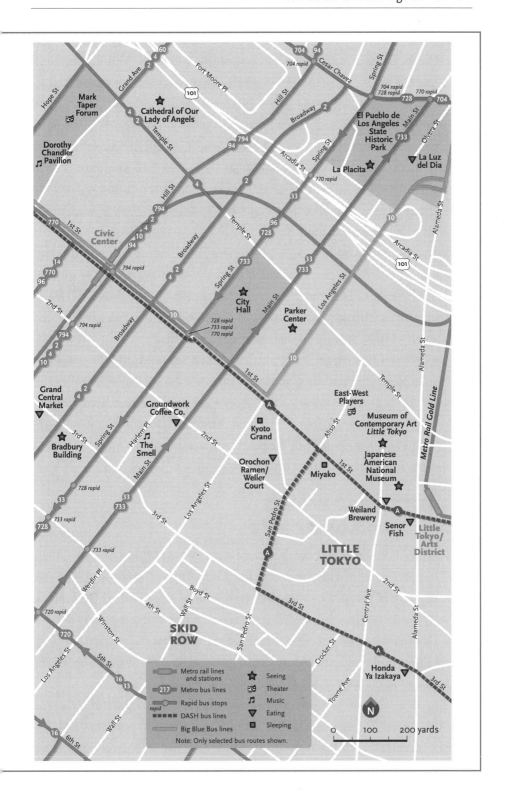

of Chavez Ravine). Public buildings were added—Disney Hall, a new police headquarters, and new state buildings, including the Ronald Reagan State Office Building (widely known—really!—as the Reagan SOB).

Despite its reputation as just a business neighborhood, Downtown has a lot of activities and attractions for visitors. Pro sports is the one activity really concentrated Downtown—the basketball Lakers and the hockey Kings play at Staples Center and the baseball Dodgers play at nearby Dodger Stadium in Chavez Ravine. Downtown has one of the city's great museums—the Museum of Contemporary Art, which has two downtown locations, on Bunker Hill and in Little Tokyo.

Upscale shopping is mostly elsewhere, but Downtown has the bargain hunter's dream, the Fashion District, where many of the clothes are actually made. Downtown is also the center of the transit network, with service reaching out to Pasadena, Hollywood, the Fairfax District, and Beverly Hills, among many other destinations.

Downtown Los Angeles is 15 miles east of Santa Monica and 7 miles southeast of Hollywood. It's bordered on the east by Boyle Heights, on the west by MacArthur Park and Echo Park, on the north by Elysian Park, and on the south by South Los Angeles. Downtown hotels are listed beginning on page 96. Restaurants are listed with each subarea of Downtown and beginning on page 91.

Transit to and within Downtown Los Angeles

Downtown Los Angeles covers a large area. From Union Station at the northeastern edge of Downtown to the Convention Center at the southwestern edge is some 2.5 miles. Though a lot of trips within Downtown are easy walks, others are not. That's why transit directions are needed *within* Downtown Los Angeles as well as to Downtown. Transit directions from Hollywood and Santa Monica are given with each of the subsections of Downtown, on page 76 and pages 81–88.

The best transit to Downtown from the northern part of LA—the San Fernando Valley—is via the Red Line subway from North Hollywood. Travelers coming from the Valley can use the directions from Hollywood.

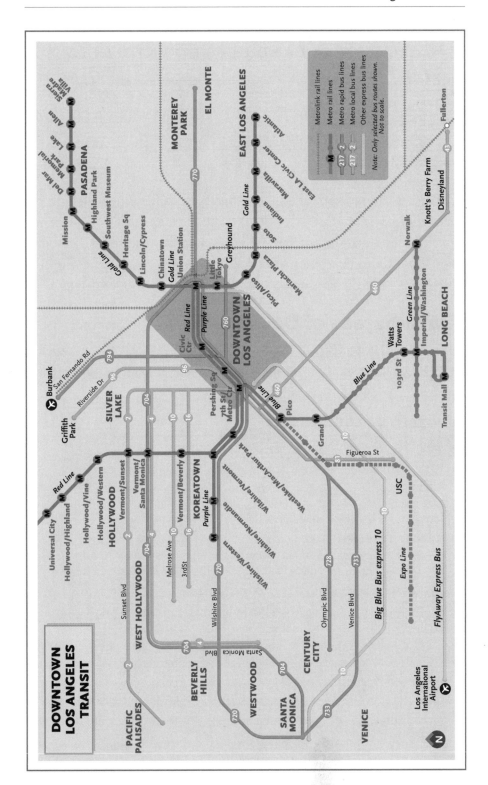

★ BIKE SHOPS IN AND NEAR DOWNTOWN LA ★

DTLA BIKES 425 S. Broadway at Fifth St.; (213) 533-8000; **dtlabikes.com**

ECHO PARK CYCLES 1928 Echo Park Blvd.; (213) 216-0515; echoparkcycles.blogspot.com

EL MAESTRO BICYCLE SHOP 806 S. Main St. at Eighth St.; (213) 627-0580; elmaestrobicycles.com

The best transit from South Los Angeles is via the Blue Line light rail to its terminus at 7th St./Metro Center. The directions within Downtown start from that station, so Blue Line travelers can use those. Traveling from South LA to Exposition Park doesn't require going all the way in to Downtown—see the Exposition Park section on page 89 for details.

The Subareas of Downtown

The subareas of Downtown LA are as follows: El Pueblo de Los Angeles, Little Tokyo, Historic Core, Bunker Hill/Financial District, South Park, Fashion District, and Exposition Park.

EL PUEBLO DE LOS ANGELES

19th-century Downtown

■ **LOCATION:** In the northeast part of Downtown Los Angeles, across Alameda Street from Union Station, between Spring Street on the west, Alameda Street on the east, Arcadia Street (Hollywood Freeway) on the south, and Cesar Chavez Avenue on the north. Visit **www.ci.la.ca.us/elp.**

■ **TRANSIT TO EL PUEBLO:**
From the Downtown Core at 7th St./Metro Center: Take the Red or Purple Line three stops to Union Station, the end of the line. El Pueblo is across Alameda Street.

From Hollywood: Take the Red Line to Union Station.

From Santa Monica: Take Big Blue Bus express 10 to Alameda and Los Angeles streets, at Union Station.

From elsewhere in Los Angeles: Go to Union Station via the Gold Line light rail from East LA, take the Red Line subway from the San Fernando Valley, or take rapid bus 740 or 745 from South Los Angeles.

EL PUEBLO IS LOS ANGELES'S OLD TOWN, with buildings that date back to the 1830s. But it does not preserve moments in time in amber. El Pueblo was

continued on page 80

▼ EL PUEBLO EATING PLACES ▼

LA LUZ DEL DIA W-1 Olvera St.; **luzdeldia.com** $

Fifty-plus-year-old Michoacán-style restaurant, known for carnitas, and widely viewed as the best on sometimes-dubious Olvera Street.

PHILIPPE THE ORIGINAL 1001 N. Alameda St. at Ord St.; **philippes.com** $

Philippe lays claim to inventing the French dip sandwich and serves a gazillion of them across its counter. It moved to this location in 1951 when due to freeway construction. A large, fun place that can get very crowded, Philippe's is a downtown landmark.

TRAXX 800 N. Alameda St.; **traxxrestaurant.com** $$$$

Fine, classic American dining in the elegant setting of Union Station. I would like all restaurants to provide transit directions on their website, but the omission is particularly glaring for this one.

UNION BAGEL CAFÉ 800 N. Alameda St.; **unionbagel.com** $

Decent bagels and chili dogs that some eaters swoon over. Union Station also has a branch of convenience store Famima, which has some decent packaged food.

TRANSIT TO CITYWIDE DESTINATIONS

DESTINATION	TRANSIT LINE TO GET THERE	WHERE TO BOARD IN DOWNTOWN LA
BEVERLY HILLS (Rodeo Drive)	Rapid bus 720 Wilshire Boulevard to Wilshire Blvd./ Beverly Blvd.	5th St./Main St., 5th St./ Broadway, and 5th St./ Grand Ave.
CHINESE THEATRE/ HOLLYWOOD historic theaters	Red Line subway to Hollywood Blvd./ Highland Ave.	Union Station, Civic Center, Pershing Square, and 7th St./ Metro Center
ECHO PARK commercial/ entertainment area	Bus 2 Sunset Blvd. or bus 4 Santa Monica Blvd. to Sunset Blvd./ Alvarado St.	Along Broadway northbound
EXPOSITION PARK	DASH F shuttle to Exposition Blvd./ Trousdale Pkwy.	Flower St. at 5th St., 7th St., 8th St., 9th St., and Olympic Blvd.
FARMERS MARKET/ THE GROVE	Bus 16 Third St. to Third St./Fairfax Ave.	Along 5th St. westbound
GETTY CENTER, Brentwood	Rapid bus 720 to Wilshire Blvd./ Westwood Ave., then rapid bus 761 to Getty Center Dr.; transfer to the tram uphill to the museum	5th St./Main St., 5th St./ Broadway, and 5th St./ Grand Ave.
HOLLYWOOD WALK OF FAME	Red Line subway to Hollywood Blvd./ Vine St.	Union Station, Civic Center, Pershing Square, and 7th St./ Metro Center
KOREATOWN	Red/Purple Line subway to Wilshire Blvd./Vermont Ave.	Civic Center, Pershing Square, and 7th St./Metro Center
LOS ANGELES COUNTY MUSEUM OF ART/MUSEUM ROW	Rapid bus 720 to Wilshire Blvd./ Fairfax Ave.	5th St./Main St., 5th St./ Broadway, and 5th St./Grand Ave.
LOS ANGELES ZOO	Bus 96 to Zoo Dr.	Along Olive St. northbound

FROM DOWNTOWN LOS ANGELES

DESTINATION	TRANSIT LINE TO GET THERE	WHERE TO BOARD IN DOWNTOWN LA
NORTON SIMON MUSEUM, Pasadena	Red/Purple Line subway to Union Station, then Gold Line light rail to Memorial Park	7th St./Metro Center, Pershing Square, and Civic Center
OLD PASADENA	Red/Purple Line subway to Union Station, then Gold Line light rail to Memorial Park	7th St./Metro Center, Pershing Square, and Civic Center
SANTA MONICA (3rd St. and pier)	Big Blue Bus express 10 to Broadway/3rd St.	Flower St./5th St., Grand Ave./7th St., and Grand Ave./Olympic Blvd.
SUNSET JUNCTION shopping area	Bus 2 Sunset Blvd. or bus 4 Santa Monica Blvd. to Hyperion Ave.	Along Broadway northbound
SUNSET STRIP entertainment area, West Hollywood	Bus 2 Sunset Blvd. to stops along Sunset Blvd. between Crescent Heights Blvd. and Doheny Dr.	Along Broadway northbound
THAI TOWN restaurant area	Red Line subway to Hollywood Blvd./Western Ave.	Union Station, Civic Center, Pershing Square, and 7th St./Metro Center
UNIVERSAL STUDIOS	Red Line subway to Universal City	Civic Center, Pershing Square, and 7th St./Metro Center
WARNER BROS. STUDIOS, BURBANK	Red Line subway to Hollywood Blvd./Vine St., then bus 222 (infrequent) to Riverside Dr./Hollywood Way	Union Station, Civic Center, Pershing Square, and 7th St./Metro Center
WATTS TOWERS	Blue Line light rail to 103rd St.	7th St./Metro Center and Pico Blvd.
WILTERN THEATER	Purple Line subway to Wilshire Blvd./Western Ave.	Civic Center, Pershing Square, and 7th St./Metro Center

continued from page 76

a living, breathing neighborhood whose residents, workers, and activities kept changing until it was made an official tourist attraction in the 1920s. As in downtown San Francisco and New York, Chinese and Italian immigrants, as well as Mexicans, once made the area their home. El Pueblo remains interesting today because it is so multilayered.

Four of the buildings at El Pueblo are museums. **Avila Adobe** is open Wednesday–Sunday, 10 a.m.–3 p.m., and **Sepulveda House** is open 9 a.m.–4 p.m. daily. Both have free admission and give glimpses of life here at various times.

The **Chinese American Museum** is located in the last standing building of LA's original Chinatown (the other buildings were demolished for Union Station). It's open Tuesday–Sunday, 10 a.m.–3 p.m., with a suggested admission of $3 for adults, $2 for students and seniors.

A new **Italian American Museum** is due to open in the former Italian Hall in 2012 but is already hosting events. The building's exterior features a mural by famed Mexican painter David Siqueiros; conservation work of the mural, which was covered over for decades, is ongoing.

The **Plaza Firehouse** was the first in Los Angeles built for that purpose, and the museum displays firefighting equipment of the late 19th century. It has free admission and is open Tuesday–Friday, 10 a.m.–3 p.m.

A new and long-awaited addition to El Pueblo is **La Plaza de Cultura y Artes,** a Smithsonian-affiliated center of Mexican American culture and history, with

▼ DIM SUM IN CHINATOWN ▼

Los Angeles's small Chinatown is directly adjacent to El Pueblo historic park. Chinatown, northwest of Union Station, is no longer LA's main Chinese restaurant and commercial area. San Gabriel Valley towns such as Monterey Park, San Gabriel, and Alhambra have superseded it. But if you're visiting sights at El Pueblo or staying nearby, you might like some dim sum (small savory pastries) in the morning. Because you'll get three or four of each dim sum, it's not great food for a solo diner.

TRANSIT: *Take the Gold Line to Chinatown station.*

CBS SEAFOOD 700 N. Spring St.

EMPRESS PAVILION RESTAURANT 988 N. Hill St. #201; empresspavilion.com

WON KOK RESTAURANT 210 Alpine St.

a particular focus on Southern California. Opening exhibits showed the early history of Los Angeles and the character of El Pueblo in the 1920s. The center also hosts events featuring performances, food, and films. Open Wednesday–Monday, noon–7 p.m., it charges $9 for adults, $7 for students and seniors, and $5 for children ages 5–18.

Olvera Street, a pedestrian-only street of vendors and restaurants, is the most popular area of El Pueblo, where Avila Adobe is located. Across Main Street from El Pueblo is **La Placita,** formally known as Our Lady Queen of Angeles Roman Catholic Church. The oldest Catholic church in the city of Los Angeles, La Placita is now run by the Claretian fathers. La Placita has long had a strong orientation toward immigrants. For a time during the civil war in El Salvador, the church declared itself a sanctuary for people fleeing the war. The small church makes an interesting contrast to the sweeping new Roman Catholic Cathedral of Our Lady of Angels a few blocks away.

LITTLE TOKYO

Postwar Downtown Rebuilding of an Old Community

■ **LOCATION:** On the east side of Downtown Los Angeles, approximately bounded by Temple Street on the north, Third Street on the south, Main Street on the west, and Alameda Street to the east.

■ **TRANSIT TO LITTLE TOKYO:**
From the Downtown Core at 7th St./Metro Center: It's about a 1.5-mile walk, long for most people, so on weekdays, take DASH A to First Street and Central Avenue. On weekends, take Metro bus 30 or 40 from Broadway and Fifth Street to Judge John Aliso Street, one block west of the museum.

From Hollywood: Take the Red Line subway to Civic Center station, and walk east on First Street four blocks.

From Santa Monica: Take Big Blue Bus express 10 to Los Angeles and Temple streets, and walk two blocks south to First Street.

From East LA: Take the Gold Line to Little Tokyo station.

From the San Fernando Valley: Take the Red Line to Civic Center station, and walk east on First Street.

From South Los Angeles: Take rapid bus 740 or 745 to Broadway and First Street.

BEFORE WORLD WAR II AND THE INTERNAL DEPORTATION of Japanese Americans, Nihonmachis (Japantowns) dotted the West Coast. Afterward, only a few, including Little Tokyo, survived. Few older buildings here, notably along First Street between Central Avenue and San Pedro Street, a National Register Historic District, survived later redevelopment. But Little Tokyo gained hotels, museums, new housing, and now, a light rail station

▼ LITTLE TOKYO EATING PLACES ▼

Little Tokyo has Japanese restaurants (and a few non-Japanese ones) of all descriptions, including sushi places, ramen places, *izakayas*, and other specialists at varying price levels.

GROUNDWORK COFFEE COMPANY   108 W. Second St. at Main St.; **lacoffee.com** $

This is an interesting two-level café on the Little Tokyo/Historic Core border, with good organic coffee from a small local chain. See listings in other neighborhoods.

HONDA YA IZAKAYA   333 S. Alameda St. at Third St.; **izakayahondaya.com**

This izakaya, a sort of Japanese tapas restaurant and sake bar, is well liked among foodies. It's part of a small local chain, with outlets in the cities of Industry, Tustin, and Fountain Valley. You can get numerous small items, so price categories don't apply, but izakaya can easily get quite pricey.

OROCHON RAMEN   123 Astronaut Ellison S. Onizuka St. (third floor of Weller Court shopping center); **orochon-ramen.com** $

Orochon sells good, big ramens, but it also allows you to set your own level of spiciness, from barely detectable to completely intolerable. If you eat the spiciest, you get a prize and free hospital care.

SENOR FISH   422 E. First St. at Alameda St.; **senorfishonline.com** $

A branch of one of LA's most famous fish taco restaurants. Also in Eagle Rock and South Pasadena.

WEILAND BREWERY   400 E. First St. at Central Ave.; **weilandbrewery.net** $$–$$$

Downtown's longest serving brewpub with quite a pickup scene on weekend nights. Also in the Financial District.

on the Gold Line. The area has become a kind of ethnic downtown for many Japanese Americans in LA, even if they don't live there. The hotels are a touchstone for tourists from Japan, though some local residents resented this when they were being built.

Little Tokyo's fragmented urban fabric doesn't always feel visitor-friendly, even though, unlike most LA neighborhoods, it has its own visitor center (307 E. First St.). Many of the streets are too wide and the buildings too large and fortresslike.

But Little Tokyo is a cultural destination and one of the livelier sections of Downtown Los Angeles, despite the damage inflicted by urban renewal. See page 206 for details about the Geffen Contemporary building of the Museum of Contemporary Art located here. The Japanese American National Museum (see page 210) is both a historical museum, with items dating back to the internment, and a museum of Japanese American art.

HISTORIC CORE

Turn of the (20th) Century Downtown

■ LOCATION: In the central area of Downtown, approximately bounded by Third Street on the north, Ninth Street on the south, Hill Street on the west, and Main Street on the east.

■ TRANSIT TO THE HISTORIC CORE:

From the Downtown Core at 7th St./Metro Center: Walk east on Seventh Street, a few blocks to the Historic Core.

From Hollywood: Take the Red Line to Pershing Square. The Historic Core begins immediately to the east of the station exits on Hill Street.

From Santa Monica: Take the Big Blue Bus express 10 to Seventh and Olive streets, and walk one block east on Seventh Street to Hill Street.

ATTRACTIONS IN THE HISTORIC CORE INCLUDE a growing number of art galleries. But the Historic Core is primarily a place you go to see the district

---

▼ HISTORIC CORE EATING PLACES ▼

The Historic Core has always had some great eateries, and as the neighborhood gentrifies, new ones are springing up.

CLIFTON'S CAFETERIA 648 S. Broadway; **cliftonscafeteria.com** $

Once a local chain, the sole remaining Clifton's serves low-priced cafeteria comfort food in a room adorned with murals of nature.

COLE'S ORIGINAL FRENCH DIP 118 E. Sixth St.; **colesfrenchdip.com** $

The other place, besides Philippe the Original, that lays claim to inventing the French dip sandwich is now restored to some of its former glory.

THE GORBALS 501 S. Spring St. at Fifth St. (Alexandria Hotel); **thegorbalsla.com** $$

The prices are decent unless you want the half-cut roasted pig head, which will set you back about $50. Where else can you get bacon-wrapped matzo balls? The cuisine has both Scottish and Jewish influences—seriously. It's now a trendy eatery at an edgy site in a moderately renovated residential hotel.

NICKEL DINER 524 S. Main St.; **nickeldiner.com** $–$$

On a block with several social service agencies, Nickel Diner turns out fine renditions of diner favorites in a meticulously restored room. Famed for bacon-covered doughnuts. It could tip over into "too hip for the likes of you," but it hasn't yet.

SYRUP DESSERTS 611 S. Spring St. near Sixth St. $

A nice hangout, open early and late, and something Downtown has long needed, it offers desserts, coffee, crêpes, and sandwiches. It has a downstairs space as well as a second-floor loft seating area. This establishment is a sign that the Downtown revival is real.

itself. Among the Downtown areas, the Historic Core has the most to see as you walk along.

Because little was built here after World War II, the area has an unusually strong and intact grouping of early 20th-century buildings. The buildings were mostly built as offices, but many are now residential. Almost 100 designated Historic Cultural Monuments (landmarks) are in Downtown LA, and the Historic Core has the largest share.

Downtown Los Angeles boomed in the early years of the 20th century, and the Historic Core is the physical reflection of that. Skyscraper office buildings were built 1900–1930, fed by one of the country's most extensive systems of local and suburban trolleys. After 1950 the Historic Core lost ground to suburban office developments and to newer buildings on the west side of Downtown LA, and it was widely considered to be blighted, almost the beginning of Skid Row. Rediscovered about 10 years ago by developers strategically using redevelopment funds, many old office buildings became lofts, apartments, and condos. Specific buildings of interest include the Bradbury Building with its atrium, often shown in movies, and the gorgeous green Eastern Columbia Building. The 2009 indie hit movie *500 Days of Summer* featured many scenes from the Historic Core.

■ **LOS ANGELES CONSERVANCY WALKING TOURS:** Saturday, 10 a.m. Visit **laconservancy.org** for exact times and meeting locations of the tours. Some tours require reservations. Adults, $10; Los Angeles Conservancy members and children age 12 and under, $5.

The Los Angeles Conservancy is LA's main citywide historic preservation organization. The conservancy has eight regular walking tours, three of them in the Historic Core—Broadway historical theaters and Historic Downtown tours are held every Saturday morning, and a Downtown Renaissance: Spring and Main tour is offered twice a month. The conservancy also tours the Biltmore Hotel, just outside the Historic Core, on Sunday afternoons and offers tours in other areas of town. The conservancy is the undisputed expert on LA's historic urban fabric.

BUNKER HILL/FINANCIAL DISTRICT

Modernist Downtown

■ **LOCATION:** On the west side of Downtown Los Angeles, approximately bounded by First Street on the north, Eighth Street on the south, the Harbor Freeway (CA 110) on the west, and Hill Street on the east.

■ **TRANSIT TO BUNKER HILL:**
From the Downtown Core at 7th St./Metro Center: This station is located in Bunker Hill.

From Hollywood: Take the Red Line to 7th St./Metro Center, Pershing Square, or Civic Center.

From Santa Monica: Take Big Blue Bus express 10 to Figueroa and Seventh, Sixth, or Fifth streets.

Angels Flight (**angelsflight.com**): Bunker Hill has a fabulous piece of mostly recreational transit, also useful for avoiding a steep hill. The Angels Flight funicular—almost like a cable car on a hill instead of a street—originally opened in 1901 and reopened in 1996 after a 9-year hiatus. In about 1 minute Angels Flight will take you in charming, historically restored cars from Hill Street up the east side of Bunker Hill to a station serving Grand Avenue and Olive Street (25-cent fare). It's been called the world's shortest railway at 298 feet in length, going up about 100 feet. The funicular is located between Third and Fourth streets and serves destinations such as the Museum of Contemporary Art, the Omni, and Disney Hall.

 ## BUNKER HILL/FINANCIAL DISTRICT EATING PLACES

BOTTEGA LOUIE   700 S. Grand Ave.; **bottegalouie.com** $$–$$$

This is a spectacular place: huge, high-ceilinged, and very, very loud. There are multiple eating opportunities from breakfast through late evening—takeout salads and entrées, a patisserie, a bar, and a full-on Italian restaurant. The place gets absolutely jammed at dinnertime, so expect long waits. More than some soulless megaproject, Bottega Louie is a real sign that there's life in Downtown LA.

CASA   350 S. Grand Ave., California Plaza concourse level; **casadowntown.com** $$–$$$

A reasonably good Mexican restaurant, though most focused on generating a party atmosphere.

BORDER GRILL   445 S. Figueroa St.; **bordergrill.com** $$$–$$$$

Part of a minichain of modern Mexican restaurants (another branch is in Santa Monica). Also an office workers' drinking spot. Lunch is served on weekdays and dinner is offered daily. Border Grill runs a free shuttle to Disney Hall and LA Live in the evenings before curtain times.

PATINA   141 S. Grand at Disney Hall; **patinarestaurant.com** $$$$$

The Patina group has long been one of LA's largest fine dining non-chains; this is their estimable Disney Hall entry. Hugely expensive, but you won't have to scramble to get to a concert. You can also get a $1 sandwich or salad at Patina Group's Concert Hall Café, open for lunch and on evenings when there are performances.

STARRY KITCHEN   350 S. Grand Ave., California Plaza concourse level; **starrykitchen.com** $

A terrific Vietnamese fusion weekday lunch place (dinner on Thursday and Friday evenings) in the bowels of California Plaza that came up from an underground North Hollywood speakeasy restaurant. The website is highly narrative.

WATER GRILL   544 S. Grand Ave.; **watergrill.com** $$$$$

A very high-end restaurant in the core of Downtown, renowned for exquisite seafood. Its website modestly claims that it is the ultimate example of fine dining in Los Angeles and has the best seafood in Southern California; some critics would agree.

THE WEST SIDE OF DOWNTOWN LA is sometimes called New Downtown. That moniker reflects the post-1960 origins of the office district on Bunker Hill and the flatlands below it. It took massive redevelopment (7,000 housing units were demolished) of the rooming house/cheap apartment district on Bunker Hill to clear a space for these towers, a trauma that is still part of LA's cultural memory.

LA doesn't have a single cultural center, but the center of official high culture is Bunker Hill. The shiny titanium pile known as Disney Hall (see page 155) is home to the Los Angeles Philharmonic and is renowned for its excellent acoustics. The Dorothy Chandler Pavilion (see page 155) in the Music Center complex up the street is home to the Los Angeles Opera. The Mark Taper Forum (see page 150), LA's longest-standing repertory theater, performs in the Music Center complex (though it has hedged its bets with another theater in Culver City). As its founders intended, the Music Center is often compared to New York's Lincoln Center.

The Museum of Contemporary Art, widely viewed as one of the world's finest modern art museums, is also on Bunker Hill in the California Plaza complex. See page 206 for more information.

The modern office towers here tend not to have stores on their ground floor, but instead have retail stores in basement-level malls. For a Downtown area, Bunker Hill is not generally a fun place to walk. The Bonaventure Hotel in particular has been criticized as an anti-urban building designed for access by cars, not people.

Below Bunker Hill, south of Fifth Street, the picture is more mixed. New towers are mixed with older structures such as the (Millennium) Biltmore Hotel on the west side of Pershing Square. One of the nicest older structures is the Los Angeles Central Library at 630 W. Fifth St., which has a wing named after the path-breaking former mayor Tom Bradley. Besides books, the library often has worthwhile art and photography exhibits.

SOUTH PARK

21st-century Downtown

■ **LOCATION:** In the southwest part of Downtown Los Angeles, bounded approximately by Eighth Street on the north, Pico Boulevard on the south (at 17th Street), the Harbor Freeway (CA 110) to the west, and Hill Street to the east.

■ **TRANSIT TO SOUTH PARK:**
From the Downtown Core at 7th St./Metro Center: Walk one to three blocks south to South Park.

From Hollywood: Take the Red Line subway to 7th St./Metro Center, and walk south one to three blocks from there.

From Santa Monica: Take Big Blue Bus express 10 to Olive and 11th streets.

YOU KNOW YOU HAVE A NEWLY DEVELOPED PART OF THE CITY when it gets a new name. Once an anonymous, semi-industrial corner of Downtown LA, notable mostly for parking lots, South Park has been transformed into a district of pricey housing, trendy restaurants, and big-time entertainment. South Park is the newest piece in the ongoing remaking of Downtown Los Angeles, still gelling as a neighborhood.

Unlike other parts of Downtown, you probably won't want to visit South Park to see the neighborhood itself, unless you're an aficionado of contemporary multifamily architecture. Only a handful of historic buildings have survived. Here it's about the attractions and the restaurants.

If Bunker Hill is the center of official high culture, then South Park, a dozen blocks south, is the unofficial center of pop culture. In fact, **LA Live,** which extends south from the corner of Figueroa Street and Olympic Boulevard, describes itself as a "one of a kind entertainment campus"—a pop culture cultural park. Check **lalive.com** for overall event listings. Major halls include the **Nokia Theatre** at 777 Chick Hearn Ct., a new venue for rock and pop concerts and events such as *American Idol Live;* Visit **nokiatheatrelalive.com** for more information. **Lucky Strike Lanes** at 800 W. Olympic Blvd., is a trendy new bowling chain (also in Hollywood). Visit **bowlluckystrike.com.** And the **Grammy**

▼ SOUTH PARK EATING PLACES ▼

South Park is becoming a trendy, if pricey, new eating neighborhood.

CORKBAR   403 W. 12th St. at Grand Ave.; **corkbar.com** $$–$$$

A wine bar with a 20-page list of wines, mostly by the glass; a good hangout for the upscale locals. It also serves dinner.

THE ORIGINAL PANTRY   877 S. Figueroa St.; **pantrycafe.com** $$

The Original Pantry is not the finest dining in town, but it's too useful to ignore (and it only accepts cash). Open 24 hours a day, 365 days a year, this diner boasts of being "never without a customer" (perhaps they keep some in reserve just in case). It's owned by former LA Mayor Richard Riordan. A slice of old LA.

RIVERA   1050 S. Flower St.; **riverarestaurant.com** $$$$–$$$$$

The food at high-priced Rivera sits on the border between Nuevo Latino and deconstructed, almost molecular cuisine. It's an attractive and interesting place to eat and drink but an unusual one. In general, my philosophy is that you can take kids anywhere to eat, but Rivera might not be the best place for them.

Museum, tracks the history of the record industry at 800 W. Olympic Blvd. It's open Monday–Friday, 11:30 a.m.–7:30 p.m., and Saturday–Sunday, 10 a.m.–7:30 p.m. Admission is $13 for adults, $12 for seniors and students over age 18 with ID, and $11 for children ages 6–17. The massive **Los Angeles Convention Center** (1201 S. Figueroa St.) rounds out and looms over the neighborhood.

■ STAPLES CENTER: 1111 Figueroa St.; **staplescenter.com**

LA's fabulously successful NBA team—the Lakers—play at Staples Center. So do the other NBA team, the Clippers, and the Women's National Basketball Association team, the Sparks. And finally there's the rather hapless pro hockey team, the Kings. Other events, such as arena rock concerts, also take place here. The center is next door to LA Live.

FASHION DISTRICT

Downtown of Our Fathers and Mothers

■ LOCATION: In the southeast part of Downtown Los Angeles, approximately bounded by Seventh Street on the north, the I-10 Santa Monica Freeway on the south, Main Street on the west, and San Julian Street on the east.

■ TRANSIT TO THE FASHION DISTRICT:

From the Downtown Core at 7th St./Metro Center: It's approximately a 1-mile walk, or take DASH E to Los Angeles and Ninth streets.

From Hollywood: Take the Red Line subway to 7th St./Metro Center, and then take DASH E to Los Angeles and Ninth streets.

From Santa Monica: Take Big Blue Bus express 10 to 11th and Olive streets and then walk east three blocks to Main Street.

THE GLOBALIZATION OF APPAREL MANUFACTURING NOTWITHSTAND-ING, Los Angeles remains a major center of garment making. Garment manufacturing, wholesaling, and retailing come together in the Fashion District in the southeastern part of Downtown LA. The district reminds me of New York's Lower East Side before it was gentrified, albeit without the tenement buildings above the stores. Stores are generally open Monday–Saturday, 10 a.m.–5 p.m., and about one-third of the stores are open Sunday.

Different kinds of clothes and accessories are sold on different blocks of the district. Not all businesses sell as retailers, and some only do so at certain times. The northeastern side of the district, Los Angeles Street from Seventh to Ninth streets, is focused on menswear. Women's wear is most of what's sold here, and it can be found along Santee Street, between Ninth Street and Pico Boulevard; Pico Boulevard, between Main Street and Santee Street; and Wall Street and Maple Street, between Olympic Boulevard and 12th Street. Kids' clothes are in the southeastern part of the district at 12th Street and Pico Boulevard,

---

▼ FASHION DISTRICT EATING PLACES ▼

Fashion District eats are, for the most part, pretty functional, designed to keep the workforce going rather than provide fine dining.

ANGELIQUE CAFÉ   840 S. Spring St.; **angeliquebistro.com** $$–$$$

At the gateway, as it were, of the Fashion District, Angelique is a pleasant, semi-French café at the triangle formed by the convergence of Main and Spring streets. Good for salads, sandwiches, and coffee, it recently started serving dinner.

TIARA CAFE   127 E. Ninth St.; **tiara-cafe-la.com** $$

Serving weekday lunch around the corner from Angelique, with a special orientation toward the cool crowd.

---

between Maple and San Julian streets. Wander freely, but if you find yourself on a deserted block with no stores, go back to where there's more life. Visit **fashion district.org** for a map that shows the different areas.

EXPOSITION PARK

Culture Park LA

■ **LOCATION:** Where 38th Street would be, about 2 miles south of the Downtown Core, and just south of the University of Southern California (USC). Bordered on the north by Exposition Blvd., on the south by Martin Luther King Jr. Blvd., on the east by Figueroa St., and on the west by Vermont Ave.

■ **TRANSIT TO EXPOSITION PARK BEFORE THE EXPO LINE OPENS:**
From the Downtown Core at 7th St./Metro Center: Take DASH F to Exposition Boulevard and Trousdale Parkway.

From Hollywood: Take the Red Line subway to Wilshire Boulevard/Vermont Avenue, and then take rapid bus 754 to Vermont Avenue and Exposition Boulevard.

From Santa Monica: Take Big Blue Bus express 10 to Olive and Eighth streets, and then take Metro bus 81 to Figueroa and State streets.

■ **TRANSIT TO EXPOSITION PARK AFTER THE EXPO LINE OPENS:**
From 7th St./Metro Center: Take the Expo light rail to Expo Park/USC station.

From Hollywood: Take the Red Line subway to 7th St./Metro Center and then the Expo light rail to Expo Park/USC station.

From Santa Monica: Take Big Blue Bus express 10 to Seventh and Olive streets, and then take the Expo light rail from 7th St./Metro Center to Expo Park/USC station.

EXPOSITION PARK IS EASILY ACCESSIBLE from Downtown by various transit lines, though it's not the most pleasant walk. By late 2011 transit to Exposition Park will get even easier—the Expo Line light rail will have a station right at the park.

▼ EXPOSITION PARK EATING PLACES ▼

CHICHÉN IZTÁ 3655 S. Grand Ave.; **chichenitzarestaurant.com** $

Serving food from Mexico's Yucatán Peninsula. You can get cochinita pibil—achiote-marinated pork, wrapped in a banana leaf—here.

LAB GASTROPUB 3500 S. Figueroa St.; **thelab.usc.edu** $$

Not all food in the neighborhood is mercado food or fast food for USC students. The Lab Gastropub serves a modern take on sandwiches, burgers, salads, and of course craft beers.

MERCADO LA PALOMA 3655 S. Grand Ave.; **mercadolapaloma.com** $–$$

A small but tasty public market in the vein of Grand Central Market or the Farmers Market at Third Street and Fairfax Avenue. About a 10-minute walk from the Exposition Park museums, just on the other side of the 110 freeway (37th Street crosses over). The market is only open until 6:30 p.m., but I don't advise doing this walk after dark. You can order food at a stand and then find a table at which to sit. From Downtown LA, take transit to Exposition Park or take bus 40, 42, or 45 or rapid bus 740 or 745 to just east of the Mercado on Broadway.

MO-CHICA 3655 S. Grand Ave.; **mo-chica.com** $–$$

A fine Peruvian establishment at the market.

Exposition Park is a much smaller-scale version of San Diego's Balboa Park—160 acres versus Balboa's 1,200. Both are cultural parks—parks with numerous cultural institutions within. Both were created during the same early 20th-century City Beautiful era. Exposition Park was initially developed in 1913. While Balboa Park encompasses a large proportion of San Diego's museums, Exposition Park just has an interesting slice of LA's. It is a particularly good destination for people traveling with children. For more information on all Exposition Park venues and activities, visit **expositionpark.org.**

■ **CALIFORNIA AFRICAN AMERICAN MUSEUM:** 600 State Dr. near Figueroa St.; **caamuseum.org;** Tuesday–Saturday, 10 a.m.–5 p.m.; Sunday, 11 a.m.–5 p.m.; Free

A permanent exhibit chronicles African Americans' journey "from the West Coast of Africa to the West Coast of America." This journey can sometimes get overlooked as the story of black movement from the South to the North is told. It also has changing exhibits.

■ **CALIFORNIA SCIENCE CENTER:** 700 Exposition Park Dr.; **californiascience center.org;** open daily (closed Thanksgiving, December 25, and January 1), 10 a.m.– 5 p.m.; Free, though the IMAX theater charges a fee

The museum describes itself as "the West Coast's largest hands-on science center." Exhibits include biology, ecology, technology, and other -ologys.

■ **MUSEUM OF NATURAL HISTORY:** 900 Exposition Blvd. near Menlo Ave.; **nhm.org;** open daily, 9:30 a.m.–5 p.m.; Adults, $9; children ages 13–17, $6.50; children ages 5–12, $2

The birds, bees, and the dinosaurs and the Lando Hall of California History. The original 1913 building has been recently restored.

■ **ROSE GARDEN:** 3990 S. Menlo Ave.; **laparks.org/exporosegarden/rosegarden. htm;** office: Monday–Friday, 9 a.m.–4 p.m.; the garden is closed January 1–March 15; Free

A 7-acre garden with 20,000 rosebushes, the Rose Garden dates back to 1908. It has survived such classic LA dangers as a proposal to tear up the garden to create an underground parking garage and a proposal to make a practice field for the Raiders football team during the brief moment they were in LA.

Eating Expeditions from Downtown LA

Besides all the tasty food in Downtown LA itself, good eating neighborhoods are a short bus or train ride away. Koreatown, a few miles west of Downtown LA, is the largest Korean business district in the country.

The San Gabriel Valley, notably the cities of San Gabriel and Monterey Park, has a huge concentration of Chinese restaurants of many varieties. This is a longer ride from Downtown LA. You may want to go at lunchtime (most restaurants are open for lunch) or earlier in the evening, though service is available later in the evening.

EAST LA EATERIES

East LA is a longtime Mexican/Mexican American neighborhood a few miles east of Downtown Los Angeles.

ANTOJITOS CARMEN 2510 E. Cesar Chavez Ave.; **antojitoscarmen restaurant.com** $ Once a street vendor, now a small restaurant known for Mexico City–style masa snacks such as sopes and gorditas; also serves quesadillas and more elaborate food. Transit: *From Downtown LA,* take the Gold Line light rail to Soto station, and then walk two blocks north on Soto Street and one block east on Cesar Chavez Boulevard.

MOLES LA TIA 4619 E. Cesar Chavez Blvd. near McDonnell Ave.; **moleslatia.com** $$–$$$$ Specializing in the cuisine of the southern Mexican state of Oaxaca, particularly its dark, rich mole sauces. Transit: *From Downtown LA on weekdays,* take rapid bus 770 on Olive Street to Cesar Chavez Boulevard and Mednik Avenue, and then walk two blocks west. *Or for daily service,* take bus 84/68 from North Main and First streets to Cesar Chavez Boulevard and Dangler Avenue, and then walk one block west on Cesar Chavez Boulevard.

LA SERENATA DE GARIBALDI 1842 E. First St. between Bailey and State streets; **laserenataonline.com** $–$$$ A longtime "fancier" Mexican restaurant in the heart of Boyle Heights, specializing in seafood. Transit: *From Downtown LA,* take the Gold Line light rail to Mariachi Plaza station, and walk two blocks east on First Street.

TACOS BAJA ENSENADA 5385 Whittier Blvd. at Oakford Dr.; **tacosbaja.us** $ Believed by many to have the best fish tacos in all LA. Transit: *From Downtown LA,* take rapid bus 720 from stops on Sixth Street to Whittier and Goodrich boulevards, and then walk one block west.

KOREATOWN RESTAURANTS

Hundreds of restaurants are located in Koreatown, and most, but not all, of them are Korean. They're thickest on the ground on Vermont Avenue between Wilshire and Olympic boulevards, and on Olympic between Vermont and Western avenues. Sixth and Eighth streets between Vermont and Western are also commercial streets; it's a very busy neighborhood. Try random restaurants here—it's hard to get a really bad meal, though it's easy to get a weird one.

BCD TOFU   3550 Wilshire Blvd. at South Kingsley Dr.; bcdtofu.com $$ Soft tofu served with a variety of things in a 24/7 diner, part of a restaurant chain that also has branches in Korea and Japan. Also has branches at 869 S. Western Ave. and 1201 S. Los Angeles St. in the downtown Fashion District. Transit: *From Downtown LA,* take the Purple Line subway to Wilshire Boulevard/Normandie Avenue.

GUELAGUETZA RESTAURANTE   3014 Olympic Blvd. near Normandie Ave.; guelaguetzarestaurante.com $–$$ From a tiny hole in the wall, favorite Guelaguetza has moved up to this cavernous site. But the moles are still great. Also in Lynwood at 11215 Long Beach Blvd., #1010. Transit: *From Downtown LA,* take bus 28 or rapid bus 728 to Olympic Boulevard/Normandie Avenue.

PARK'S BBQ   955 S. Vermont Ave. at San Marino St.; parksbbq.com $$$ In the inevitable strip mall, behind the inevitable overcrowded parking lot, is Park's, one of the prettiest and best Korean barbecue restaurants around. Its prices approach fine dining levels, but at lunch very affordable specials come with their full share of *banchan.* Transit: *From Downtown LA,* take bus 28 or rapid bus 728 to Olympic Boulevard/ Vermont Avenue.

POLLO A LA BRASA   764 S. Western Ave. at Eighth St. $ Peru is famous for rotisserie-roasted chicken, and this is probably LA's best example of it. The food is cheap here too. You may have to wait, and there's not really any place to sit, so you'll need to take your food somewhere—back to your hotel, or to a perching place on an office building plaza on Wilshire.

■ SHORT EXPEDITION TO LANGER'S ■

Historic (it opened in 1947), oddly located Langer's (at 704 S. Alvarado St. at Seventh St.) is the shrine of LA Jewish deli-dom. It's been lauded by critics from the James Beard Foundation to Jonathan Gold, a great restaurant critic and the only one to ever win a Pulitzer Prize. Gold seems to regard the Red Line subway as primarily a mechanism to deliver diners to Langer's. Needless to say, it has terrific pastrami, corned beef, and so on. Open Monday–Saturday, 8 a.m.–4 p.m. only; **langersdeli.com.** Transit: *From Downtown LA,* take the Red/Purple Line subway to Westlake/MacArthur Park station (one station west of 7th St./Metro Center), and then walk one block south to Langer's. *From Hollywood,* take the Red Line subway to Westlake/MacArthur Park, and then walk one block south to Langer's. *From Santa Monica,* take Big Blue Bus express 10 to 7th St./Metro Center. From there, take the Red/Purple Line subway to Westlake/MacArthur Park, and then walk one block south to Langer's.

Transit: *From Downtown LA,* take the Purple Line subway to Wilshire Boulevard/Western Avenue.

SOOT BULL JEEP 3136 W. Eighth St. at Catalina St. $$ Highly regarded, but very smoky, Korean barbecue restaurant. You barbecue the meat over a charcoal fire rather than the usual gas-powered one. Transit: *From Downtown LA,* take the Red/Purple Line subway to Wilshire Boulevard/Vermont Avenue.

SAN GABRIEL VALLEY RESTAURANTS

The San Gabriel Valley is a vast suburban zone, encompassing a half-dozen towns. Its residents and restaurants are largely, but not exclusively, Asian, with a particularly large Chinese population. The big restaurant centers are San Gabriel and Monterey Park. They look like standard, aging suburban strips, but they're laced with great food. San Gabriel's restaurants line Valley Boulevard, with San Gabriel Square being a particularly large concentration in a mall. In Monterey Park, Garvey Avenue is the main food drag, though some eateries are also found along north-south Atlantic Avenue (Garvey and Valley run east–west).

BABITA   1823 S. San Gabriel Blvd. near Valley Blvd., San Gabriel $$$ Babita is widely considered one of the finest Mexican restaurants in all LA. Transit: *From Downtown LA,* take bus 76 to Valley and San Gabriel boulevards.

BEIJING DUCK HOUSE   250 W. Valley Blvd. near Abbott Ave., San Gabriel $ We're in pretty heavy eating country now; a Hilton hotel is nearby if you just can't go any farther. Beijing is a noodle specialist on the second floor of a strip mall with some hard-to-find dishes. Transit: *From Downtown LA,* take bus 76 to Valley Boulevard and Abbott Avenue.

DUCK HOUSE   501 S. Atlantic Blvd. at Harding Ave., Monterey Park; **pearlcatering.com** $$ This restaurant specializes in Peking (or Beijing) duck, which is pricier than most of the other items. Transit: *From Downtown LA,* take rapid bus 770 to Garvey Avenue and Atlantic Boulevard.

ELITE RESTAURANT   700 S. Atlantic Ave. at El Portal Pl., Monterey Park; **elitechineserestaurant.com**   Almost across the road from Duck House. A huge favorite for dim sum; expect to wait. Transit: *From Downtown LA,* take rapid bus 770 to Garvey Avenue and Atlantic Boulevard, and then walk 0.5 mile south.

SEA HARBOUR SEAFOOD RESTAURANT   3939 N. Rosemead Blvd. near Valley Blvd., Rosemead $$–$$$ They do dim sum in this cavernous place, but they're particularly noted for seafood dinners, coming right out of those tanks. Rosemead is east of Monterey Park. Transit: *From Downtown LA,* take bus 76 to Valley and Rosemead boulevards.

THIEN AN BO BAY MON   8837 Valley Blvd. near Ivar Ave., Rosemead $$–$$$ This Vietnamese restaurant specializes in a meal known as "seven courses of beef." Come hungry, and worry that Americans eat too much beef another day. Transit: *From Downtown LA,* take bus 76 to Valley Boulevard and Muscatel Avenue.

YU GARDEN   107 E. Valley Blvd. at Del Mar Blvd., San Gabriel $–$$ Shanghai-style restaurants such as this were once rare but now have blossomed. Transit: *From Downtown LA,* take bus 76 to Valley and Del Mar boulevards.

Grocery Stores and Markets in Downtown Los Angeles

FAMIMA   Six of these upscale Japan-based convenience stores are in Downtown: at Union Station, 350 S. Grand Ave. (California Plaza, Bunker Hill), 505 S. Flower St. (City National Plaza), 700 Wilshire Blvd., 727 W. Seventh St. (Roosevelt Building, open 24 hours), and 525 W. Sixth St.

GRAND CENTRAL MARKET   317 S. Broadway   Downtown LA's public market, with almost 40 merchants selling fresh and prepared foods.

RALPH'S (FRESH FARE) SUPERMARKET   645 W. Ninth St. (between Hope and Flower streets)   Large, attractive, well-stocked supermarket, a store beyond the typical Ralph's.

6TH STREET MARKET   212 W. Sixth St. near Spring St.   Downtown superette in the Historic Core, larger than a convenience store.

Where to Stay in Downtown Los Angeles

Car-free travelers have many good hotel choices in Downtown LA.

BUNKER HILL AND HISTORIC CORE

HILTON CHECKERS   535 S. Grand Ave.; **hiltoncheckers.com** $$$$ The Checkers, across Grand Avenue from the Biltmore, was an independent hotel before it was a Hilton, and it still has more of a boutique quality than most Hiltons. The rooftop swimming pool is neat.

LOS ANGELES ATHLETIC CLUB   431 W. Seventh St.; **laac.com** $$$ With the renovation of its dark-toned, consciously clubby hotel rooms, the Los Angeles Athletic Club has emerged as a really good hotel. And the athletic facilities—including exercise machines, gym, and pool—are spectacular. Near the Red/Purple and Blue lines at 7th St./Metro Center.

MILLENNIUM BILTMORE   506 S. Grand Ave.; **thebiltmore.com** $$$ A historic, classic downtown city hotel overlooking Pershing Square. Rooms vary greatly in size and amenities. It often has good deals on the weekend. One block from the Red Line Pershing Square station.

O (ORCHID) HOTEL   819 S. Flower St.; **ohotelgroup.com** $ The O is on the $/$$ borderline, and the Historic Core/South Park borderline, but it is certainly one of the cheaper hip hotels around. It's about the closest you'll find to the older budget hotels of other West Coast cities (rooms can be on the small side). Near the Red/Purple Line subway and Blue Line light rail at 7th St./Metro Center station.

OMNI LOS ANGELES HOTEL AT CALIFORNIA PLAZA   251 S. Olive St.; **omnihotels.com** $$$$ A hotel where things seem to work flawlessly, complete with a pool actually designed for swimming. It's up on Bunker Hill among office buildings, often discounted on the rather quiet weekends. Near the Red/Purple Line Civic Center station.

SHERATON LOS ANGELES DOWNTOWN   711 S. Hope St.; **sheraton.com/losangeles** $$$$ Large, modern high-rise business-oriented hotel right at the 7th St./Metro Center rail station.

WESTIN BONAVENTURE   404 S. Figueroa St.; **thebonaventure.com** $$$ Shiny modern high-rise on Bunker Hill, frequently cited as the epitome of defensive 1970s design. Near the Red/Purple and Blue lines at 7th St./Metro Center; numerous buses.

SOUTH PARK

LUXE CITY CENTER   1020 S. Figueroa St.; **luxecitycenter.com** $$$–$$$$ Downtown (LA Live) entry of the international boutique hotel company, in a thoroughly renovated former Holiday Inn a bit south of the Downtown Core.

THE RITZ-CARLTON, LOS ANGELES   900 W. Olympic Blvd.; **ritzcarlton.com** $$$$$ New outpost of the super-luxury chain, in a tall high-rise at LA Live south of the Downtown Core.

LITTLE TOKYO

MIYAKO   328 E. First St.; **miyakoinn.com** $$ Moderate-priced hotel mostly catering to Japanese but fine for all. Near the Gold Line Little Tokyo station and 0.5 mile from Union Station.

KYOTO GRAND HOTEL AND GARDENS 120 S. Los Angeles St.; **kyotograndhotel.com** $$$ Good value high-rise that has a mostly but not exclusively Japanese clientele. Near the Gold Line Little Tokyo station and Red/Purple Line Civic Center station.

CHINATOWN

BEST WESTERN DRAGON GATE INN 818 N. Hill St.; **dragongateinn.com** $ A bit less fancy than other Best Westerns, but clean, surrounded by stores, and very near the Chinatown Gold Line light rail station.

ROYAL PAGODA MOTEL 995 N. Broadway; *royalpagodamotel.com* $ Very, very basic hotel (that is, no radios) at the northern end of Chinatown, a mile from the Historic Core. But possibly the cheapest clean hotel in central LA, and good for budget travelers.

■ 5 Pasadena

Los Angeles's Historic Spot

PASADENA IS CUT FROM RATHER DIFFERENT CLOTH than most of Los Angeles. While much of Los Angeles first boomed after World War I, or World War II, Pasadena first came into prominence in the 1880s. It was the Southern California city that beckoned wealthy Midwesterners, where they could come to live among the orange groves. The first Festival of Roses, the precursor to today's Rose Bowl football game and parade, was held in 1890.

Geographically too, Pasadena stands apart from most of Los Angeles's main attractions. While most visitor-attracting neighborhoods are in the stretches west of Downtown LA, Pasadena is some 10 miles northeast of Downtown. Pasadena is not along Wilshire or Sunset boulevards, but instead follows the Arroyo Seco—the dry river. It's a far older travel corridor along which roads, then a freeway (one of the nation's first), and now light rail have been built. For a brief period in the early 20th century, a dedicated bikeway was located here.

Transit

Because Downtown LA is closer to Pasadena, it's preferable to visit Pasadena from Downtown rather than Westside if you're splitting your stay between the two.

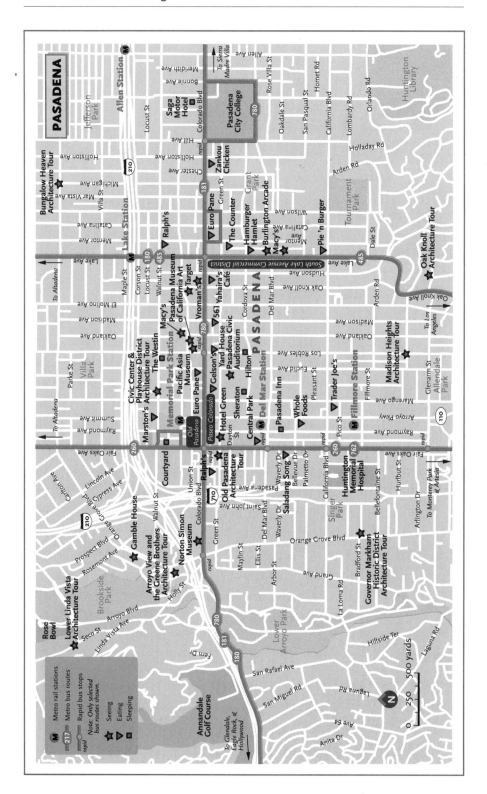

From Downtown Los Angeles, take the Red or Purple Line subway to Union Station, and then the Gold Line light rail from Union Station to Del Mar or Memorial Park station in Pasadena.

From Hollywood, it's generally faster to take the Red Line subway to Union Station, and then the Gold Line light rail to Pasadena. However, during the week, rapid bus 780 provides a one-seat ride from Hollywood Boulevard and Highland Avenue in the daytime, but it starts farther east at Hollywood Boulevard and Vine Street on weekends during the day.

From Santa Monica, take Big Blue Bus express 10 to Union Station, and then the Gold Line light rail to Memorial Park.

From the San Fernando Valley, take rapid bus 794 to San Fernando Road and Central Avenue in Glendale, and then take rapid bus 780 east to Pasadena.

From South Los Angeles, take the Blue Line light rail north to 7th St./Metro Center, and then the Red or Purple Line subway to Union Station, and then the Gold Line light rail to Pasadena.

From East LA, take the Gold Line light rail to Pasadena.

Note: These transit directions apply to all destinations in this chapter, except where noted.

Pasadena has published a map showing transit provided by all transit agencies. Visit **tinyurl.com/pasadenatransit.** Unlike others in SoCal (some of them occupying land owned by Metro), many Pasadena businesses include transit information on their websites.

Bicycling

Pasadena is a more bike-friendly city than Los Angeles. The city has just completed a new plan calling for significant expansion of bike lanes and bike routes. For a bicycle map of Pasadena, visit **ci.pasadena.ca.us/transportation/bicycling.** Outside of the northwestern hills, Pasadena is mostly flat and has a grid pattern of streets, facilitating biking. If you want to go past Pasadena, put your bike on the Gold Line light rail or the rapid bus 780, and then resume riding at the other end.

★ BIKE SHOPS IN PASADENA ★

EMPIRE BIKE SHOP 546 N. Fair Oaks St.; (626) 578-9350; **empirebikeshop.net**

INCYCLE BICYCLES 175 S. Fair Oaks St.; (626) 577-0440; **incycle.com**

PASADENA CYCLERY 1670 E. Walnut St.; (626) 584-6391; **pasadenacyclery.com**

PERFORMANCE BICYCLE 323 S. Arroyo Pkwy.; (626) 395-9796; **performancebike.com**

Seeing Pasadena

CENTRAL PASADENA

Pasadena's central area, where most of the city's attractions are, is long and narrow. It's more than 1.5 miles, or a 30-minute walk, from the Norton Simon Museum on the west to the delicious original Euro Pane on the east. Colorado Boulevard was the old Route 66, and the city's activities and attractions stretch out along it. But the core is really only about 0.5 mile wide (a 10-minute walk), from Walnut to Cordova streets. (The Del Mar light rail station lies just beyond this boundary.)

If you come on the Gold Line to Memorial Park station, walk south on Arroyo Parkway to Colorado Boulevard. You'll be in Old Pasadena, about two-thirds of the way west within the central area. Most of Old Pasadena, along with the Norton Simon, will lie to the west (to the right, walking out from the Gold Line). To the east (left) will be Paseo Colorado, the Playhouse District including Vroman's bookstore, as well as Lake Avenue and Euro Pane. You can certainly walk pleasurably within this area; there are relatively few dead spots.

The best way to get around within Pasadena, generally, is to walk, and it's usually pleasant enough. There is internal transit—Metro bus 180/181 makes local stops along Colorado. Rapid bus 780 stops at Orange Grove Boulevard, Fair Oaks Avenue, Los Robles

TIP **PASADENA VISITOR CENTER** 300 E. Green St. at the Pasadena Civic Auditorium; (626) 795-9311; (800) 307-7797; Monday–Friday, 8 a.m.–5 p.m.; Saturday, 10 a.m.–4 p.m.; **visitpasadena.com**

Avenue, and Lake Avenue. Pasadena's 25-cent local ARTS bus loops westbound on Colorado Boulevard to Orange Grove Boulevard and the Norton Simon, eastbound on Green Street, and one block south of Colorado Boulevard.

OLD PASADENA

Old Pasadena is the turn-of-the-20th-century commercial district around Colorado Boulevard and Raymond Avenue, the city's oldest commercial district. In recent years, the Victorian/Edwardian commercial buildings on and off Colorado Boulevard between Pasadena Avenue and Arroyo Parkway have been rescued from decrepitude and become a hot dining and shopping area. You'll find unique buildings here, but with success and rising rents, chain stores and restaurants have taken over, especially on the Colorado Boulevard frontage. Side streets are more varied. Distant Lands at 56 S. Raymond Ave. is a travel outfitter and bookstore, one of the last ones around. Old Pasadena is a pleasant environment for strolling and a busy one for people-watching. For a directory map, visit **oldpasadena.org**.

MUSEUMS

Pasadena has long been a center of culture for SoCal culture, so not surprisingly it has some of SoCal's most interesting museums. **Huntington Library,** actually in San Marino, has beautiful gardens in addition to its art collection. See page 208 for more details. The **Norton Simon Museum** showcases South Asian art, Edgar Degas dancers, and other holdings. See page 208 for more details. **Pasadena Museum of California Art** is a quirky little museum devoted solely to California art, spotlighting both famous and obscure, historic and modern California artists and art movements. Your view of California art will expand. See page 212 for full details.

PACIFIC ASIA MUSEUM

46 N. Los Robles Ave. near Union St.; **pacificasiamuseum.org**

■ Wednesday–Sunday, 10 a.m.–6 p.m.

■ Adults, $9; students and seniors, $7

SOUTHERN CALIFORNIA'S LONGTIME MUSEUM OF ASIAN ART, with an international collection of some 15,000 objects. **Transit:** *From Union Station,* take the Gold Line light rail to Memorial Park station. *From Memorial Park station,* head south on Arroyo Parkway one block to Union Street. Turn left and go east on Union for about six blocks to Los Robles Avenue. The Pacific Asia Museum will be to your right; PMCA will be straight ahead.

PASADENA ARCHITECTURE TOURS

Pasadena is justly proud of its historic architecture and has 23 historic districts in its 16 square miles. The Pasadena Convention and Visitors Bureau has assembled a booklet of fine historic architecture tours throughout the city at **visitpasadena.com,** or pick up a copy at the visitor center.

Most of the routes listed below have transit directions from central Pasadena to the starting and ending location (the tours are loops). The ones listed have reasonably good transit or particularly strong historic and architectural significance. Some bus routes listed operate infrequently; check the Metro Trip Planner.

GAMBLE HOUSE

4 Westmoreland Pl.; (626) 793-3334; **gamblehouse.org**

▓ Thursday–Sunday, tours start noon–3 p.m. Bookstore: Tuesday–Saturday, 10 a.m.–5 p.m.; Sunday, 11:30 a.m.–5 p.m.

▓ Adults, $10; children under age 12, free

YOU CAN TAKE A GUIDED TOUR of the Gamble House by itself or view it as part of the Arroyo View tour. The 1908 structure is considered to be Charles and Henry Greene's masterpiece not only of Arts and Crafts architecture but also of furniture design. It's been rated one of the best house tours in America.

Transit: Take rapid bus 780 or bus 180/181 on Colorado Boulevard, which are about a 10-minute walk away at Colorado and Orange Grove boulevards. They will take you into central Pasadena or over to Hollywood. To go back to Downtown LA, get off at Fair Oaks Avenue (one stop on the rapid) and stroll over to the Memorial Park Gold Line light rail station four blocks away.

ARROYO VIEW AND THE GREENE BROTHERS (northwest Pasadena)   Starts at Holly Street and Grand Avenue. Take bus 180/181 or rapid bus 780 to Colorado and Orange Grove boulevards, walk north on Orange Grove (over freeway), and then west on Holly Street.

BUNGALOW HEAVEN (northeast Pasadena)   Starts at Orange Grove Boulevard and Michigan Avenue. Take Pasadena ARTS bus 40 to Villa Street and Michigan Avenue, and then walk north on Michigan Avenue.

CIVIC CENTER AND PLAYHOUSE DISTRICT (central Pasadena)   Starts at Walnut and Garfield avenues. Take the Gold Line light rail to Memorial Park, walk east on Holly Street, and then north on Garfield Avenue, or take bus 180/181 or rapid bus 780 to Colorado Boulevard and Los Robles Avenue and walk west on Colorado, and then north on Garfield. The playhouse referred to is the Pasadena Playhouse, which is currently closed.

GOVERNOR MARKHAM VICTORIAN DISTRICT (southern Pasadena)   Starts at Orange Grove Boulevard and Markham Place. Take the 686 or 687 bus to Fair Oaks Avenue and Congress Street (more than 0.5 mile from tour start). The buses also goes to Fillmore station. The tour booklet notes that this is one of the few Pasadena neighborhoods with large numbers of pre-1900 homes in good repair.

LOWER LINDA VISTA (northwest Pasadena)   Starts at Linda Vista Avenue and Seco Street. Take ARTS bus 51 to Linda Vista Avenue and Seco

Street, which runs once an hour; Colorado Boulevard buses are about 1 mile away. This tour includes the Rose Bowl exterior; the interior is accessible when there is an event.

MADISON HEIGHTS (southern Pasadena)   Starts at El Molino Avenue and Alpine Street. Take Metro bus 485 from Colorado Boulevard and Lake Avenue to Oak Knoll Avenue and Alpine Street; walk one short block west. The bus also runs from Downtown LA.

OAK KNOLL (southern Pasadena)   Starts at Hillcrest and Wentworth avenues. Take Metro bus 485 from Colorado Boulevard and Lake Avenue to Oak Knoll and Hillcrest avenues; walk one block east. The bus also runs from Downtown LA.

OLD PASADENA (central Pasadena)   Starts at Fair Oaks Avenue and Green Street. Take bus 180/181 or rapid bus 780 to Colorado Boulevard and Fair Oaks Avenue or take the Gold Line light rail to Del Mar station.

Shopping

Pasadena is not known as a shopper's mecca, but it offers some intriguing venues for shoppers.

PASEO COLORADO

As a shopping mall, Paseo Colorado is pretty typical. It has a lot of the stores you'd expect in an upper middle-class mall—such as Macy's, Harry and David, and Sephora. But as a mall, it's a cut above. Some stores front Colorado Boulevard, not just the interior mall. The main walkway of the mall gives a route—and a view—between Pasadena's gorgeous Beaux Arts Civic Center and the Convention Center. Apartments in striking modernist buildings are above. Paseo Colorado replaces the 1970s suburban-style Plaza Pasadena, which cut downtown Pasadena in half. The mall is located on Colorado Boulevard between Marengo Avenue and Los Robles Avenue, two blocks east of Old Pasadena.

SOUTH LAKE AVENUE COMMERCIAL DISTRICT

South Lake, located on Lake Avenue from Green Street to California Boulevard, was one of the first post-World War II commercial districts, kick-started by the opening of Bullocks department store in 1947. Today South Lake is a pleasant, somewhat genteel shopping district where you can find Macy's (yep, another one), Talbot's, or cute children's clothes. Plenty of eateries. Transit: *From Downtown LA,* to go directly to the Lake Avenue retail area, take the Gold Line light rail from Union Station to one stop past Memorial Park to Lake station, and then walk south 0.5 mile (approximately 10 minutes' walk). *From Hollywood,* take the Red Line subway to Union Station and follow the directions from Downtown LA. *From Santa Monica,* take Big Blue Bus express 10 to Union Station and follow the directions from Downtown LA.

VROMAN'S

Vroman's is one of the last, best independent bookstores in Southern California. It has a fine selection of real books, and it also has a news-stand, a little café, and rather too much gifty, cutesy stuff. It hosts a lot of readings too. Despite the fluff and clutter, this bookstore is the real deal. It's located at 695 E. Colorado Blvd. at El Molino Ave.

Rose Parade

The Rose Parade and Rose Bowl football game on New Year's Day are still Pasadena's biggest annual event. The parade wends through Pasadena to the Rose Bowl stadium, where the Rose Bowl football game is played between two leading college football teams. Organizations work all year to make elaborate floats that drive along the parade. People camp out all night to get spots on the parade route, or you can pay for a bleacher seat. The entire event is officially known as the Tournament of Roses. Transit: The Tournament of Roses is a time of special transit and special snarls; check the Metro website at **metro.net** or **tournamentofroses.com.**

Where to Eat in Central Pasadena

Old Pasadena is a big restaurant area, but it has suffered from rent infla-tion and an invasion of cookie-cutter chain eateries. Much of the best food in Pasadena is in other parts of the city's central area. All sites are accessible from Colorado Boulevard buses, as well as the Gold Line light rail if noted.

CENTRAL PARK 219 S. Fair Oaks Ave. at Orange Pl. (near Del Mar Gold Line station); **centralparkrestaurant.net** $$–$$$ You could call Central Park a California cuisine eatery, perhaps the best of that type in central Pasadena. Adjacent to Pasadena's Central Park, it serves three meals a day.

THE COUNTER 140 Shoppers Ln. west of Mentor Ave.; **thecounter burger.com** $ It's now a national/international chain, but its build-your-own-burger approach makes it popular.

EURO PANE 950 E. Colorado Blvd. near Mentor Ave. and 300 E. Colorado Blvd. across from Paseo Colorado (near Euclid Ave.) $ A fabulous bakery. The only criticism of its croissants is that they're not as good as those in Paris. They also serve famed egg salad sandwiches and light meals, as well as breads. Either branch is a good place to hang out.

MARSTON'S 151 E. Walnut Ave. near Raymond Ave. near Memorial Park Gold Line station (also in Valencia); **marstonsrestaurant.com** $$$ A pretty, tasty place in a cottage for all meals (dinner Wednesday–Saturday), but especially breakfast. Expect long lines on weekend mornings.

PIE 'N BURGER 913 E. California Blvd. near Lake St.; **pienburger.com** $ In the southeast corner of central Pasadena, this three-meal place has been Pasadena's homegrown diner for 40 years.

SALADANG AND SALADANG SONG 353 and 383 S. Fair Oaks Ave. at Waverly Dr. (near Del Mar Gold Line station) $$ Modern Thai food in interesting settings, especially the highly modernist and pricier Saladang Song to the south.

YAHAIRA'S CAFÉ 698 E. Colorado Blvd.; **yahairascafe.com** $ It serves breakfast and lunch daily, and dinner Thursday–Saturday. Nuevo Latino food near El Molino Avenue (across the street from Vroman's) at reasonable prices. What's not to like?

ZANKOU CHICKEN 1296 E. Colorado Blvd. near Holliston Ave.; **zankou chicken.com** $ Slightly east of the central area but worth the trip. SoCal minichain Zankou has the world's greatest rotisserie chicken and garlic sauce.

EXPEDITION TO SAN GABRIEL VALLEY RESTAURANTS

You can also take Metro bus 260 or rapid bus 762 down Fair Oaks Avenue to San Gabriel or Monterey Park restaurants. Some of them are near Atlantic Boulevard, where the bus operates, but for others you'd need to transfer. See "Eating Expeditions from Downtown Los Angeles" on page 91.

Grocery Stores and Markets in Central Pasadena

GELSON'S 245 E. Green St. in Paseo Colorado shopping center Gelson's is Southern California's largest high-end grocery chain, known for high quality, not affordability.

RALPH'S 320 W. Colorado Blvd. at St. John Ave. Your basic grocery store. Also at 160 N. Lake St. (near Lake Gold Line station).

TRADER JOE'S 610 S. Arroyo Pkwy. at California Blvd. (near Fillmore Gold Line station) TJs are either very small supermarkets or overgrown gourmet stores. Great for beer, snacks, candy, cookies, dried fruit, and so on. Also at 345 S. Lake St. at Del Mar Blvd.

WHOLE FOODS MARKET 465 S. Arroyo Pkwy. at Bellevue Ave. (near Del Mar Gold Line station) The folks who did for organic food what Starbucks did for coffee.

Where to Stay in Pasadena

If you want to focus your visit on the Pasadena area for a day or two, which is eminently worth doing, then staying in Pasadena for a night or two makes sense. Otherwise, Pasadena is not a good base for seeing the rest of Los Angeles. Pasadena is at the very northeastern edge of visitors' LA, so transit trips to the Westside can wind up taking 90 minutes or even longer.

Pasadena's few hotels cluster in the downtown area, and then stretch out along Colorado Boulevard. I generally don't recommend the eastern Colorado Boulevard motels; it's a highway strip environment (one budget exception below). And sorry, visitors, that grand old pile that was the Green Hotel is now seniors' housing and is no longer a hotel. Look for wintertime deals, but not in the Christmas–New Year's week, which is Rose Bowl season. Prices spike dramatically during that week, and hotels that are not usually crowded fill up.

COURTYARD BY MARRIOTT 180 N. Fair Oaks Ave. at Holly St.; **courtyardpasadena.com** $$$$ This is the only hotel in Old Pasadena, and it's also very close to the Memorial Park Gold Line station (and Colorado Boulevard buses, as all the hotels are). The rooms follow the Courtyard formula.

HILTON 168 S. Los Robles Ave. near Cordova Ave.; **hilton.com** $$$ The rare middle ground price wise and a centrally located property.

PASADENA INN 400 S. Arroyo Pkwy.; **oldpasadenainn.com** $ Central Pasadena's budget choice. Located by the Del Mar Gold Line station and Whole Foods, it is within easy walking distance. Not to be confused with the Best Western Pasadena Inn, which is on the strip.

SAGA MOTOR HOTEL 1633 E. Colorado Blvd.; **thesagamotorhotel.com** $ The Saga is a pleasant, reasonably priced motel on the western (near town) end of the Colorado Boulevard strip, across from Pasadena City College. It's a good family or budget choice, with Colorado Boulevard buses right at hand and the Allen Gold Line station about a 10-minute walk away. Most important, Zankou Chicken is within walking distance.

SHERATON 303 E. Cordova Ave. near Marengo Ave.; **starwoodhotels.com** $$$$ A business-oriented hotel and the closest hotel to the Pasadena Civic Auditorium, where many meetings are held.

THE WESTIN PASADENA 191 N. Robles Ave.; **starwoodhotels.com** $$$$ Rooms are generously proportioned, with a bit of 1980s grandiosity, and it's quiet. It's located a couple blocks north of Colorado Boulevard, in the central area but east of Old Pasadena. It has a swimming pool.

■ 6 Griffith Park

A Patch of Green

GRIFFITH PARK IS LOS ANGELES'S LARGEST PARK, but it's not like New York's Central Park or San Francisco's Golden Gate Park, with their carefully constructed landscapes. Rather, it is mostly a wildland park that happens to be within the city of Los Angeles. It comes down and touches the developed city at the edge of the Los Feliz district.

The city calls Griffith Park, at 4,210 acres (6.5 square miles), "the largest municipal park with urban wilderness area in the United States." Elevations in the park range from 384 feet above sea level to 1,625 feet—the hilly park is at the eastern end of the Santa Monica Mountains. Griffith Park is a rare patch of (public) green in the seemingly endless city. The park (measured at the Autry Museum) is 7 miles northwest of Downtown Los Angeles and 7 miles northeast of Hollywood. Much of the park is without roads, inaccessible by any motorized mode.

Transit

If you're splitting your stay, it's easier and faster to go to Griffith Park when you're staying in Downtown or Hollywood, rather than in Santa Monica or Westwood.

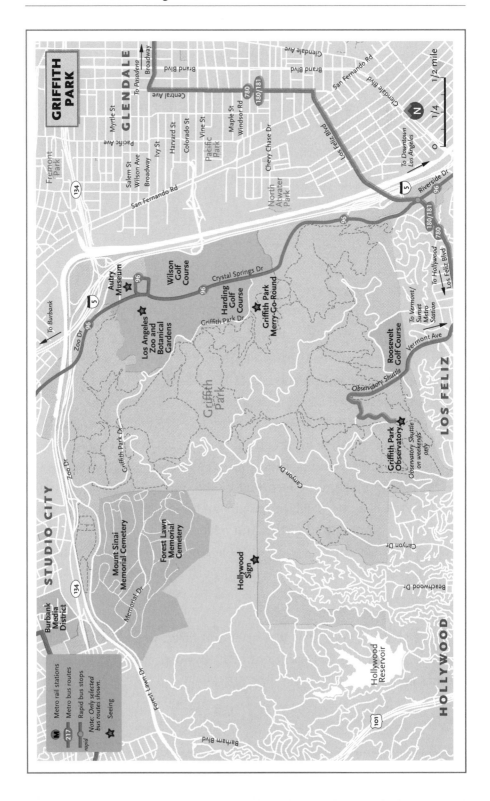

GRIFFITH PARK

GLENDALE

To Pasadena

Broadway

Brand Blvd

Glendale Ave

Central Ave

Brand Blvd

San Fernando Rd

780

180/181

N

1/4 1/2 mile

0

Myrtle St

Pacific Ave

Salem St

Wilson Ave

Broadway

Ivy St

Harvard St

Colorado St

Vine St

Maple St

Windsor Rd

Chevy Chase Dr

Pacific Park

Glendale Blvd

Los Feliz Blvd

To Downtown Los Angeles

To Los Angeles

Fremont Park

134

San Fernando Rd

North Atwater Park

5

Riverside Dr

96

180/181

780

To Hollywood

Los Feliz Blvd

Wilson Golf Course

Crystal Springs Dr

96

Harding Golf Course

Griffith Park Dr

Griffith Park Merry-Go-Round

To Burbank

5

96

Autry Museum

96

Los Angeles Zoo and Botanical Gardens

Zoo Dr

To Vermont/ Sunset Metro Station

Roosevelt Golf Course

Vermont Ave

Observatory Shuttle

Griffith Park

Griffith Park Dr

Zoo Dr

LOS FELIZ

Griffith Park Observatory

Observatory Shuttle on weekends only

Canyon Dr

STUDIO CITY

Burbank Media District

134

Memorial Dr.

Mount Sinai Memorial Cemetery

Forest Lawn Memorial Cemetery

Hollywood Sign

Canyon Dr

Beachwood Dr

Forest Lawn Dr

Barham Blvd

Hollywood Reservoir

101

HOLLYWOOD

M Metro rail stations

217 Metro bus routes

rapid Rapid bus stops

Note: Only selected bus routes shown.

★ Seeing

★ BICYCLE RENTALS IN GRIFFITH PARK ★

SPOKES 'N' STUFF 4730 Crystal Springs Dr. (ranger station parking lot); **laparks.org/dos/parks/griffithpk/bikeride.htm;** Saturday–Sunday, 10 a.m.–sunset, year-round; Monday–Friday, 2–6 p.m., Memorial Day–Labor Day. Cash only on weekdays.

Most transit to Griffith Park is provided by Metro bus 96, which operates from Downtown LA to the park and on to Burbank and Sherman Oaks. Local bus 96 runs every 30 minutes on weekdays and Saturdays and every 45 minutes on Sundays. *From Hollywood,* take bus 180/181 or rapid bus 780 to Los Feliz Boulevard and Riverside Drive, just outside the park, and transfer to bus 96. *From distant Santa Monica,* take Big Blue Bus express 10 downtown and transfer at Olive and Ninth streets to bus 96, which you take to Western Heritage Way at the museum entrance. Depending on wait time, that trip could take about an hour and 45 minutes. *From elsewhere in LA,* find connecting points to bus 96, mostly in Downtown LA.

Transit-accessible Attractions

The **Autry Museum,** officially the Museum of the American West, may be one of the more underrated in Los Angeles. It features changing exhibits on topics such as images of Yellowstone, saints' names in Los Angeles streets, and women in the American West. The museum has a fine bookstore of both popular and scholarly Western Americana. See page 209 for more information.

GRIFFITH PARK MERRY-GO-ROUND

HAS A CHILD BEEN BORN THAT DOESN'T LIKE A MERRY-GO-ROUND? This is Griffith Park's version, built in 1926 and brought to the park in 1937. Transit: Take local bus 96 to Crystal Springs and Griffith Park.

GRIFFITH PARK OBSERVATORY

2800 E. Observatory Rd.; **griffithobs.org**
■ Wednesday–Friday, noon–10 p.m.; Saturday–Sunday, 10 a.m.–10 p.m.
■ Free admission; planetarium show: adults, $7; students and seniors, $5; children ages 5–12, $3

COURTESY OF GRIFFITH PARK OBSERVATORY

IF YOU'RE AROUND ON A WEEKEND, you should definitely visit the beautifully restored 1935 observatory building. You can look through telescopes and get some of the most spectacular views of Los Angeles. **Transit:** Transit runs only on weekends. There's a 25-cent DASH bus—the DASH Observatory Shuttle runs from the Vermont Avenue/Sunset Boulevard subway station on weekends only. It runs the same hours that the observatory is open, so you can go for an evening look if you want. It actually stops much closer to the entrance than cars are able to park.

LOS ANGELES ZOO

5333 Zoo Dr.; **lazoo.org**

■ Open daily, 10 a.m.–5 p.m.; closed December 25

■ Adults age 13 and older, $14; seniors age 62 and older, $11; children ages 2–12, $9; children under age 2, free. And if you have proof of payment for Metro, you'll get $3 off adult admission and $2 off a child's. Kudos to the zoo—if only this program were in effect at cultural institutions with better transit.

**A NOTE ABOUT THE HOLLYWOOD SIGN:
NO ACCESS. REALLY.**

The famed Hollywood sign once promoted the Hollywoodland subdivision but at some point lost its final letters; it is located in a remote area of Griffith Park. The trails to the sign are closed so that it won't be damaged by vandalism or pranks. Because the sign is so high up on Mount Lee, you can see it from many vantage points, such as the back of the Hollywood & Highland Center, or at the corner of Franklin Avenue and Gower Street, and many other locations.

SOUTHERN CALIFORNIA'S GREAT, WORLD-CLASS ZOO is in San Diego. But the LA Zoo is here and has a pretty respectable collection of more than 250 species, 29 of which are endangered, as well as a children's zoo. The zoo considers its grounds to be a botanical garden—its official name is Los Angeles Zoo and Botanical Gardens. Transit: Take local bus 96 to Western Heritage Way/LA Zoo.

Where to Eat in Griffith Park

No freestanding restaurants are in the transit-accessible part of Griffith Park. However, the Golden Spur Café is located within the Autry Museum, and the zoo has a number of snack bars. The Griffith Park Observatory features the Café at the End of the Universe (Douglas Adams would be proud). You'll get the most choices by taking local bus 96, transferring to a westbound rapid bus 780, and riding to Vermont and Prospect avenues in Los Feliz, a foodie hot spot.

■ 7 Hollywood

Fun City Once More

HOLLYWOOD IS, OF COURSE, AN INDUSTRY, but it is also a place, a neighborhood—the neighborhood where the film industry first settled in Los Angeles. (Hollywood the neighborhood still provides services for film-making, but the key production areas are now mainly elsewhere, notably in Burbank and other San Fernando Valley areas.)

Hollywood Boulevard, for the mile or so between Gower Street and La Brea Boulevard, is probably the one real tourist-dominated zone in Los Angeles. The tourist population also means that crowds of pedestrians are here—day and night—walking on wide, decorated sidewalks. Hollywood Boulevard is a place to look back on and participate in 80 years of Los Angeles movie history.

Hollywood Boulevard is a distinctive street, a street for grand gestures, in a city where most streets just disappear into the mix. The historic movie theaters on the street are tall and mostly covered in architectural ornament. The Hollywood & Highland Center is built around grand stairways and escalators. The Walk of Fame has put more than 2,400 stars on the sidewalk and shows no sign of stopping. The only thing that's skimpy is the underwear in the lingerie stores that still dominate the first few blocks west of Vine Street.

Hollywood is a good place for car-free travelers to stay. It's central to visitor attractions and has good subway and bus service to many areas. The Red Line subway can take you to Universal Studios, Thai Town, Koreatown, and Downtown Los Angeles. Fairfax Avenue buses from Hollywood go to the Farmers Market/The Grove, the LA County Museum, and Museum Row. Other buses go to Westwood (UCLA) and the Warner Brothers Studio in Burbank.

Like Downtown LA, and the hero(ine)s of many Hollywood films, Hollywood the neighborhood has come back from a fallen state. Glamorous from the 1920s through 1940s, Hollywood was seen as the home of runaways and junkies by the 1970s. Liberal applications of redevelopment money, the Red Line subway (after a rocky construction period), and changing times and attitudes have made the neighborhood a star once again. The (slower) rebirth of Hollywood was accomplished with much less of the slash-and-burn urban renewal clearance that scarred Downtown, though some small businesses have complained about being pushed out.

Hollywood is 8 miles west of Downtown Los Angeles and 12 miles east of downtown Santa Monica. It's bounded on the east by East Hollywood, on the west by West Hollywood, on the north by the Hollywood Hills, and on the south by Larchmont Village and Hancock Park.

Transit

If you're splitting your stay, but not staying in Hollywood, Hollywood is a quick ride from Downtown and not too long from Westwood, but at least an hour from Santa Monica.

From Downtown Los Angeles, take the Red Line subway to Hollywood Boulevard/Highland Avenue or Hollywood Boulevard/Vine Street station.

From Santa Monica, check the Metro Trip Planner for the best routing at the specific time you want to go, as several routes travel here. During the day and early evening, take Metro express bus 534 to Washington Boulevard/Fairfax Avenue, and then rapid bus 780 or local bus 217 to Hollywood Boulevard/Highland Avenue or Hollywood Boulevard/

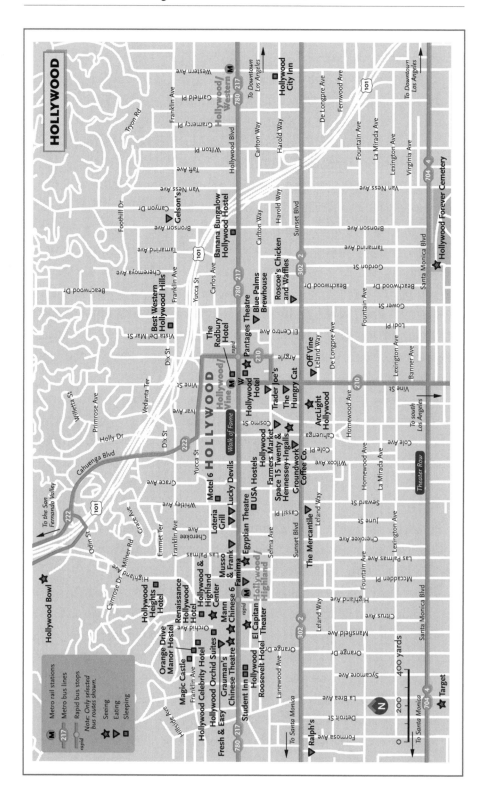

HOLLYWOOD

★ BIKE SHOPS IN AND NEAR HOLLYWOOD ★

BICYCLE KITCHEN 706 Heliotrope Dr., East Hollywood; **bicyclekitchen.com**
The Bicycle Kitchen is not a bike store but "a nonprofit bicycle repair educational organization." It's considered to be a center of LA bike culture.

ORANGE 20 BIKES 4351 Melrose Ave., East Hollywood; **orange20bikes.com**

SAFETY CYCLE 1014 N. Western Ave., East Hollywood; **safetycycle.com**

Vine Street. This is the fastest route, if the connections work well. During the day take rapid bus 704 to Santa Monica Boulevard/Highland Avenue or Santa Monica Boulevard/Vine Street, and then walk north about 15 minutes. Rapid bus 704 runs every 40 minutes from Santa Monica on weekdays and every 20 minutes on weekends. On this route, you don't have to transfer. Also during the day and evening, you can take Big Blue Bus 1 to Santa Monica and Westwood boulevards, and then take Metro bus 4 or rapid bus 704 to Santa Monica Boulevard/ Highland Avenue or Santa Monica Boulevard/Vine Street. This routing has the most frequent service. Midnight–5 a.m., take Metro bus 4 from Santa Monica to Highland Avenue or Vine Street, and then walk 0.75 mile north (approximately 15 minutes' walk).

From the San Fernando Valley, catch any bus that serves the North Hollywood or Universal City stations, such as Metro buses 152, 154, 155, 156/656, 222, 224, or 240; rapid bus 750; or Burbank Buses NoHo–Media District or NoHo–Empire. Then catch the Red Line subway to Hollywood Boulevard/Highland Avenue or Hollywood Boulevard/Vine Street station. *From South Los Angeles,* take bus 210 up Crenshaw Boulevard to Hollywood Boulevard, or take the Blue Line light rail to 7th St./ Metro Center and catch the Red Line subway to Hollywood Boulevard/ Vine Street or Hollywood Boulevard/Highland Avenue station. *From East Los Angeles,* take the Gold Line light rail to Union Station and catch the Red Line subway to Hollywood Boulevard/Vine Street or Hollywood Boulevard/Highland Avenue station.

Note: These transit directions apply to all destinations in this chapter, except where noted.

Seeing Hollywood

THE WALK OF FAME

The Walk of Fame (**hollywoodchamber.net**), the procession of stars' names and handprints set into the sidewalk of Hollywood Boulevard and some side streets, turned 50 in 2010. It's not just movie stars, but TV folks, singers, comedians, radio folks, and so on.

The Walk seems to have grown without a discernible plan, so there are remarkably random juxtapositions of stars. For example, TV actor Barbara Hale, radio broadcaster Ted Malone, bandleader Johnny Mercer, and orchestra conductor Arthur Fiedler are next to one another on the east side of Vine Street south of Hollywood Boulevard. And then there are, as The Kinks point out, stars you have never even heard of. The Walk of Fame alone keeps a walk down Hollywood Boulevard interesting, if sometimes strange (and that's before you start looking

at the folks around you). The Walk of Fame has spawned imitators around the country, including the Talladega Walk of Fame in Talladega, Alabama; the Advertising Walk of Fame on Madison Avenue in New York City; and the Motorsports Walk of Fame (shouldn't it be a road of fame?) in nearby Long Beach.

HOLLYWOOD BOWL

The Hollywood Bowl (2301 N. Highland Ave.; **hollywoodbowl.com**) is one of LA's longest running and best-loved summer music venues. Everyone from the LA Philharmonic to world-music artists to ABBA tribute bands (arguably a kind of world music) play there. Bowl performances happen June–September.

Transit: *From Hollywood Boulevard and Highland Avenue hotels,* it's a shade under a mile walk, probably the best method if you're up to it. Shuttles also run from Hollywood Boulevard/Highland Avenue and Universal City Red Line stations. Also look on the venue's website for park-and-ride buses from around the city, including Pasadena, Westwood, and (eastern) Santa Monica.

PARAMOUNT STUDIO TOUR

Paramount (5555 Melrose Ave.; **paramountstudios.com**) is the one major studio still in the physical neighborhood of Hollywood. You can take a tour of its studio (see page 141).

Transit: *From Hollywood Boulevard/Vine Street,* take either Metro bus 210 to Vine Street/Melrose Avenue or the Hollywood-Wilshire DASH to Melrose Avenue/Windsor Boulevard at the studio.

GOING TO THE MOVIES IN HOLLYWOOD

You might think that going to a movie on your vacation is a bit of waste. But the restored Hollywood theaters are very grand, never more so when decorated for a premiere. Check the *Los Angeles Times, LA Weekly,* or their websites for showtimes and features. All listed locations are on Hollywood Boulevard between Gower Street and La Brea Avenue unless otherwise noted.

ARCLIGHT HOLLYWOOD   6360 W. Sunset Blvd. near Vine St.; **arclight cinemas.com**   A couple of blocks off Hollywood Boulevard, the ArcLight is known as a plush place to see a movie, at a premium price.

EL CAPITAN THEATER   6838 Hollywood Blvd.; **elcapitan.go.com**   Disney's own movie palace.

GRAUMAN'S CHINESE THEATRE   6925 Hollywood Blvd.; **chinese theatres.com**   An architectural riot of chinoiserie, a major visitor attraction in its own right, at Hollywood Boulevard and Highland Avenue.

MANN CHINESE 6   6801 Hollywood Blvd.; **chinesetheatres.com**   New theaters built with the Hollywood & Highland Center adjacent to the original Chinese Theatre.

■ *Repertory and Revival Movies*

EGYPTIAN THEATRE   6712 Hollywood Blvd.; **americancinematheque.com** The Egyptian claims the first Hollywood premiere showing. Now it is part of American Cinematheque and shows classic movies, film festivals, avant-garde movies, and so on. A good place to see a film.

HOLLYWOOD FOREVER CEMETERY   6000 Santa Monica Blvd. at Gordon St., about a mile southeast of Hollywood Blvd.; **hollywoodforever.com** On Saturday nights in summer, classic movies are shown outdoors here—it's extremely popular. Transit: *From Downtown LA,* take Metro bus 4 to Santa Monica Boulevard and Bronson Avenue. Then walk two blocks farther to Gordon Street. *From Hollywood,* take Metro bus 210 on Vine Street to Santa Monica Boulevard, and then walk three blocks left (east) to Santa Monica Boulevard and Gordon Street. *From central Hollywood,* a cab might make sense, at least on the way back.

■ *Live Theater*

Like everything else, live theater is spread around LA. But Hollywood remains the single-most concentrated location for seeing live theater. The best way to keep track is to check listings in the *LA Weekly, Los Angeles Times,* or through the LA Stage Alliance (**lastagealliance.com**), which also sells discounted tickets.

PANTAGES THEATRE   6233 Hollywood Blvd.; **broadwayla.org**   This theater, at the eastern end of the Hollywood Boulevard strip near Vine Street, is where big Broadway shows and the like tend to play in LA.

THEATER ROW **theaterrowhollywood.com** Theater Row is on Santa Monica Boulevard between El Centro Avenue (one block east of Vine Street) and Highland Avenue, about 0.75 mile south of Hollywood Boulevard. It doesn't look like a grand entertainment district on the outside because it's really part of Hollywood's movie production and technical services district, which is actually a special type of industrial district. Still, Hollywood Theater Row has 20 stages for live theater, the largest concentration in the region outside of the North Hollywood Arts District. They're small theaters for generally intimate works, not the sites for grand spectaculars. Transit: *From Hollywood Boulevard and Highland Avenue,* take Hollywood DASH to the theater if leaving by 6:30 p.m.; otherwise, take the Red Line subway to Hollywood Boulevard/Vine Street, and then take local bus 210 to Vine Street and Santa Monica Boulevard. On the return trip to Hollywood Boulevard and Highland Avenue, take local bus 210 to Hollywood Boulevard and Vine Street, and then take the Red Line subway one stop to Hollywood/Highland station, or walk the whole way—about a 30-minute walk.

From Downtown LA, take rapid bus 704 or local bus 4 (evenings) to Santa Monica Boulevard and Vine Street.

From Santa Monica, take rapid bus 704 or local bus 4 (evenings) to Santa Monica Boulevard and Vine Street.

From the San Fernando Valley, take the Red Line subway to Hollywood Boulevard/Vine Street, and then take local bus 210 to Vine Street and Santa Monica Boulevard, or walk south about 0.8 mile to Vine Street and Santa Monica Boulevard. *From East Los Angeles,* take the Gold Line light rail to Union Station, and then take the Red Line subway to Hollywood Boulevard/Vine Street. *From South Los Angeles,* take local bus 210 on Crenshaw Boulevard to Vine Street and Santa Monica Boulevard.

Bars and Clubs

One of contemporary Hollywood's big attractions is bars and clubs. Each night, seemingly thousands of young (mostly) Angelenos converge on

Hollywood to drink, dance, and mate (and a small number, alas, come to fight). The proximity of bars and clubs is a major reason for some travelers, car-free and otherwise, to stay in Hollywood. The most concentrated strip of clubs is on Cahuenga Boulevard between Sunset Boulevard and Franklin Avenue, on both sides of Hollywood Boulevard. But clubs are also scattered along Hollywood Boulevard and the other side streets between Vine Street and Highland Avenue.

Unfortunately, it's impossible to direct you to a club in Hollywood. They simply change too quickly—they go in and out of business, change music genres, and change intended audiences. By the time you read the information, it would probably be out of date. Some of the rock clubs on the Sunset Strip in West Hollywood have been more stable—see page 133 for those.

So what are your information sources? Publications include the *Los Angeles Times, Brand X* (a spin-off from the discontinued Thursday entertainment section of the *Times*), and *LA Weekly*. If you're at a hotel with a concierge, that person may be able to help you. On page 154, some of the city's leading live music venues, which tend to stay in place more, are listed.

HOLLYWOOD'S ARCHITECTURAL HISTORY

As you're probably gathering, Hollywood is one of LA's most historic neighborhoods, recalling the cinematic splendor of the 1920s and '30s. Angel's Walk Hollywood (**angelswalkla.org**) is a self-guided tour—you'll also see informative signs along the way.

Where to Eat in Hollywood

Eating in Hollywood has gotten a lot better in recent years, though it's still not one of the city's culinary hot spots. One conspicuous gap if you're staying here is breakfast places—I suggest getting on the bus and going to The Griddle Cafe at Sunset Boulevard and Fairfax Avenue. If you crave Thai food, head for Thai Town. Take the Red Line subway—or a Hollywood Boulevard bus (180/181 or rapid bus 780 during the day on a weekday)—to Hollywood Boulevard/Western Avenue.

The Koreatown restaurants listed on page 93 are accessible from Hollywood via the Red Line subway to Wilshire Boulevard/Vermont Avenue.

GROUNDWORK COFFEE CO. 1501 Cahuenga Blvd. at Sunset Blvd.; **lacoffee.com** $ Hollywood runs more to bars than coffeehouses, but Groundwork is part of a small citywide chain.

HOLLYWOOD FARMERS' MARKET **farmernet.com** $–$$ Centered on the intersection of Ivar and Selma avenues between Hollywood and Sunset boulevards and between Cahuenga Boulevard and Vine Street. Open Sunday, 8 a.m.–1 p.m.

THE HUNGRY CAT 1535 Vine St. near Sunset Blvd.; **thehungrycat.com** $$$ Hollywood's spot for seafood.

LOTERIA GRILL 6627 Hollywood Blvd.; **loteriagrill.com** $–$$ Loteria started life as a very popular modern Mexican food stand at the Farmers Market at Fairfax Avenue, and then spun off this simple but pretty sit-down restaurant (there's also a branch in Studio City now).

LUCKY DEVILS 6613 Hollywood Blvd. near Whitley Ave.; **luckydevils-la.com** $–$$ Bar and grill refined for the trendy set—craft beers and upscale burgers and pizzas. A good place though not cheap. Not to be confused with Lucky Strike Bowling on Highland Avenue.

THE MERCANTILE 6600 Sunset Blvd. at Seward St.; **themercantilela.com** $$ Wine bar and French gourmet market; simpler French foods (for example, onion soup, salads, sandwiches, and so on) at the counter or upstairs dining room.

MUSSO & FRANK 6667 Hollywood Blvd. at Cherokee Ave.; **mussoandfrank.com** $$$ Hollywood's great historic restaurant; it's been open since 1926. More famed for ambience than food.

OFF VINE 6263 Leland Way just east of Vine St., one block south of Sunset Blvd.; **offvine.com** $$$ Back from a devastating fire with fine California cuisine, with a side of comfort food.

ROSCOE'S CHICKEN AND WAFFLES 1512 N. Gower St. at Sunset Blvd.; **roscoeschickenandwaffles.com** $ Roscoe's, a small Los Angeles chain, is right at the southeastern edge of Hollywood's core. As the name suggests, Roscoe's focuses on fried chicken and waffles. Call it mental health food.

Grocery Stores and Markets in Hollywood

It has become much easier to buy real food in Hollywood in recent years.

FAMIMA   6759 Hollywood Blvd. just east of Highland Ave.   Open daily, 6 a.m.–2 a.m. The convenience store that sells good food, not just junk food.

FRESH & EASY   7021 Hollywood Blvd. at Sycamore Ave.   Relatively small supermarket with a variety of low-priced items (including produce), just west of Hollywood Boulevard and Highland Avenue.

GELSON'S   5877 Franklin Ave. at Bronson Ave.   The gourmet-oriented grocery has a location on the northeastern edge of Hollywood near the Best Western Hollywood Hills.

RALPH'S   7257 Sunset Blvd. at Poinsetta Pl. and 5429 Hollywood Blvd. at Western Ave., Thai Town   LA's leading supermarket chain. On the west side of the neighborhood. Open 24 hours.

TRADER JOE'S   1600 N. Vine St. south of Hollywood Blvd.   The famed grocery store has gone into the Hollywood Boulevard/Vine Street complex—it's the closest TJs to any Metro rail station citywide.

Where to Stay in Hollywood

As previously mentioned, Hollywood is definitely a good base for the car-free traveler. If you're looking for a really cheap option, Hollywood has a few hostels; see page 129.

HOTELS NEAR HOLLYWOOD BOULEVARD AND HIGHLAND AVENUE (RED LINE STATION)

HOLLYWOOD CELEBRITY HOTEL   1775 N. Orchid Ave. at Yucca St.; **hotel celebrity.com** $$ Next door and similar to the Orchid. Some rooms have kitchens.

HOLLYWOOD HEIGHTS HOTEL 2005 N. Highland Ave.; **hollywood heightshotel.com** $$$$ A pleasantly renovated former Holiday Inn that doesn't quite reach the heights of trendiness to which it aspires. Rooms facing Highland Avenue get a lot of traffic noise, so ask for a room on the back side.

HOLLYWOOD ORCHID SUITES 1753 N. Orchid Ave. at Yucca St.; **orchid suites.com** $$ This hotel is a terrific value, on a quiet street right behind the Hollywood & Highland Center, less than a 5-minute walk through the mall to the Hollywood Boulevard/Highland Avenue Metro station. Rooms aren't elegantly decorated, but many have kitchens. No online booking.

HOLLYWOOD ROOSEVELT HOTEL 7000 Hollywood Blvd. at Orange Dr.; **thompsonhotels.com** $$$$ Hollywood's historic hotel, festooned with Oscar paraphernalia. Thompson Hotels has made the Roosevelt highly trendy again, and guests complain that the pool is often closed for private parties.

MAGIC CASTLE 7025 Franklin Ave. at Sycamore Ave.; **magiccastlehotel.com** $$$ Visit the Magic Castle club where you can watch magicians perform (a tough ticket if you're not staying there). The building also houses a well-liked hotel.

MOTEL 6 HOLLYWOOD 1738 Whitley Ave. near Yucca St.; **motel6.com** $ Motel 6 as a chain is about as low as you can go, price and amenity-wise, and still have a clean and acceptable motel.

RENAISSANCE HOLLYWOOD HOTEL 1755 N. Highland Ave. at Yucca St.; **renaissancehollywood.com** $$$$ The glitziest hotel in the Hollywood Boulevard and Highland Avenue area—a high-rise with a color scheme of bright blues and purples and a large outdoor pool. Great views.

HOTELS NEAR HOLLYWOOD BOULEVARD AND VINE STREET (RED LINE STATION)

BEST WESTERN HOLLYWOOD HILLS 6141 Franklin Ave. at Vista Del Mar Ave.; **bestwestern.com** $$$ Quiet motor inn out of the center of Hollywood a bit, on residential Franklin Avenue east of Vine Street. Near the Red Line.

THE REDBURY HOTEL   1717 N. Vine St. at Hollywood Blvd.; **theredbury. com** $$$$$ A new boutique entry on the Hollywood glam hotel scene as of early 2011. Across the street from the Hollywood Boulevard/Vine Street Red Line station.

W HOLLYWOOD HOTEL   6250 Hollywood Blvd.; **starwoodhotels. com** $$$$$ This W, like the others, is known for glitz. This brand-new hotel is over at Vine Street, at the eastern end of the main Hollywood Boulevard strip. Literally on top of the Hollywood Boulevard/Vine Street Red Line station.

BUDGET MOTELS ALONG THE RED AND PURPLE LINES

These motels offer good deals in locations with good transit along the Red and Purple subway lines between Downtown LA and Hollywood. None of the neighborhoods would be called fancy, but they're all fine—especially for city-savvy travelers—and just a few subway stops away from Hollywood.

HOLLYWOOD CITY INN   1615 N. Western Ave.; **hollywoodcityinn.net** $ It is a well-kept property just south of the Hollywood Boulevard/Western Avenue Red Line Metro station. It is a mile—or one subway stop—east of Hollywood Boulevard and Vine Street, the eastern end of the Hollywood Boulevard strip.

SHELTER HOTEL   457 S. Mariposa Ave. at Fifth St.; **shelterhotels. com** $$ A Days Inn reworked to be a cool, simple hotel. The hotel definitely has rough spots, but it also has a great location in a Koreatown residential neighborhood near the Wilshire Boulevard/Normandie Avenue Purple Line station. It's also near Koreatown shopping.

TRAVELODGE VERMONT/SUNSET   1401 N. Vermont Ave.; **travelodge hollywood.com** $ It's practically on top of the entrance to the Red Line Vermont Avenue/Sunset Boulevard station. Simple as it is, I particularly like this place—it's within walking distance of the Los Feliz commercial district, not very far from Sunset Junction, and pretty close to the Hollywood branch of Zankou Chicken. Several hospitals in the area can

create a certain amount of noise, but they also assure that people are around at all hours.

WILSHIRE HOTEL (formerly the Wilshire Plaza) 3515 Wilshire Blvd.; **thewilshirehotel.com** $$ Across the street from the Purple Line Wilshire Boulevard/Normandie Avenue station in Koreatown—a favorite of car-free travelers.

HOSTELS

BANANA BUNGALOW HOLLYWOOD HOSTEL 5920 Hollywood Blvd. at North Bronson Ave.; **bananabungalow.com** The location is a dead spot halfway between Hollywood Boulevard/Western Avenue and Hollywood Boulevard/Vine Street Red Line stations (it's a little livelier coming from Western). $24–$32 per night in summer; private rooms available.

CHATEAU DE SOLEIL 11621 Burbank Blvd.; **chateaudesoleil.com** Within walking distance of the North Hollywood Red Line subway station, to get to Hollywood or Downtown LA. Be clear on the geography—large hills, or small mountains, between North Hollywood and Hollywood prevent walking. $225 per week in summer; private rooms and monthly rates available.

NORMANDIE MIDTOWN HOTEL AND HOSTEL 605 S. Normandie Ave. at Sixth St., Koreatown A block from Wilshire Boulevard, the Wilshire Boulevard/Normandie Avenue Purple Line subway station, and Wilshire Boulevard buses. Closest hostel to Downtown LA. $25–$36 per night in summer.

ORANGE DRIVE MANOR HOSTEL 1764 N. Orange Dr.; **orangedrive hostel.com** Just north of Hollywood Boulevard and one block from Hollywood Boulevard/Highland Avenue Red Line subway station and buses. $25–$35 per night year-round; private rooms and small dorms for groups available.

STUDENT INN 7038 Hollywood Blvd. near Sycamore Ave. Two blocks west of the Hollywood Boulevard/Highland Avenue Red Line subway station and buses, and down the block from the Roosevelt Hotel. $25 per night in summer; weekly and monthly rates available.

USA HOSTELS 1624 Schrader Blvd.; **usahostels.com/hollywood** Just off Hollywood Boulevard, a few blocks west of the Hollywood Boulevard/ Vine Street Red Line subway station. Served by tour buses. $38–$42 per night in summer; private rooms available.

■ **8** West Hollywood

Urban Pleasure Dome

WEST HOLLYWOOD IS A SMALL PLACE WITH A BIG REP (or maybe several big reps). Only 1.9 square miles (or 4.9 square kilometers) in area, West Hollywood is the most densely populated city in Southern California and has two of the region's leading nightclub zones, its top home design center, numerous treasured Art Deco buildings, and countless restaurants. The city is rightly known for its gay community, but among its 35,000 residents are many Russian émigrés and other urbanites. West Hollywood promotes itself as "the creative city." It is one of the most recently formed cities in Los Angeles County, incorporated in 1984, as a result of a creative gay-Russian alliance to support rent control.

West Hollywood is also a city that wants transit. It had the highest vote (84%) in favor of transit tax Measure R of any city in Los Angeles County.

Despite its small size, West Hollywood is very diverse as a place. Each of the main east-west streets—Sunset Boulevard, Santa Monica Boulevard, Melrose Avenue, and Beverly Boulevard (listed from north to south)—have a distinct character. Some areas in the eastern part of the city are struggling, while penthouse condos on the western edge can fetch millions.

The nicest thing about West Hollywood is that it's a genuinely walkable community, where people do in fact walk. Santa Monica Boulevard, with its wide sidewalks, makes for particularly good strolling, despite significant volumes of traffic.

West Hollywood is just west of Hollywood, 9 miles northwest of Downtown LA and 9 miles northeast of downtown Santa Monica. It's bounded on the east by Hollywood, on the west by Beverly Hills, on the north by the Hollywood Hills, and on the south by the Fairfax District. Note, however, that the main visitor areas of Hollywood and West Hollywood are 2–3 miles apart, so don't expect to walk between them unless you like good, long walks.

Transit

If you're splitting your stay and spending part of your time in Hollywood, visit West Hollywood from Hollywood. West Hollywood is also a reasonably short trip from Westwood. Travel time is about even from Downtown LA or Santa Monica, but more service is available from Downtown.

From Downtown Los Angeles, take local bus 2 to Sunset and La Cienega boulevards or local bus 4 to Santa Monica and La Cienega boulevards.

From Union Station, take rapid bus 704 (it runs every 20 minutes) to Santa Monica and La Cienega boulevards. There are also rapid stops in active parts of West Hollywood at Santa Monica Boulevard and Sweetzer Avenue and Santa Monica and San Vicente boulevards.

From Hollywood, take local bus 2 from Sunset Boulevard and Highland Avenue to Sunset and La Cienega boulevards.

From Santa Monica, check the Metro Trip Planner to find the best routing for when you're going. During the day, take rapid bus 704 to Santa Monica and La Cienega boulevards. It runs every 40 minutes from Santa Monica on weekdays and every 20 minutes on weekends. During the day and evenings Monday–Friday, more frequent service is available via Big Blue Bus 1 to Santa Monica and Westwood boulevards, and then Metro bus 4 or rapid bus 704 to Santa Monica and La Cienega boulevards. During the evening and overnight (7 p.m.–5 a.m.), take Metro bus 4 from Santa Monica city to La Cienega Boulevard.

From the San Fernando Valley, take the Red Line subway from the North Hollywood station to Hollywood Boulevard/Highland Avenue, and then walk 5 minutes south (downhill) to Highland Avenue/Sunset Boulevard. Then catch bus 2 Sunset Boulevard westbound to Sunset and La Cienega boulevards.

From South Los Angeles, buses 105, 550, and 705 provide direct service.

Note: These transit directions apply to all destinations in this chapter, except where noted.

Seeing West Hollywood

SUNSET STRIP

Including the area from Fairfax Avenue west to the Beverly Hills line (though it trails off west of Doheny Drive), the Sunset Strip is just under 2 miles long. You might call the Strip the classic rock of entertainment areas, and indeed, banners proclaim Sunset to be "The Street That Rock Built."

But Sunset's history as a nightclub zone dates back to the 1920s Prohibition era. As an unincorporated, county-governed locality, the rules on the Strip were much looser than in the city of Los Angeles. The Strip took its more or less modern form in the 1960s and 1970s, when it became LA's hotbed of rock. It remains a major music locale today, even as Echo Park, Silver Lake, and Hollywood have emerged as other rock lands.

The (first) **House of Blues, the Key Club, the Rainbow Bar and Grill, The Roxy,** and **The Viper Room** are all major venues on the Strip. Check **laweekly.com** for listings.

In addition to rock clubs, the Sunset Strip has restaurants, hotels, and a typical range of establishments but no grocery stores. **Book Soup** is a fine bookstore on the Strip. The Sunset Plaza stores, a 1930s development lined up along Sunset Boulevard at Sunset Plaza Drive, include some elite retailers such as Nicole Miller and BCBG, as well as some less elevated brands. This isn't one of LA's major shopping areas, but it's one of the more pleasant, with sidewalk cafés providing a resting spot for shoppers.

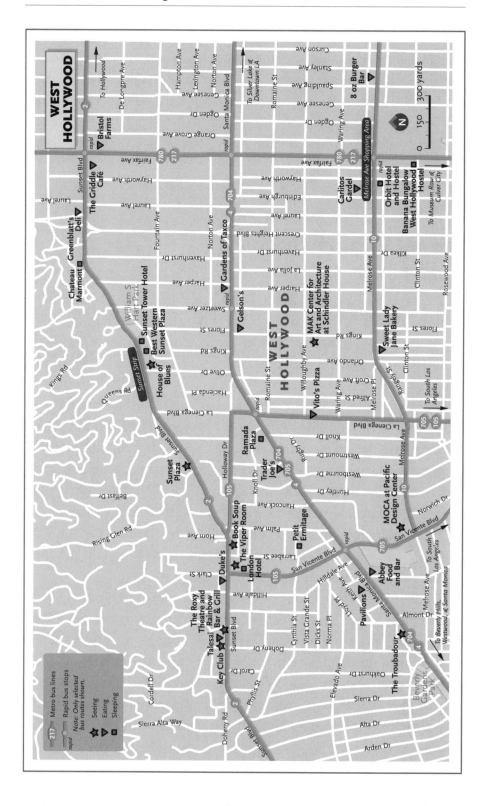

★ BIKE SHOP NEAR WEST HOLLYWOOD ★

SPOKES 'N' STUFF 7777 Melrose Ave. near Ogden Ave.; **spokes-n-stuff.com**

SANTA MONICA BOULEVARD AND "BOYS TOWN"

As a city of entertainment and excitement, West Hollywood doesn't exactly have a classic Main Street. But Santa Monica Boulevard, an urban backbone just under 3 miles long, is as close as it gets. Once part of Route 66, the street stretches the length of the little city from La Brea Boulevard at the edge of Hollywood to Doheny Drive at the Beverly Hills line. The street is lined with storefront businesses virtually that entire length.

The character of Santa Monica Boulevard changes as you go west. The eastern third, from La Brea Boulevard to Fairfax Avenue, has been lower income, with many businesses catering to the long-standing Russian émigré community. The western part, from Fairfax Avenue to Doheny Drive, focuses on gays, the urban hip, and entertainment industry folk. The practical stores of West Hollywood—the groceries and hardware stores, along with the fun spots—are on Santa Monica Boulevard. It's known as "Boys Town" for its gay bars, especially on the westernmost third between La Cienega Boulevard and Doheny. It's an unusual case (especially in LA) of a wide street with moderate speed traffic, slowed down by frequent traffic lights. It's an enjoyable stretch and one of LA's best urban neighborhoods, whatever your sexual persuasion.

MOCA AT PACIFIC DESIGN CENTER

The Pacific Design Center is highly visible in West Hollywood—it's made up of the huge, striking, angular blue, green, and red buildings on the west side of the city. The original blue building is known as the "blue whale." It's the wholesale showplace for furniture and home design in Southern California and is closed to the general public. Unless you're in that trade, or have a friend who is, you can only ogle PDC from the outside. You can go in to the small, separate building on-site that is a branch of Downtown LA's fine Museum of Contemporary Art, where a single exhibit and store are located. The museum can be found at 8687

Melrose Ave. at San Vicente Blvd. Admission is free, and the museum is open Tuesday–Friday, 11 a.m.–5 p.m. and Saturday–Sunday, 11 a.m.–6 p.m. Visit **moca.org** for more information.

Transit: *From Downtown LA,* take Metro bus 10 to Melrose Avenue and San Vicente Boulevard. *From Hollywood,* take rapid bus 780 to Fairfax Avenue and Santa Monica Boulevard, and then take local bus 4 or rapid bus 704 to Santa Monica and San Vicente boulevards. *From Santa Monica,* take rapid bus 704 to Santa Monica and San Vicente boulevards; it operates every 40 minutes. More frequent service is available Monday–Friday via rapid bus 720 to Wilshire and La Cienega boulevards, and then take rapid bus 705 to San Vicente and Santa Monica boulevards.

MAK CENTER FOR ART AND ARCHITECTURE AT SCHINDLER HOUSE

The MAK Center (835 N. Kings Rd. near Willoughby Ave.; **makcenter.org**) is an architectural exhibit space in an experimental two-family house that famed German modernist R. M. Schindler built in 1922. If you're interested in modern architecture, this structure is still pretty striking and worth a visit. It's tucked into the midst of an ordinary West Hollywood apartment neighborhood. It's open Wednesday–Sunday, 11 a.m.–6 p.m. Admission is $7 for adults and $6 for students and seniors.

Transit: *From Downtown LA,* take rapid bus 704 Santa Monica Boulevard or local bus 4 (two blocks north). *From Hollywood,* take bus 217 or rapid bus 780 to Fairfax Avenue and Santa Monica Boulevard, and then take local bus 4 or rapid bus 704. *From Santa Monica,* take rapid bus 704, which runs every 40 minutes, or rapid bus 720 to Wilshire and La Cienega boulevards, and then take bus 105, which has more frequent service, to La Cienega Boulevard and Waring Avenue.

Shopping

Though West Hollywood isn't usually thought of as a big shopping town, portions of the Melrose Avenue shopping strip and the adjacent Beverly Center shopping area are in West Hollywood. They're described beginning on page 172.

Where to Eat in West Hollywood

As a movie industry hangout and home of many urban hipsters, West Hollywood is a big eating town, though not particularly an ethnic eating area or a cheap eats area.

ON OR NEAR SANTA MONICA BOULEVARD

ABBEY FOOD AND BAR   692 N. Robertson Blvd.; **abbeyfoodandbar.com** **$$**   Back in the day, I could sit at Abbey sipping coffee and watching my daughter play in the playground at adjacent West Hollywood Park.

GUITAR ART AT BUS STOP IN ROCKIN' WEST HOLLYWOOD

They've ramped up a bit since then, functioning more as a gay bar with good food and drinks.

GARDENS OF TAXCO 1113 N. Harper Ave.; **gardensoftaxco.com** $$ Longtime Mexican restaurant known as much for its lavish decor as for its Mexico City–style food. It sometimes offers an early-bird special 4:30–7 p.m., Tuesday–Friday.

VITO'S PIZZA 846 N. La Cienega Blvd. at Willoughby Ave.; **vitopizza.com** $ East Coast–style pizza in West Hollywood.

ON OR NEAR THE SUNSET STRIP

DUKE'S 8909 Sunset Blvd. near San Vicente Blvd.; **dukeswest hollywood.com** $ Duke's has also morphed, from Duke's Coffee Shop into Duke's West Hollywood. Hopefully its character as a music industry hangout and "little slice of unreality" won't change. The food is perfectly fine, but not really the reason you go there.

THE GRIDDLE CAFE 7916 W. Sunset Blvd. near Fairfax Ave.; **thegriddle cafe.com** $$ Technically, The Griddle is within the city of Los Angeles, but it sits physically and psychologically at the beginning of the Sunset Strip, so it's listed here with West Hollywood. It's a fun, fast, but genuinely friendly place for big orders of pancakes or French toast at breakfast (it also serves lunch) and a great place to see young Hollywood at ease. Expect a wait on weekend mornings, unless you get there close to the 8 a.m. opening time (7 a.m. on weekdays).

TALESAI 9043 Sunset Blvd. near Doheny Dr.; **talesai.com** $$$ One of the first upscale or fusion Thai restaurants in Los Angeles, and still a quiet, elegant place for a good meal, though without the macho spicing that some Thai restaurant diners seek.

Grocery Stores and Markets in West Hollywood

BRISTOL FARMS 7880 W. Sunset Blvd. at Fairfax Ave. LA's leading (pricey) produce and other foods purveyor. Prepared foods deli.

GELSON'S 8330 W. Santa Monica Blvd. at Kings Rd. The upscale supermarket chain of LA. Has prepared sandwiches and grab-and-go Wolfgang Puck Express.

PAVILIONS 8969 W. Santa Monica Blvd. at Robertson Blvd. A large supermarket, somewhere on the scale between mid-scale Ralph's and upscale Gelson's.

TRADER JOE'S 7304 W. Santa Monica Blvd. at Genessee Ave. and 8611 W. Santa Monica Blvd. at Westmount Dr. The grocery for snacks, candy, water, beer, wine, and dried fruit, though it carries a small selection of all types of items, including produce.

Where to Stay in West Hollywood

West Hollywood is a great fun town, busy day and night, but it's not the top place for car-free travelers to stay. Transit is pretty good, especially during the day, and it's a great place to walk around. But West Hollywood doesn't have the range of connections that Hollywood to the east or Westwood (or even Beverly Hills) to the west have. Rapid buses on Santa Monica and La Cienega boulevards serve West Hollywood during the day but don't run in the evenings. Sunset Boulevard is also sharply uphill from Santa Monica Boulevard, the strongest transit spine.

Here are some West Hollywood choices if you do want to stay and partake of the scene.

BEST WESTERN SUNSET PLAZA 8400 W. Sunset Blvd. at Kings Rd.; **bestwestern.com** $$$$ It's not all glamour on the Strip. Stay here if you want a decent, regular (if pricey) hotel in glitz land. Within walking distance of La Cienega Boulevard buses.

CHATEAU MARMONT 8221 W. Sunset Blvd. at Marmont Ln.; **chateau marmont.com** $$$$$ This is old West Hollywood, built in 1928 as a hotel for the stars and still (or again) catering to them after a famous period of decrepitude. It's a good place to spot celebrities and is featured in many stories. Within walking distance—about 10 minutes—to Fairfax Avenue buses (217 and rapid bus 780), a significant plus. On Sunset Strip.

LONDON HOTEL 1020 N. San Vicente Blvd. just below Sunset Blvd.;

thelondonwesthollywood.com $$$$ A hotel for modern luxury and to see and be seen in West Hollywood. Within walking distance of La Cienega Boulevard buses.

PETIT ERMITAGE 8822 Cynthia St. at Larrabee St.; **petitermitage. com** $$$ This converted apartment building is on a quiet residential street one block from Santa Monica Boulevard. Within walking distance of La Cienega Boulevard buses.

RAMADA PLAZA 8585 Santa Monica Blvd. at West Knoll Dr.; **ramada weho.com** $$–$$$ The most affordable decent hotel in West Hollywood, right on the Santa Monica Boulevard transit spine. Within walking distance of La Cienega Boulevard buses.

SUNSET TOWER HOTEL 8358 Sunset Blvd. at Kings Rd.; **sunsettower hotel.com** $$$$–$$$$$ The prime Art Deco landmark of West Hollywood. Within walking distance of La Cienega Boulevard buses.

HOSTELS

BANANA BUNGALOW WEST HOLLYWOOD HOSTEL 603 N. Fairfax Ave.; **bananabungalow.com** They call this West Hollywood, but it's about a block outside the main Fairfax commercial district. Best bus lines are 217 and rapid bus 780 on Fairfax Avenue north to Hollywood Boulevard and south to Wilshire Boulevard. $24–$32 per night in summer; private rooms available.

ORBIT HOTEL AND HOSTEL 7950 Melrose Ave. at North Hayworth Ave.; **orbithotel.com** It's two blocks west of Fairfax Avenue, so it's really in the Fairfax district. Best bus lines are 217 and 780 on Fairfax Avenue north to Hollywood Boulevard and south to Wilshire Boulevard. It's a couple of blocks from Banana Bungalow West Hollywood. $22–$28 per night in summer; private rooms available.

■ 9 Culture Explorer Los Angeles

LOS ANGELES'S ABUNDANT CULTURAL AND ENTERTAINMENT SCENE can be found in many neighborhoods, so you might be considering a play, concert, or film in multiple parts of the city. You may decide to attend an event closer to where you're staying, especially for events at night, for easier transit. If you plan to stay in more than one area of Los Angeles during your trip, you may have more events from which to choose, though concerts and special films tend to only run for one or two nights. This chapter lists many types of cultural venues in and across Los Angeles, including leading shopping areas.

Film Studio Tours

Many people want to see how the dream factory operates and how movies are made. Studios are happy to oblige, up to a point, and for a price.

PARAMOUNT   5555 Melrose Ave. at Gower St., Hollywood; **paramount studios.com/special-events/tours.html** $35   Similar to the Warner Brothers' tour, you'll be taken into the studio, but hours are more restricted. The only major studio that's still operating in the Hollywood neighborhood. Tours leave at 10 a.m., 11 a.m., 1 p.m., and 2 p.m. Monday–Friday. Transit: *From Hollywood,* take local bus 210 from Vine Street/ Hollywood Boulevard to Vine Street/Melrose Avenue (1.3 miles). *From Downtown LA,* take Metro bus 10 Melrose Avenue to Melrose Avenue/

Gower Street. *From Santa Monica,* take rapid bus 720 to Wilshire and Santa Monica boulevards, and then take local bus 4 to Santa Monica Boulevard and Gower Street.

SONY 10202 Washington Blvd. at Overland Ave., Culver City; **sony picturesstudiostours.com** $33 Promises a trip back to Hollywood's glory days along with a visit to a state-of-the-art movie studio. Tours run every hour 9:30 a.m.–2:30 p.m. plus a twilight tour at 6:30 p.m. Transit: *From Downtown LA,* take local bus 33 or rapid bus 733 to Venice Boulevard and Motor Avenue. *From Hollywood,* take local bus 217 or rapid bus 780 to Fairfax Avenue/Venice Boulevard, and then take local bus 33 or rapid bus 733 to Motor Avenue. *From Santa Monica,* take rapid bus 733 to Venice Boulevard and Motor Avenue.

UNIVERSAL STUDIOS Universal City Plaza; **universalstudioshollywood. com** $62–$77 Universal is the best known of the studio tours, but it's not really a tour of a studio at all. Instead it's a theme park based on a movie studio. The tram you ride there never stops. Many people find it very entertaining, and millions visit, but it's not really the place to learn how movies are made. The basic 1-day ticket is $62 for Southern California residents (zip code required), and $77 for out-of-area people. Transit: *From Downtown LA or Hollywood,* take the Red Line subway to Universal City station, and then take a free tram across Lankershim Boulevard on Universal Terrace Parkway. *From Santa Monica,* it's quickest to take the Big Blue Bus express 10 to Seventh and Hope streets in Downtown LA (7th St./Metro Center station), and then the Red Line subway to Universal City station. Then take a free tram across Lankershim Boulevard on Universal Terrace Parkway.

WARNER BROTHERS 3400 Riverside Dr., Burbank; **vipstudiotour.warner bros.com** $48 Widely considered to be the best studio tour. You're taken on electric carts in groups of 12 through Warner's soundstages, shops, and sets. Tours are offered Monday–Friday, 8:20 a.m.–4 p.m. Transit: *From Hollywood,* take Metro bus 222 to Hollywood Way/Riverside Drive. *From Downtown LA,* take the Red Line subway to Hollywood Boulevard/Vine Street, and connect to Metro bus 222 to Hollywood Way and Riverside Drive. *From Santa Monica,* take Metro bus 534 to Washington Avenue/

Fairfax Avenue, then take local bus 217 or rapid bus 780 to Hollywood Boulevard/Highland Avenue, and then take Metro bus 222 to Hollywood Way and Riverside Drive. Check Trip Planner for other routings.

Special Film

Most of the movies shown in Los Angeles are the same as what's shown around the country, although the theaters here might be more interesting. But some films shown in LA aren't shown in many other cities. LA buzzes with film festivals year-round—far more than I can list. Repertory cinemas are devoted to old movies while other venues focus on current movies that haven't found a commercial distributor. Foreign countries create LA showcases for the films of their nation. If you want to search out unique cinema, LA is the place.

For the most part, special film programs are shown at night, making it more challenging (but certainly not impossible) for transit-using travelers. Some cinemas, such as the New Beverly and the LACMA film series, occasionally have matinees. Film festivals typically run all day, making it easier to get to daytime and early evening screenings.

FILM FESTIVALS

Because so many film festivals are in Los Angeles, I'm listing an arbitrary, ideally somewhat representative, selection of festivals. Some are based on particular demographic groups while others are not. Venues and dates may change year to year for film festivals; check current information at the time.

AFI FEST   Grauman's Chinese Theatre, Hollywood & Highland Center; early November; **afi.com**   AFI stands for American Film Institute, the folks whose mission is the propagation of film as art. Both a major film festival and a global film marketplace, this festival is probably the closest thing LA has to the Cannes Film Festival in France. (Beverly Hills is Cannes's sister city.)

DOWNTOWN FILM FESTIVAL   Various venues; September; **dffla. com**   Here's how these folks describe their festival: "Our programming reflects downtown LA's vibrant new urbanism, the unique ethnic and cultural diversity of its communities and neighborhoods, and its seminal role in the early days of American cinema."

HOLLYWOOD FILM FESTIVAL ArcLight Cinema, Hollywood; October; **hollywoodawards.com** The Hollywood Film Festival is made up of a series of subfestivals, such as documentaries, independent, international, and so on. It seems to place a heavy emphasis on awards and declares its October run as the start of the Hollywood awards season. Near the Hollywood Boulevard/Vine Street Red Line subway station.

LAST REMAINING SEATS Various venues; Wednesday nights in May–June; **laconservancy.org** This series of films combines a film and a historical preservation event. The Los Angeles Conservancy, LA's leading historical preservation organization, sponsors classic movies in historic theaters in Downtown Los Angeles, some of them endangered. Buy tickets early if possible; these often sell out.

LOS ANGELES ASIAN PACIFIC FILM FESTIVAL Split between West Hollywood and Little Tokyo venues; late April–early May; **asianfilm festla.org** Large festival of Asian Americans and Asian films, running for almost three decades.

LOS ANGELES FILM FESTIVAL Various venues; June; **lafilmfest.com** It presents more than 200 features, shorts, and music videos—a hefty festival. The festival is held at multiple venues, all Downtown and transit accessible, except the John Anon Ford Theatre, where they run a shuttle from Universal City Red Line to there.

LOS ANGELES INTERNATIONAL SHORT FILM FESTIVAL Laemelle Sunset 5, West Hollywood; July; **lashortsfest.com** It's a sad fact, but the shorts often don't get respect in this world. LAISF goes long on shorts, presenting what it says is the world's largest festival of short films. Take the 2 Sunset Boulevard bus, the 4 Santa Monica Boulevard bus, or the 704 Santa Monica Boulevard rapid bus to get there.

LOS ANGELES LATINO INTERNATIONAL FILM FESTIVAL Mann Chinese 6, Hollywood; August; **latinofilm.org** This festival seeks to connect the Hollywood movie world with the Latino world, inside and outside the United States. Near the Hollywood Boulevard/Highland Avenue Red Line station.

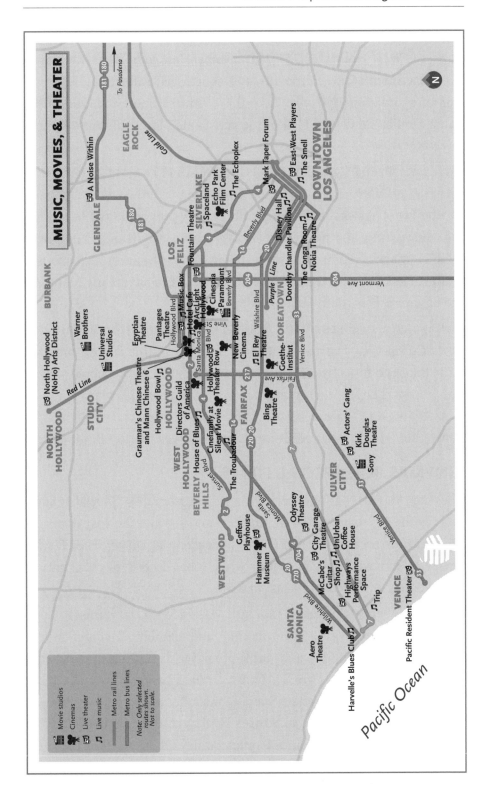

LOS ANGELES WOMEN'S INTERNATIONAL FILM FESTIVAL Laemelle Sunset 5, West Hollywood; March; **lawomensfest.com** Presents narratives, documentaries, animation, and shorts that inform audiences of women's situations globally. Take the 2 Sunset Boulevard bus, the 4 Santa Monica Boulevard bus, or the 704 Santa Monica Boulevard rapid bus to get there.

OUTFEST Primarily at Directors' Guild of America and Laemelle Sunset 5 theater, West Hollywood; July; **outfest.org** Outfest describes itself as "the Los Angeles–based nonprofit organization dedicated to nurturing, showcasing, and protecting lesbian, gay, bisexual, and transgender (LGBT) images." Their big film fest is in early July—they also sponsor Outfest Fusion, focused on gays and lesbians of color, in early March, at the Egyptian Theatre in Hollywood.

PAN-AFRICAN FILM FESTIVAL Culver Plaza Cinema, 9919 Washington Blvd., Culver City; February; **paff.org** Every year, this festival presents more than 100 films from around the world that focus on people of African descent. The festival is presented in Los Angeles in February, as well as in Atlanta and Nigeria. It's accessible by Metro bus 33 or rapid bus 733 Venice Boulevard lines and Culver City bus 1 Washington Boulevard.

CINEMAS FOR SPECIAL FILMS

These are venues that have recurring movie programs. Special venues, such as the Directors Guild of America and the Goethe Institute, also show movies occasionally. REDCAT (**redcat.org**) at Disney Hall Downtown shows movies once or twice a week; it has other types of events as well. Venues are listed from east to west.

ECHO PARK FILM CENTER 1200 N. Alvarado St. at Sunset Blvd.; **echoparkfilmcenter.org** A filmmaking and exhibition center where experimental, no budget, and punk films live, including open screening nights. Most events are $5. Transit: *From Downtown LA,* take the 2 Sunset Boulevard bus or the 4 Santa Monica Boulevard bus westbound. *From Hollywood,* take the 2 Sunset Boulevard bus eastbound. *From Santa Monica,* take the 4 Santa Monica Boulevard bus eastbound, or for daytime and early evening events Monday–Saturday, take the 704 Santa Monica Boulevard rapid bus.

CINESPIA outdoor summer screenings at Hollywood Forever Cemetery; 6000 Santa Monica Blvd. (enter off Gordon Ave.); **cinespia.org** You want to get there really early to get a decent spot on the lawn. Bring a picnic; this isn't just a movie—it's an event. Cost is $10. Transit: *From Hollywood,* take the 210 Vine Street bus southbound or just walk the 0.75 mile from Hollywood Boulevard. *From Downtown LA,* take bus 4 Santa Monica Boulevard westbound. *From Santa Monica,* take bus 4 Santa Monica Boulevard eastbound.

EGYPTIAN THEATRE (American Cinematheque)   6712 Hollywood Blvd. near Highland Ave.; **americancinematheque.com** Magnificently restored classic cinema showing American independent and world cinema. *Forever Hollywood,* shown on weekends, is a 1-hour repeated movie that celebrates the history of Hollywood film. Transit: *From Downtown LA,* take the Red Line subway to Hollywood Boulevard/Highland Avenue. *From Santa Monica,* take rapid bus 720 Wilshire Boulevard to Wilshire Boulevard and Fairfax Avenue, and then take local bus 217 or rapid bus 780 to Hollywood Boulevard/Highland Avenue.

NEW BEVERLY CINEMA   7165 Beverly Blvd. near La Brea Blvd.; **newbev cinema.com** The New Beverly describes itself as LA's "premiere" revival movie house. It's practically the only one at this point. Programming is highly knowledgeable. Transit: *From Downtown LA,* take bus 14 Beverly Boulevard or bus 16 Third Street at Third Street and La Brea Boulevard east to Downtown (Third Street is farther away but much more frequent). *From Hollywood,* take the 212 La Brea Boulevard bus to Beverly Boulevard, but be forewarned that it has unusually poor 60-minute service after 9:20 p.m. *From Santa Monica,* take rapid bus 720 east to Wilshire and La Brea boulevards, and then take bus 212 north to La Brea and Beverly boulevards, or you could walk the 1 mile from Wilshire Boulevard to Beverly Boulevard.

BING THEATRE AT LOS ANGELES COUNTY MUSEUM OF ART   5905 Wilshire Blvd. near Fairfax Ave.; **lacma.org** Saved from elimination by public protest, LACMA continues to show classic films on Friday, Saturday, and Tuesday. Tickets are $10 and $2 for Tuesday matinees. **Transit:** *From Downtown LA,* take rapid bus 720 Wilshire Boulevard to Wilshire Boulevard and Fairfax Avenue. *From Hollywood,* take local bus 217 or rapid bus 780 Fairfax Avenue to Fairfax Avenue/Wilshire Boulevard. *From Santa Monica,* take rapid bus 720 Wilshire Boulevard to Wilshire Boulevard/Fairfax Avenue.

CINEFAMILY AT SILENT MOVIE 611 N. Fairfax Ave. near Clinton St.; **cinefamily.org** Cinefamily describes itself as an organization of moviegoers showing a variety of rare, comic, and sometimes but not always silent films. **Transit:** *From Hollywood,* take local bus 217 or rapid bus 780 to Fairfax Avenue/Melrose Boulevard. *From Downtown LA,* take bus 14 Beverly Boulevard to Beverly Boulevard/Fairfax Avenue. *From Santa Monica,* take bus 4 Santa Monica Boulevard to Fairfax Avenue/Santa Monica Boulevard, and then walk 0.5 mile south. *For day and early evening events Monday–Saturday,* take rapid bus 704 Santa Monica Boulevard.

HAMMER MUSEUM 10899 Wilshire Blvd. at Westwood Blvd.; **hammer.ucla.edu; cinema.ucla.edu** Two different film series go on here, and they don't seem to have a joint calendar. The Hammer itself offers Hammer Screenings, related to the work of the art museum. The UCLA Film and Television Archive, one of the world's leading film conservation organizations, also presents many, though not all, of its screenings of historic and archival films at the Hammer. The archive does a free Family Flicks series one Saturday morning per month. **Transit:** *From Downtown LA,* take rapid bus 720 to Wilshire and Westwood boulevards. *From Hollywood,* take local bus 2 from Sunset Boulevard/Highland Avenue to Le Conte Avenue/Westwood Boulevard. *From Santa Monica,* take rapid bus 720 to Wilshire and Westwood boulevards.

AERO THEATRE 1328 Montana Ave. at 14th St.; **americancinematheque.com** A 1940 theater that, along with the Egyptian Theatre in Hollywood, is part of the American Cinematheque. It focuses on classic American movies from the 1920s through the 1980s, shown Wednesday–Sunday. **Transit:** *From downtown Santa Monica (about a 30-minute walk),* take Big Blue Bus

3 to Montana Avenue and 14th Street, or take Big Blue Bus 2 or Metro rapid bus 720 eastbound to Wilshire Boulevard/14th Street. *From Downtown LA,* take rapid bus 720 westbound to Wilshire Boulevard/14th Street.

Live Theater

Live theater is one of LA's great, often overlooked cultural strengths. The only U.S. cities that compare are New York and Chicago. In LA, a virtually limitless pool of acting talent hangs around hoping for a big break in movies or television. Almost all of LA theater is nonprofit (or more accurately, profitless), though a few big commercial productions take place every year. LA is notable not so much for one great theater but for a brace of them across the city.

Hollywood is definitely the top theater neighborhood, but notable theaters are also located in North Hollywood, Downtown LA, Westwood, and elsewhere. To see what's playing now, check the *LA Weekly* or *Los Angeles Times,* especially their websites, as well as theater websites. Listings are usually available about a month in advance, but many individual theaters have their schedules planned much longer.

Theater happens mostly at night, so plan your transit trips carefully. Websites will often list the running time of a play or you can call the theater, so you can figure out when the play will be over. That way you can use the Trip Planner to plan your trip back—the best route may depend on exactly when the play lets out. In some cases, the transit listed below is different for getting to the theater as opposed to getting home from the theater because some buses stop running in the evening.

Most theaters have matinees on Sunday, but not on Thursday or Saturday, as Broadway in New York does. LA does not have a discount theater ticket booth à la Times Square, but for discounts on tickets, check Plays 411 (**plays411.net**). Some theaters may have their own discount/rush tickets (the Mark Taper Forum has); it's always worth asking. I've listed some leading Los Angeles live theaters, arranged from east to west.

EAST-WEST PLAYERS   120 Judge John Aliso St., Downtown LA (Little Tokyo); **eastwestplayers.org**   East-West Players is one of the longest-standing Asian American theater companies, which has premiered more than 100 plays in 45 years. Transit: *From 7th St./Metro Center,* take DASH A to First Street/Central Avenue. *From Hollywood,* take the Red Line subway to Civic Center station, and walk east on First Street four blocks. *From Santa Monica,* take Big Blue Bus express 10 to Los Angeles and Temple streets, and walk two blocks south to First Street. *From East LA,* take the Gold Line light rail to Little Tokyo station. *From the San Fernando Valley,* take the Red Line subway to Civic Center station and walk east on First Street 0.5 mile (10 minutes). *From South Los Angeles,* take rapid bus 740 or 745 to Broadway/First Street.

MARK TAPER FORUM/CENTER THEATRE GROUP   The Music Center, 135 N. Grand Ave. at Temple St., Downtown LA (Bunker Hill); **center theatregroup.org**   The Taper started as Los Angeles's repertory theater when that movement was just starting. Transit: *From Hollywood or from the Downtown Core,* take the Red Line subway to the Civic Center station, and then walk two blocks west on First Street to Grand Avenue. *From Santa Monica,* take Big Blue Bus express 10 to Hope at First Street, which is at the back of Disney Hall. If you're on or near Hill Street, you can take Angels Flight up the hill, and then walk north on Grand Avenue. Some Downtown restaurants provide shuttle service to Disney Hall/The Music Center; it's worth asking if you're eating dinner Downtown before the concert.

A NOISE WITHIN   234 S. Brand Blvd. at Colorado St., Glendale; **anoise within.org**   This well-regarded company focuses on classic plays, including those by William Shakespeare. Transit: *From Downtown LA,* take Metro bus 92 to Brand Boulevard/Harvard Street. *From Hollywood,* take Metro bus 180/181 or rapid bus 780 eastbound to Broadway/Brand Boulevard. *From Pasadena,* take westbound bus 180/181 or rapid bus 780 to Brand Boulevard/Broadway. *From Santa Monica,* use Metro Trip Planner to determine which of the multiple connecting options for Santa Monica to take.

FOUNTAIN THEATRE   5060 Fountain Ave. at Normandie Ave., (East) Hollywood; **fountaintheatre.com**   A small theater that's tackled big plays, including several American premieres of leading South African playwright Athol Fugard. Among major theaters this is probably the location where you have to be most careful of personal safety. Transit: *From Downtown LA,* take bus 2 westbound to Sunset Boulevard/Normandie Avenue. *From Hollywood,* take bus 2 eastbound to Sunset Boulevard/Normandie Avenue. *From Santa Monica,* take rapid bus 704 to Santa Monica Boulevard/Normandie Avenue; this route will take you to all plays and from matinees; take bus 4 Santa Monica Boulevard back from evening plays.

PANTAGES THEATRE   6233 Hollywood Blvd., Hollywood; **broadwayla.org** Where the big shows such as *Wicked* go when they come to Los Angeles. Transit: *From Downtown LA,* take the Red Line subway to Hollywood Boulevard/Vine Street. *From Santa Monica,* take rapid bus 704 to Santa Monica Boulevard/Vine Street, and then walk north 0.8 mile or take local bus 210 to Vine Street/Hollywood Boulevard.

HOLLYWOOD THEATER ROW   6200–6700 Santa Monica Blvd. from El Centro Ave. to McCadden Pl., Hollywood; **theaterrowhollywood. com**   The Hollywood Media District (the place where support functions for TV and film production are located) has about a dozen small theaters with 20 stages. Some theaters belong to specific companies while others are rental stages. At any given time, some stages are likely to be active. Theaters here include Hudson Theatre, Open Fist, and Celebration Theatre. Transit: *From Downtown LA,* take local bus 4 to Santa Monica Boulevard/Vine Street. *From Hollywood,* take local bus 210 to Vine Street/Santa Monica Boulevard or walk 0.8 mile from Hollywood Boulevard. *From Santa Monica,* take rapid bus 704 to Santa Monica Boulevard/Vine Street to all plays and from matinees; take local bus 4 Santa Monica Boulevard back from evening plays.

NORTH HOLLYWOOD (NOHO) ARTS DISTRICT   Centered on Lankershim and Magnolia boulevards, North Hollywood is in the southeastern corner of the San Fernando Valley. A couple dozen theater stages are here, though not all are going at once. You can get information on the various companies and performances at **nohoartsdistrict.com**. Transit: *From Downtown LA and Hollywood,* take the Red Line subway to North

Hollywood. *From Santa Monica,* take Metro bus 534 to Washington Boulevard/Fairfax Avenue, and then take local bus 217 or rapid bus 780 to Hollywood Boulevard/Highland Avenue, and then Red Line subway to North Hollywood. Check Trip Planner for other routings.

ACTORS' GANG   9070 Venice Blvd. (Ivy Substation), Culver City; **theactorsgang.com**   Actors' Gang, which sees itself as working in the Italian *commedia dell'arte* tradition, is a politically engaged theater company led by movie actor Tim Robbins. The theater is about 0.5 mile from the Kirk Douglas Theatre. Transit: *From Downtown LA,* take bus 33 or rapid bus 733 westbound to Venice Boulevard and Bagley Avenue, and then walk two blocks west to the theater. *From Santa Monica,* take rapid bus 733 eastbound to Venice Boulevard and Bagley Avenue, and then walk two blocks west to the theater. *From Hollywood,* take bus 217 to Fairfax Avenue and Venice Boulevard, and then transfer to bus 33 or rapid bus 733 westbound to Venice Boulevard and Bagley Avenue. Then walk two blocks west to the theater. Once the Expo Line light rail Culver City station opens, take the Expo Line from Downtown LA to the Venice Boulevard/Robertson Boulevard station in Culver City, and then walk straight ahead along Venice Boulevard to the theater.

KIRK DOUGLAS THEATRE   9820 Washington Blvd., Culver City; **centertheatregroup.org**   The Center Theatre Group's Westside outpost, a smaller theater where they test out edgier plays. Transit: See the Actors' Gang entry above. Once the Expo Line Culver City station opens, the Expo Line will be the best route from Downtown LA; the station is about a 10-minute walk from the theater.

GEFFEN PLAYHOUSE   10886 Le Conte Ave. near Westwood Blvd., Westwood; **geffenplayhouse.com**   The Geffen (endowed by movie mogul David Geffen) is plush and pricey, as befits its Westside digs, but serious nonetheless, often presenting good plays done well. Transit: *From Downtown LA,* take rapid bus 720 to Wilshire and Westwood boulevards. *From Hollywood,* take bus 2 from Sunset Boulevard/Highland Avenue to Le Conte Avenue/Westwood Boulevard. *From Santa Monica,* take rapid bus 720 to Wilshire and Westwood boulevards.

ODYSSEY THEATRE 2055 S. Sepulveda Blvd. near Mississippi Ave., West Los Angeles; **odysseytheatre.com** The space is an unprepossessing old city warehouse, but Odyssey has three stages of new and recent good-quality theater in here. Transit: *From Westwood,* take Culver City bus 6; get off at Westwood Boulevard between Le Conte Avenue and Wilshire Boulevard. *From Santa Monica,* take Big Blue Bus 5 to Olympic and Sepulveda boulevards for matinees; for evening shows take Big Blue Bus 1 or Metro bus 4 or rapid bus 704 to Santa Monica and Sepulveda boulevards. *From Hollywood,* take bus 4 or rapid bus 704 Santa Monica Boulevard (a 0.8-mile walk from Hollywood Boulevard) to Santa Monica and Sepulveda boulevards. *From Downtown LA,* take Big Blue Bus express 10 to Bundy Drive/Santa Monica Boulevard, and then take Big Blue Bus 1 or Metro rapid bus 704 to Santa Monica and Sepulveda boulevards to and from matinees and to evening performances; for evening performances, take Metro bus 4 Santa Monica Boulevard to Santa Monica and Sepulveda boulevards, and then walk south 0.5 mile to the theater, which is on the west side of Sepulveda.

HIGHWAYS PERFORMANCE SPACE 18th Street Arts Center, 1651 18th St., Santa Monica; **highwaysperformance.org** In the 1980s Highways Performance Space was ground zero in the culture war, the home base of gay artists that the National Endowment for the Arts was desperately trying to defund. Out of the spotlight, Highways continues to function as a home for experimental theater, dance, and solo performance. Transit: *From Santa Monica,* take Big Blue Bus 1 to Santa Monica Boulevard/18th Street. *From Hollywood,* consult the Metro Trip Planner as there are multiple bus routings. *From Downtown LA,* to and from matinees and to evening performances, take Big Blue Bus express 10 to Santa Monica Boulevard/22nd Street; returning from evening performances, take Metro bus 4 Santa Monica Boulevard to Santa Monica Boulevard and 17th Street.

CITY GARAGE THEATRE 2525 Michigan Ave., Building C1 at Bergamot Station, Santa Monica; **citygarage.org** City Garage does classic European plays and the occasional premiere in a building that was indeed a city garage. Transit: *From Santa Monica,* take Big Blue Bus 2 or rapid bus 704 to Santa Monica Boulevard and 26th Street. *From Hollywood,* take Metro bus 217 or 780 to Fairfax Avenue/Pico Boulevard, and then take Big Blue Bus 5 to Olympic Boulevard/26th Street, or take Big Blue Bus 7 to Cloverfield and Pico boulevards. Line 5 gets you closer; line 7 is more frequent. *From Downtown LA,* take Big Blue Bus express 10 to Santa Monica Boulevard and 26th Street.

PACIFIC RESIDENT THEATER   703 Venice Blvd. near Shell Ave., Venice; **pacificresidenttheater.com**   Great theater in a tiny space, judged to be one of the city's 10 best companies by *LA Weekly.* Transit: *From downtown Santa Monica,* take Metro bus 33 Venice Boulevard or rapid bus 733 Venice Boulevard to Lincoln Avenue/Venice Boulevard (a 0.5-mile walk). *From Hollywood,* take Metro bus 217 or 780 to Venice Boulevard/Fairfax Avenue, and then take bus 33 or 733 to Lincoln Avenue/Venice Boulevard. *From Downtown LA,* take bus 33 or 733 west to Lincoln Boulevard.

Music

Los Angeles lays down many tracks as a music town. Aside from country music in Nashville, much of what remains of the ailing American commercial music industry is based in Los Angeles. That has helped support rock and hip-hop scenes, with Echo Park and Silver Lake being an especially prominent area for rock clubs. In classical music, the Los Angeles Philharmonic, playing in the acoustically fine (if aesthetically challenged) Disney Hall, has became a major classical music orchestra. The LA Phil's music director, Venezuelan-born Gustavo Dudamel, has achieved almost rock star status in the city.

As with theater, Hollywood is the single-most concentrated neighborhood for live music. But as in so many things, major music venues are scattered across the city. Still, almost 40% of the live music venues listed by the *Los Angeles Times* are in four areas—Downtown, Hollywood, West Hollywood, and Santa Monica.

Live music is probably the toughest art form to access as a car-free visitor. Many performances are late at night, when many buses run infrequently or not at all. Most locations are safe to wait for a bus, but almost nowhere is as safe at 1 a.m. as it is at 1 p.m. or even 8 p.m. You may have to walk a lot farther to catch the bus (trains don't run after about 1 a.m.).

There's also the question of going from club to club. Some (especially within Hollywood or West Hollywood) are within walking distance, but others are spread farther. One advantage of using public transit or cabs is that many people want to drink while they're clubbing, and not driving avoids drinking and driving problems. Live music is probably the activity that most justifies spending money on cab fare.

Below are some of LA's major live music venues, in various genres. Things can change very quickly in music land, so be sure to check for current listings before heading somewhere. The listings are north to south Downtown and then east to west.

DISNEY HALL   111 S. Grand Ave. at First St., Downtown; **laphil.com**   This is the big, shiny titanium pile where the Los Angeles Philharmonic Orchestra plays in acoustical splendor, led by charismatic music director Gustavo Dudamel. Also hosts other events from varying musical genres. Transit: *From Hollywood or the Downtown Core,* take the Red Line subway to the Civic Center station, and then walk two blocks west on First Street to Grand Avenue. *From Santa Monica,* take Big Blue Bus express 10 to Hope at First Street, which is at the back of Disney Hall. If you're on or near Hill Street, you can take Angels Flight up the hill, and then walk north on Grand Avenue. Some Downtown restaurants provide shuttle service to Disney Hall/The Music Center; it's worth asking if you're eating dinner Downtown before the concert.

DOROTHY CHANDLER PAVILION   135 N. Grand St. at Temple St., Music Center, Downtown; **musiccenter.org**   Across the street from Disney Hall is the older, more Lincoln Center–like version. The Los Angeles Opera performs here, as do visiting groups. Transit: See Disney Hall above for transit directions.

THE SMELL   247 S. Main St. at Third St., Downtown; **thesmell.org**   Enter from Harlem Place alley between Spring and Main streets. The Smell is a small, nonprofit punk club showcasing bands from around the country; most shows have only a $5 admission. Shows open to all ages (no alcohol). **Transit:** *In Downtown LA, from 7th St./Metro Center station,* walk 1 mile, first east on Seventh Street six blocks, and then north on Main Street five blocks. There's no good evening transit alternative for this because most have you walking almost halfway. *From Hollywood,* take the Red Line subway to Pershing Square. *From Santa Monica,* take rapid bus 720 Wilshire Boulevard to Sixth and Main streets. Owl service after 1 a.m. is available via the 2 Sunset bus, which runs on Hollywood Boulevard west of Vermont Avenue, and the 20 Wilshire Boulevard bus at Seventh and Main streets. You might feel more comfortable waiting for the bus farther west on Seventh Street.

THE CONGA ROOM   Figueroa St. and Olympic Blvd., Downtown; **congaroom.com**   The Conga Room thinks of itself as "the House of Blues for Latin music." It plays salsa, rock en español, and just plain rock from the likes of Los Lobos. **Transit:** *In Downtown LA, from 7th St./Metro Center station,* walk south 0.4 mile on Figueroa Street to Olympic Boulevard. *From Hollywood,* take the Red Line subway to 7th St./Metro Center, and then walk 0.5 mile or take Blue Line light rail to Pico Boulevard. *From Santa Monica in the early evening,* take Big Blue Bus express 10 to Olympic Boulevard/Olive Street; in the later evening, take bus 720 to Sixth Street/ Grand Avenue. Owl service after midnight is available to Hollywood via the 2 Sunset bus at Broadway/Olympic Boulevard and to Santa Monica via bus 20 Wilshire Boulevard at Wilshire Boulevard/Flower Street.

NOKIA THEATRE   777 Chick Hearn Ct., LA Live complex, Downtown; **nokiatheatrelalive.com**   A 7,100-seat theater that's a central part of the LA Live complex. It seeks to present 120 events a year. It has a very detailed transit page found under parking (bravo!). **Transit:** See the Conga Room entry above.

THE ECHOPLEX AND THE ECHO   1822 Sunset Blvd. and 1154 Glendale Blvd. (adjacent), Echo Park; **attheecho.com**   A top indie rock venue, even up to Dave Alvin and the Guilty Men, under the same management as Silver Lake's Spaceland. Kudos to these folks for putting bus stops on their website's directional map. **Transit:** *From Downtown LA,* take the 2 Sunset bus or the 4 Santa Monica Boulevard bus; both local lines run all night.

From Hollywood, take the 2 Sunset bus (24-hour service). *From Santa Monica,* take Metro bus 4 Santa Monica Boulevard (24-hour service).

SPACELAND   1717 Silver Lake Blvd. near Effie St., Silver Lake; **club spaceland.com**   This 260-seat club has been a mainstay of LA's indie rock scene for years. Age 21 and over. Transit: The nearest nighttime transit is at Sunset and Silver Lake boulevards approximately 0.7 mile away, where there's both regular and owl service. *From Downtown LA,* take the 2 Sunset bus or 4 Santa Monica Boulevard bus westbound. *From Hollywood,* take the 2 Sunset bus eastbound. *From Santa Monica,* take Metro bus 4 Santa Monica Boulevard.

EL REY THEATRE   5515 Wilshire Blvd. near Dunsmuir Ave., Mid-Wilshire; **theelrey.com**   An all ages, standing-room (no seats) Art Deco theater for rock. It's good (and all too unusual) that they have transit information on the website; alas, as of publication of this book, it was outdated. Transit: *From Hollywood,* take the 212 La Brea Boulevard bus (hourly service after 9:30 p.m.). *From Downtown LA,* take rapid bus 720 Wilshire westbound. *From Santa Monica,* take rapid bus 720 Wilshire eastbound. Owl service to Downtown LA (after 2 a.m.) is available via local bus 20 Wilshire Boulevard eastbound and to Santa Monica via local bus 20 Wilshire Boulevard westbound. No owl service is available to Hollywood.

MUSIC BOX   6126 Hollywood Blvd. (at the Henry Fonda Theater) at Gower St., Hollywood; **henryfondatheater.com**   Here we have a historic theater in the heart of Hollywood where Concrete Blonde plays, with the Blue Palms (microbrew) brewhouse next door. What more could you want? Transit: *In Hollywood,* it's three blocks east of the Hollywood/Vine Red Line subway station. *From Downtown LA,* take the Red Line subway to Hollywood Boulevard/Vine Street, and then walk three blocks east. *From Santa Monica,* use the Metro Trip Planner because you'll need to take two buses, and different combination of routes is better at different specific times. Owl service after 1 a.m. to Downtown LA is available via the 2 Sunset bus at Sunset Boulevard/Vine Street and to Santa Monica via the 4 Santa Monica Boulevard bus, which is 0.8 mile south of Hollywood Boulevard.

HOTEL CAFE   1623½ N. Cahuenga Blvd. near Selma Ave., Hollywood; **hotel cafe.com**   Neither a hotel nor a café but a top venue for singer/songwriter folks. Age 21 and over. Transit: Use Music Box directions on page 157, but walk west on Hollywood Boulevard from Hollywood/Vine Red Line subway station, and then south a half block on Cahuenga Boulevard.

HOLLYWOOD BOWL   2301 N. Highland Ave. at Odin St., Hollywood; **hollywoodbowl.com**   The Hollywood Bowl is an outdoor concert site within LA, instead of out in the countryside where you would have to drive. The Bowl is the summer home of the Los Angeles Philharmonic Orchestra, but other events, such as the Playboy Jazz Festival, are held there too. Transit: The Bowl has a well-used set of buses from park-and-rides across the city, as well as local shuttles from Hollywood Boulevard/Highland Avenue and Universal City Red Line stations. It's about a 20-minute walk from Hollywood Boulevard/Highland Avenue. You don't have to park to ride. The buses cost $5 round-trip if paid in advance, $8 exact change if paid at the lot. The bus locations most likely to be useful to car-free travelers are in Westwood at 11000 Wilshire Blvd. at Veteran Avenue in the Federal Building parking lot; Pasadena at 240 Ramona St. at the northeast corner of Ramona Avenue and Marengo Street in the Pasadena Civic Center; and (eastern) Santa Monica at 2235 Colorado Ave. at the DMV parking lot. Buses will leave 5:30–7:30 p.m. at various times, depending on the time of the concert.

HOUSE OF BLUES   8430 Sunset Blvd. at Olive St., Sunset Strip (West Hollywood); **houseofblues.com**   Opened in 1994 and still a significant rock and blues venue. Covered in tin like a Mississippi Delta shack. Also known for its Sunday gospel brunches. Transit: *From Hollywood and Downtown LA,* take the 2 Sunset bus to Sunset Boulevard and Kings Road, and then walk one block west. *From Santa Monica,* take the 4 Santa Monica Boulevard bus to Santa Monica Boulevard and Kings Road, and then walk up Kings Road to Sunset Boulevard. Owl service is available to Hollywood and Downtown LA via the 4 Santa Monica Boulevard bus eastbound and then a 0.8-mile walk up Highland Avenue, and to Santa Monica via the 4 Santa Monica Boulevard bus westbound.

THE TROUBADOUR   9081 Santa Monica Blvd. near Doheny Dr., West Hollywood; **troubadour.com**   Very few music clubs in the U.S. have lasted more than 50 years, especially in Los Angeles. The Troubadour is one. Transit: *From Downtown LA,* take the 4 Santa Monica Boulevard bus (24-hour service) to Santa Monica Boulevard and Doheny Drive. *From Hollywood,* take the 2 Sunset bus to Sunset Boulevard/Doheny Drive (use the 4 Santa Monica Boulevard bus after 1:30 a.m.).

UNURBAN COFFEE HOUSE   3301 Pico Blvd. at Urban St., Santa Monica   I dislike the name, but it's a significant music venue, just up the street from McCabe's, with live entertainment most nights and eclectic decor every night. Transit: *From downtown Santa Monica,* take Big Blue Bus 7 eastbound to Pico Boulevard and 30th Street, and then walk one block east. *From Hollywood,* take Metro bus 217 to Fairfax Avenue/ Pico Boulevard, and then take Big Blue Bus 7 westbound to Dorchester Avenue/30th Street, and walk one block east. *From Downtown LA,* take Big Blue Bus express 10 to Bundy Drive/Pico Boulevard; return in the later evening via Big Blue Bus 7 to Pico Boulevard/Rimpau Boulevard terminal, and then take bus 33 to stops along Spring Street between Eight Street and Fifth Street, or take rapid bus 733 to stops along Spring Street between Eighth Street and Cesar Chavez Avenue.

McCABE'S GUITAR SHOP   3101 Pico Blvd., Santa Monica; **mccabes.com**   McCabe's is in fact a guitar shop; it's also a longtime music venue on the east side of Santa Monica. Shows on Sunday are $10 and start at 7 or 8 p.m., making it easier to catch transit home. Past acts have included Dave Alvin, Richard Thompson, and Kinky Friedman. Transit: See directions for UnUrban Coffee House above.

TRIP   2101 Lincoln Blvd. at Grant Ave., Santa Monica; **tripsantamonica. com**   Dive bar rock venue on a nondescript commercial strip. It's a longtime bar, but with a frequently changing name. Transit: *To and from downtown Santa Monica,* take Big Blue Bus 3 or 7 and connect to Metro buses 704 or 720 for Hollywood or Downtown LA, respectively. No service after 12:30 a.m.; walk 1 mile to downtown Santa Monica and connect to owl buses 4 Santa Monica Boulevard or 20 Wilshire.

HARVELLE'S BLUES CLUB   1432 Fourth St. between Santa Monica Blvd. and Broadway, Santa Monica; **harvelles.com**   Harvelle's is the Westside's oldest live music venue, in business since 1931. It features blues, soul, and R&B. Transit: *From Downtown LA,* take Big Blue Bus express 10 and get off on Broadway at the Third Street Promenade; leaving Downtown LA 8:30 p.m.–midnight, take Metro rapid bus 720 Wilshire on Sixth Street to Wilshire Boulevard and Fourth Street in Santa Monica and walk south three blocks. *From Hollywood,* take rapid bus 780 to Fairfax Avenue/Wilshire Boulevard, and then take rapid bus 720 westbound to Wilshire Boulevard and Fourth Street in Santa Monica and walk south three blocks. Check the Metro Trip Planner for other combinations of routes that may be faster depending on what times you are traveling.

Art Galleries

Note: *For art museums, see "An Art Lover's Trip" on page 202.*

Sometime between the 1950s and the 1970s, Los Angeles emerged as a leading visual arts city, one that even New York critics would eventually have to take seriously. Today, LA is clearly the second city of American contemporary art, with a thriving art gallery scene to match. If you're interested in contemporary art, you should visit some LA galleries and do what's known as a gallery crawl.

Galleries are spread across LA, but the largest number are concentrated into five clusters: Chung King Road and adjacent in Chinatown, the Downtown Historic Core, Wilshire Boulevard near the Los Angeles County Museum of Art, Culver City, and the Bergamot Station Complex in Santa Monica. See **artscenecal.com/maps** for detailed maps or see page 204.

Gallery exhibitions tend to last only about a month or two, so you'll need to check the *Los Angeles Times, LA Weekly, Art Scene,* or the gallery websites to see what's on now. Typical gallery hours are 11 a.m.–5 p.m., Tuesday–Saturday, the time of day when transit service is generally at its highest.

CHINATOWN

There is a tight cluster of more than a dozen galleries on tiny, car-free Chung King Road and accessing Chung King Court (also car free), west of Hill Street and north of College Street. Some galleries are located on Hill Street between College Street and Bamboo Lane. While some galleries have a connection to Chinese or Chinese American art, most do not. Transit: *From the Downtown Historic Core,* take bus 45 to Broadway/ Bernard Street. *From Hollywood,* take the Red and Purple Line subway to Union Station and then Gold Line light rail one stop to Chinatown. *From Santa Monica,* take the Big Blue Bus express 10 to Union Station, and then Gold Line light rail one stop to Chinatown.

DOWNTOWN HISTORIC CORE

The Downtown LA gallery area focuses on a roughly 10-square-block area of the Historic Core, between Third and Sixth streets, east of Broadway to Los Angeles Street. A handful of galleries is also in the Arts District along Third and Fourth streets east of Alameda Street. A Downtown LA Art Walk (**downtownartwalk.com**) is held in the gallery core area on the second Thursday of each month, with some galleries staying open as late as 9 p.m. Some have complained that the walk has become more street fair than art event, but there certainly are plenty of people in the galleries. Transit: *From the easterly Hope Street exit of 7th St./Metro Center station,* walk four blocks east to Broadway. *From Hollywood,* take the Red Line subway to Pershing Square. The Historic Core district begins immediately to the east of the station exits on Hill Street. *From Santa Monica,* take the Big Blue Bus express 10 to Seventh and Olive streets, and walk one block east on Seventh Street to Hill Street.

LOS ANGELES COUNTY MUSEUM OF ART AREA

A cluster of four galleries is in the 6150 Wilshire Boulevard building (near Fairfax Avenue), with additional galleries scattered along Wilshire from Burnside in the east to Crescent Heights in the west. Transit: *From Downtown LA,* take rapid bus 720 Wilshire Boulevard west to Wilshire Boulevard/Fairfax Avenue. *From Santa Monica,* take rapid bus 720 east to Wilshire Boulevard/Fairfax Avenue. *From Hollywood,* take local bus 217 or rapid bus 780 to Fairfax Avenue/Wilshire Boulevard.

CULVER CITY

The Culver City Art District, as it is called, has galleries on two crossing streets—Washington Boulevard from Sentney Avenue west to Cattaragus Avenue, and on South La Cienega Boulevard (not to be confused with La Cienega Avenue) from Venice Boulevard to Washington Avenue. One confusing fact—Washington east of La Cienega Avenue has street numbers in the 6000s, but at La Cienega Avenue, they jump to 8500. Visit **ccgalleryguide.com** for a list of galleries. Transit: *From Downtown LA or Santa Monica,* take local bus 33 or rapid bus 733 west to Venice and La Cienega boulevards. *From Hollywood,* take rapid bus 780 or local bus 217 Fairfax to Washington and Fairfax avenues. Once the Expo Line opens, take it from 7th St./Metro Center station Downtown to the La Cienega station.

BERGAMOT STATION

Southern California's largest art complex, with dozens of galleries and related businesses, and the only major gallery complex on the far Westside. Located in eastern Santa Monica off 26th Street between Olympic Boulevard and Michigan Avenue—most transit riders should enter near Olympic. Visit **bergamotstation.com.** Transit: *From Santa Monica,* take Big Blue Bus 2 or rapid bus 704 to Santa Monica Boulevard and 26th Street. *From Hollywood,* take local bus 217 or rapid bus 780 to Fairfax Avenue and Pico Boulevard, and then take Big Blue Bus 5 to Olympic Boulevard/26th Street, which gets you the closest. Or you can take more frequent Big Blue Bus 7 from Olympic Boulevard and Fairfax Avenue to Cloverfield and Pico boulevards, which is slightly farther away. *From Downtown LA,* take Big Blue Bus express 10 to Santa Monica Boulevard and 26th Street.

WATTS TOWERS

Located at 1761 E. 107th St., Watts Towers is a unique and massive work of folk art metal sculpture in a working-class South LA neighborhood, constructed over years by local craftsman Simon Rodia. A gallery and art center are on-site. There are no directional signs from the train station, though at certain points you'll be able to see the towers. Open Wednesday–Sunday (admission, $7); docent tours available Thursday–Sunday. Visit **wattstowers.us** for more information. Transit: *From Downtown LA,* take the Blue Line light rail to 103rd Street station, and then walk south 0.6 mile on Graham Avenue (just east of the Blue Line tracks). *From Hollywood,* take the Red Line subway to 7th St./Metro Center, and then take the Blue Line light rail to 103rd Street. *From Santa Monica,* take Big Blue Bus express 10 to Figueroa and Seventh streets, and then take Blue Line light rail to 103rd Street.

TRANSIT TO AND BETWEEN GALLERY AREAS

The gallery areas are listed from east to west. The easiest art crawl route, with best connections between areas, would be Chinatown to Downtown (via rapid bus 794) to Los Angeles County Museum of Art (via rapid bus 720 Wilshire) to Culver City (via rapid bus 780) to Bergamot Station (via Metro express bus 534 and Big Blue Bus 5). Once the Expo Line opens, it will provide a good, quick connection from Downtown to Culver City, creating more options for gallery crawl routes. When the Expo Line opens, take it from 7th St./Metro Center station in Downtown Los Angeles to the La Cienega/Jefferson station, and then walk 0.5 mile (10 minutes) north on La Cienega Boulevard to La Cienega and Washington boulevards, in the heart of the Culver City Art District.

Los Angeles Architecture

Los Angeles has been an architectural showcase since at least the early 20th century. The city has often had conditions that nurture architectural flowering—fast growth, image consciousness, willingness to experiment, and activist governments. Here's a sample of some notable buildings with different types of uses, from different eras, listed across the city from east to west. In addition to the usual transit directions, this includes transit directions from site to site, so you could do it (or more likely parts of it) as a tour.

HOTEL GREEN 50 E. Green St. at Fair Oaks Ave., Pasadena Now apartments, the great Victorian pile of the Hotel Green was built in 1898, then expanded in 1903 as a home for well-off Midwesterners escaping the cold in Pasadena. Transit: *From Downtown LA,* take the Red/Purple Line subway to Union Station and then the Gold Line light rail to Memorial Park. *From Hollywood,* take the Red Line subway to Union Station and then the Gold Line light rail to Memorial Park. *From Santa Monica,* take Big Blue Bus express 10 to Union Station and then the Gold Line light rail to Memorial Park.

LA PLACITA (Our Lady Queen of Angels Church) 535 N. Main St. near New High St., Downtown LA Built in 1861 and subsequently renovated, La Placita, a Catholic Church in El Pueblo de Los Angeles (the "old town"), has long been considered a people's church, a church of the poor and immigrants. Transit: *From the Downtown Historic Core,* take the Red/Purple Line subway to Union Station. *From Hollywood,* take the Red Line subway to Union Station. *From Santa Monica,* take Big Blue Bus express 10 to Union Station, and then cross Alameda Street into the El Pueblo historic park.

LOS ANGELES CITY HALL 200 N. Spring St. at Temple St., Downtown LA The building on the *Dragnet* TV show shield, completed in 1928 in an assertion of Los Angeles's growing prominence. Ask for directions to the cool observation deck. Transit: *From the Downtown Historic Core,* walk north on Spring Street past First Street to City Hall, approximately 0.9 mile from Seventh and Spring streets, or take the Red/Purple Line subway to Civic Center station, and then walk two blocks east to Spring Street and half a block north to City Hall. *From Hollywood,* take the Red Line subway to Civic Center station, and then walk two blocks east to Spring Street and half a block north to City Hall. *From Santa Monica,* take Big Blue Bus express 10 to Temple and Spring streets, and then walk half a block south to City Hall.

PARKER CENTER 150 N. Los Angeles St. at First St., Downtown LA Until recently the headquarters of the Los Angeles Police Department, the "corporate modernist" Parker Center, built in 1955, embodied the department's "just the facts" stance, behind which lay a police force that was often seen as racist and brutal into the 1990s. The new police headquarters building a block away strives to appear much friendlier. The city is currently considering what to do with the now empty Parker Center. Transit: *From the Downtown Historic Core,* walk north 1 mile via Main Street, First Street, and Los Angeles Street or take the Red/Purple Line subway to Civic Center station, and then walk three blocks east on First Street and half a block north on Los Angeles Street. *From Hollywood,* take the Red Line subway to Civic Center station, and then walk three blocks east on First Street and half a block north on Los Angeles Street. *From Santa Monica,* take Big Blue Bus express 10 to Temple and Los Angeles streets.

CATHEDRAL OF OUR LADY OF ANGELS   555 W. Temple St. at Grand Ave., Downtown LA   A surprisingly self-effacing, or bland, new home (built in 2002) for the Los Angeles diocese of the Roman Catholic Church, the largest diocese in the nation. The former diocesan church, St. Vibiana's (now an event space) was part of the Little Tokyo neighborhood, but the new cathedral stands farther apart on a hill over a freeway. Transit: *From the Downtown Historic Core,* take the Red/Purple Line subway to Civic Center station, and then walk one block north on Hill Street to Temple Street and then west half a block on Temple Street. *From Hollywood,* take the Red Line subway to Civic Center station, and then walk one block north on Hill Street to Temple Street and then west half a block on Temple Street. *From Santa Monica,* take Big Blue Bus express 10 to Temple Street/Grand Avenue.

DISNEY HALL   111 S. Grand Ave. at First St., Downtown LA   A great piece of Downtown architecture by Frank Gehry, this is a shiny titanium pile with great acoustics. The 2003 structure is home to the LA Philharmonic Orchestra. Transit: See directions to Cathedral of Our Lady of Angels above.

BRADBURY BUILDING   304 S. Broadway at Third St., Downtown LA   A much-filmed building with its interior balconies and metal stairways, the elegant 1893 Bradbury is one of the few surviving commercial buildings from 19th-century Los Angeles. Transit: The building is in the

■ DOWNTOWN LA ARCHITECTURAL ■
WALKING TOUR

If you wish to view these architectural landmarks as part of a walking tour, visit them in the following order.

LA PLACITA (Our Lady Queen of Angels Church)   535 N. Main St. near New High St., Downtown LA   Built in 1861 and remodeled and expanded in later years

LOS ANGELES CITY HALL   200 N. Spring St. at Temple St., Downtown LA   Built in 1928

PARKER CENTER   150 N. Los Angeles St. at First St., Downtown LA   Built in 1955

CATHEDRAL OF OUR LADY OF ANGELS   555 W. Temple St. at Grand Ave., Downtown LA   Built in 2002

DISNEY HALL   111 S. Grand Ave. at First St., Downtown LA   Built in 2003

BRADBURY BUILDING   304 S. Broadway at Third St., Downtown LA   Built in 1893

BONAVENTURE HOTEL   404 S. Figueroa St., Downtown LA   Built in 1976

BILTMORE HOTEL   506 S. Grand Ave. at Fifth St., Downtown LA   Built in 1923

Downtown Historic Core. *From Hollywood,* take the Red Line subway to Pershing Square (use Fourth Street exit), and then walk one block east on Fourth Street and one block north on Broadway. *From Santa Monica,* take Big Blue Bus express 10 to Hope and First streets, and then walk four blocks east to Broadway and two blocks south to Third Street.

BONAVENTURE HOTEL   404 S. Figueroa St., Downtown LA   Considered a landmark of city-hostile architecture when it was opened in 1976, the mirrored-glass Bonaventure is still easier to enter by car than on foot. It's a blot on Downtown LA's escutcheon. Transit: *From the Downtown Historic Core,* walk west four blocks from Hill Street to Figueroa Street, and then walk half a block north on Figueroa Street. *From Hollywood,* take the Red Line subway to 7th St./Metro Center, and then walk three and a half blocks north on Figueroa Street. *From Santa Monica,* take Big Blue Bus express 10 to Figueroa and Fifth streets, and then walk a block and a half north on Figueroa.

BILTMORE HOTEL   506 S. Grand Ave. at Fifth St., Downtown LA   A grand Downtown hotel in the 1920s manner (1923 to be exact), where the generous public spaces often outshined the hotel rooms. The first home of the Academy Awards. Transit: *From the Downtown Historic Core,* walk one block west from Fifth and Hill streets to Fifth and Olive streets. *From Hollywood,* take the Red Line subway to Pershing Square, and then walk one block west on Fifth Street. *From Santa Monica,* take Big Blue Bus express 10 to Figueroa and Fifth streets, and then walk three blocks east on Fifth Street.

WILSHIRE BOULEVARD TEMPLE   3663 Wilshire Blvd. at Hobart Blvd., Koreatown   Wilshire Boulevard's Rabbi Edgar Magnin was the "rabbi to the stars," serving at the temple for 69 years. The magnificent, Byzantine-style, domed temple was an unmistakable statement that LA's Jews had arrived. The 1929 building is still very much in use, though the temple has also established a Westside branch. Transit: *From Downtown LA,* take the Purple Line subway to Wilshire Boulevard/Western Avenue. *From Holly-wood,* take the Red Line subway to Wilshire Boulevard/Vermont Avenue, and then the Purple Line subway to Wilshire Boulevard/Western Avenue. *From Santa Monica,* take rapid bus 720 Wilshire to Wilshire Boulevard/ Western Avenue, and then walk three blocks east to Hobart Avenue.

THE WILTERN   3790 Wilshire Blvd. at Western Ave., Koreatown   The emerald city—a gorgeous Art Deco/Streamline Moderne theater and office building. The 1931 theater was rescued from dereliction and is now a major rock venue. Transit: See directions to Wilshire Boulevard Temple above.

GRAUMAN'S CHINESE THEATRE   6925 Hollywood Blvd. at Orange Dr., Hollywood   A riot of chinoiserie, built in the golden age of cinemas in 1927 in the Hollywood neighborhood, and later added on to. Transit: Grau-man's is on the same block as the Hollywood Boulevard/Highland Ave-nue station. *From Downtown LA,* take the Red Line subway to Hollywood Boulevard/Highland Avenue; Grauman's is on the same block. *From Santa*

Monica, take Big Blue Bus 2 to Westwood Boulevard/Le Conte Avenue, and then take Metro bus 2 to Sunset Boulevard and Highland Avenue. From there, walk 0.25 mile north to Highland Avenue and Hollywood Boulevard. *From Wilshire Boulevard Temple or The Wiltern,* take the Purple Line subway from Wilshire Boulevard/Western Avenue to Wilshire Boulevard/Vermont Avenue, and then the Red Line subway to Hollywood Boulevard/Highland Avenue, on the same block as Grauman's.

PARK LA BREA   Bounded on the north by Third St., on the south by Sixth St., on the west by Fairfax Ave., and on the east by Cochrane Ave., Fairfax District   A large apartment and town house complex, one of several built in the country by the Metropolitan Life Insurance Company. Despite its near Westside location, Park La Brea, built 1942–1949, feels very central to the urban life of Los Angeles. Some new apartment buildings are being added. Observe from the outside as entry is controlled. Transit: *From Downtown LA,* take local bus 16 to Third Street and Fairfax Avenue; walk one block south on Fairfax. *From Hollywood,* take local bus 217 or rapid bus 780 to Fairfax Avenue and Third Street, and then walk half a block south. *From Santa Monica,* take rapid bus 720 to Wilshire Boulevard and Fairfax Avenue, and then walk 0.6 mile north on Fairfax Avenue, or take local bus 217 or rapid bus 780 to Fairfax Avenue and Third Street. *From Grauman's Chinese Theatre,* take local bus 217 or rapid bus 780 from Hollywood Boulevard and Highland Avenue to Fairfax Avenue and Third Street.

SUNSET TOWER   8358 Sunset Blvd. at Kings Rd., West Hollywood   Gorgeous, high-priced Art Deco hotel (originally built in 1931 as apartments) on the Sunset Strip, iconic and much filmed. There's a very chic bar and restaurant at the top. Transit: *From Downtown LA or Hollywood,* take the 2 or 302 bus to Sunset Boulevard and Kings Road. *From Santa Monica,* take Big Blue Bus 2 to Westwood Boulevard/Le Conte Avenue, and then take Metro bus 2 to Sunset Boulevard and Kings Road. If you are touring the architecture sites, it is easier to get to Sunset Tower from the Chinese Theatre via Metro bus 2 than from Park La Brea. *From Park La Brea,* you need to take local bus 217 or rapid bus 780 north from Fairfax

Avenue and Third Street to Fairfax Avenue and Sunset Boulevard. Then take the 2 Sunset bus west to Sunset Boulevard and Kings Road.

BEVERLY HILLS HOTEL 9641 Sunset Blvd. at Crescent Dr., Beverly Hills This sprawling hotel was built in 1912 to entice home buyers to purchase sprawling homes in Beverly Hills. It was later remodeled by leading black architect Paul Williams. Williams designed the wonderful little Fountain Coffee Room in the hotel's basement, which serves good coffee shop food at less than insane prices—well worth a visit. **Transit:** See directions for Sunset Tower above. *From Sunset Tower,* take Metro bus 2 to Sunset Boulevard and Beverly Drive, adjacent to the hotel.

CENTURY PLAZA HOTEL 2025 Avenue of the Stars at Constellation Blvd., Century City A recent proposal to demolish this austere but gracefully curved modernist landmark triggered a surprising historic preservation battle, which ended with an agreement to preserve the 1966 building and develop elsewhere in Century City. **Transit:** *From Downtown LA,* take Metro bus 28 or rapid bus 728 to Constellation Boulevard/Avenue of the Stars. *From Hollywood,* take local bus 217 or rapid bus 780 to Fairfax Avenue/Santa Monica Boulevard, and then take local bus 4 or rapid bus 704 to Santa Monica Boulevard/Century Park East. Then walk one block south on Century Park East and one block west on Constellation Boulevard. *From Santa Monica,* take Big Blue Bus 5 to Constellation Boulevard/Avenue of the Stars. If doing this as a tour, it is easier to get to Century City from Park La Brea via local bus 28 or rapid bus 728 from Olympic Boulevard/Fairfax Avenue than to get from the Beverly Hills Hotel to Century City.

JANSS INVESTMENT COMPANY BUILDING 1045 Westwood Blvd. at Kinross Ave., Westwood Westwood was planned and developed by the Janss Company, which made the brilliant move of offering the University of California free land for its growing Los Angeles campus. This 1929 domed building, now used by a Japanese restaurant, was Janss's first commercial structure in the area. **Transit:** *From Downtown LA,* take rapid bus 720 Wilshire to Wilshire and Westwood boulevards, and then walk two blocks north into Westwood Village on Westwood Boulevard. *From*

Hollywood or the Beverly Hills Hotel, take the 2 Sunset bus to Westwood Boulevard/Le Conte Avenue, and then walk two blocks south through Westwood Village to the building. *From Santa Monica,* take rapid bus 720 Wilshire to Wilshire and Westwood boulevards, and then walk two blocks north on Westwood. *From the Century Plaza Hotel,* take local bus 4 or rapid bus 704 to Santa Monica and Westwood boulevards, and then take Big Blue Bus 1, 8, or 12 to Westwood and Wilshire boulevards. Then walk two blocks north on Westwood Boulevard.

J. PAUL GETTY MUSEUM   1200 Getty Center Dr., Brentwood   More impressive as a work of grand, neoclassical architecture and landscape architecture than as a museum. Built in 1997. Transit: *From Downtown LA and Santa Monica,* take rapid bus 720 Wilshire to Wilshire and Westwood boulevards, and then take rapid bus 761 to Sepulveda Boulevard and Getty Center Drive, and then catch the tram to get to the museum. *From Hollywood,* take bus 2 Sunset Boulevard to Sunset Boulevard/ Hilgard Avenue, and then take rapid bus 761 to Sepulveda Boulevard and Getty Center Drive. *From the Janss Building,* take rapid bus 761 from Westwood and Wilshire boulevards to Sepulveda Boulevard and Getty Center Drive.

SANTA MONICA PLACE   Broadway at Third Street Promenade   The Santa Monica Place shopping center, which anchors the southern end of the Third Street Promenade and was originally built in 1981, was rebuilt in 2010 from a mid-scale mall that ignored its surroundings to an upscale facility that takes full advantage of Santa Monica's ocean air, complete with rooftop food court and drinking deck. It's still a selling machine, but a pleasant one. Transit: *From Downtown LA,* take Big Blue Bus express 10 to Second Street/Broadway. *From Hollywood,* take Metro bus 2 to Le Conte Avenue/Westwood Boulevard, and then take Big Blue Bus 2 to Broadway/Second Street. *From the Getty Museum,* take rapid bus 761 to Westwood and Wilshire boulevards, and then Big Blue Bus 1 or 2 to Broadway/ Second Street.

CHIAT-DAY BUILDING   340 Main St. at Dudley Ave., Venice   The poster child for LA postmodernism, this three-part building was designed by

Frank Gehry in 1991. (In)famous building-size "binoculars" designed by artists Claes Oldenberg and Coosje Van Bruggen serve as its auto entrance. Transit: *From Downtown LA,* take rapid bus 733 to Main Street and Pier Avenue in Santa Monica and walk back 0.33 mile to the building. *From Hollywood,* take local bus 217 or rapid bus 780 to Fairfax Avenue/Venice Boulevard, and then take local bus 33 or rapid bus 733 to Main Street and Pier Avenue in Santa Monica and walk back 0.33 mile to the building. *From Santa Monica,* take Big Blue Bus 1 to Main and Rose streets, and then walk two blocks farther to the building.

Professional Sports

Los Angeles is not known as a sports crazy town like New York or Boston, but some teams draw strong crowds, especially when they're winning. The good news is that LA's main pro sports venues are now in or near downtown. Los Angeles does not have a professional football team, which caused much wailing and gnashing of teeth in some quarters but hasn't seemed to stress out most Angelenos. As of this writing, proposals are underway for an NFL stadium deep in the eastern suburbs and in Downtown LA; both are controversial and years away from fruition, though the downtown stadium appears to be gaining momentum.

BASEBALL: LA DODGERS

The Dodgers play April–September at Dodger Stadium in Chavez Ravine, about 2 miles northwest of the Downtown Historic Core. The Dodgers games are well-attended and have been known for relatively cheap tickets. Visit **losangeles.dodgers.mlb.com.** Transit: *From Downtown LA,* take the Red and Purple Line subway to Union Station, and then Dodger Stadium Express. *From Hollywood,* take the Red Line subway to Union Station, and then Dodger Stadium Express. *From Santa Monica* in the day and early evening, take Big Blue Bus express 10 to Union Station, and then Dodger Stadium Express; in the later evening, take local bus 4 Santa Monica Boulevard from Sunset Boulevard/Innes Avenue out to Santa Monica city.

BASKETBALL: LA LAKERS, CLIPPERS, AND SPARKS

The regular basketball season runs October–April, though a long series of playoffs extend two more months into June. If any pro sports team inspires strong support in LA, it's the National Basketball Association (NBA) champion Lakers. The Lakers and the Clippers both play at Staples Center (1111 Figueroa St.) at the southern edge of Downtown LA. The Women's National Basketball Association (WNBA) Los Angeles Sparks also play at Staples Center in the summer. Visit **nba.com/lakers, nba.com/clippers,** or **wnba.com/sparks.** Transit: *From 7th St./Metro Center,* walk about 15 minutes south or take the Blue Line light rail one stop to Pico Boulevard , and then walk one block west on Pico to Figueroa, and one block north on Figueroa to Staples Center. *From Hollywood,* take the Red Line subway to 7th St./Metro Center, and then walk about 15 minutes south or take the Blue Line light rail to Pico Boulevard, and then walk one block west on Pico to Figueroa, and one block north on Figueroa to Staples Center. *From Santa Monica* in the daytime or early evening, take Big Blue Bus express 10 to Olive and 11th streets; in the later evening, take rapid bus 733 to Venice Boulevard/Figueroa Street, and then walk north on Figueroa to 12th Street and Staples Center.

HOCKEY: LA KINGS

The hockey season is pretty much the same as basketball's—fall and winter, October–April. Hockey definitely takes a back seat to basketball and baseball in Americans' affections, but it has its rabid fans. The Kings also play at Staples Center (1111 Figueroa St.). Transit: See the directions in the basketball entry above. Visit **kings.nhl.com.**

Shopping

Los Angeles is a shopping capital, with shopping areas ranging from the gritty to the glittery (and some with a bit of both). Some might say that LA is the capital of conspicuous consumption, which is hardly surprising in the city that makes images for the world. No single street or transit route captures all of LA's shopping, but you can certainly stitch together more than one area using various trains and buses. Rapid bus 704 Santa Monica Boulevard serves many shopping areas. Racked LA (**la.racked.com**) is a good site for keeping up with the ever-changing LA shopping scene. From east to west, here are 10 notable shopping areas.

1. SOUTH LAKE AVENUE, Pasadena

Many retail stores are just boxes in which to sell, but Bullocks Pasadena (now Macy's) at 401 South Lake Ave. was more. A Streamline Moderne building built in 1947, it was instantly acclaimed as fine architecture. It's now been restored and seismically upgraded.

Lake Avenue as a whole is more elegant than many SoCal shopping districts and serves the affluent southern part of Pasadena and city of South Pasadena. There's even a shopping arcade, or a passage within a building, known as the Burlington Arcade (presumably named for the one in London) at 380 S. Lake Ave. Eateries include one of SoCal's last Hamburger Hamlets at 214 S. Lake Ave. South Lake Avenue is about a mile east of the Old Pasadena shopping district around Colorado and Raymond boulevards, where mostly chain stores are located in meticulously restored historic buildings. Visit **southlakeavenue.org/business-center.**

Transit: *From Downtown LA,* take the Red and Purple Line subway to Union Station, and transfer to the Gold Line light rail to Lake station; from there, walk approximately 0.75 mile south. Or take express bus 485, which is more direct but less frequent. *From Hollywood,* take rapid bus 780 or local bus 180/181 to Colorado Boulevard/Lake Avenue and walk south on Lake Avenue 0.75 mile. *From Santa Monica,* take a large book to read for your long trip. Take Big Blue Bus express 10 to Union Station, and then transfer to the Gold Line light rail to Lake station; from there, walk approximately 0.75 mile south.

2. FASHION DISTRICT, Downtown LA

The core area is Eighth Street to Pico Boulevard and Los Angeles Street to San Julian Street, though some businesses are beyond these boundaries. The Fashion District is an old-fashioned bargain district, the kind of place folks went before there were warehouse stores and outlet malls. The long economic stagnation of Downtown Los Angeles from the 1950s through the 1990s allowed businesses like these to stay, while in other cities they were forced out by rising rents.

Many of the clothes sold in the Fashion District are made in the immediate area, while others are just imported there. You can get great deals, or you can get taken by the fake designer labels often sold there. Clothes for men, women, kids, and other specializations are on different blocks. New Yorkers may be reminded of the Lower East Side in the days before it housed trust funders. The Fashion District is a fun place to shop, but caveat emptor. Visit **fashiondistrict.org.**

Transit: *From 7th St./Metro Center,* walk approximately 1 mile south and east or take DASH E to Los Angeles Street and Olympic Boulevard. *From Hollywood,* take the Red Line subway to 7th St./Metro Center, and then take DASH E to Los Angeles Street and Olympic Boulevard. *From Santa Monica,* take the Big Blue Bus express 10 to 11th and Olive streets, and then walk east four blocks. *From Lake Avenue,* take the Gold Line light rail to Union Station, and then (on weekdays) DASH D to Main and Ninth streets. On weekends, take Metro bus 40 or 45, or rapid bus 740 or 745 and walk one block east to Ninth and Main streets.

3. SUNSET BOULEVARD, Echo Park, Silver Lake, and Sunset Junction Sunset Boulevard, from Echo Park Avenue to Vermont Avenue, has become the home of the cool, the funky, and the just plain weird. Look for unusual, sometimes punky fashion. These stores don't cover every inch of this 2.7-mile stretch but instead coexist with dollar stores, auto repair shops, and taquerias, particularly in the eastern part of the street. It's better that way. The areas around Alvarado Street in Echo Park, Hyperion Avenue in Silver Lake, and Hillhurst Avenue in Sunset Junction are particularly active.

Brite Spot diner (clearwaterst.com/britespot) at 1918 Sunset Blvd., near the overpass over Glendale Boulevard, manages to be simultaneously punky, tasty, and friendly. They're open 6 a.m.–4 a.m., so if you've indulged too much at the Echoplex around the corner, you can stagger over here. **Millie's (milliescafe.net)**, located at 3524 Sunset Blvd. at Maltman Avenue, is an old-time breakfast and lunch place that made the transition to the modern era of organic food and French press coffee. Later in the

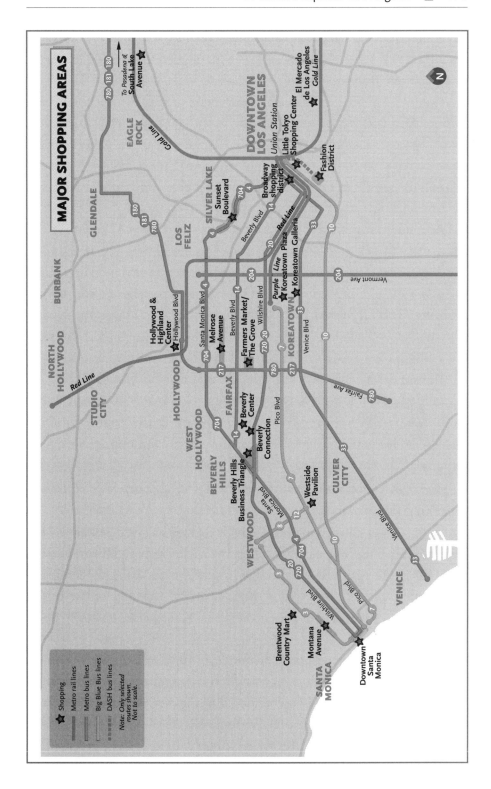

day you might try **Alegria** (**alegriaonsunset.com**), a California-style Mexican restaurant. This stretch of Sunset has a lot of good food, and a lot of restaurants more devoted to being cool than serving good food.

I've long been a fan of **Soap Plant/Wacko**—4633 Sunset Blvd. near Rodney Dr. just east of Vermont Ave. Soap Plant (**soapplant.com**) sells soap, low-cost artwork through the La Luz de Jesus art gallery, and a quite remarkable selection of high- and low-culture books. I bought a fabulous pamphlet on the history of LA's boulevards there. Also see the Sunset Boulevard ride on page 191.

A trendy commercial district is located along Silver Lake Boulevard from Effie Street to the lake (reservoir) itself. This is about 0.5 mile north of Sunset Boulevard. The 201 bus goes to this area but runs infrequently, so you're probably best off spending 15 minutes or so walking up from Sunset Boulevard. Another great detour is up Vermont Avenue into the Los Feliz district, a lively, trendy stretch up to Franklin Avenue, including 24-hour eatery Fred 62, and fine bookstore Skylight Books.

Transit: *From Downtown LA,* take the 2 Sunset bus westbound, the 4 Santa Monica Boulevard bus, or rapid bus 704 Santa Monica Boulevard westbound. (All three are on Sunset Boulevard in this segment.) *From Hollywood,* take the 2 Sunset bus eastbound. *From Santa Monica,* take rapid bus 704 Santa Monica Boulevard eastbound.

4. FARMERS MARKET AND THE GROVE (AND ADJACENT RETAIL), Fairfax District

Farmers Market (**farmersmarketla.com**) is located at Third Street/Fairfax Avenue, and The Grove is adjacent on the same property. It's where the retailing of the 1930s meets the retailing of the 2000s. The former, in the Farmers Market, consists of simple, partially open, shedlike buildings that house food stores and food stands. You can sit and eat at tables in a common area.

The Grove (**thegrovela.com**), a mid-level modern outdoor shopping mall, has the razzle-dazzle of dancing fountains and even a recreational "trolley" that glides across the center. Both appear to be very popular and economically healthy. At the Farmers Market, look for the modern Mexican Loteria Grill and throwback diner DuPar's. The Grove offers

American Girl Place (dolls), Apple, Barnes & Noble, Nordstrom, and Victoria's Secret among others. Fairfax Avenue, a few blocks north of the mall (a stretch sometimes called Fairfax Village), is pretty lively, as is Third Street across from the Farmers Market and to the west.

Transit: *From Downtown LA,* take the 16 Third Street bus to Fairfax Avenue and Third Street. *From Hollywood,* take local bus 217 or rapid bus 780 southbound to Fairfax Avenue and Third Street. *From Santa Monica,* take the 720 bus to Wilshire Boulevard/Fairfax Avenue, and then walk 0.6 mile north—a little more than 10 minutes' walk—or take local bus 217 or rapid bus 780 northbound to Fairfax Avenue and Third Street. *From Sunset Junction,* take the 2 Sunset bus to Sunset Boulevard/Fairfax Avenue, and then take local bus 217 or rapid bus 780 southbound to Third Street.

5. MELROSE AVENUE from Highland Ave. to San Vicente Blvd., Westside

This 2.5-mile shopping street has one of LA's longest stretches of essentially continuous storefronts, though there are a few gaps toward the western end. Melrose is less than a mile north of Third Street and the Farmers Market; the street is partially located in the city of Los Angeles and partially in West Hollywood. The main shopping area of the street divides roughly into three main parts:

1. A section of restaurants and fairly high-priced boutiques between La Brea and Fairfax avenues

2. Very high-priced boutiques between Fairfax Avenue and La Cienega Boulevard

3. Furniture and home stores between La Cienega and the Pacific Design Center at San Vicente Boulevard

The street has mostly independent and designer stores, while major chains are largely absent. Melrose Avenue is a nicer place to walk than many, with moderate traffic volumes and stores to browse.

Melrose Avenue is a food magnet. Eateries include Pizzeria (and Osteria) Mozza at 641 N. Highland Ave. (equivalent to 6600 Melrose Ave.), All About the Bread bakery and sandwiches at 7111 Melrose Ave. at La Brea Ave., Pink's famed hot dog stand at 709 N. La Brea Ave., Angeli

Caffe at 7274 Melrose Ave. at Poinsettia Pl., Village Idiot gastropub at 7383 Melrose Ave. at Martel Ave., 8 Oz Burger Bar at 7661 Melrose Ave. at Spaulding Ave., Carlitos Gardel Argentinian at 7963 Melrose Ave. at Edinburgh Ave., and Sweet Lady Jane bakery at 8360 Melrose Ave. at Orlando Ave.

Transit: *From Hollywood,* a short trip, use local bus 217 or rapid bus 780 to Fairfax Avenue/Melrose Avenue. *From Downtown LA,* Metro bus 10 operates along Melrose, but only once every 40 minutes to the shopping area. The better choice is bus 14 on Beverly Boulevard to Beverly Boulevard and Fairfax Avenue, approximately a 10-minute walk from the south. *From Santa Monica,* take rapid bus 720 Wilshire to Wilshire Boulevard/Fairfax Avenue, and change to local bus 217 or rapid bus 780. (Or use the 704 Santa Monica Boulevard rapid bus, approximately a 10-minute walk from the north. The 704 rapid bus runs only once every 40 minutes from Santa Monica.) *From The Grove,* it is an approximately 1-mile walk, or take local bus 217 or rapid bus 780 from Melrose and Fairfax avenues to Third Street/Melrose Avenue.

6. BEVERLY CENTER AREA, Westside

This area is located around Beverly Boulevard at La Cienega Boulevard. From the name, you might logically think that Beverly Center (**beverly center.com**) is in the center of Beverly Hills. It's not—it's about 2 miles east of downtown Beverly Hills in the city of Los Angeles, a jurisdiction that was willing to approve this megastructure. (The more restrictive city of Beverly Hills would not have approved it, which is one reason that so much development is clustered on the edge of Beverly Hills.) Beverly Center is a little more than 1 mile west of The Grove and Farmers Market complex and less than 0.5 mile south of Melrose Avenue, though the three shopping areas are definitely distinct.

Beverly Center is a multilevel mall perched atop tier upon tier of parking structure. This creates an overly tall structure that makes it abundantly clear that pedestrians are low priority—the *Architectural Guidebook to Los Angeles* calls the 1982 building "monstrous." The escalators from street level—added after the building's construction—do provide an interesting ride of sorts.

Inside you'll find Macy's, Bloomingdale's, and middle to high-end fashion chains such as Ann Taylor, Diesel, Kenneth Cole, and Banana Republic. Beverly Center serves as an anchor for ground-level shopping around it on adjacent and nearby streets—Robertson Boulevard, Third Street, La Cienega Boulevard, and to a lesser extent Beverly Boulevard. These streets (**westthirdstreet.com**) cater to a more upscale economic level with boutiques and independent, non-chain restaurants. Celebrity watchers apparently prowl the stretch of Robertson between Third Street and Beverly Boulevard looking for famous moms with famous babies.

Beverly Connection (**thebeverlyconnection.com**), on the northeast corner of Third and La Cienega, has more affordable shopping with Loehmann's, Marshall's, Nordstrom Rack (Nordstrom's discount outlet), Old Navy, Ross, Staples, and others.

Transit: *From Downtown LA,* take the 14 Beverly Boulevard bus or the 16 Third Street bus to La Cienega Boulevard. *From Hollywood,* see the Metro Trip Planner as different routes are available. *From Santa Monica,* take the 720 Wilshire Boulevard rapid bus to La Cienega Boulevard/Wilshire Boulevard, and then walk north 0.5 mile to Beverly Center. *From Melrose Avenue,* walk from Melrose and La Cienega 0.5 mile to Beverly Center.

7. BEVERLY HILLS BUSINESS (OR GOLDEN) TRIANGLE

Bounded by Santa Monica Boulevard on the north, Wilshire Boulevard on the south, and Canon Drive on the east, this area includes the famous Rodeo Drive as well as other somewhat more practical shopping streets. Rodeo Drive (**rodeodrive-bh.com**) provides an A to V of international luxury brands: Avakian (no apparent relation to the Berkeley revolutionary), Brooks Brothers, Cartier, Dolce & Gabbana, Ermenegildo Zegna, Frette, Gucci, Harry Winston, Ilori, Jimmy Choo, Lacoste, Montblanc, Omega, Prada, Ralph Lauren, St. John, Tiffany, and Versace, as well as other stores.

Many of the Rodeo Drive stores are intended more as "billboards"—places to show off their wares—than as real sales outlets. On other streets in the Triangle, you might actually buy something, especially on Beverly Drive, which becomes more neighborhood-oriented (remembering that

Beverly Hills is the neighborhood) as it moves south and continues as a commercial street south of Wilshire Boulevard. Visit **lovebeverlyhills.com** and click on "Shopping," but note that not all listings on this page are in the Business Triangle Area. For an utterly unpretentious, but often star-attended, meal, try Nate 'n Al's (Jewish) deli at 414 N. Beverly Dr.

Transit: *From Downtown LA,* take rapid bus 720 Wilshire to Wilshire Boulevard/Beverly Boulevard. *From Hollywood,* take local bus 217 or rapid bus 780 to Fairfax Avenue/Santa Monica Boulevard, and then take local bus 4 or rapid bus 704 to Canon Drive. *From Santa Monica,* take rapid bus 720 Wilshire to Wilshire Boulevard/Beverly Drive. *From Beverly Center,* take the 16 bus from Third Street/La Cienega Boulevard to Santa Monica Boulevard/Canon Drive (only take buses with a Century City destination, not Cedars-Sinai).

8. BRENTWOOD COUNTRY MART, Brentwood/North of Montana
Shopping areas tend to be in downhill and flatland neighborhoods, which are usually easier to get to and have better roads. Brentwood Country Mart (**brentwoodcountrymart.com**) and the adjacent shopping district on 26th Street in northern Santa Monica, nestled partway up the hill, are an exception. It's the kind of "country" shopping where local resident movie stars have a cup of coffee and übertrendy *Monocle* magazine has its store, sort of a smaller-scale successor to the Sharper Image franchise. Yet this irregular cluster of mostly small stores is genuinely low-key and seems authentic somehow, a far more pleasant environment than a standard-issue mall. For the lovers of unusual ice cream, try Sweet Rose Ice Cream. More substantial fare is available at Reddi Chick (rotisserie chicken) and Frida, one of a small chain of upscale taquerias. The mart is located at 26th Street and San Vicente Boulevard in Brentwood.

Transit: Sshh, it's not well publicized, but Big Blue Bus 4 San Vicente from downtown Santa Monica runs here every 30 minutes on weekdays. Or you can walk up about 0.5 mile from bus 3 on Montana Avenue, or walk about 1 mile up—moderately but definitely up—from the 720 rapid bus or Big Blue Bus 2 on Wilshire Boulevard. It's best to go from Santa Monica if possible. *From Downtown LA,* take Big Blue Bus express 10 to Broadway/Fourth Street, and then Big Blue Bus 4 to 26th Street/San Vicente Boulevard. *From Hollywood,* take the 2 Sunset bus to Sunset Boulevard/Burlingame Avenue. *From Sunset and Burlingame,* walk left on Burlingame, right on Marlboro Street, left on Rockingham Avenue, and left on 26th Street for a total of 0.7 mile. *From Beverly Hills,* take rapid bus 720 to Wilshire Boulevard/Bonsall Avenue (Veterans Administration area), and then take Big Blue Bus 4 to San Vicente Boulevard/26th Street.

9. MONTANA AVENUE, Santa Monica
From Lincoln Boulevard to 17th Street, Montana Avenue is the most posh 10 blocks of shopping street in Santa Monica, and thus one of the most posh in all LA. Yet Montana remains somehow non-crazy, a place for the neighborhood rich, not so much a place to see and be seen. (North of Montana is considered to be the truly elite part of Santa Monica.) Montana's boutiques and designer shops are almost all independent stores,

MAJOR GENERAL RETAILERS IN SOUTHERN CALIFORNIA NEIGHBORHOODS

MACY'S	Macy's Plaza	750 W. Seventh St., Downtown Los Angeles
	Macy's Beverly Center	8500 Beverly Blvd., Westside
	Macy's Paseo Colorado	400 E. Colorado Blvd., Pasadena
	Macy's Pasadena Plaza	401 S. Lake Ave., Pasadena

TARGET	777 E. Colorado Blvd., Pasadena
	7100 Santa Monica Blvd., West Hollywood

with few chains found among them. Regroup with coffee at small, high-quality, pricey Café Luxxe at 925 Montana Ave. (also in Brentwood Country Mart).

Transit: This is another trip to do from downtown Santa Monica, if you can. *From downtown Santa Monica,* take Big Blue Bus 3. (*Note:* Some trips on bus 3 end before going to Montana Avenue, so make sure you're on a through bus, which run every 30 minutes.) About 0.5 mile away are the more frequent Big Blue Bus 2 Wilshire Boulevard and Metro rapid bus 720 Wilshire, which stops at Wilshire Boulevard/14th Street. *From Hollywood,* take the 2 Sunset bus to Le Conte Avenue/Tiverton Drive, and then take Big Blue Bus 3 to Montana Avenue/14th Street.

From Downtown LA, take Big Blue Bus express 10 to Santa Monica Boulevard/14th Street, and then take the Crosstown Ride or walk approximately 15 minutes north. (The Crosstown Ride is a one-way loop bus; on the way back it takes you to 20th Street/Santa Monica Boulevard.)

10. DOWNTOWN SANTA MONICA

Downtown Santa Monica shopping got a big boost with the "re-visioning" of Santa Monica Place (**santamonicaplace.com**), the shopping mall along Broadway between Second and Fourth streets. Once a walled fortress, the mall has been opened up to the neighborhood and was made more upscale with the addition of a Nordstrom and a Bloomingdale's.

Downtown Santa Monica (**downtownsm.com**) has a nice variety of shopping environments. Besides the mall, Third Street Promenade, the pedestrian-only shopping street, caters to youth and visitors. The street

A SAMPLING OF SHOPPING MALLS ■ ORIENTED TO PARTICULAR NATIONALITIES ■

CHINESE   San Gabriel Square 140 W. Valley Blvd., San Gabriel   Metro bus 76 (more frequent) or express bus 487 from Downtown LA to Valley Boulevard/Del Mar Avenue

JAPANESE   Little Tokyo Shopping Center 333 S. Alameda St., Downtown LA Gold Line light rail to Little Tokyo station

KOREAN   Koreatown Galleria 3250 W. Olympic Blvd. near Oxford St. Metro bus 28 or rapid bus 728 to Olympic Boulevard and Western Avenue

   Koreatown Plaza 928 S. Western Ave. at Ninth St.   Metro bus 28 or rapid bus 728 to Olympic Boulevard and Western Avenue

LATINO/MEXICAN   El Mercado de Los Angeles 3455 E. First St. at Lorena St., East Los Angeles   Near Indiana Gold Line light rail station

   Plaza Mexico 3100 E. Imperial Hwy., Lynwood   Near Long Beach Boulevard Green Line light rail station

   Broadway shopping district Second St. to Ninth St., Downtown LA   Civic Center, Pershing Square, or 7th St./Metro Center Red/Purple Line subway stations

is pedestrian-only for three (long) blocks from Wilshire Boulevard to Broadway at Santa Monica Place. Artists can sell artwork they make in carts on the promenade. Downtown also has shopping and eating opportunities more oriented to adults on surrounding streets, such as Second Street, Fourth Street, and connecting east-west streets such as Arizona Avenue and Santa Monica Boulevard east to roughly Fifth Street.

Transit: *From Downtown LA,* take Big Blue Bus express 10 during the day; in the evenings take rapid bus 720 Wilshire to Ocean Avenue/ Colorado Avenue. *From Hollywood,* take rapid bus 780 or local bus 217 to Fairfax Avenue/Wilshire Boulevard, and then take rapid bus 720 to Ocean Avenue/Colorado Avenue.

OUTLET MALLS

Outlet malls feature the reduced-price outlet stores of national brand retailers. The goods may not have sold well, may be discontinued styles, and so on. Bargain hunters love outlet malls. Outlet malls, however, tend to be in fairly remote locations because retailers often won't allow an out-let store within a certain distance (such as 30 or 40 miles) of a full-price store. Some companies have freestanding outlets that aren't part of malls; you should check for any retailer that you particularly like.

The one LA outlet mall with relatively good transit access is **Citadel Outlets** (**citadeloutlets.com**) southeast of Downtown Los Angeles in the city of Commerce at 110 The Citadel Dr. Benetton, Corningware, and Levi's are among the retailers that have outlets here. See page 284 for an outlet mall in Orange County.

Transit: Take Metro bus 62 from stops on Sixth Street in Downtown Los Angeles to Telegraph Road/Citadel Drive. The service runs approximately every 30 minutes.

■ **10** Riding LA: More Rides about Buildings, Food, and Art

LOS ANGELES, MORE THAN MOST AMERICAN CITIES, was built along long, straight streets. Much of the visitors' city was built up between 1920 and 1950, when long boulevards carried streetcars, buses, and cars but before freeways had been developed. So to really see Los Angeles, you need to ride those corridors. If you really get into exploring corridors, other interesting ones with good bus service include Santa Monica Boulevard, Pico Boulevard (it takes two buses to go from Downtown LA to the ocean), and Vermont Avenue.

These rides cover portions of Sunset Boulevard, Wilshire Boulevard, and Fairfax Avenue—three of the most important and interesting streets in Los Angeles. Wilshire Boulevard is known as Los Angeles's linear downtown, the city's great street of the 20th century. Sunset Boulevard has long been the top corridor of entertainment, glamour, and hipness. Fairfax Avenue is a major urban crosstown street, a place where city life happens.

The rides are good for familiarizing yourself with more of the city. They're also good activities for the afternoon when you might be a bit tired and don't necessarily want to keep walking. You can take them in the early evening if you wish, though you obviously won't see as much, and the Wilshire corridor is less lively then.

If you want to take all three together, they form a loop. Starting in Downtown LA, you could take the Wilshire Boulevard bus west to Fairfax Avenue, the Fairfax Avenue bus north to Sunset Boulevard, and the Sunset Boulevard bus east to Downtown, or do it in the other direction. You can also begin the loop in Hollywood along Sunset Boulevard, or in the Fairfax District along either Fairfax Avenue or Wilshire Boulevard. You could do the whole thing in about 2 hours time in transit and waiting time, though it gets to be a lot of riding all at once.

The ride on the 780 bus connects a series of key streets, notably Fairfax Avenue, Hollywood Boulevard, and Colorado Boulevard. They too are important parts of linear LA, especially for foodies.

Wilshire Boulevard: LA's Linear Downtown

Begin the ride at Fifth Street and Grand Avenue in Downtown LA. *From Hollywood,* take the Red Line subway to Westlake/MacArthur Park station. *From Santa Monica,* take rapid bus 720 in the opposite direction of the ride to Wilshire Boulevard and Alvarado Street (a 70- to 85-minute ride).

You'll probably ride a bus along Wilshire Boulevard sometime in the course of your trip. It would be hard to travel car-free in LA and not use Wilshire. But if you want to see more of Wilshire's striking architecture, head over to the northwest corner of **Fifth Street and Grand Avenue,** across the street from the elegant Central Library. On Wilshire you can see important buildings built anytime from 1920 to 2010. It's about a 7-mile trip out to Wilshire and Fairfax.

Get on a very long, very red 720 Wilshire Boulevard rapid bus heading westbound. Try to avoid rush hour or the bus will probably be very crowded. Feel free to get off along the way and investigate the places that strike your fancy. The Wilshire rapid bus runs frequently, so it will be easy to get back on, and with a day pass you won't pay more fare. This ride is really meant for daylight, though you can see some nifty neon at night, particularly between MacArthur Park and Western Avenue.

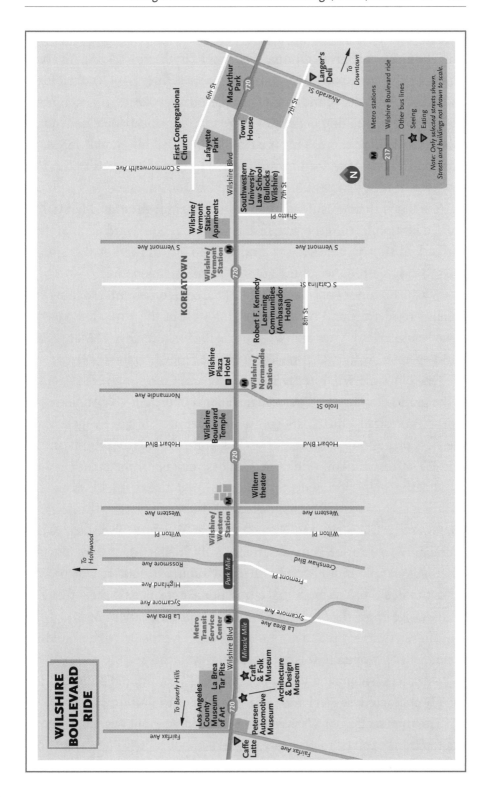

WILSHIRE BOULEVARD RIDE

Metro stations

M Wilshire Boulevard ride
217 Other bus lines
☆ Seeing
▷ Eating

Note: Only selected streets shown.
Streets and buildings not drawn to scale.

N

To Downtown

Langer's Deli
MacArthur Park
720
Alvarado St
6th St
7th St

First Congregational Church
Lafayette Park
Town House
S Commonwealth Ave
Wilshire Blvd
Southwestern University Law School (Bullocks Wilshire)
7th St
Shatto Pl

Wilshire/Vermont Station Apartments
S Vermont Ave
KOREATOWN
Wilshire/Vermont Station
720
Robert F. Kennedy Learning Communities (Ambassador Hotel)
S Catalina St
8th St
S Vermont Ave

Wilshire Plaza Hotel
Normandie Ave
Wilshire/Normandie Station
M
Irolo St

Wilshire Boulevard Temple
Hobart Blvd
720
Hobart Blvd

Wiltern theater
Western Ave
Wilshire/Western Station
M
Wilton Pl
Western Ave

To Hollywood

Rossmore Ave
Highland Ave
Sycamore Ave
La Brea Ave
Park Mile
Wilton Pl
Crenshaw Blvd
Fremont Pl
Sycamore Ave
La Brea Ave

Metro Transit Service Center
M
Wilshire Blvd
Miracle Mile

WILSHIRE BOULEVARD RIDE

To Beverly Hills
720
Los Angeles County Museum of Art
La Brea Tar Pits
☆ Craft & Folk Museum
☆ Petersen Automotive Museum
Architecture & Design Museum
Fairfax Ave

▷ Caffe Latte
Fairfax Ave

The first 1.5 miles of the bus ride out to **MacArthur Park** is not terribly scenic, but it gives glimpses of inner city life in LA. At Alvarado Street, by the park, you'll see lines of vendors selling fruit, cooked food, and CDs. You'll see hundreds of people on the street, in a neighborhood whose population density of more than 40,000 people per square mile exceeds Brooklyn's. This is a classic "first neighborhood" for Mexican and Central American immigrants. The famed **Langer's Deli** is one block south of Wilshire at Seventh and Alvarado streets.

You'll see that Wilshire Boulevard slices right through MacArthur Park, a bit uphill from the lake in the park. The boulevard went around the park until 1934 when it was straightened out and rerouted, a sign of the growing dominance of the automobile in Angeleno life.

Wilshire's zone of once-fashionable (and sometimes still or again fashionable) residences and buildings begins west of the park. The 13-story **Town House** at Park View and Wilshire (at the western edge of MacArthur Park) operated as the Sheraton Town House Hotel into the 1990s.

One block off Wilshire, at Sixth Street and Commonwealth Avenue, is the grand Gothic-style **First Congregational Church** of Los Angeles, the oldest Protestant church in continuous service in Los Angeles. It's the first of a group of grand churches and religious buildings in the Mid-Wilshire area. You won't see it unless you get off the bus.

But the neighborhood's architectural and urban highlight is the building that formerly housed **Bullocks Wilshire** and is now the home of **Southwestern University Law School,** at 3050 Wilshire Blvd. near Westmoreland Ave. In 1928 Bullocks, then an elite department store, opened what is generally thought to be the first suburban (out of Downtown) department store. The store had a traditional entrance on the street and an entrance from the parking lot in back, an innovation. Many of the building's Art Deco features remain intact. The inside of the building is not generally open to the public, though you can see the exterior and the entrances. Alongside Wilshire Boulevard's soulful old buildings are mostly characterless steel-and-glass modern office buildings.

The intersection of **Wilshire Boulevard and Vermont Avenue** is one of the top transit corners in the city. Underneath is a busy subway station, served by the Red and Purple lines. The **Wilshire Boulevard/Vermont Avenue Station Apartments** have risen on Metro-owned land on the northeast corner, providing stores, a café, and a little pool inside. By now, you're solidly into **Koreatown,** a neighborhood with a majority Latino population. It's called Koreatown for the hundreds of businesses and restaurants owned by Korean Americans who serve Koreans from throughout LA. See page 93 for some Koreatown eating choices, though it's hard to get a really bad meal here.

West of Vermont, you move seriously into the big church district, reminders of the 1920s and 1930s when Mid-Wilshire was the city's elite district. At 3400 Wilshire Blvd., near Catalina Avenue, you'll see an odd juxtaposition of apparently old and new buildings. This was the site of the **Ambassador Hotel,** for years the city's most elegant. Now it is the home of the **Robert F. Kennedy Learning Communities** (the senator was killed here), no less than six schools with a total intended enrollment of more than 4,000 students. The demolition of the Ambassador was intensely controversial and fought bitterly by historic preservationists for years. School space was desperately needed for the densely populated neighborhood's badly overcrowded schools. The Wilshire Boulevard frontage of the site is now the Robert F. Kennedy Inspirational Park, displaying a series of quotes from the much-loved senator.

At Normandie Avenue, there's another subway station and the **Wilshire Hotel,** a subway-adjacent budget choice (see page 129). A few blocks west at Hobart Boulevard is the grand, domed **Wilshire Boulevard Temple.** Hollywood connections were strong—the temple's rabbi from 1914 to 1984, Edgar Magnin, was known as the "rabbi to the stars."

Wilshire Boulevard and Western Avenue is the end of the Purple Line subway (for now) and home to the absolutely gorgeous emerald-green **Wiltern theater.** It's a leading mid-size music venue. On the northeast corner, more new housing, in a rather simpler mode than at Wilshire Boulevard and Vermont Avenue, is rising. We're still in Koreatown, although streets south of Wilshire—especially Olympic Boulevard—are the main business streets. Still Wilshire here is lined with storefronts.

West of **Wilton Place,** a couple blocks past Western Avenue, the character of the street changes. Towers disappear; storefronts drop away; and long, low office buildings dominate the street, more suburban office park than linear downtown. Large houses can be glimpsed on the side streets, some of which (such as Fremont Place) are old-time private streets, the original gated communities. Wilshire continues in this mode roughly 1.5 miles to **Highland Avenue,** which leads up through the affluent Hancock Park neighborhood to Hollywood. Special zoning and planning protections kept the **Park Mile** this way.

The last mile or so of the ride, from Highland Avenue west to Fairfax Avenue, is the most active retail section of Wilshire Boulevard east of the city of Santa Monica. Until it reaches Museum Row, the street is dominated by one- and two-story retail buildings, punctuated by the occasional Art Deco tower. The section between Sycamore Avenue (a few blocks west of Highland Avenue) and Fairfax Avenue is known as the **Miracle Mile** and was developed in the 1920s in the face of zoning meant to keep the street residential. Coming up to **Fairfax Avenue** is the **Los Angeles County Museum of Art**'s multi-building complex on the north side of Wilshire, sharing its park space with the **La Brea Tar Pits.** If you visit only one art museum in Los Angeles, make it the county museum, with its world-spanning collection.

Your ride is done, but Wilshire goes on and on, for almost another 10 miles, out through Beverly Hills, forming the southern edge of the famed Business Triangle, through a golf course, and then an amazing zone of nothing but high-rise condos, along the southern edge of the Westwood area and out into the development-calmed low-rise city of Santa Monica. You can ride rapid bus 720 as far out as you like. At the transfer point of Wilshire Boulevard and Fairfax Avenue, you may be ready for some refreshment. Try **Caffe Latte** at 6354 Wilshire Blvd. It's a comfortable breakfast/lunch restaurant one long block west in a strip mall, just east of Crescent Heights.

From the end of the ride at Wilshire Boulevard and Fairfax Avenue, return to Downtown LA the way you came; take rapid bus 720 east to Downtown LA. To Hollywood, take rapid bus 780 or local bus 217 north on Fairfax Avenue to Hollywood Boulevard/Highland Avenue. To Santa Monica, continue on rapid bus 720 Wilshire Boulevard to Fourth Street/ Wilshire Boulevard or Colorado and Ocean avenues in Santa Monica.

Sunset Boulevard: Let the Good Times Roll

The Sunset Boulevard ride begins at Broadway and Sixth Street in Downtown Los Angeles. *From Hollywood,* take the Red Line subway to Pershing Square, and catch the 2 or 302 bus on Broadway to Sixth Street. *From Santa Monica,* take Big Blue Bus express 10 to Seventh and Olive streets in Downtown LA, three blocks from your starting point at Broadway and Sixth Street.

Sunset Boulevard is a great retail, restaurant, and entertainment street—the street where you'd go to have fun. This ride is about an hour, or a few minutes less, depending on what time of day you ride. It's an almost 10-mile trip, more than 8 miles of which are along Sunset Boulevard itself. Bus service is frequent enough, at least until about 8 p.m., so feel free to get on and off if you wish.

The ride on Sunset Boulevard is roughly parallel to the ride on Wilshire Boulevard, some 1–2 miles to the north (Sunset angles northwestward, away from Wilshire's course almost due west). But Sunset has a very different character and is interesting for very different reasons. Wilshire is a street of grand buildings, reflecting much of the 20th-century history of LA's leading city residents. Sunset has relatively few grand buildings east of Fairfax Avenue, with storefronts, mini-malls, and motels setting the physical tone.

Wilshire is the staid province of offices and apartments, a street for workaday life more than good times. The Wilshire ride only makes sense in the daytime, but Sunset could be especially entertaining in the evening, particularly with some of the characters on the bus itself. If there's a glamour-puss of LA bus lines, it would be the Sunset Boulevard bus. And while Wilshire is a straight arrow across the city, bending only occasionally, Sunset twists and turns on its route at the base of the hills.

The ride starts at **Sixth Street and Broadway.** Catch bus 2 or 302 along Broadway anywhere from Venice Boulevard north to Cesar

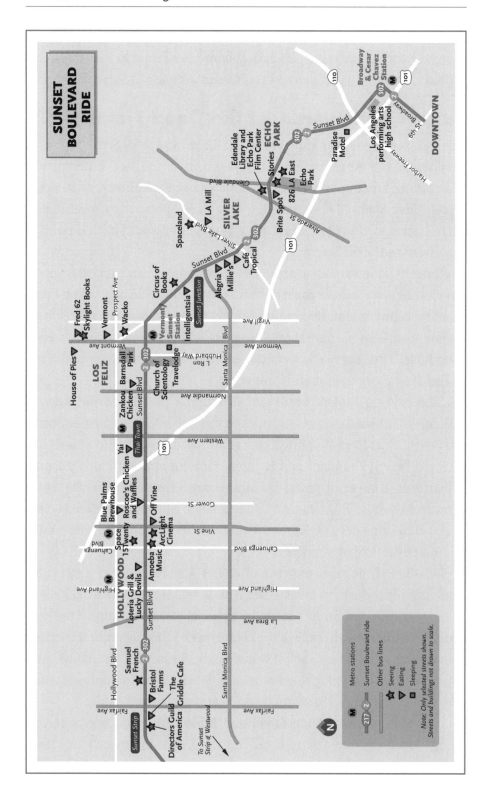

Chavez Avenue near Union Station. The bus takes you up through Broadway's vibrant discount shopping district, through LA's massively stolid civic center, across the usually crawling 101 freeway, and onto Cesar Chavez Avenue.

At **Figueroa Street,** almost the western edge of downtown, the street changes names—Cesar E. Chavez to the east and Sunset Boulevard to the west. This tells you something about where eastern LA and western LA are psychologically located. The rather artsy pile on the left at Grand Avenue is **Los Angeles's new performing arts high school.**

Crossing the **Harbor (110) Freeway,** you leave the well-organized, thoroughly redeveloped downtown zone. Just past the freeway and Bellevue Avenue is the **Paradise Motel.** It looks like a non-Edenic place to stay, but its neon is kept in lovely working order, and it's sometimes used for filming. Sunset seems like a street from some other place or time here—a street of tumbledown repair shops and garages and a canyon between two hills. Occasional public stairways, originally built for the Sunset streetcar, climb the hills to the neighborhoods above (the Echo Park Historical Society leads walks on these stair streets).

Sunset as Fun Street really begins in the **Echo Park** neighborhood (the park itself is just a couple blocks to the south, to the left). Working-class Latinos and hip young Anglos share the neighborhood, depicted in films such as *Quinceañera*. At 1716 Sunset Blvd. at Lemoyne St., **Stories** bookstore/café combines two of life's great pleasures. It's next to **826 LA East,** a writing program for kids modeled on San Francisco's famed 826 Valencia Street writing center.

The artsy presence in the neighborhood is not new—in the early 20th century an artistic and intellectual community, with a strong gay element, was located in what was then called Edendale. The name Edendale is rarely used now, except at the attractive new **Edendale Public Library** branch on Sunset Boulevard just east of Alvarado Street. Just around the corner on Alvarado Street is the **Echo Park Film Center,** a hub of do-it-yourself filmmaking.

Retail stores briefly thin out west of Echo Park Avenue but pick up again by Silver Lake Boulevard. The highly decorated **Café Tropical** at that corner serves you Cuban sandwiches and coffee strong enough to see you through any journey. North (right) on Silver Lake about 0.5 mile is **LA Mill** (1636 Silver Lake Blvd.), a temple of single-origin coffee that could probably produce the coffee grower in person if you asked. LA Mill is in a groovy little commercial district that also includes the **Spaceland** rock club (1717 Silver Lake Blvd.).

The epicenter of Sunset's hip commercial strip is in the **Sunset Junction** area, starting at approximately Maltman Avenue, centered on Hyperion Avenue, and out to about Fountain Avenue and Hoover Street, a roughly 0.5-mile segment. The area has trendy restaurants, bars, and the scene-heavy coffeehouse **Intelligentsia** (3922 Sunset Blvd.; also in Venice and Pasadena). An older flavor of the neighborhood can be found up the block at **Circus of Books** (also in West Hollywood), a pioneering gay erotica store (4001 Sunset Blvd.). Sunset Junction is also the home of a now enormous street fair with rock concerts each August.

West of Sunset Junction, at **Hillhurst Avenue,** Sunset ends its curving and angling path and heads due west across a flatter landscape. A few blocks north on Hillhurst, beginning at about Prospect Avenue, is another trendy commercial street—one of the two main ones in the **Los Feliz** neighborhood. The other Los Feliz commercial district is **Vermont Avenue,** heading north from Sunset past Hollywood Boulevard and up to Franklin Avenue.

At L. Ron Hubbard Way (named for the founder of Scientology), two blocks west of Vermont Avenue, sits the massive and vividly blue compound of the **Church of Scientology,** known as Saint Hill. The Scientologists have bought and restored numerous historic buildings in Hollywood.

Sunset has a Thai-oriented zone around Western Avenue. (The Thais who run LA Thai restaurants are mostly ethnic Chinese from Thailand.) The core of **Thai Town** is three blocks up on Hollywood Boulevard from Western Avenue east. Movie studio buildings are a notable, if blank-walled, presence along Sunset between Western Avenue and Vine Street.

Sunset Boulevard and Vine Street has been reshaped as Hollywood has been rebuilt. The tower of trendiness—the **W Hollywood Hotel**—rises above a Red Line subway station on the northeast corner. A massive new apartment complex holds down the northwest corner. Now we're entering **Hollywood** the neighborhood, though Hollywood Boulevard is definitely the district's main street. Some might find the relatively low-key nature of Sunset here a relief.

A block west of Vine Street is the **ArcLight Cinema,** a plush, premium-priced movie theater at the former Cinerama Dome. Originally slated for demolition, the dome was saved after a historic preservation fight. The blocks of **Cahuenga Boulevard** north of Sunset are the epicenter of club land Los Angeles. **Amoeba Music,** a transplant from Berkeley and one of America's largest surviving record stores, rocks the corner. Just north of Sunset at 1520 N. Cahuenga Blvd. is a small shopping mall that bids to be the coolest mall of all—**Space 15Twenty.** Anchored by an Urban Out-fitters store, the complex has a small branch of Santa Monica's great art and architecture bookstore—**Hennessey + Ingalls.**

West of **La Brea Avenue,** Sunset becomes a neighborhood shop-ping street for a Hollywood neighborhood. Theatrical publisher **Samuel French** has a bookstore at 7623 Sunset Blvd. (between Curson and Stan-ley avenues), which must be one of the world's best places to buy copies of plays. The Motion Picture Editors union has its modest headquarters here (7715 Sunset Blvd.). A small cluster of Hollywood unions lead up to the "film can" building, the headquarters of **Directors Guild** just west of Fairfax Avenue.

At Fairfax Avenue, you've reached the end of the ride. You can head home, loop down Fairfax Avenue, or keep going on Sunset. A couple blocks past Fairfax and you're on West Hollywood's Sunset Strip, with its oversize billboards, oversize clubs, and oversize hair. The Strip boasts a few historic structures—notably **Chateau Marmont** and the dazzling Art Deco **Sunset Tower.** Once you pass Doheny Drive, it's Beverly Hills's linear park and walled mansions. Beyond that you'll mostly see an afflu-ent suburban landscape for the 12 more miles to the Pacific Ocean.

At the transfer point of Sunset Boulevard and Fairfax Avenue, get some pricey but excellent fruit and vegetables for a snack from the **Bris-tol Farms** grocery store, or down some huge pancakes at **The Griddle Cafe,** just west of the intersection, at 7916 Sunset Blvd.

The end of this Sunset Boulevard ride is at Sunset and Fairfax Avenue. From here to Downtown LA, ride the other direction on the 2 bus. To Hollywood, take rapid bus 780 or local bus 217 north on Fairfax Avenue to Hollywood Boulevard/Highland Avenue. To Santa Monica, take rapid bus 780 or local bus 217 south on Fairfax Avenue, or walk approximately 0.5 mile to Santa Monica Boulevard; then take the 704 Santa Monica Boulevard rapid bus or the 4 Santa Monica Boulevard local bus.

Fairfax Avenue: Deep in the City

This trip can be done as a ride from Wilshire to Sunset boulevards, approximately 2.5 miles, or as a walk from Wilshire Boulevard to Melrose Avenue (approximately 1.5 miles). It's better appreciated as a walk unless you're doing it as part of a bigger loop trip with the Wilshire or Fairfax buses.

This ride or walk begins at Fairfax Avenue and Wilshire Boulevard. *To get there from Downtown LA,* take the 720 Wilshire rapid bus to Wilshire Boulevard/Fairfax Avenue. *From Hollywood,* take the 780 rapid bus or local bus 217 to Fairfax Avenue/Wilshire Boulevard. *From Santa Monica,* take the 720 rapid bus to Wilshire Boulevard/Fairfax Avenue.

Fairfax Avenue is geographically toward the western end of LA, but in this urban and ethnic neighborhood, it feels deep in the city. The street was known for urban experiences, such as walking and shopping, even in the era when LA wasn't. Fairfax developed as the great street of Jewish LA after World War II. It then took on a more Orthodox Jewish character, as many secular Jews moved farther out into the Westside and into the San Fernando Valley. Fairfax today is the terrain of urban hipsters as well as Orthodox Jews, who themselves have a larger retail center in the Pico/Robertson neighborhood to the southwest.

Start at the corner of Wilshire Boulevard and Fairfax Avenue, a strongly cultural locale. The shining, golden former May Company department store, now the western end of the **Los Angeles County Museum of Art** (LACMA), is located on the northeast corner. LACMA is the region's largest and most comprehensive art museum, the "Metropolitan Museum of Southern California." Across Wilshire are the giant "fins" of the **Petersen**

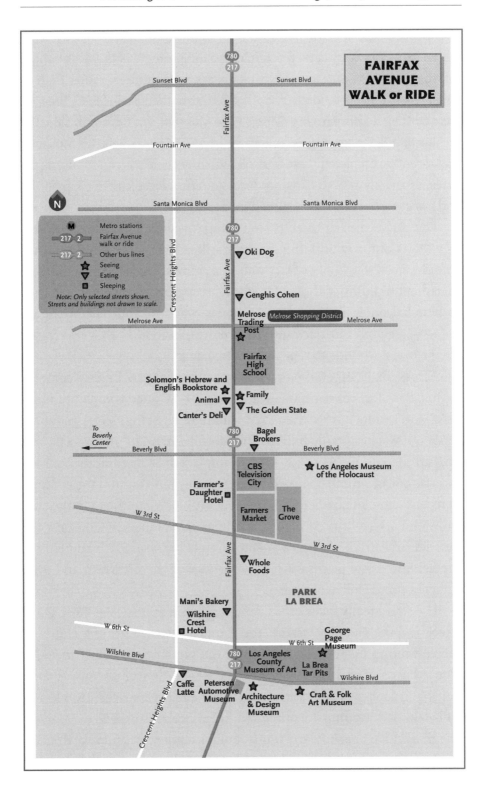

FAIRFAX AVENUE WALK or RIDE

Sunset Blvd

Fountain Ave

Santa Monica Blvd

N

M — Metro stations
217 2 — Fairfax Avenue walk or ride
217 2 — Other bus lines
☆ — Seeing
▽ — Eating
◻ — Sleeping
Note: Only selected streets shown. Streets and buildings not drawn to scale.

Crescent Heights Blvd

Fairfax Ave

780 217

▽ Oki Dog

▽ Genghis Cohen

Melrose Ave

Melrose Trading Post ☆

Melrose Shopping District

Fairfax High School

Solomon's Hebrew and English Bookstore ☆
Animal ▽
☆ Family
▽ The Golden State
Canter's Deli ▽

To Beverly Center

Beverly Blvd

780 217

Bagel Brokers ▽

☆ Los Angeles Museum of the Holocaust

CBS Television City

Farmer's Daughter Hotel ◻

Farmers Market

The Grove

W 3rd St

W 3rd St

Fairfax Ave

▽ Whole Foods

PARK LA BREA

Mani's Bakery ▽

Wilshire Crest ◻ Hotel

W 6th St

W 6th St

George Page Museum ☆

Wilshire Blvd

780 217

Los Angeles County Museum of Art

La Brea Tar Pits

Wilshire Blvd

Crescent Heights Blvd

Caffe Latte ▽

Petersen Automotive Museum ☆

☆ Architecture & Design Museum

☆ Craft & Folk Art Museum

Automotive Museum. I'm not sure how many car-free travelers want to see an exhibit of nifty cars, though Metro did promote it as a destination. (Maybe the idea was that you'd think of cars as sculptures, rather than as a means of transportation.) East of LACMA are the fossil-rich **La Brea Tar Pits** and their accompanying **George Page Museum.** On the south side, the **Architecture & Design Museum,** adjacent to the **Craft & Folk Art Museum,** was recently completed. Just west on Wilshire there's a clutch of art galleries, especially at 6150 Wilshire Blvd. And the closed coffee shop on the northwest corner is a much-filmed property.

The ride begins at the bus stop along the side of the gilt-edged former May Company building on the northeast corner. Get on a northbound 217 or 780 bus, or start walking. Across Fairfax notice the new apartment building with its blue glass, struggling to gain traction with its blue balconies and windows. If you're walking, your sidewalks are unfortunately all too narrow. The only consolation is that the traffic often slows down due to repeated traffic jams.

Across Sixth Street, the exclusively residential **Park La Brea** complex begins. Park La Brea is unique within LA, a now gated complex of more than 4,000 units in 160 acres (0.25 square mile) of high-rises and town houses. It was originally built by the Metropolitan Life Insurance company in the late 1940s in an effort to provide first-rate in-city housing and was one of several complexes the company built around the country. In recent years, the owners have been adding new buildings to the site.

With Park La Brea taking up (and fencing off) the east side, only the west side of Fairfax is left as a business street between Sixth and Fourth streets. Still a few places such as **Mani's Bakery** have thrived and even attracted some Hollywood types.

The street really takes off as a retail site as it approaches West Third Street and the **Farmers Market.** You'll probably see a healthy clutch of people waiting for the bus in front of the big strip mall that includes Whole Foods. The Farmers Market is a collection of dozens of food stores and food-service stands in partially enclosed spaces. It's akin to Philadelphia's Reading Terminal Market or Seattle's Pike Place Market. The market isn't particularly pretty, but it's a great, down-to-earth place to eat that attracts all kinds, especially for lunch.

The Grove shopping center is set behind, east of, the Farmers Market; its developers had originally proposed the unpopular idea of demolishing the Farmers Market. You won't really see much of the shopping center from Fairfax Avenue itself. The Grove describes itself not merely as a mall but as an entertainment destination, with its "trolley" that runs 1,000 feet through the complex and its Las Vegas–style dancing fountains. The Grove has been immensely popular from the day it opened—it provides a safe and visually stimulating place to walk around.

Just across The Grove Drive is a far more somber site—the newly built **Los Angeles Museum of the Holocaust.** Both the museum's architecture and its exhibits have already been both lauded and criticized.

North of the Grove, behind enormous parking lots, is the box of **CBS Television City.** Civilians mostly go there for tapings of shows, notably *The Price is Right*. Show contestants (**cbs.com/daytime/the_price_is_right**) often stay along with the hipsters at the retro-kitschy **Farmer's Daughter Hotel** across the street (115 S. Fairfax Ave.), a makeover of a once decaying motel.

At **Beverly Boulevard,** Television City's parking lot mercifully ends, and the pedestrian scale **Fairfax Village** begins. But don't miss **Bagel Brokers** (7825 Beverly Blvd.) one block east of Fairfax, which is among LA's finer bagel bakeries (takeout only). If you head west on Beverly from Fairfax, toward Beverly Center a mile away, stores become fancier and more expensive, although Third Street is the more intense retail street closest by.

The core Fairfax commercial district covers the next three blocks, up to Clinton Street, but in that short stretch, you get a nice walking experience. Traffic is slow, and sidewalks are decent. You'll find a curious mix of stores along here. One of the most famous is **Canter's Deli** on the block north of Beverly (419 N. Fairfax Ave; not that you'd miss it). Though it's not particularly beloved by foodies, its bakery is quite good. Lovers of craft beer and sandwiches might be found across the street at **The Golden State** (426 N. Fairfax Ave.), a simple pleasant showcase for California food. If you're a meat-lover, try the well-regarded **Animal** (435 N. Fairfax Ave.), which seems to serve a creature in every dish. If you wanted a magazine or offbeat novel to read while you eat, you might stop by groovy **Family** (436 N. Fairfax Ave.). Or visit **Solomon's Hebrew**

and English Bookstore (447 N. Fairfax Ave.), though not on Friday afternoons or Saturday when it is closed.

Fairfax High School is at the end of the strip at Melrose Avenue. Every Sunday it hosts a flea market known as **Melrose Trading Post,** whose website quotes the *Los Angeles Times* describing the market as a flea market "for the sexy, hip and groovy crowd." Melrose is a major retail street; see page 177. If you're walking, you've finished.

From the end of the walk or bus ride at Fairfax and Melrose avenues, return to Downtown LA by taking the 10 Melrose Avenue bus to Downtown LA. To Hollywood, take rapid bus 780 or local bus 217 on Fairfax Avenue to Hollywood Boulevard/Highland Avenue. To Santa Monica, take rapid bus 704 at Santa Monica Boulevard or local bus 4.

FAIRFAX AVENUE NORTH OF MELROSE AVENUE

The main reason to keep going the extra mile north of Melrose Avenue is to connect up with the Sunset Boulevard ride. The street through this mile has a scatter of residential and commercial buildings—Santa Monica Boulevard is a major retail corner. The stretch has two notable eateries. One is **Genghis Cohen,** a Kosher Chinese restaurant (740 N. Fairfax Ave.), and the other is the **Oki Dog** stand (860 N. Fairfax Ave.). An Oki Dog is—believe it or not—a hot dog with pastrami, chili, and cheese wrapped in a tortilla. You see lots of signs for pastrami, burrito, and hamburger eateries in Los Angeles, and this rolls them all into one dish. Fortunately, a lot of cardiologists live in West LA.

To complete the loop, get off at Sunset Boulevard to transfer to the 2 or 302 bus. To return to Downtown LA from Fairfax and Sunset, take the 2 or 302 Sunset bus to Downtown LA. To Hollywood, take rapid bus 780 or local bus 217 on Fairfax Avenue to Hollywood Boulevard/ Highland Avenue. To Santa Monica, take rapid bus 704 at Santa Monica Boulevard or local bus 4.

Food Bus 780

Tons of good food can be found in Los Angeles, but a special concentration of it is along the 780 rapid bus route, which wends its way from the edge of Culver City through Little Ethiopia, the Jewish/hipster Fairfax District, Hollywood, trendy Los Feliz, heavily Armenian Glendale, groovy Eagle Rock, and into the middle of Pasadena. Each of these areas has its signature eateries. It's a fascinating ride for more reasons than just food—you'll see a whole cross-section of LA's neighborhoods spool by.

You can get off at just about any stop along this route and find terrific food. You might try having a drink at one stop, your main meal at another, and dessert at a third. I've starred five stops that I see as particular standouts, but all the ones I've listed are good (I've skipped a few less gastronomic stops). Restaurants are further described in their neighborhood chapters. Crossing transit routes are noted. You will travel the route from the southwest in Culver City to the northeast in Pasadena.

Start the ride at Washington Boulevard and Fairfax Avenue. *To get there from Downtown LA,* take the 37 or 14 bus from Fifth Street/Grand Avenue to Washington Boulevard/Fairfax Avenue. *From Hollywood,* take rapid bus 780 or local bus 217 south; the ride will take you back north on this route. *From Santa Monica,* take express bus 534 from Santa Monica Boulevard and Second Street (30-minute frequency), almost nonstop to the Washington/Fairfax transit center.

Line 780 runs as a through rapid on Monday–Friday during the day and early evenings only; on weekends and at night, the 217 bus covers the portion of the route up through Hollywood Boulevard and Vine Street, where you can catch the 180/181 bus for the rest of the trip.

From the end of the ride at Colorado Boulevard and Hill Street in Pasadena, return to Downtown LA via the Gold Line light rail from Allen station to Union Station, and then take the Red Line subway into Downtown Los Angeles. To Hollywood, take the Gold Line light rail from Allen to Union Station, and then take the Red Line subway to Hollywood/Vine or Hollywood/Highland station. To Santa Monica, take the Gold Line light rail from Allen to Union Station, and then take Big Blue Bus express 10 (30-minute frequency) to Santa Monica.

▼ FOOD BUS 780 STOPS ▼

Note: Transit in parentheses crosses the bus 780 route at the intersection listed.

Fairfax Ave./Pico Blvd., MID-CITY (Big Blue Bus 5 or 7)   Bloom Café

Fairfax Ave./Olympic Blvd., LITTLE ETHIOPIA (Metro bus 28 or 728)   Nyala Café and Little Ethiopia restaurants

Fairfax Ave./Wilshire Blvd., FAIRFAX DISTRICT (Metro bus 20 or 720)   Caffe Latte

★ **Fairfax Ave./Third St., FAIRFAX DISTRICT** (Metro bus 16)   Farmers Market (multiple eateries and food stands), DuPar's, and Black Cat Bakery

Fairfax Ave./Beverly Blvd., FAIRFAX VILLAGE (Metro bus 14)   Canter's Deli, Bagel Brokers, and Golden State (craft beer). This stop is good for bakeries.

★ **Fairfax Ave./Melrose Ave.** (Metro bus 10)   Melrose is a big eat-street for the tony neighborhoods—try 8 Oz. Burger Bar and Carlitos Gardel.

Fairfax Ave./Santa Monica Blvd., WEST HOLLYWOOD (Metro bus 4 or 704) Oki Dog

Fairfax Ave./Sunset Blvd., HOLLYWOOD (Metro bus 2)   The Griddle and Greenblatt's Deli. This stop is good for breakfast.

Hollywood Blvd./Highland Ave., HOLLYWOOD (Red Line or Metro bus 212) Loteria Grill and Lucky Devils

Hollywood Blvd./Argyle St. near Vine St., HOLLYWOOD (Red Line or Metro bus 210)   Off Vine, Blue Palms (craft beer), and Roscoe's. This stop is good for bars.

An Art Lover's Trip

LA is a great city of culture and visual art, with the West Coast's finest collection of art museums. If you're really interested, these can be the focus of your trip with the museum-a-day plan. Each day visit a different museum. After visiting the museum, eat lunch (or dinner) and see the neighborhood. It wouldn't take your whole day, but it would be a major chunk.

This schedule works best if you start on Thursday; otherwise you may have to adjust the order to compensate for museums' closed days. The suggested plan starts with the biggest museums and moves to smaller ones as the days go on. If you are staying in Hollywood, visit the museums in the following order.

Hollywood Blvd./Normandie Ave., EAST HOLLYWOOD (Metro bus 206)   Zankou Chicken (on Sunset Blvd.) has the best, most garlicky rotisserie chicken you'll ever eat. It's cheap too.

★ **Hollywood Blvd./Western Ave.** (Red Line or Metro bus 207)   Thai Town restaurants

★ **Prospect Ave./Vermont Ave., LOS FELIZ** (Red Line Vermont Ave./Sunset Blvd. or Metro bus 204 or 754)   Yai, Vermont, Fred 62, and House of Pies. This stop is good for desserts, among other things.

Los Feliz Blvd./San Fernando Rd., GLENDALE   Tam O'Shanter Inn

Broadway/Verdugo Rd., GLENDALE   Zankou Chicken

Broadway/Brand Blvd., GLENDALE   Raffi's Place (Persian kabobs)

★ **Colorado Blvd./Eagle Rock Blvd., EAGLE ROCK**   In the heart of this lively, happening neighborhood, you will find The Oinkster (fast food reinvented), Blue Hen, Senor Fish, and Casa Bianca Pizza.

Colorado Blvd./Los Robles Ave., PASADENA   Yard House (multistate chain with many beers) and 561 (Le Cordon Bleu cooking school restaurant)

Colorado Blvd./Lake Ave., PASADENA   Euro Pane bakery (pastries and light meals). Euro Pane's critics only complaint is that its croissants are not as good as the ones in Paris.

Colorado Blvd./Hill St., PASADENA   Zankou Chicken

DAY 1 (THURSDAY)

LOS ANGELES COUNTY MUSEUM OF ART

5905 Wilshire Blvd. at Ogden Dr., Fairfax District; **lacma.org**

▨ Monday, Tuesday, and Thursday, noon–8 p.m.; Friday, noon–9 p.m.; Saturday–Sunday, 11 a.m.–8 p.m.; closed Wednesday

▨ Adults, $15; seniors, $10; students age 18 and older with ID, $10; children age 17 and under, free

THE COUNTY MUSEUM IS LA'S BIG COMPREHENSIVE ART MUSEUM, with particular strengths in Californian, Latin American, and Japanese art, as well as numerous changing exhibitions. The museum has playground space in Hancock Park behind it, good for art lovers with young children.

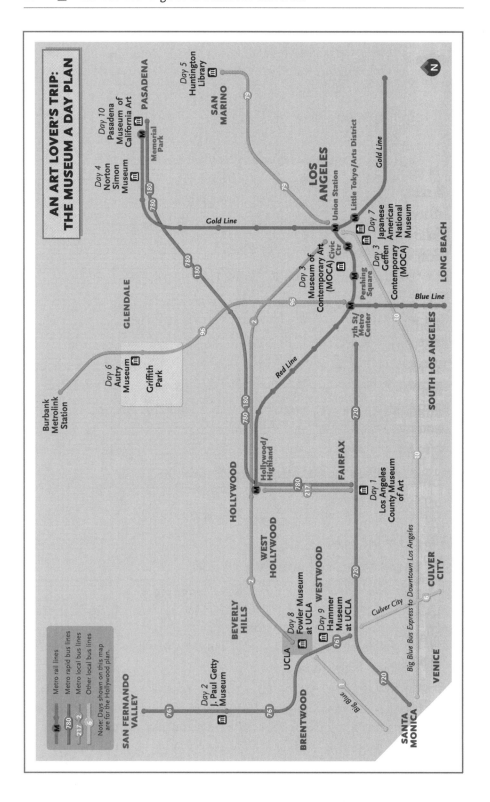

AN ART LOVER'S TRIP:
THE MUSEUM A DAY PLAN

Note: Days shown on this map
are for the Hollywood plan.

Metro rail lines
Metro rapid bus lines
Metro local bus lines
Other local bus lines

URBAN LIGHT BY CHRIS BURDEN AT THE LOS ANGELES COUNTY MUSEUM OF ART

■ *Food*

Take about a 15-minute walk up Fairfax Avenue (or take the 217 or 780 bus) to the Farmers Market, where a wealth of stands cook great food.

■ *Transit*

From Hollywood Boulevard/Highland Avenue, take rapid bus 780 or local bus 217 to Wilshire Boulevard/Fairfax Avenue. *From Downtown LA or Santa Monica,* take rapid bus 720 Wilshire to Wilshire Boulevard/Fairfax Avenue.

DAY 2 (FRIDAY)

J. PAUL GETTY MUSEUM

1200 Getty Center Dr., Brentwood; **getty.edu**

■ Tuesday–Friday and Sunday, 10 a.m.–5:30 p.m.; Saturday, 10 a.m.–9 p.m.; closed Monday

■ Free

A BIG, ARCHITECTURALLY IMPRESSIVE MUSEUM (with large gardens) on the hills above the Westside, with a focus on classical and European art and exhibitions on the process of art-making.

■ *Food*

No off-site restaurants are in this strictly residential neighborhood, but you can eat in pleasant surroundings at the Getty.

■ *Transit*

All visitors take the tram up from Getty Center Drive. *From Hollywood,* take the 2 Sunset bus to Hilgard and Westholme avenues at UCLA, and then transfer to rapid bus 761 to Getty Center Drive. *From Santa Monica,* take the 720 Wilshire rapid bus or Big Blue Bus 1 or 2 to Wilshire Boulevard/Westwood Boulevard, and then take rapid bus 761 to Getty Center Drive.

DAY 3 (SATURDAY)

MUSEUM OF CONTEMPORARY ART (MOCA)

California Plaza on Bunker Hill at 250 S. Grand Ave. and the Geffen Contemporary in Little Tokyo at 152 N. Central Ave. at First St., Downtown LA; **moca.org**

■ Monday and Friday, 11 a.m.–5 p.m.; Thursday, 11 a.m.–8 p.m.; Saturday, 11 a.m.–9 p.m.; Sunday, 11 a.m.–6 p.m.; closed Tuesday and Wednesday

■ Adults, $10; seniors and students with ID, $5; children under age 12, free; free Thursday, 5–8 p.m.

MOCA IS ONE OF THE WORLD'S LEADING MUSEUMS of post-1940 art, and art lovers around the world rallied when it faced financial trouble in 2009.

■ *Food*

Little Tokyo has several restaurants; try Honda Ya Izakaya, Orochon Ramen, Senor Fish, Weiland Brewery, or Groundwork. At the Bunker Hill location, Bottega Louie, Casa, Border Grill, Patina, Starry Grill, and Water Grill are good choices. See pages 82 and 85 for more information.

■ *Transit*

From Hollywood to California Plaza, take the Red Line subway to Pershing Square. *From Hollywood to Geffen Contemporary,* take the Red Line subway to Union Station. It's about a mile walk between the two sites. *From Santa Monica,* take Big Blue Bus express 10 to Hope and Third streets for California Plaza. *For MOCA in Little Tokyo,* take Big Blue Bus express 10 to

■ THE MUSEUM A DAY PLAN ■

If you split your stay between Downtown Los Angeles and the Westside, tackle each museum in the suggested orders. See page 202 for details on each museum.

FROM DOWNTOWN LA OR THE WESTSIDE

DAY 1: Los Angeles County Museum of Art

DAY 2: J. Paul Getty Museum

DAY 3: Fowler Museum at UCLA

DAY 4: Hammer Museum at UCLA

FROM HOLLYWOOD

DAY 1: Los Angeles County Museum of Art

DAY 2: J. Paul Getty Museum

DAY 3: Museum of Contemporary Art

DAY 4: Norton Simon Museum

DAY 5: Huntington Library

DAY 6: Autry Museum

DAY 7: Japanese American National Museum

DAY 8: Fowler Museum at UCLA

DAY 9: Hammer Museum at UCLA

DAY 10: Pasadena Museum of California Art

Los Angeles and Temple streets. *From the 7th St./Metro Center,* walk about 15 minutes to the California Plaza branch; walk straight north (and uphill) on Grand Avenue. But from the 7th St./Metro Center to the Little Tokyo branch, it's about a 1.5-mile, 30-minute walk. If you do want to walk, head east on Seventh Street, north on Broadway, and east on First Street. Instead, on weekdays, take the DASH A local bus to First Street and Central Avenue, and enter the museum in the courtyard. On weekends, take Metro bus 30 or 40 from Broadway and Fifth Street to Judge John Aliso Street, one block west of the museum.

DAY 4 (SUNDAY)

NORTON SIMON MUSEUM

411 W. Colorado Blvd. near Orange Grove Blvd., Pasadena; **nortonsimon.org**

■ Wednesday–Thursday and Saturday–Monday, noon–6 p.m.; Friday, noon–9 p.m.; closed Tuesday

■ Adults, $10; seniors, $5; students with ID and children age 17 and under, free

IT WAS ORIGINALLY THOUGHT THAT NORTON SIMON'S COLLECTION— particularly strong on South Asian art and Edgar Degas dancers—would go to the County Museum, but instead he set up his own museum on the west side of Pasadena.

■ *Food*

Central Park, The Counter, Euro Pane, Marston's, Pie 'n Burger, Saladang, Saladang Song, Yahaira's Café, and Zankou Chicken are all in the Pasadena area. See page 107 for more information.

■ *Transit*

From Hollywood, take rapid bus 780 to Colorado and Orange Grove boulevards, about an hour ride. *From Downtown LA,* take the Red and Purple Line subway to Union Station, and then take Gold Line light rail to Memorial Park. Then walk west 0.7 mile or about 15 minutes). *From Santa Monica,* take Big Blue Bus express 10 to Union Station, and then take the Gold Line light rail to Memorial Park (this requires patience because the trip is over 90 minutes).

DAY 5 (MONDAY)

HUNTINGTON LIBRARY

1151 Oxford Rd., San Marino; **huntington.org**

■ Wednesday–Monday, 10:30 a.m.–4:30 p.m.; closed Tuesday

■ Weekday admission: Adults, $15; seniors, $12; students ages 12–18, $10; children ages 5–11, $6; children under age 5, free. Weekend admission: Adults, $20; seniors, $15; children age 18 and younger pay weekday price.

THE HUNTINGTON LIBRARY INCLUDES, despite its name, an art museum and a major botanic garden, with 207 acres of grounds. There is also a research library. Henry E. Huntington made his fortune largely from real estate development based on trolley lines he owned. The art collection focuses on 19th-century British and American work, as well as Renaissance paintings.

■ *Food*

A tearoom is at the museum, and a few restaurants are on Huntington Drive, but your best bets are probably in central Pasadena or Downtown LA.

■ *Transit*

The Huntington is the hardest of these museums to reach on transit, with the least frequent service (every 30 minutes). *From Hollywood,* take the Red Line subway to Union Station, and then catch the 79 bus to San Marino Avenue, about a 90-minute ride with the transfer and wait time. Point yourself the way the bus came, and then follow the (auto) way-finding signs for Huntington Library, an approximately 1-mile (20-minute) walk. *From Downtown LA,* take the 79 bus to San Marino Avenue and make the 1-mile walk. *From Santa Monica,* take Big Blue Bus express 10 to Union Station, and then take the 79 bus to Huntington Drive and San Marino Avenue; then walk following the way-finding signs.

DAY 6 (TUESDAY)

AUTRY MUSEUM

4700 Western Heritage Way, Griffith Park; **theautry.org**

■ Tuesday–Friday, 10 a.m.–4 p.m.; Saturday–Sunday, 11 a.m.–5 p.m.; closed Monday

■ Adults, $10; seniors and students with ID, $6; children ages 3–12, $4; children under age 3, free

YES, THIS IS THE MUSEUM FUNDED BY GENE AUTRY, the movies' "singing cowboy," but it has taken pains to mount serious exhibits on art and history of Western America, as well as having a statue of Autry (and a great bookstore of Western Americana). It has merged with the Southwest Museum—the cowboys and the Indians getting together.

■ *Food*

The Autry is in Griffith Park, which has limited eating facilities. Go elsewhere, such as the Los Feliz area, for food.

■ *Transit*

From Hollywood, take rapid bus 780 or local bus 217 to Los Feliz Boulevard/Riverside Drive, and then transfer to a northbound 96 bus to Western Heritage Way (by the zoo). *From Downtown LA,* take the 96 bus from stops along Olive Street to Western Heritage Way.

DAY 7 (WEDNESDAY)

JAPANESE AMERICAN NATIONAL MUSEUM

369 E. First St. at Central Ave., Downtown LA; **janm.org**

◼ Tuesday–Wednesday and Friday–Sunday, 11 a.m.–5 p.m.; Thursday, noon–8 p.m.; closed Monday

◼ Adults, $9; seniors, students with ID, and children ages 6–17, $5; children age 5 and younger, free. Free every Thursday, 5–8 p.m.

LOS ANGELES HAS ALWAYS BEEN ONE OF THE MOST IMPORTANT CITIES for Japanese Americans. The Japanese American National Museum is a high-quality, accredited, engaging museum about the Japanese American experience, as seen in art, artifacts, and historical material. The museum is down the block from the Geffen Contemporary.

◼ *Food*

Little Tokyo has several restaurants; try Honda Ya Izakaya, Orochon Ramen, Senor Fish, Weiland Brewery, or Groundwork. See page 82 for more information.

◼ *Transit*

From Hollywood, take the Red Line subway to Union Station. From there walk down Alameda Street (the major street in front of the station) over the freeway and to the museum, a little more than a 10-minute walk. Alternatively, take the Gold Line light rail (toward East Los Angeles) one station to Little Tokyo, which is directly across Alameda Street from the museum. *From Santa Monica,* take Big Blue Bus express 10 to Los Angeles and Temple streets, three blocks from the museum. *From Seventh and Flower streets,* at the 7th St./Metro Center subway station in the Downtown Core, it's about a 1.5-mile, 30-minute walk to the museum. Instead, on weekdays, take the DASH A local bus to First Street and Central Avenue right at the museum. On weekends, take Metro bus 30 or 40 from Broadway and Fifth Street to Judge John Aliso Street, one block west of the museum.

DAY 8 (THURSDAY)

FOWLER MUSEUM AT UCLA

308 Charles E. Young Dr. North, UCLA campus (not to be confused with Charles E. Young Dr. East!); **fowler.ucla.edu**

◼ Wednesday and Friday–Sunday, noon–5 p.m.; Thursday, noon–8 p.m.; closed Monday and Tuesday

◼ Free

THE FOWLER DESCRIBES ITS SUBJECT AS GLOBAL ARTS AND CULTURES, past and present. It's somewhere between an art museum and an anthropology museum, but it's all wonderful. The Fowler is always well curated and treats its subjects with great respect.

■ *Food*

Walk down to Westwood Village for food. See page 232 for suggestions.

■ *Transit*

From Hollywood, take the 2 Sunset bus to Hilgard and Wyton avenues, on the northeast side of UCLA. *From Santa Monica,* take Big Blue Bus 1 or 2 to Ackerman Terminal, UCLA, and then walk on campus. *From Downtown LA,* take rapid bus 720 Wilshire to Wilshire and Westwood boulevards, and then walk approximately 1 mile or take Big Blue Bus 1, 2, 8, 11, or 12 to Hilgard Terminal. From Hilgard Terminal walk up the steps behind the terminal onto the UCLA campus and straight ahead until Charles E. Young Drive East, the first crossing street. Turn left there, and then turn left again at Dickson Court, an internal street with a lawn ahead. Follow the street, go down the Janss Steps, and then turn right—the Fowler Museum will be the first building on your right. It's about a 10-minute walk. *From Wilshire and Westwood boulevards,* walk north on Westwood Boulevard past where it crosses Le Conte Avenue and becomes Westwood Plaza. Continue north on this path as it becomes walk only, past the Ackerman (student) Union until Charles E. Young Drive North. Turn right; the Fowler Museum is the second building on your right.

DAY 9 (FRIDAY)

HAMMER MUSEUM AT UCLA

10899 Wilshire Blvd. at Westwood Blvd., Westwood Village (not on the UCLA campus); **hammer.ucla.edu**

▨ Tuesday–Wednesday and Friday–Saturday, 11 a.m.–7 p.m.; Thursday, 11 a.m.– 9 p.m.; Sunday, 11 a.m.–5 p.m.; closed Monday

▨ Adults, $10; seniors and UCLA alumni with ID, $5; students with ID, UCLA faculty and staff, and children under age 17 accompanied by adult, free. Free to all on Thursday.

ANOTHER CASE OF A WEALTHY MAN (Armand Hammer) deciding to start his own museum, the Hammer focuses mostly on modern art, with occasional forays further back.

■ *Food*

Try Westwood Village or south along Westwood Boulevard. Many Iranian restaurants are located a few blocks south. See page 232 for suggestions.

■ *Transit*

From Hollywood, take the 2 Sunset bus to Westwood Boulevard/Le Conte Avenue. *From Santa Monica,* take Big Blue Bus 1 or Metro bus 720 to Wilshire and Westwood boulevards. *From Downtown LA,* take rapid bus 720 Wilshire to Wilshire and Westwood boulevards.

DAY 10 (SATURDAY)

PASADENA MUSEUM OF CALIFORNIA ART

490 E. Union St. at Oakland Ave., Pasadena; **pmcaonline.org**

■ Wednesday–Sunday, noon–5 p.m.; closed Mondays and Tuesdays

■ Adults, $7; seniors and students, $5

JUST MORE THAN A MILE EAST OF THE NORTON SIMON, this quirky little museum devotes the upper floors of a building to exhibits about California artists and the California art world going back to the beginning of the state. You're bound to learn something fascinating that you didn't know.

■ *Food*

Central Park, The Counter, Euro Pane, Marston's, Pie 'n Burger, Saladang, Saladang Song, Yahaira's Café, and Zankou Chicken are all in the Pasadena area. See page 107 for more information.

■ *Transit*

From Hollywood, take rapid bus 780 on the 60-minute trip to Los Robles Avenue. Walk across Colorado Boulevard, and walk one block north to Union Street. Turn right, and the museum is on your right in the next block. *From Downtown LA,* take the Red and Purple Line subway to Union Station, and then take the Gold Line light rail to Memorial Park. From Memorial Park station, walk south on Arroyo Parkway one block to Union Street. Turn left and go east on Union for about six blocks. The museum is on the south side of Union, just before Oakland Avenue. *From Santa Monica,* take Big Blue Bus express 10 to Union Station, and then take the Gold Line light rail to Memorial Park. From Memorial Park station, walk south on Arroyo Parkway one block to Union Street. Turn left and go east on Union for about six blocks. The museum is on the south side of Union, just before Oakland Avenue.

iii. los angeles's westside

■ 11 Introduction to the Westside

THOM ANDERSON, THE DIRECTOR OF *Los Angeles Plays Itself,* scornfully (or angrily) dismisses "Westside movies," where the filmmaker acts as if the Westside is all of Los Angeles. Many TV shows, and even some travel writing, perpetuate this illusion.

While the Westside isn't all of Los Angeles, it is an important part of the city, especially for a visitor. Because so many wealthy people live there and have lived there for decades, the Westside has more than its share of cultural amenities such as museums and live theaters. Shopping concentrates here, where the well-heeled customers are. Many of the city's top hotels and restaurants are here. And of course the Westside ends at the beach, the most desirable location of all. Parts of the Westside definitely suffer from "affluenza," but there's a lot more to it than that. Look past the trendiness and see the complexity of the Westside on the bus.

City planners might say that the Westside was one of America's first "edge cities"—a place away from downtown with downtown-type activities as well as corporate offices, major hotels, and dense apartment buildings.

Getting to the Westside from Central Los Angeles

To Santa Monica from Downtown LA, take Big Blue Bus 10 from Union Station. The stops on the line that are closest to most hotels are Flower Street at Fourth Street, Flower at Fifth Street, Wilshire Boulevard at Hope Street, and Wilshire Boulevard at Grand Avenue. To Santa Monica from Hollywood, take rapid bus 780 to Fairfax Avenue/Wilshire Boulevard, and then take rapid bus 720 Wilshire to Wilshire Boulevard/Fourth Street or Ocean Avenue/Colorado Avenue. See the map on page 217.

Seeing the Westside

Geographically, the Westside is the western end of the core metropolitan area of Los Angeles, roughly between Sunset Boulevard on the north and Washington Boulevard on the south. So the Westside is about 8 miles east-west and 5 miles north-south. The Westside includes parts of the city of Los Angeles—notably Westwood, Brentwood, Bel Air, and Venice—along with the independent cities of Beverly Hills, Santa Monica, and Malibu. The Westside has many miles of beach, sweeping from Malibu in the west (the coast runs east-west there) to Venice in the south.

Westside has no officially or universally agreed-upon eastern border. Some would say that the Westside goes east all the way to La Brea Avenue and the edge of Hollywood. No clear border—no body of water, large park, or freeway—defines this edge of the Westside. In 2010 the *Los Angeles Times* asked its readers where the Westside ends and received more than 400 often passionate, sometimes vitriolic responses. Where the Westside ends is clearly a state of mind as well as a physical place.

The Westside is a distinct area within LA because of its unique transit, its distance from central Los Angeles, and even its distinctive weather. Downtown LA could be sweltering while Santa Monica is balmy and pleasant, with westerly winds blowing much of the smog inland. For car-free travelers, the fact that bus service west of Beverly Hills is largely provided by Santa Monica's Big Blue Bus provides a

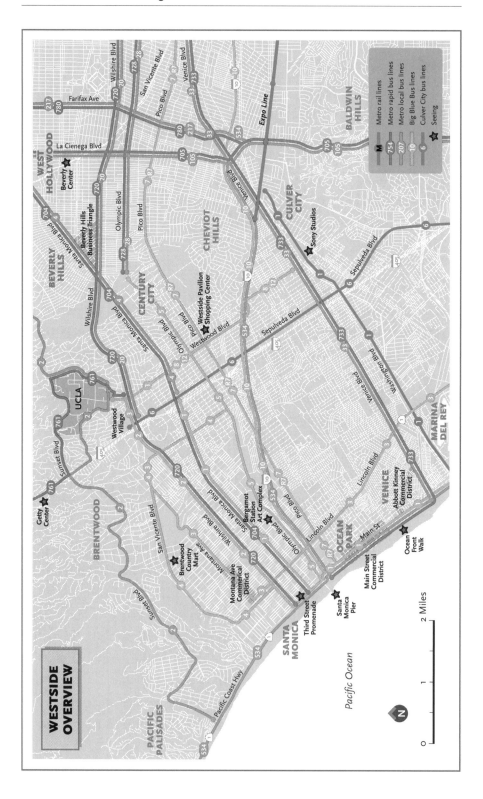

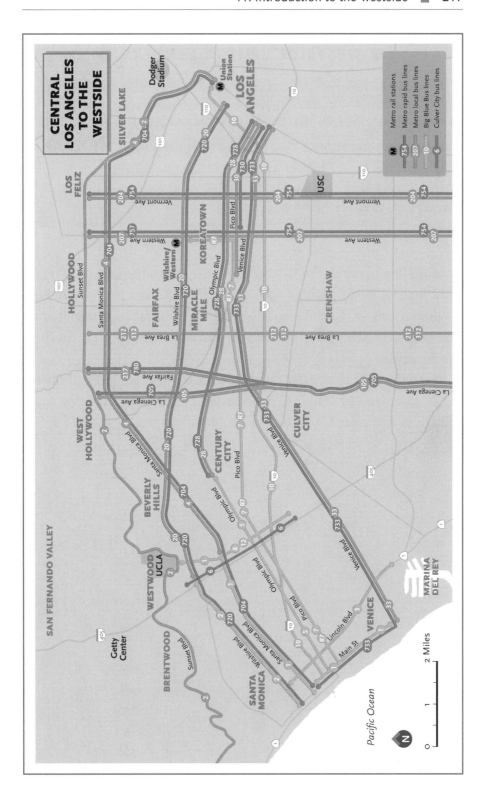

CENTRAL LOS ANGELES TO THE WESTSIDE

■ WESTSIDE VISITOR CENTERS ■

BEVERLY HILLS 239 S. Beverly Dr. near Charleville Blvd. (two blocks south of Wilshire Blvd). Monday–Friday, 8:30 a.m.–5 p.m.

MARINA DEL REY 4701 Admiralty Way. Monday–Friday, 10 a.m.–4 p.m.

SANTA MONICA MAIN STREET 1920 Main St. #8 near Pico Blvd. Daily, 9 a.m.–6 p.m.

SANTA MONICA PALISADES PARK 1400 Ocean Ave. at Santa Monica Blvd. Daily, 10 a.m.–5 p.m. (until 4 p.m. in the winter)

dividing line between the Westside and the Metro-focused central city. But I include Beverly Hills in the Westside because it is closer, in both geography and spirit, to Westside centers than central Los Angeles ones. The eastern border of the Westside for this book thus becomes La Cienega Boulevard.

The Westside is smaller than central Los Angeles but still far too big to cover just by walking. A dedicated cyclist, especially one brave enough to ride eight-lane arterials, could probably tackle most of it.

■ **12** Transit and Getting around on the Westside

BELIEF THAT LA CAN'T BE NEGOTIATED BY TRANSIT runs strongest on the Westside, sometimes among globe-trotters who have the London tube or Paris subway map as their screen saver. The Westside does have the challenge of multiple centers and destinations, and it doesn't (yet) have a train. The grid of bus routes, particularly north-south lines, isn't as strong as in central Los Angeles. But the system is good enough for a car-free visitor to move around comfortably, especially to major destinations.

Frequent bus service links Santa Monica and Westwood with most major destinations. Downtown Santa Monica is one of the best served locations in all LA. Westwood, the home of UCLA, has a lot of service as well. Santa Monica's Big Blue Buses are generally attractive, clean, and well-stocked with timetables. The worst Westside travel problem hits auto drivers and bus passengers alike—horrendous congestion, especially near the 405 freeway. The reasons for this traffic can and have filled books, but what is principally driving it now is the tendency of Westside cities to add fiscally lucrative workplaces in their communities without providing tax-consuming homes for the added workers to live in.

Metro Buses and Santa Monica's Big Blue Buses

Both Metro buses and Santa Monica's Big Blue Buses provide important transit service on the Westside. Metro runs the rapid buses on the long east-west corridors—rapid bus 720 on Wilshire Boulevard, rapid bus 704 on Santa Monica Boulevard, and rapid bus 733 on Venice Boulevard and Main Street. Metro also runs express bus 534 to Malibu (really an east-west route), the 2 Sunset bus, and the north-south service on La Cienega Boulevard (bus 105 and rapid bus 705). Big Blue Bus pretty much handles the rest—local service in Santa Monica, Venice, and adjacent communities, with some service (for example, the 7 Pico Boulevard bus) going as far east as mid-city Los Angeles.

WESTSIDE TRANSIT HUBS

Two main transit hubs are on the Westside—Downtown Santa Monica and Westwood Village. They're hubs for both Metro and Big Blue Bus.

The Santa Monica hub is made up of multiple stops on Santa Monica Boulevard (eastbound) between Second and Fourth streets and, one block to the south, Broadway (westbound and southbound) between Second and Fourth streets. Big Blue Bus routes radiate out from downtown Santa Monica. You can ride to destinations in eastern Santa Monica (for example Bergamot Station), West LA, Westwood, and Venice. Metro's regional service heads east on Venice, Santa Monica (rapid), and Wilshire (rapid) boulevards, as well as west along Pacific Coast Highway to Malibu.

The most important bus transfer point in Westwood is at Wilshire and Westwood boulevards, at the base of Westwood Village. The Santa Monica (Big Blue) buses serving Westwood all stop here, as do Metro's Wilshire Boulevard rapid buses and Van Nuys Boulevard rapid bus to Getty Center. At Westwood Boulevard and Le Conte Avenue, three blocks up from Wilshire Boulevard, you'll find Big Blue Bus stops as well as stops for Sunset Boulevard buses.

TRANSIT CORRIDORS AND FREQUENCY OF SERVICE

In Central LA, between Downtown and Hollywood, most major streets have good bus service. As you get out into the Westside, there are still many strong transit corridors, but they are farther apart. Strong corridors serve downtown Santa Monica, Westwood Village, Venice Beach,

---

★ **MOST IMPORTANT CORRIDORS FOR VISITORS** ★

EAST–WEST TRANSIT CORRIDORS

Wilshire Blvd. Downtown LA–Beverly Hills–Westwood–Santa Monica
(Metro and Big Blue Bus)

Santa Monica Blvd. Downtown LA–Beverly Hills–Santa Monica
(Metro and Big Blue Bus)

Venice Blvd. Venice–Culver City–Downtown LA (Metro only)

NORTH–SOUTH TRANSIT CORRIDORS

La Cienega Blvd. West Hollywood–Beverly Center–Culver City (Metro only)

Westwood Blvd. UCLA–Westwood Village–Westside Pavilion (Big Blue Bus only)

Ocean Ave./Main St. Downtown Santa Monica–Venice Beach (Metro and Big Blue Bus)
Another key transit link is Big Blue Bus's express 10 from Santa Monica to Downtown
Los Angeles, which is the fastest way to make that trip.

Bergamot Station, and other destinations. The Getty Center and Malibu,
locations off the main grid, have less frequent service.

WESTSIDE SERVICE BY TIME

As in central Los Angeles, Westside service is pretty good during the
day on weekdays but is less frequent in the evening. There's a particular falloff on north-south corridors such as La Cienega and Westwood
boulevards. During the day, La Cienega has a bus on average every 12
minutes (counting locals and rapids); in the evening, that becomes once
every 30 minutes, and then once every 50 minutes, with no service at all
after midnight.

★ **STREETS WITH 24-HOUR SERVICE** ★

(Metro routes only; Big Blue Bus has no 24-hour routes)

FAIRFAX AVENUE	**WILSHIRE BOULEVARD**
MAIN STREET/SANTA MONICA BOULEVARD (*one route runs on these two streets*)	**SANTA MONICA BOULEVARD**
MAIN STREET/VENICE BOULEVARD	**VENICE BOULEVARD**

Your evening travel options are 1) stick close to your hotel, within walking distance, 2) stick close to good bus lines, 3) walk to get to better bus lines (such as Wilshire and Santa Monica boulevards), or 4) take taxis.

There is no midnight–5 a.m. service on Westwood, Lincoln, or Pico boulevards (Westside segment). Nor is there any rapid bus service during those hours.

WESTSIDE WEEKDAY AND WEEKEND SERVICE

Weekend service on the Westside, like elsewhere in Los Angeles, is reduced from weekday levels, but generally not drastically. Lines that might run every 10–15 minutes during the middle of day on weekdays may drop to 15–20 minute frequencies on weekends. None of the major Westside bus lines run less frequently than that on weekends, except Big Blue Bus express 10 from Santa Monica to Downtown LA, which only runs every 30 minutes on both weekdays and weekends. The Westside's top rapid buses—704 on Santa Monica Boulevard, 720 on Wilshire Boulevard, and 733 on Venice Boulevard—run on weekends, though less frequently than during the week.

METRO BUS AND BIG BLUE BUS FARES

If you're spending any time on the Westside, you'll probably be using both Big Blue Bus and Metro. That means you'll have to juggle their separate, only slightly connected fare systems.

■ Metro Bus

Metro's cash fare is $1.50, good for a ride on a single bus or train only; its day passes are $5. If you want to transfer from a Metro bus to a Santa Monica Big Blue Bus, you can get a Metro-Muni transfer for 35 cents. You need to have a TAP card to buy a pass on the bus (see page 64 for an explanation of TAP cards).

■ Big Blue Bus

The base fare is $1, or $2 to ride Big Blue Bus express 10. A day pass is $4, which allows unlimited rides on local lines and the express. A transfer to get on either a Big Blue or Metro bus is 50 cents. You can buy a Big Blue Bus day pass on the bus. You don't need a TAP card.

■ Day Passes

It's sort of a borderline call whether it's worth buying day passes under these circumstances of split service. You'll probably use both Big Blue Bus and Metro, but maybe not enough to cover the cost of a pass on both. If you purchase a day pass for both, you break even with four rides on Metro plus four rides on Big Blue Bus (unless you use Big Blue Bus express 10, in which case it only takes two rides). It's a lot more convenient to have a day pass because you don't have to deal with cash and change.

GETTING TRANSIT INFORMATION

There are five basic ways to get information about what transit to take to get around.

■ 1. Directions in This Guidebook

This book has transit directions from transit hubs for each destination—from downtown Santa Monica and Westwood on the Westside to Downtown LA and Hollywood in central LA.

■ 2. Trip Planner on the Metro Website

The Metro Trip Planner (**mta.net**) will give you the transit information for your specific trip—from your starting point to your destination, at the time of day you want to go (regardless of which transit agency or agencies you need to use). Big Blue Bus service is included on the Metro Trip Planner, and you'll find a link to the Trip Planner on the Big Blue Bus website.

Type in your starting point, your ending point, and what time and day you want to go (or want to get there). The Trip Planner will ask you to confirm in which city your starting point and ending point are. Then, voilà, you'll get one or more routes, telling you the fastest way to go, listing the bus or train you need to take, and where you need to transfer (if you do). If you ask for the Advanced Trip Planner, you'll get a few more options. For example, it will ask you how far you're willing to walk to the bus stop. You can also use the Google Transit trip planner at **google.com/transit**.

■ 3. Telephone Information (Daytime)

You can get timetable information and routes, in English and Spanish, from (323) GO-METRO. Its hours are Monday–Friday, 6:30 a.m.–7 p.m. and Saturday–Sunday, 8 a.m.–4:30 p.m. Big Blue Bus has its own information line: (310) 451-5444, that operates Monday–Friday, 6:30 a.m.–5:30 p.m., and Saturday noon–6 p.m.

■ 4. Metro on Your Mobile Device

Metro now provides extensive transit information for Internet-enabled smartphone users. Versions of the Trip Planner, map and timetable information, and real-time arrival information for rapid buses are available. They're summarized at Metro on Your Mobile: **metro.net/around/mobile-resources**.

■ 5. Map and Timetable Information

You can plan your trip using system maps and bus and rail timetables. All of the maps and timetables for both Metro and Big Blue Bus are available online. Big Blue Bus timetables, and sometimes its system map, are available on the buses and at the Transit Store at 223 Broadway in downtown Santa Monica. It's best to get both the Metro map and the Big Blue Bus map because neither does a very good job of showing the other's routes.

TRANSIT INFORMATION LOCATIONS IN SANTA MONICA

Unlike Metro schedules, paper copies of Big Blue Bus timetables are easy to come by—most buses carry a complete set. Some buses even have copies of the Big Blue Bus system map. You can also get this information at the Transit Store at 223 Broadway, just off the Third Street Promenade, in downtown Santa Monica (open Monday–Saturday), as well as at the Santa Monica Main Library at Sixth Street and Santa Monica Boulevard. Unfortunately, the Transit Store doesn't carry copies of Metro maps or timetables. You might be able to get the Metro timetable you need on the bus, if you're lucky, or from the Tourist Information Center at Palisades Park. Metro's closest Metro Customer Service Center for the Westside is back at Wilshire Boulevard and La Brea Avenue.

Bicycling

Like Metro, Big Blue Buses all have bike racks. But off the bus, it's not such a pretty picture. Cycling has been a low priority in Los Angeles. The bikeway network is fragmented, and traffic on major streets can be incredible. The city of Los Angeles's new 2011 bike plan is a major commitment to improve its bikeway network. We'll see how well that gets implemented in the years ahead.

The bright spot for bikes is the city of Santa Monica, which has been designated a bike-friendly community. Santa Monica has a pretty complete network of bike lanes and bikeways, as well as a bike (and pedestrian) path along the city's oceanfront. Within Santa Monica, trips are quite manageable for cyclists, as few are more than 3 miles. Santa Monica also publishes an excellent biking plus transit map, available at visitor information booths or online at **tinyurl.com/smbikemap**.

No bike-sharing program exists, but there are a number of bike rental possibilities. On Ocean Front Walk, the bike places typically rent beach cruisers—slow, heavy, one-speed bikes—which are fine if all you want to do is cruise the beach. See the neighborhood chapters for bike stores in each area.

Taxis

Taxis don't really work as a major mode of travel on the Westside, with its long distances between active areas. For the most part, the taxi rules here are the same as in central Los Angeles. The basic fare is $2.85 to start, plus $2.70 a mile, or $16.05 for a 5-mile trip. Westwood, West Los Angeles, Brentwood, and Venice (among other neighborhoods) are all within the city of Los Angeles. The city of Beverly Hills has taxis that charge the same rates as in Los Angeles, and it authorizes some of the same companies to make pickups in Beverly Hills.

Just to make things more confusing, in Santa Monica, cab companies can charge whatever they want, though the large companies authorized in LA charge the same rates. As in central Los Angeles, you could be facing a long, expensive trip in a cab, so most visitors will want to save them for trips such as late-night rides home from the bar.

■ **13** Westwood

Gateway to the Westside

WESTWOOD IS THE NEIGHBORHOOD ADJACENT to the University of California, Los Angeles (always referred to as UCLA). Westwood Village was once an upscale retail district, like many others on the Westside, but in recent years the Village has become more student-oriented and less fancy. Westwood was the leading place for movie premieres and still hosts them, but other premieres have decamped to Hollywood and Westwood's premier movie-premiering theater was demolished. There's just not as much going on in Westwood as in Santa Monica or Hollywood.

Despite these losses, Westwood can still be a good base for a transit-based traveler, even if you don't have business at UCLA or UCLA Medical Center. Some people like to tour university campuses, though the ever-expanding and rebuilding UCLA is not very architecturally coherent. Westwood is a main hub of the Westside transit system, with direct buses to Santa Monica, Beverly Hills, the Getty Center, Hollywood, and LAX, among other places. You can also hop on a bus and go eat at restaurants along Westwood Boulevard or in the Sawtelle district. No other place on the Westside has direct buses to so many places. So even if the Westwood Village neighborhood is not the most exciting, it is the hub from which you can easily access all those other places. And it's also a pretty good locale for movies, live theater, and art museums.

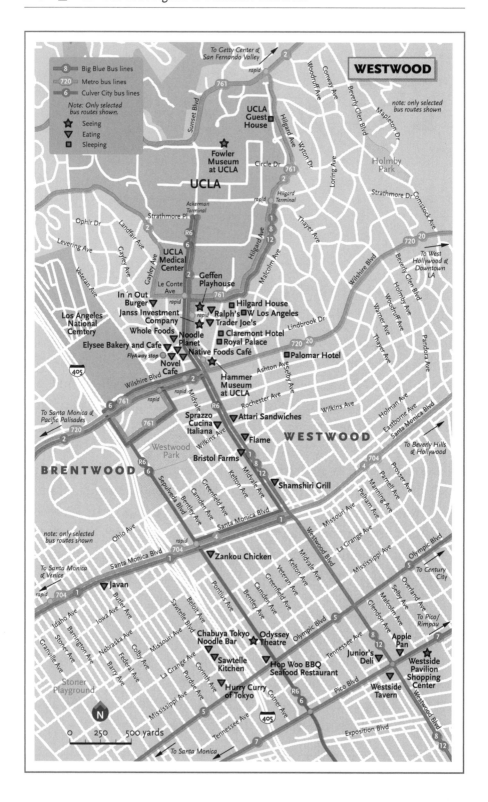

WESTWOOD

Legend:
- 8 Big Blue Bus lines
- 720 Metro bus lines
- 6 Culver City bus lines

Note: Only selected bus routes shown.

- ☆ Seeing
- ▽ Eating
- ■ Sleeping

To Getty Center & San Fernando Valley

note: only selected bus routes shown

UCLA Guest House

Fowler Museum at UCLA

UCLA

Holmby Park

Ackerman Terminal

Hilgard Terminal

Strathmore Pl

Ophir Dr

Levering Ave

UCLA Medical Center

Geffen Playhouse

Le Conte Ave

In 'n Out Burger

Los Angeles National Cemtery

Janss Investment Company

Whole Foods

Elysee Bakery and Cafe

FlyAway stop

Noodle Planet

Novel Cafe

Hilgard House

Ralph's

W Los Angeles

Trader Joe's

Claremont Hotel

Royal Palace

Native Foods Café

Palomar Hotel

Hammer Museum at UCLA

Wilshire Blvd

To Santa Monica & Pacific Palisades

Sprazzo Cucina Italiana

Attari Sandwiches

Westwood Park

Flame

WESTWOOD

To Beverly Hills & Hollywood

BRENTWOOD

Bristol Farms

Shamshiri Grill

note: only selected bus routes shown

To Santa Monica & Venice

Javan

Zankou Chicken

To Century City

To Pico/ Rimpau

Chabuya Tokyo Noodle Bar

Odyssey Theatre

Stoner Playground

Sawtelle Kitchen

Hop Woo BBQ Seafood Restaurant

Junior's Deli

Apple Pan

Westside Pavilion Shopping Center

Hurry Curry of Tokyo

Westside Tavern

N

0   250   500 yards

To Santa Monica

To West Hollywood & Downtown LA

Westwood is 12 miles west of Downtown Los Angeles, 8 miles southwest of Hollywood, and 5 miles east of downtown Santa Monica. It's bordered on the north by Bel Air, on the south by West Los Angeles and Century City (southeast), on the east by Beverly Hills, and on the west by Veterans Administration (VA) land.

If you're splitting your stay and staying some days on the Westside—for example in Santa Monica or Venice—it's easier to get to Westwood from there than from locations in central Los Angeles, such as Downtown LA.

Transit

Westwood Village and UCLA locations are within a short walk of these stops.

From Downtown Los Angeles, take rapid bus 720 to Wilshire Boulevard/Westwood Avenue.

From Hollywood, take the 2 Sunset bus from Sunset Boulevard/Highland Avenue to Le Conte Avenue/Westwood Avenue in Westwood Village.

From Santa Monica, take rapid bus 720 to Wilshire Boulevard/Westwood Avenue.

From the San Fernando Valley, take rapid bus 761 Van Nuys Boulevard. *From South Los Angeles*, use north-south routes to Wilshire Boulevard and catch rapid bus 720. *From East LA*, take the Gold Line light rail to Union Station and then rapid bus 704 or take rapid bus 720 along Whittier Boulevard directly to Westwood.

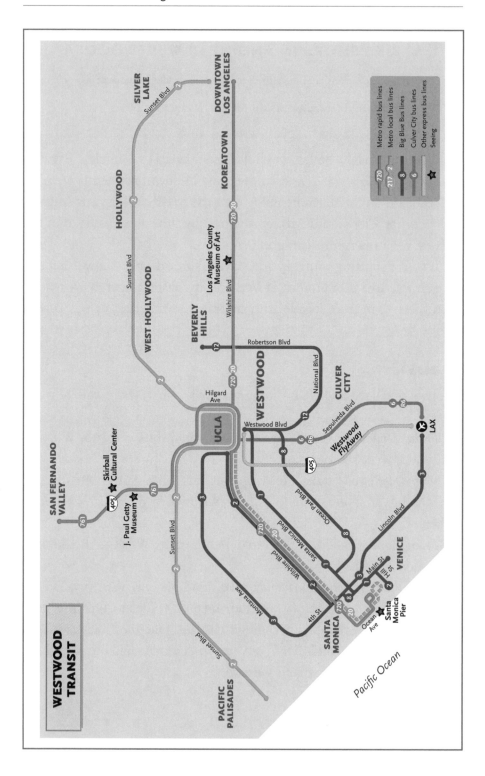

Seeing Westwood

MUSEUMS

FOWLER MUSEUM AT UCLA

308 Charles E. Young Dr. North

A FREE, FASCINATING MUSEUM OF GLOBAL ARTS AND CULTURES, past and present, with changing exhibits ranging from Iranian Americans in LA to rice as a global crop. See page 210 for full details. It is within walking distance of Westwood Village.

HAMMER MUSEUM AT UCLA

10899 Wilshire Blvd. at Westwood Blvd.

THE HAMMER, WHICH HOUSES THE COLLECTION OF ARMAND HAMMER, focuses mostly on modern art, with occasional forays back. The Hammer Museum is also the venue for special film series. See page 211 for full details. It is within walking distance of Westwood Village.

J. PAUL GETTY MUSEUM

1200 Getty Center Dr., Brentwood

THE GETTY, FREE FOR THE CAR-FREE, has a grand set of buildings and a less impressive, though growing collection of Western art from the middle ages to modern times. See page 205 for full details.

THE SKIRBALL CULTURAL CENTER

2701 N. Sepulveda Blvd.; **skirball.org**

▦ Tuesday–Friday, noon–5 p.m.; Saturday–Sunday, 10 a.m.–5 p.m.

▦ Adults, $10; children ages 2–12, $5

THE SKIRBALL CULTURAL CENTER, LA'S JEWISH MUSEUM, is farther up Sepulveda Boulevard than the Getty, toward the San Fernando Valley. The Skirball has a fairly small museum but also hosts numerous literary and cultural events, including nonsectarian items such as National Public Radio game shows.

Transit: *From Westwood,* take rapid bus 761—the only bus line that serves the museum (it runs every 20 minutes midday Monday–Friday). Catch the 761 bus at Westwood Avenue/Wilshire Boulevard or Westwood Avenue/Le Conte Avenue. It stops at Sepulveda Boulevard and Skirball Center Drive, slightly north of the Getty.

LIVE THEATER

GEFFEN PLAYHOUSE

10886 Le Conte Ave. near Westwood Blvd., Westwood Village; **geffenplayhouse.com**

THE GEFFEN (ENDOWED BY MOVIE MOGUL DAVID GEFFEN) is plush and pricey, but serious nonetheless, often presenting good plays done well.

Where to Eat in Westwood

Though Westwood Village itself is not a top eating area, a number of good eating zones are a short ride away. I have listed restaurants in Westwood Village as well as nearby areas.

RESTAURANTS IN WESTWOOD VILLAGE

ELYSEE BAKERY AND CAFÉ 1099 Gayley Ave. at Kinross Ave.; **elysee bakery.com** $–$$ French bakery with light entrées and sandwiches. It is open long hours and is a nice hangout spot.

IN 'N OUT BURGER 922 Gayley Ave. near Le Conte Ave.; **in-n-out.com** $ In 'n Out is Southern California's own iconic fast food chain—it has 200 outlets across California and a few out of state. Some people swear that In 'n Out is vastly superior to McDonald's and its ilk, while others find less difference. Most In 'n Out stores are in suburban locations, so the only other one that's in a main visitor area is Hollywood.

NATIVE FOODS CAFÉ 1110½ Gayley Ave. near Kinross Ave.; **nativefoods.com** $ One of a small Southern California chain of lower-priced, all-vegan restaurants.

NOODLE PLANET 1118 Westwood Blvd.; **noodleplanet.com** $ Noodle Planet, serving the increasingly Asian student body of UCLA, was one of the first of the pan-Asian noodle bars. They serve noodle soups and plates from Vietnam, China, Taiwan, and Japan. The food is good and cheap, and the restaurant is open until at least 10:30 p.m. every night. Also in Monterey Park.

NOVEL CAFÉ 1101 Gayley Ave. at Kinross Ave.; **novelcafe.com** $ Straightforward, unfussy café where you can drink strong coffee and write your novel. Or your screenplay. Novel Café is also on Main Street in Santa Monica, in the Downtown LA Arts District, and in Pasadena.

RESTAURANTS ON WESTWOOD BOULEVARD

The 1.5-mile stretch of Westwood Boulevard south of Westwood Village and Wilshire Boulevard down to Pico Boulevard is a classic LA neighborhood shopping street. Westwood Boulevard has become increasingly identified with the Iranian (or Persian) community, whose bookstores and restaurants cluster here. It's a key location within a city sometimes known as Tehrangeles. Still, Westwood Boulevard is by no means monoethnic. Westwood isn't necessarily the greatest walking street—it's a little too fast and wide, and there are too many dead stretches are among the stores.

Transit: *From Westwood Village,* it is a quick ride on Santa Monica's Big Blue Bus 8 or 12.

APPLE PAN   10801 Pico Blvd. near Westwood Blvd.; **applepan.com** (unofficial website)   **$**   Straightforward dining, breakfast, lunch, and dinner, for more than 60 years, particularly famous for its burgers.

ATTARI SANDWICHES   1388 Westwood Blvd. near Wilkins Ave.; **atari sandwiches.info $**   A pretty courtyard setting, *osh* soup, and great falafel make Attari a worthy and affordable deli.

FLAME   1442 Westwood Blvd. near Ohio Ave.; **flamepersiancuisine.com $$–$$$**   Flame says that it makes the best kabobs in LA, and who are we to argue? Do a taste test.

JUNIOR'S DELI   2379 Westwood Blvd. at Pico Blvd.; **jrsdeli.com $$**   LA's Jewish delis are gradually fading into the sunset, but Junior's is one of the grand survivors, an expansive temple of corned beef, pastrami, and lox. Junior's has been proving that life is good for more than 50 years.

SHAMSHIRI GRILL   1712 Westwood Blvd. near Massachusetts Ave.; **shamshiri.com $$–$$$**   Fine Persian cuisine for lunch or dinner. Lamb cooked 10 ways and an even longer list of vegetarian dishes using saffron and basmati rice. Lunch specials. Makes me hungry just reading it.

SPRAZZO CUCINA ITALIANA   1389 Westwood Blvd. near Rochester Ave.;

sprazzo.net $$$ Small, not too expensive Italian restaurant just a bit south of Wilshire Boulevard, particularly known for gnocchi.

WESTSIDE TAVERN 10850 Pico Blvd. at Westwood Blvd., Westside Pavilion Shopping Center; **westsidetavernla.com** $$$–$$$$ It's unusual to find good eateries in a major indoor mall (as opposed to a small strip mall), but Westside Tavern offers (pricey) high-quality versions of tavern sandwiches and meals, plus wine, tequilas, and craft beers.

ZANKOU CHICKEN 1716 S. Sepulveda Blvd. at Santa Monica Blvd.; **zankouchicken.com** $ OK, it's off Westwood Boulevard, but it's within a few minutes' walk, and you don't want to miss Zankou. It has wonderful garlic chicken, lamb shawarma, and other specialties, for dirt-cheap prices in a clean but less than beautiful environment. Also in Hollywood, Pasadena, and Glendale.

RESTAURANTS ON AND NEAR SAWTELLE BOULEVARD

Sawtelle Boulevard in West Los Angeles, in the blocks from south of Santa Monica Boulevard to Olympic Boulevard, is a Japanese American commercial district. It developed before World War II, survived the internment of the Japanese, and has grown into a lively, modern commercial district, complete with two-story mini-malls, whose height is an important sign of commercial success in LA. It's not as historic as Little Tokyo, but it's on the Westside and offers a wide range of restaurants and stores. Sawtelle Boulevard is about 10 blocks, or 0.75 mile, west of Westwood Boulevard, just on the west side of the perpetually jammed 405 freeway. Overall, the Sawtelle area is about 2 miles from Westwood Village.

Transit: *From Westwood Village,* take Culver City bus 6 or rapid bus 6 (fare $1) from Westwood Boulevard/Weyburn Avenue to Olympic Boulevard/Sepulveda Boulevard, and walk four blocks west (under the 405 freeway) to Sawtelle Boulevard.

CHABUYA TOKYO NOODLE BAR 2002 Sawtelle Blvd. at La Grange Ave. $ One of several ramen restaurants on or near Sawtelle, this one distinguishes itself by having nicer decor and following California cuisine practices, such as trying to locally source ingredients.

HOP WOO BBQ SEAFOOD RESTAURANT 11110 Olympic Blvd. at Sawtelle Blvd.; **hopwoowestla.com** $–$$ Check out this unusually authentic Chinese restaurant for the Westside, instead of schlepping to the San Gabriel Valley.

HURRY CURRY OF TOKYO 2131 Sawtelle Blvd. near Mississippi Ave.; **hurrycurryoftokyo.com** $ Curry is apparently very popular in Japan— this group aims to spread Japanese curry dishes around the world. (Its other franchise is in Jakarta, Indonesia.)

JAVAN 11500 Santa Monica Blvd. at Butler Ave.; **javanrestaurant.com** $$$ The very well-regarded Javan is seeking to provide fine Persian cuisine at a non-outrageous price.

SAWTELLE KITCHEN 2024 Sawtelle Blvd. near LaGrange Ave.; **sawtelle kitchen.com** $$–$$$ Very popular, moderately priced Japanese-Western bistro that has been around for almost 20 years (an eternity on the Westside).

Grocery Stores and Markets in Westwood

BRISTOL FARMS 1515 Westwood Blvd. at Ohio Ave. High-quality produce, at a price.

RALPH'S 10861 Weyburn Ave., Westwood Village The solid middle-of-the-road supermarket.

TRADER JOE'S 1000 Glendon Ave., Westwood Village Everybody's favorite grocery store. For visitors, it's good for beer, wine, juice, nuts, and candy.

WHOLE FOODS 1050 Gayley Ave., Westwood Village The Westwood outlet of that nationwide natural foods supermarket generally known as "Whole Paycheck." Lots of prepared foods.

Where to Stay in Westwood

Surprisingly few hotels are in Westwood, given its central and convenient location.

CLAREMONT HOTEL 1044 Tiverton Ave.; **claremonthotel.net** $ Sorry, northern Californians, this exceedingly modest hotel has no relationship or resemblance whatsoever to the Claremont Hotel in the Berkeley Hills.

HILGARD HOUSE 927 Hilgard Ave.; **hilgardhouse.com** $$$ Across the street from the W, but pretty much its opposite: small, quiet, and well-regarded for a long time.

PALOMAR HOTEL 10740 Wilshire Blvd. at Selby Ave.; **hotelpalomarlawestwood.com** $$$$ Completely remodeled a few years ago, the Palomar is one of the more recent additions to the hip (but not over-the-top) Kimpton boutique hotel empire. It's a short walk away from Westwood Village along highway-like Wilshire Boulevard. Check for bargains—Kimpton often does promotions.

ROYAL PALACE 1052 Tiverton Ave.; **royalpalacewestwood.com** $$ A fairly basic motel on a pleasant residential block adjacent to Westwood Village.

UCLA GUEST HOUSE 330 Charles E. Young Dr. East; **www.hotels.ucla.edu** $$$ If you're affiliated with, or doing business with, UCLA (including the medical center), you can stay in its on-campus Guest House, a small hotel. It's a bit remote in the northeast section of the campus, but bus lines and campus shuttles are nearby.

W LOS ANGELES 930 Hilgard Ave.; **starwoodhotels.com** $$$$$
W Hotels are known for glitz and glam. Judging from the weekend night scene here, the W Los Angeles is no exception. Still it's a high-rise with a fine view just a couple of blocks from Westwood stores and from UCLA, especially the medical center. Not to be confused with the W Hollywood.

■ 14 Santa Monica

Where the City Comes to the Sea

SANTA MONICA IS WHERE THE CITY—THE URBAN PART—of Los Angeles meets the sea. Someday, if LA Mayor Antonio Villaraigosa is successful, you'll be able to take the subway to the sea—plans are to extend the Purple Line subway all the way down Wilshire Boulevard to Santa Monica.

Funding is in place to extend the Purple Line almost 10 miles from Wilshire Boulevard and Western Avenue to Westwood Boulevard; the Westwood Boulevard–city of Santa Monica section is less certain. In the meantime, Santa Monica is one of the nicest areas in all LA, as well as a very useful locale for car-free travelers. It's a walkable, bike-able zone, well served by the city's own Big Blue Buses and by Metro. There's wading in the ocean and walking and shopping and strolling, and even, over at Bergamot Station, some art. If LA were a house, then Santa Monica would be its sunlit front parlor.

Sociologically, Santa Monica has been described as "the home of the homeless," an affluent suburb, a laid-back beach town, a haven for career women (because of the availability of rent-controlled apartments), and even as a barrio. (Satirist Harry Shearer proclaims the label "home of the homeless" each week on his radio show, which originates from Santa Monica–based public radio station KCRW. Shearer could be talking about the spiritually homeless as well as the physically homeless.) All of these are aspects of a small but complex city.

Downtown Santa Monica is 15 miles west of Downtown Los Angeles and 12 miles southwest of Hollywood. Santa Monica is bordered on the north by Pacific Palisades, on the south by Venice, on the east by the West Los Angeles district, and on the west by the Pacific Ocean.

Seeing Santa Monica

THIRD STREET PROMENADE AND SANTA MONICA PLACE

People come from all around Southern California for a rare treat—strolling, shopping, and socializing on a car-free street—Third Street between Wilshire Boulevard and Broadway. The city says that almost 5 million visitors a year, or 13,000 a day, come to downtown Santa Monica, equally split between American and foreign visitors. That would make it the third-biggest attraction in the region, after Disneyland and Universal Studios, and roughly double the Dodgers' 2.5 million attendants.

> **TIP** *Street numbers in Santa Monica go up from west to east, from the ocean inland, the opposite direction from street numbers in Los Angeles, which go up from downtown west toward the ocean. When you cross the LA–Santa Monica line, all the street numbers change.*

Once an ordinary commercial street, Third Street Promenade (**downtownsm.com**) was made a car-free street in 1965 and remade, with spectacular success, in 1989. On weekend evenings Third Street is jammed with people—shopping, eating, and watching street performers, some quite talented. It seems like a place one could get discovered. Third Street is also famed for its giant topiaries (pruned bushes) in the shape of dinosaurs and other animals. With a few exceptions, the architecture along Third Street is unexceptional. Instead, the promenade shines as an urban place. Some homeless people hang out here, but not in overwhelming numbers, and they're vastly outnumbered by visitors. Third Street can be a lively environment, too much so for some.

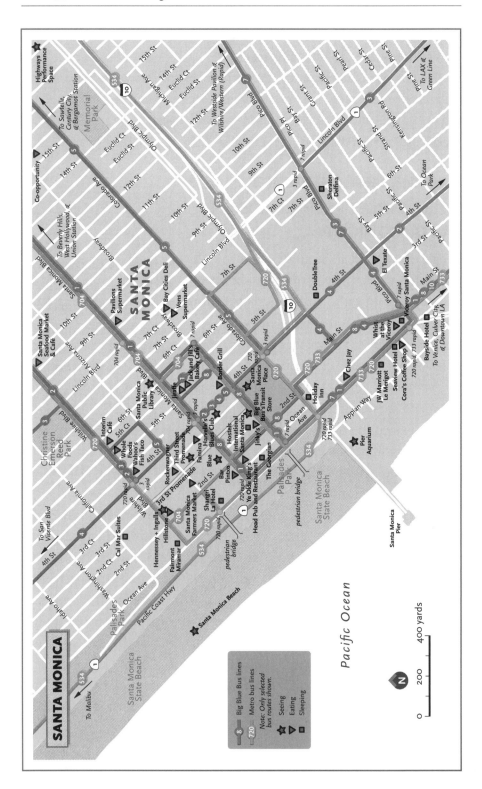

Each block on both sides is solidly lined with stores, with some kiosks and outposts in the middle. The stores mostly hew to the mainstream of American youth-oriented shopping—clothing stores include Abercrombie & Fitch, American Apparel, Banana Republic, The Gap, Old Navy, Benetton, Urban Outfitters, and Victoria's Secret. Local, independent stores, such as the bookstores that once clustered here, have been largely priced out.

Just south of the promenade, across Broadway, the Santa Monica Place shopping mall (**santamonicaplace.com**) has been rebuilt from a Frank Gehry–designed indoor mall to a more contemporary open-air structure. It has become more upscale, with Bloomingdale's, Nordstrom, and chef-designed restaurants in the new structure. The mall features rooftop eating and bar areas and seems very popular. It is definitely an above-average shopping mall experience.

Numerous food stands and restaurants are on the promenade. About 25 eateries—restaurants, coffee shops, and takeout windows—front the promenade. Many have outdoor dining spaces. You certainly can eat along the promenade, but some of the area's best eats are along nearby streets (see page 250).

THE REST OF DOWNTOWN SANTA MONICA

Third Street is famed far and wide, but it doesn't sit isolated from other businesses. Third Street is the main retail street of downtown Santa Monica (also sometimes known as the Bayside District). The downtown covers the area from Ocean Avenue on the west to Sixth Street on the east (five blocks), from Wilshire Boulevard on the north to Colorado Avenue on the south (four longer blocks).

The east side of Ocean Avenue is lined with hotels; the west side is Palisades Park, overlooking the ocean. Stores on the east-west streets, such as Broadway, Santa Monica Boulevard, and Wilshire Boulevard, appeal more to the general upscale audience, with less of an entertainment feel than those on Third Street. And we mustn't forget **Big Blue Bus's Transit Store** at 220 Broadway, between Second and Third streets (open Monday–Saturday). You can geek out on the Blue Bus here with maps, schedules, passes, toy buses, T-shirts, and so on.

Some useful places are located in the broader downtown: the main Santa Monica Post Office is at Fifth Street and Arizona Avenue, and the new main library is at Sixth Street and Santa Monica Boulevard, across from the YMCA. Like Third Street, downtown Santa Monica overall shines not as an architectural showcase but as a high-quality urban environment.

Transit: If you're splitting your stay, but not staying in Santa Monica, it's easier to get to Santa Monica from Beverly Hills or Westwood than from Downtown LA or Hollywood.

From Westwood/UCLA, take Metro rapid bus 720 to Fourth Street/ Wilshire Boulevard, or take Big Blue Bus 1 or 2 from Westwood Boulevard stops and get off at Broadway/Third Street or Fourth Street/ Wilshire Boulevard.

From Downtown LA, take Big Blue Bus express 10 and get off on Broadway at the Third Street Promenade. Leaving Downtown LA 8:30 p.m.–midnight, take Metro rapid bus 720 Wilshire from stops on Sixth Street in Downtown LA.

From Hollywood, take rapid bus 780 to Fairfax Avenue/Wilshire Boulevard, and then take westbound rapid bus 720 to Ocean and Colorado avenues. Check the Metro Trip Planner, as other combinations of routes may be faster depending on when you are traveling.

From the San Fernando Valley, catch rapid bus 761 Sepulveda to Westwood and Wilshire boulevards, and then take rapid bus 720 Wilshire Boulevard to downtown Santa Monica. *From South Los Angeles,* connect to the Washington Boulevard/Fairfax Avenue Transit Center and take express bus 534 or connect to 7th St./Metro Center and take Big Blue Bus express 10 to Broadway and Third Street Promenade. *From East Los Angeles,* take the Gold Line light rail to Union Station and catch Big Blue Bus express 10 to Broadway and Third Street Promenade, or take rapid bus 720 from East LA directly to Ocean and Colorado avenues in downtown Santa Monica.

SANTA MONICA PIER

Enter at Ocean Avenue and Colorado Avenue (or from Appian Way walkway on Santa Monica Beach). There is no admission charge for the pier—amusements have individual fees. Different activities have different hours, with activities approximately 9 a.m.–1 a.m. in summer. Visit **santamonicapier.org.**

■ *Retro Recreation*

In ever so trendy Santa Monica, the pier is an old-time survivor. More than 100 years old, the pier still lures thousands of visitors to walk out over the ocean, ride on the Ferris wheel, and play the New Jersey arcade games of my youth such as Skee-Ball. No matter that the amusement park—Pacific Park—was missing from the pier between the 1930s and the 1980s. The Ferris wheel—dubbed Pacific Wheel—is the world's only solar-powered Ferris wheel and is lit in terrific patterns at night. Many of the rides on the pier are ideal for little kids.

Toward the beginning of the pier is the carousel, a vintage merry-go-round inside the historic Hippodrome building. The area also has takeout and sit-down eateries, though no one has ever nominated the pier as Santa Monica's gourmet hot spot.

The Pacific shoreline was once dotted with piers—Santa Monica, for instance, also had the Ocean Park Pier. But as inland amusement parks such as Disneyland grew in popularity, piers fell out of favor. Santa Monica Pier was proposed for demolition in 1973, but residents quickly mounted a campaign to save it—one of modern Santa Monica's first political stirrings—and the council quickly rescinded the action.

■ *Pier Aquarium*

Heal the Bay—an environmental advocacy group—runs a small aquarium literally below the pier. You enter it from the beach level, with a $5 suggested donation and $3 minimum; children age 12 and under are free. Visit **healthebay.org/smpa.**

Transit: Use the same routes as downtown Santa Monica, but get off at slightly different stops.

From downtown Santa Monica hotels, walk. All hotels are within 15 minutes of the pier.

From Westwood/UCLA, take Metro rapid bus 720 from Wilshire Boulevard/Westwood Avenue to Ocean Avenue/Colorado Avenue. Or

take Big Blue Bus 1 from Westwood Avenue stops to Ocean Avenue/ Colorado Avenue.

From Downtown LA, take Big Blue Bus express 10 to the last stop at Second Street/Colorado Avenue, and then walk one block west to Ocean Avenue. If you are leaving Downtown LA 8:30 p.m.–midnight, take Metro rapid bus 720 Wilshire to Ocean and Colorado avenues.

COURTESY OF DENNIS FINN/FILMEYE.COM

From Hollywood, take the 217 or 780 bus to Fairfax Avenue/Wilshire Boulevard, and transfer to westbound rapid bus 720 on Wilshire Boulevard to Ocean Avenue/Colorado Avenue. Check the Metro Trip Planner; other combinations of routes may be faster depending on when you are traveling.

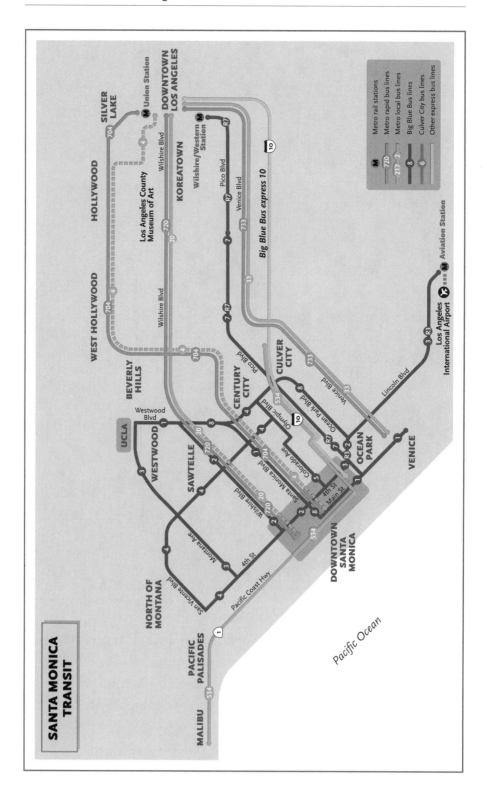

SANTA MONICA BEACH

No transit stops directly along Santa Monica Beach, though Metro semi-express bus 534 travels along Pacific Coast Highway next to it. So you have to get off uphill from the beach, in downtown Santa Monica, or along Main Street in the Ocean Park neighborhood.

If you're not staying near the beach, it's easiest to reach the beach via downtown Santa Monica, served by multiple bus routes (see directions under Santa Monica Pier above). Downtown Santa Monica sits on a cliff, or a palisade, above the beach. To get to the beach on foot, you'll need to either go out on Santa Monica Pier and take the steps from the pier to the beach, or use the pedestrian bridge over Pacific Coast Highway at Broadway or Arizona Avenue.

The American Planning Association has deservedly declared Santa Monica Beach to be one of the nation's "Great Public Spaces," along with places such as New York's Central Park and Savannah's famous squares. The planners noted how Santa Monica Beach has always been everybody's beach. In the 1920s when racially restrictive covenants were common on Southern California beaches, Santa Monica Beach was open to all. Santa Monica's racial record was not always so good. In the early 1960s, when the Santa Monica Freeway was being built, it destroyed much of the city's small African American community.

Santa Monica Beach is wide, sandy, and well-used, and in the summer is sometimes very well-used. The normal range of California beach activities here includes walking, swimming, sunbathing, surfing (though this isn't typically a high surf spot), and even some volleyball courts south of the pier. The water is not typically that warm, even in summer. You can fish from the pier, though pay attention to water-quality advisories if you're planning to eat what you catch. For little kids, a nice playground at Beach Park, just inland of the beach itself at Ocean Park Boulevard, will be entertaining.

Recreational bicycling is a huge activity along the beach. The concrete path next to the beach is separated by a stripe into well-respected bicycle and pedestrian sections. The path is 22 miles long along the beach, from Pacific Palisades to Redondo Beach.

BERGAMOT STATION

Bergamot Station, which includes the Santa Monica Museum of Art, is in southeastern Santa Monica, about 2 miles inland from downtown Santa Monica. It's not a touristy or beachy area at all. Instead, you'll find low-rise light industrial parks. The address is 2525 Michigan Ave., but the most convenient place for most car-free travelers to enter is the vehicle exit on 26th Street just south of Olympic Boulevard, which is closer to bus lines on Olympic and Santa Monica boulevards.

Bergamot Station (**bergamotstation.com**) was in fact a station on an early rail line from Los Angeles and Santa Monica. A station will be here once again when the Expo light rail line, now under construction from South Los Angeles to Culver City, is extended to Santa Monica.

But now there's a complex of some 40 art galleries that show art of all descriptions. Just wander around until you see something that you like. The buildings are low-slung industrial/warehouse buildings renovated for art—it's an interesting place to wander around even without sidewalks between the buildings. Think of it as a horizontal version of New York's West Chelsea gallery district. Most galleries are open Tuesday–Friday, 10 a.m.–6 p.m. and Saturday, 11 a.m.–5:30 p.m. The Santa Monica Museum of Art—a small museum of contemporary art—is located in the complex (suggested adult donation $5; open Tuesday–Saturday, 11 a.m.–6 p.m.).

Transit: From downtown Santa Monica, take Metro rapid bus 704 to Santa Monica Boulevard/26th Street, and walk four blocks down to Bergamot Station. It is not the closest bus, but it is the fastest.

From Downtown LA, take Big Blue Bus express 10 to Santa Monica Boulevard/26th Street, and walk four blocks down to Bergamot Station.

From Hollywood, take Metro bus 217 Fairfax Avenue or rapid bus 780 to Fairfax Avenue/Santa Monica Boulevard, and then take Santa Monica Boulevard rapid bus 704 to Santa Monica Boulevard/26th Street. Then walk four blocks down to Bergamot Station. Different combinations of two buses are possible, so check the Metro Trip Planner for the fastest route at any given time.

A Trip to Malibu

If you want to go to the famed beachside suburb (not that they'd ever call it that) of Malibu, Santa Monica is your takeoff point. Malibu's long beaches are very pretty, but accessing them can be difficult because most of the beachfront land is occupied by very pricey homes. Beaches in California, up to the high-tide line, are legally public, but the issue is how to get there. The California Coastal Commission has waged a long and somewhat successful battle with Malibu residents, including movie stars, to create coastal access, but it still can be difficult.

Some public parks and piers, such as Malibu Pier, offer opportunities along the route where you can get out and walk along the beach. The main advantages people see for Malibu beaches over Santa Monica and Venice beaches are that fewer people are on the beach (though it's hardly deserted) and surf tends to be bigger in Malibu. There are numerous bus stops along the beach in Malibu, but typically you won't be able to walk to much except the beach itself. Malibu stores are actually fairly limited and often disappoint visitors who expect a glamorous shopping environment. For that, go to Montana Avenue in Santa Monica instead (see page 181). Malibu is where the stars go when they want to chill.

The bus wends through downtown Santa Monica, and a couple of stops are along Ocean Avenue. Counterintuitively, you have to catch the bus going south on Ocean Avenue (on the park side of the street) to go to Malibu. The schedule is irregular, but the bus runs roughly every 30 minutes Monday–Saturday, and every 45–60 minutes on Sunday.

The Getty Villa, the Getty's Disneyland-ish re-creation of an ancient Roman villa, is along this route, but I don't recommend trying to go there. The villa can only be accessed by shuttle, not on foot. Shuttle service is not set up to provide timely or respectful access for car-free travelers.

Transit: Metro bus 534 is the only bus to Malibu. It goes out some 20 miles west of downtown Santa Monica to Trancas Canyon Road, essentially the far end of the developed area. Except for a brief stretch around Cross Creek Road shopping centers and Pepperdine University, the bus stays right on Pacific Coast Highway the whole time—it's pretty just as a ride.

★ BIKE SHOPS IN SANTA MONICA ★

BICYCLE AMBULANCE 2212 Lincoln Blvd. at Pacific St.; (310) 395-5026

BIKE ATTACK 2400 Main St. at Hollister Ave.; **bikeattack.com**

CYNERGY CYCLES 2300 Santa Monica Blvd. at 23rd St.; **cynergycycles.com**

HELEN'S CYCLES 2501 Broadway at 25th St.; **helenscycles.com**

From Downtown LA, take Big Blue Bus express 10 to Ocean and Colorado avenues in the city of Santa Monica, and transfer to bus number 534 to all Malibu stops. *From Hollywood,* take the 217 bus or rapid bus 780 to Fairfax Avenue/Washington Boulevard, and transfer to bus 534 to all Malibu stops.

Where to Eat in Santa Monica

You have loads of choices, especially toward the more expensive end. Don't be shocked if you encounter some attitude, particularly in trendier, pricier places; it's all part of your Westside experience (eating early may get you friendlier service because the restaurants are less busy).

RESTAURANTS IN DOWNTOWN SANTA MONICA

Non-chain coffeehouses are elsewhere—east on Wilshire Boulevard, south on Main Street, or to the north on Montana Avenue. In downtown, try Starbucks at Barnes & Noble and down the promenade, or the surprisingly grim branch of the Coffee Bean & Tea Leaf at Second Street and Santa Monica Boulevard. All listings are accessible by all downtown Santa Monica buses.

Restaurants near the Santa Monica Pier (see page 252), in Sawtelle (see page 234), along Westwood Boulevard (see page 233), and in Venice (see page 264) are all also within reasonable bus or bike riding distance of downtown Santa Monica.

BAR PINTXO 109 Santa Monica Blvd.; **barpintxo.com** Tapas by the sea in a small bar/restaurant. Tapas are $5–$10.

BORDER GRILL   1445 Fourth St. between Broadway and Santa Monica Blvd.; **bordergrill.com** $–$$ A favorite of mine. Before there was Nuevo Latino food, Border Grill served modern Mexican food. The same chefs put together Ciudad downtown.

HILLSTONE   202 Wilshire Blvd.; **hillstone.com** $$$$$ The chain that people don't regard as a chain, with a range of California-style food.

INTERIM CAFÉ   530 Wilshire Blvd. at Sixth St.; **interimcafe menu.info** $ A vegan joint; "home of the Maui veggie burger."

JACK AND JILL'S BAKERY CAFÉ   510 Santa Monica Blvd.; **eatatjackn jills.com** $$ Pleasant but small at the eastern edge of the downtown, and thus the bakery and café generates lines for its breakfast and lunch. Also in Beverly Hills and near Beverly Center.

JINKY'S   1447 Second St. between Broadway and Santa Monica Blvd.; **jinkys.com** $–$$ Jinky's is a breakfast and lunch place that manages to have a pleasant space, and it is both good and reasonably priced. Also in Sherman Oaks and Studio City.

JIRAFFE   502 Santa Monica Blvd.; **jirafferestaurant.com** $$$$$ A French-oriented restaurant, one of Santa Monica's finest and priciest. Dishes based on what's available seasonally. Make a reservation online if you want to go.

ROCKENWAGNER   311 Arizona Ave.; **rockenwagner.com** $ Bread, goodies, sandwiches, and stuff in a smallish space across from the Santa Monica Farmers Market.

SANTA MONICA SEAFOOD MARKET & CAFÉ   1000 Wilshire Blvd.; **santa monicaseafood.com** $$$ About a 15-minute walk or a short ride east of downtown Santa Monica. Santa Monica Seafood Market & Café is the gleaming restaurant and fish market of a wholesale seafood distributor. Very popular.

WAHOO'S FISH TACO   418 Wilshire Blvd.; **wahoos.com** $ Now a multistate chain with dozens of locations, Wahoo is still considered by many to be the defining spot for fish tacos.

YE OLDE KING'S HEAD PUB AND RESTAURANT   116 Santa Monica Blvd.; **yeoldekingshead.com** $ Santa Monica has a little British thing going,

■ LA MONARCA BAKERY ■

La Monarca Bakery (**lamonarcabakery.com**), which recently opened at 1300 Wilshire Blvd. at Euclid Ave., deserves special mention. The first Westside site of a Southern California minichain of *panaderias* (combination bakeries and coffeehouses), it's a neat place with terrific pastries. And it gives money to help save Mexico's monarch bakeries. Purists complain that it's not as authentic (and more expensive) than panaderias in the hood, but I think it's a terrific addition to Santa Monica. It is about a 20-minute walk or a 5-minute bus ride to downtown Santa Monica on Big Blue Bus 2 or Metro rapid bus 720.

with two English pubs and a British shop (maybe it's all those British actors coming over). It's the place for traditional English foods such as steak and kidney pie, tikka masala, and (Irish) Guinness on draft.

RESTAURANTS NEAR SANTA MONICA PIER

Plenty of good places are within a short walk of the pier. All of the downtown places are within reasonable walking distance.

CHEZ JAY   1657 Ocean Ave.; **chezjays.com** $$$$ Sometimes Westsiders want elegant restaurants that befit their elevated station in life. Sometimes they want to feel like regular folks in (pricey) dive bars with meat and seafood, like this establishment that is more than 40 years old next to the Ocean Lodge Motel.

CORA'S COFFEE SHOP   1802 Ocean Ave. north of Pico Blvd.; **coras coffee.com** $$ They say that chef Bruce Marder has incorporated Capo's high-quality food into Cora's at a fraction of the cost. Actually, Cora's is fairly pricey for a coffee shop, but everything is beautiful and top-notch, the opposite of a greasy spoon. The outdoor seating area is quite pleasant too. Breakfast and lunch only.

EL TEXATE   316 Pico Blvd.; **eltexate.com** $$ Somehow, as famed LA restaurant critic Jonathan Gold says, restaurants from the Oaxacan region of Mexico migrated a little farther west than ethnic restaurants usually do. This is definitely your gain in spendy Santa Monica because you can get a cheap hit of mole here.

WHIST AT THE VICEROY   Viceroy Hotel, 1667 Ocean Ave.; **viceroyhotels andresorts.com/santamonica** $$$$$ If you're able and willing to spend $60 per person or more on dinner, Whist will deliver a very good California-Mediterranean meal.

RESTAURANTS NEAR BERGAMOT STATION

Note that these restaurants are also fairly close to the Comfort Inn and Days Inn in eastern Santa Monica, though you'll usually need to take a crosstown walk to get to them—north-south bus connections are limited here. Outside of the complex it gets rather scattered in non-visitor neighborhoods, but some decent possibilities are within walking distance.

THE BERGAMOT CAFE   2525 Michigan Ave., Unit A3, Bergamot Station; **bergamotcafe.com** $ Located in the complex, the café is quite decent for salads, sandwiches, and such for breakfast and lunch.

GILBERT'S EL INDIO   2526 Pico Blvd.; **gilbertselindiorestaurant menu.info** $–$$ Mexican American, not deep Mexican, food. Hey, it's taste that's important, not authenticity, right?

JOSIE   2424 Pico Blvd. (If you are coming from Bergamot Station, go out the Michigan Avenue exit); **josierestaurant.com** $$$$$ Josie is one of the best regarded and most expensive "progressive American" restaurants on the Westside. Dinner only.

RESTAURANTS NEAR SANTA MONICA BEACH

There are stands are along the oceanfront walk, and quite a few around Santa Monica Pier. I'd pass these by for the many good options in downtown Santa Monica or along Main Street in the Ocean Park section, two blocks inland.

Grocery Stores and Markets in Santa Monica

ALBERTSON'S   3105 Wilshire Blvd.   The cheap supermarket, convenient to east Santa Monica motels.

BAY CITIES DELI   1517 Lincoln Blvd. at Colorado Ave.   Mostly known for (huge and wonderful) sandwiches, it's also an Italian gourmet shop with bread, olives, desserts, and so on.

CO-OPPORTUNITY   1525 Broadway   Santa Monica's independent natural food store; it's the size of a small supermarket.

FAMIMA   1348 Third Street Promenade near Santa Monica Blvd.   The fast food store that sells food that's actually good for you and tasty.

PAVILIONS SUPERMARKET   820 Montana Ave.   Upscale supermarket in an upscale neighborhood.

SANTA MONICA FARMERS MARKET   Arizona Ave. and Second St. on Wednesday   There are several, actually; this is the biggest one downtown.

VONS SUPERMARKET   710 Broadway at Seventh St. and 1311 Wilshire Blvd. at 13th St.   Mid-range mart.

WHOLE FOODS   500 Wilshire Blvd. at Fifth St. and 2200 Wilshire Blvd. at 22nd St.   Also known as "Whole Paycheck," the pricey but comprehensive natural food store.

Where to Stay in Santa Monica

DOWNTOWN SANTA MONICA HOTELS

Transit: *From Westwood/UCLA,* take Metro rapid bus 720 to Fourth Street/Wilshire Boulevard, or take Big Blue Bus 1 or 2 from Westwood Boulevard stops and get off at Broadway/Third Street or Fourth Street/ Wilshire Boulevard.

From Downtown LA, take Big Blue Bus express 10 and get off on Broadway at the Third Street Promenade. Leaving Downtown LA 8:30 p.m.–midnight, take Metro rapid bus 720 Wilshire from stops on Sixth Street in Downtown LA.

From Hollywood, take rapid bus 780 to Fairfax Avenue/Wilshire Boulevard, and then take westbound rapid bus 720 to Ocean and Colorado avenues. Check the Metro Trip Planner, as other combinations of routes may be faster depending on when you are traveling.

BAYSIDE HOTEL   2001 Ocean Ave.; **baysidehotel.com** $$$ Pleasant budget (especially in winter) property on a quieter stretch of Ocean Avenue within a short walk of both downtown Santa Monica and the Main Street Ocean Park retail area.

CAL MAR SUITES   220 California Ave.; **calmarhotel.com** $$$ A converted 1960s apartment building in a downtown residential neighborhood at Third Street and California Avenue (a block away from the pedestrian mall). Large rooms with kitchens.

DOUBLETREE   1707 Fourth St.; **doubletree.com** $$$$ A modern hotel just south of the freeway and the downtown core, DoubleTree is one of Hilton's fancier brands.

FAIRMONT MIRAMAR   101 Wilshire Blvd.; **fairmont.com/santamonica** $$$$$ A historic 1927 independent hotel that became part of the Fairmont group. The Fairmont is ideally situated at the end of Wilshire Boulevard, where it meets Ocean Avenue at a palisade (cliff) overlooking the beach.

THE GEORGIAN   1415 Ocean Ave.; **georgianhotel.com** $$$$ A gem, a rare historic hotel in Santa Monica.

HOLIDAY INN   120 Colorado Ave.; **holidayinn.com** $$$$ A well-located mid-range property, but the freeway side of the building gets very noisy in the morning. Ask for a room on the other side.

JW MARRIOTT LE MERIGOT   1740 Ocean Ave.; **marriott.com** $$$$$ Like the Viceroy, one of a string of luxury hotels (and a few dives) on Ocean Avenue south of Santa Monica Pier.

SEA SHORE MOTEL   2637 Main St. at Ocean Park Blvd.; **seashoremotel. com** $$ The Sea Shore is a well-regarded budget motel 1 mile south of downtown Santa Monica, the only one on the trendy Main Street commercial strip. You have to reserve by e-mail or phone (they don't reserve online), and reserve early because this motel fills up fast. Transit: *From downtown Santa Monica,* take Big Blue Bus 1 to Main Street and Ocean Park Boulevard. *From Downtown LA,* take Metro rapid bus 733 to Main and Marine streets, and then walk 0.5 mile north on Main Street. *From Hollywood,* take Metro bus 217 or rapid bus 780 to Fairfax Avenue and Venice Boulevard, then take Metro rapid bus 733 to Main and Marine streets, and then walk 0.5 mile north on Main Street.

SEAVIEW HOTEL 1760 Ocean Ave. at Pacific Ter. (a pedestrian street); **seaviewhotel.com** $–$$ This is a great little find in pricey Santa Monica—a clean, older motel close to both the beach and the downtown that is gradually renovating. Rooms away from busy Ocean Avenue will be quieter.

SHANGRI LA HOTEL 1301 Ocean Ave.; **shangrila-hotel.com** $$$$ Recently renovated Art Deco property aiming to attract the beautiful people. Ah, Shangri La, I knew you when you were a gently fading beauty.

SHERATON DELFINA 530 Pico Blvd.; **sheratondelfina.com** $$$$–$$$$$ A few blocks away from the ocean and the downtown core.

VICEROY SANTA MONICA 1819 Ocean Ave.; **viceroyhotelsandresorts. com/santamonica** $$$$$ A trés chic choice a few blocks south of the downtown core.

HOSTEL

HOSTELS INTERNATIONAL SANTA MONICA 1436 Second St.; **hilosangeles.org** A well-located hostel in downtown Santa Monica, a block from Palisades Park above the beach. Served by all downtown Santa Monica buses and also by tour buses. About $30 per night in summer; private rooms available.

EASTERN (INLAND) SANTA MONICA HOTELS

Eastern Santa Monica is roughly midway between downtown Santa Monica and Westwood, 2–3 miles from each. You can save money by staying there, reducing your transit access and your walking amenity, but not to an unacceptable degree. The motels are right on rather drab Santa Monica Boulevard. Wilshire Boulevard in this area has a number of restaurants, plain and fancy.

Transit: These motels give you access to good bus routes, including rapids, along Wilshire (Big Blue Bus 2 or Metro rapid bus 720) and

Santa Monica boulevards (Big Blue Bus 1 or Metro rapid bus 704), and to the Big Blue Bus express 10 to Downtown LA (stops on Santa Monica Boulevard). Your transit hubs, as it were, are the Wilshire Boulevard rapid stops at 14th and 26th streets, and the Santa Monica Boulevard rapid stops at 20th and 26th streets.

AMBROSE HOTEL   1255 20th St. at Arizona Ave.; **ambrosehotel.com** $$$$ In the medical center area of mid–Santa Monica; a luxury hotel that advertises its ecofriendliness, though not its bus connections.

BEST WESTERN GATEWAY   1920 Santa Monica Blvd. at 20th St.; **gateway hotel.com** $$$ Around the corner from the Ambrose.

COMFORT INN   2815 Santa Monica Blvd. at Harvard St.; **comfortinn santamonica.com** $$ Almost at the eastern city line, on a sort of commercial strip, and you'll have been to Harvard.

DAYS INN   3007 Santa Monica Blvd. at Stanford St.; **daysinn.com** $$ In the same area as the Comfort Inn, a couple of blocks farther east.

■ 15 Venice

Hip or Hippie?

VENICE IS ONE OF THE MOST DISTINCTIVE PLACES in LA, a "signature district," the planning department would call it. With its narrow streets and vendor-lined oceanfront walkway, parts of the neighborhood look a bit like Haight-Ashbury by the sea. Venice has had a reputation as a center of bohemian countercultural life since at least the 1950s. Today Venice is marked by extremes—million-dollar townhomes rising above tiny, aging bungalows. As a result, Venice, always a politically active neighborhood, has seen some of LA's fiercest battles over the character of development in the community.

Venice once was an independent city that, in the early 20th century, agreed to be absorbed into Los Angeles to get access to LA's water supply. Traces of a distinctive development pattern remain, especially the canals that form marine streets in a section of the community. Venice is also a place where big crowds of people walk along Ocean Front Walk. Venice is an intriguing place for visitors, if not always a comfortable one.

Visitors are most interested in the area bounded by Navy Street (the city of LA/city of Santa Monica line) on the north, Washington Street and the Venice Pier on the south, the diagonal Lincoln Boulevard on the east, and the ocean on the west. Most visitors will be in the western part of that area, west from Abbott Kinney Boulevard. It's no more than a 15-minute walk from the beach to Abbott Kinney.

Venice is 2 miles south of downtown Santa Monica and 15 miles southwest of Downtown Los Angeles. Venice is bordered on the north by Santa Monica, on the south by Marina del Rey, on the east by Mar Vista, and on the west by the Pacific Ocean.

Transit

If you're splitting your stay, it's easier to get to Venice from Santa Monica (especially) or Westwood than from Downtown Los Angeles or Hollywood.

From Downtown Los Angeles, take rapid bus 733 to Main Street and Windward Avenue or local bus 33 on Spring Street to stops along Main Street between Venice Boulevard and Sunset Avenue.

From Hollywood Boulevard/Highland Avenue, take Metro rapid bus 780 or the 217 bus to Fairfax Avenue/Venice Boulevard, and transfer to westbound rapid bus 733 or local bus 33 to Venice Boulevard/Main Street and stops along Main Street.

From Santa Monica or Westwood, take Big Blue Bus 1 to stops along Main Street.

From the San Fernando Valley, take the 761 Van Nuys rapid bus to Westwood Boulevard/Wilshire Boulevard, and transfer to Big Blue Bus 1 to stops along Main Street. *From East Los Angeles,* take the Gold Line light rail to Union Station, and then transfer to rapid bus 733 to Main Street and Windward Avenue. *From South Los Angeles,* take any north-south bus such as line 207 or 757 along Vermont Avenue or the 40 or 740 bus along Crenshaw Boulevard to Venice Boulevard, and transfer to rapid bus 733 to Main Street and Windward Avenue.

Seeing Venice
VENICE BEACH

Venice Beach is a wide swath of beach with all sorts of people walking, lying, and exercising on it, and even sometimes surfing next to it (though it's not considered a top surfing spot). Like most Southern California beaches, the water usually isn't warm enough to swim in without

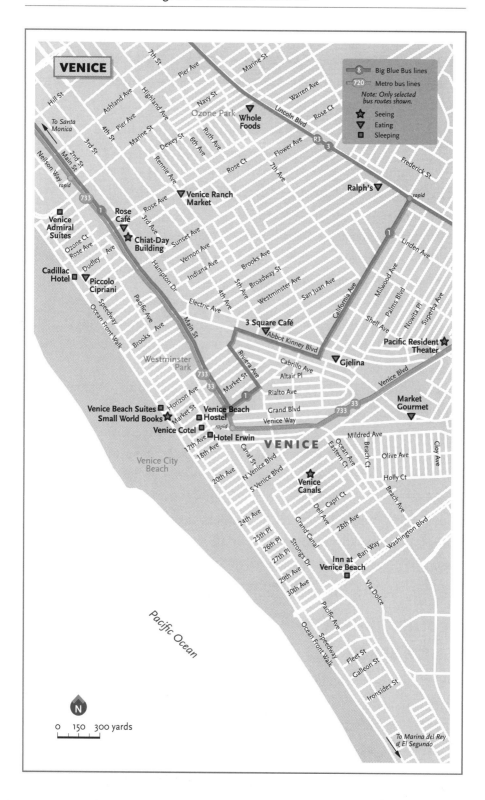

VENICE

| 8 | Big Blue Bus lines |
| 720 | Metro bus lines |

Note: Only selected bus routes shown.

☆ Seeing
▽ Eating
■ Sleeping

7th St
Pier Ave
Marine St
Warren Ave
Rose Ct

Hill St
Ashland Ave
Highland Ave
Navy St
Lincoln Blvd

To Santa Monica
4th St
Pier Ave
Marine St
Ozone Park
Whole Foods
R3
3

Neilson Way rapid
2nd St
3rd St
Main St
Dewey St
Ruth Ave
6th Ave
Rose Ct
Flower Ave
7th Ave
Frederick St

733
Rennie Ave
Rose Ave
Venice Ranch Market
Ralph's ▽
rapid

Venice Admiral Suites
Rose Café ▽
3rd Ave
Sunset Ave
Linden Ave

Ozone Ct
Rose Ave
Ave
Dudley
Chiat-Day Building ☆
Vernon Ave
Indiana Ave
Brooks Ave

Cadillac Hotel ■ ▽ Piccolo Cipriani
Hampton Dr
5th Ave
Broadway St
San Juan Ave
Milwood Ave
Palms Blvd
Novita Pl
Superba Ave

Speedway
Pacific Ave
4th Ave
Electric Ave
Westminster Ave
California Ave
Shell Ave

Ocean Front Walk
Brooks Ave
Main St
Westminster Park
3 Square Café ▽
Abbot Kinney Blvd
Pacific Resident ☆ Theater

733
33
Riviera Ave
Market St
Cabrillo Ave
Altair Pl
Gjelina ▽
Venice Blvd

Rialto Ave
Market Gourmet ▽

Venice Beach Suites ■
Small World Books ☆
Horizon Ave
Market St
Venice Beach Hostel ■
Grand Blvd
Venice Way
33
733

Venice Cotel ■
rapid
Hotel Erwin ■
VENICE
Mildred Ave
Ocean Ave
Beach Ct
Olive Ave
Cloy Ave

Venice City Beach
17th Ave
18th Ave
Canal St
N Venice Blvd
S Venice Blvd
Venice Canals ☆
Eastern Ct
Holly Ct
Beach Ave

20th Ave
24th Ave
25th Pl
26th Pl
27th Pl
29th Ave
30th Ave
Capri Ct
28th Ave
Washington Blvd
Bari Way

Grand Canal
Dell Ave
Strongs Dr
Inn at Venice Beach ■
Via Dolce

Pacific Ocean
Pacific Ave
Speedway
Ocean Front Walk
Fleet St
Galleon St
Ironsides St

To Marina del Rey & El Segundo

N
0   150   300 yards

a wet suit. The Muscle Beach Weight Training Facility at 1800 Ocean Front Walk near 18th Place, operated by the LA City Parks Department, provides weight-lifting and strength-training equipment. The fee for a day's use is $10.

VENICE OCEAN FRONT WALK

This is what Venice has instead of a boardwalk. It's a wide path with no motorized vehicles (except patrolling police cars) with tons of pedestrians, bicyclists, in-line skaters, and other conveyances. In the miles between the Santa Monica line at Navy Street and about 27th Street, the ocean side of the walk is lined with vendors of sunglasses, henna tattoos, T-shirts, and other items necessary for human existence. The colorfully attired, mostly young crowds are definitely part of the attraction too. Performing and sales spaces are so prized—and sometimes so offensive to nearby residents—that a special city ordinance regulates how spaces are allotted. Cheap eateries abound, but don't look for any foodie favorites here.

Small World Books, an independent bookstore specializing in fiction and poetry (1407 Ocean Front Walk near Horizon Ave.), has survived, even with a noisy outdoor restaurant right in front of it.

ABBOTT KINNEY BOULEVARD

The sleek and hip stores and eateries (some foodie favorites) of Abbott Kinney Boulevard are stylistically the opposite of the studied funk of the Venice oceanfront. Taking a walk one day in Venice, my daughter expressed surprise that houses were getting less fancy as we approached the ocean, rather than the usual pattern of them becoming more upscale. A decade or so ago, Abbott Kinney was the main line of a crime-ridden ghetto, but now it ranks among LA's seriously fashionable streets. Some people remember the old proletarian Abbott Kinney and find the new street hard to take. Abbott Kinney was the name of the original developer of Venice at the turn of the 20th century.

Abbott Kinney starts at Main Street near Brooks Avenue and then slants inland, southwesterly. The commercial section is about 0.75 mile long, down to Venice Boulevard, though the street continues past there.

Transit: *From downtown Santa Monica,* take Big Blue Bus 1 (Pacific Avenue/Wilshire Boulevard) to stops on Abbott Kinney between Riviera and California avenues. *From Downtown LA,* take Metro bus 33 Venice Boulevard to Venice Boulevard/Abbott Kinney Boulevard, or take Metro rapid bus 733 Venice Boulevard to Main Street and Windward Avenue, the closest rapid stop. From there, walk three blocks east on Windward, turn right into the intersection with Cabrillo Avenue, make an immediate left onto Andalusia Avenue, and walk two blocks east to Abbott Kinney (total walk 0.4 mile).

CANALS

When Abbott Kinney developed Venice, California, he really wanted it to replicate Venice, Italy, complete with canals. So Kinney developed a community with a widespread network of canals. But the town struggled

financially and the growth of automobiles demanded more space for roads, so most canals were filled in.

But a small, picturesque tract of canals remains. The canals are a few blocks inland from the beach, south of Venice Boulevard, north of 28th Avenue, east of Strongs Drive, and west of Ocean Avenue. Four small canals run east-west, and two run north-south, with small streets called canal courts in between them. Like much of Venice, the neighborhood had become run-down by the 1960s, but in the decades since, it has been restored to pricey glory, with new houses built alongside older cottages. Just take a walk around the area, crossing over the little steep bridges and marveling at what some folks do with small spaces, such as a vest-pocket playground adjacent to a canal.

Transit: *From Downtown LA or Santa Monica,* take Metro bus 33 or rapid bus 733 Venice Boulevard to Washington Way, and then walk west on South Venice Boulevard to Eastern Court (total walk 0.2 mile). *From Hollywood,* take Metro bus 217 or rapid bus 780 to Fairfax Avenue/ Venice Boulevard, and then take local bus 33 or rapid bus 733 to Venice Boulevard/Washington Way.

Where to Eat in Venice

If you want different choices than what Venice offers, you're a walk or short ride from Santa Monica eateries on Main Street in the Ocean Park district or a short ride to downtown Santa Monica. **Transit:** *From downtown Santa Monica or Westwood,* take Big Blue Bus 1 to stops on Abbott Kinney Boulevard between Riviera and California avenues, take Metro bus 33 to Venice and Abbott Kinney boulevards, or take Metro rapid bus 733 to Venice and Lincoln boulevards.

From Downtown LA, take rapid bus 733 to Venice and Lincoln boulevards, or take local bus 33 to Venice and Abbott Kinney boulevards. *From Hollywood,* take Metro bus 217 or rapid bus 780 to Fairfax Avenue/ Venice Boulevard, and then take rapid bus 733 to Venice and Lincoln boulevards, or take local bus 33 to Venice and Abbott Kinney boulevards.

To get to Piccolo Cipriani or Rose Café from downtown Santa Monica, take Big Blue Bus 1 to Main and Rose streets. *From Downtown LA,* take Metro rapid bus 733 to Main and Marine streets, and then walk south 0.2 mile from Rose Street. *From Hollywood,* use Metro's Trip Planner, as two buses will be required, and the best routing will vary depending on the time of your trip.

3 SQUARE CAFÉ 1121 Abbott Kinney Blvd. at San Juan Ave.; **rocken wagner.com** $$ High-quality food from the Rockenwagner folks with a minimum of attitude. The related bakery next door is also terrific.

GJELINA 1429 Abbott Kinney Blvd.; **gjelina.com** $$$–$$$$ It is very trendy but has quickly emerged as a top-rate plaza for modern pizza. Lunch and dinner are served daily, and it offers a weekend brunch.

JOE'S 1023 Abbott Kinney Blvd. at Broadway St.; **joesrestaurant.com** $$$$$ Fine dining Joe's describes itself as mixing formal French techniques with Asian- and California-influenced aesthetics while using the best ingredients.

PICCOLO CIPRIANI   5 Dudley Ave. just off Ocean Front Walk; **piccolo venice.com** $$$$$ A real Italian restaurant in an unexpected location.

ROSE CAFÉ   220 Rose Ave. near Main St.; **rosecafe.com** $$ A lively inclusive place—my lodestar in Venice. Once considered upscale for Venice, but no more. You can order coffee, pastries, and food at the counter, or in a pricier sit-down section that includes outdoor seating.

Grocery Stores and Markets in Venice

MARKET GOURMET   1800 Abbott Kinney Blvd. near Washington Way (a bit south of the main commercial area)   A small store with top-notch foods in each category. Not open past 7 p.m. Makes sandwiches.

RALPH'S   910 Lincoln Blvd. near Broadway St.   LA's ubiquitous supermarket chain.

VENICE RANCH MARKET   426 Rose Ave. at Fifth St.   A pleasant superette that also makes sandwiches and has Mexican specialties.

WHOLE FOODS MARKET   225 Lincoln Blvd. near Rose Ave.   Venice is definitely heading from crunchy granola to designer granola—Whole Foods has arrived. This is the location of the YouTube hit "Whole Foods Parking Lot."

Where to Stay in Venice

Venice doesn't have many tourist-grade hotels. Transit service is moderately good to Santa Monica and Westwood, as well as Downtown Los Angeles (an hour-plus ride), but other destinations such as Hollywood require a long ride and a transfer. Still, it's not a transit hub like Santa Monica, and it is south of the strongest part of the transit grid. Two hostels are located in Venice. Still, you have some choices if you have your heart set on staying in groovy Venice.

If you are looking for a Venice hotel, make sure that it is actually in Venice, from Washington Boulevard and the Venice Pier north, not in Marina del Rey to the south, a fancier and newer but much less pedestrian and transit-friendly zone.

CADILLAC HOTEL 8 Dudley Ave.; **thecadillachotel.com** $$ A relatively budget choice just off Ocean Front Walk. If the presence of colorful characters in the neighborhood disturbs you, don't stay here.

HOTEL ERWIN 1697 Pacific Ave.; **jdvhotels.com/hotels/losangeles/ Erwin** $$$$ Recently renovated by the Joie de Vivre boutique hotel group, just a half block away from Ocean Front Walk. The Erwin is a fun hotel, clearly catering to (well-off) twentysomethings, with its rooftop bar High, its eatery Hash, and its general party atmosphere.

INN AT VENICE BEACH 327 Washington Blvd.; **innatvenicebeach.com** $$$$ A Pacifica group hotel, at the more mainstream southern edge of the Venice neighborhood, complete with a bus stop outside.

VENICE ADMIRAL SUITES 29 Navy St.; **veniceadmiralsuites.com** $$–$$$ A renovated older building half a block from the beach, with the world's tiniest elevator. The rooms are like little studio or one-bedroom apartments, with a full kitchen. Hardly a high-gloss property, but well located near the Venice/Santa Monica border, with easy walking access to Santa Monica's Main Street shops and restaurants.

VENICE BEACH SUITES 1305 Ocean Front Walk; **venicebeachsuites.com** $$$ Managed by the same folks that manage the Venice Admiral, the Venice Beach Suites is another renovated building right in the heart of the Venice action.

HOSTELS

VENICE COTEL 25 Windward Ave.; **venicebeachcotel.com** Just off Ocean Front Walk, right in the heart of Venice Beach. Served by Big Blue Bus 1, Metro rapid bus 733, and Metro local bus 33. $22–$26 per night in summer; private rooms available.

VENICE BEACH HOSTEL 1515 Pacific Ave. at Market St.; **planetvenice.com** Around the corner from Cotel in Venice. Offers free airport pickup. Served by Big Blue Bus 1, Metro rapid bus 733, and Metro local bus 33. $19–$27 per night in summer; private rooms available.

iv. south of los angeles

■ 16 Long Beach

LA's Gritty City

LONG BEACH IS A LONG WAY FROM LOS ANGELES'S main visitor neighborhoods, almost 25 miles south of Downtown Los Angeles, even 15 miles south of South Los Angeles's Watts Towers. Still, Long Beach is worth the trip for a different kind of Southern California experience. Long Beach is also a good place to stay the night if you're taking an ocean cruise from San Pedro, where visitor facilities and attractions are more limited. Long Beach today might be a rather different kind of place if Walt Disney had been able to build Disneyland here, as he'd originally planned, instead of in Anaheim.

Once known as "the seacoast of Iowa" for all the Midwesterners who'd moved there (in that era, the annual Iowa Day picnic would draw thousands), Long Beach has evolved into a multiethnic city of almost half a million people, the third-largest in Southern California and seventh-largest in the state. With neighboring San Pedro, Long Beach is one of the world's largest ports. It has been a center of aircraft manufacturing and oil production and is home to the retired ocean liner *Queen Mary.* Long Beach also offers visitors a major aquarium, a historic but unpretentious downtown, and one of the nation's few clusters of Cambodian restaurants.

Cara Mullio and Jennifer M. Volland wrote and photographed the lavish *Long Beach Architecture: The Unexpected Metropolis* about the city's leading structures—extant and demolished—in 2004 (published by Santa Monica architectural bookstore Hennessey + Ingalls). "The unexpected metropolis" is a good characterization for Long Beach—a city often overlooked and somewhat squeezed between Los Angeles's big city glamour and Orange County's suburban affluence.

Transit

TRANSIT FROM LOS ANGELES TO DOWNTOWN LONG BEACH

From Downtown Los Angeles, take the Blue Line light rail from 7th St./ Metro Center to Transit Mall station, Long Beach (last stop).

From Hollywood Boulevard/Highland Avenue, take the Red Line subway eastbound to 7th St./Metro Center, and transfer to the Blue Line light rail to Transit Mall station, Long Beach (last stop).

From Santa Monica, take Big Blue Bus express 10 to Seventh and Figueroa streets. Walk one block to 7th St./Metro Center, and take the Blue Line light rail to Transit Mall station, Long Beach (last stop).

From elsewhere in Los Angeles, you'll need to go downtown and catch the Blue Line. Direct bus service goes from the LAX Transit Center and Manhattan Beach and Redondo Beach (bus 232), though it's a very long ride. An express bus (bus 577X) from transit centers in El Monte and Norwalk to eastern Long Beach requires a connection into downtown Long Beach.

TRANSIT FROM SAN DIEGO TO LONG BEACH

You can use the Greyhound station at 120 W. Broadway in San Diego, which will take you to the Long Beach station at 1498 Long Beach Blvd. (near the Anaheim Blue Line stop). It's the most direct route from Long Beach to San Diego. But keep your wits about you in that area of Long Beach at night.

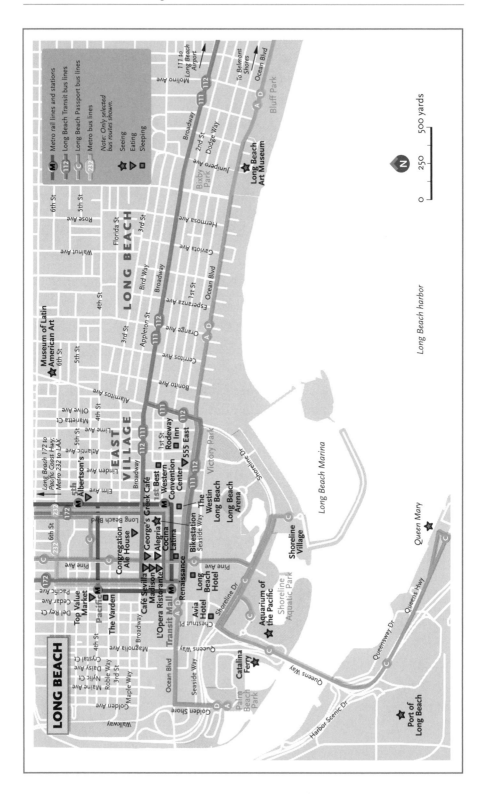

TRANSIT IN LONG BEACH

Metro reaches Long Beach, notably with the Blue Line light rail to Downtown Los Angeles, but transit within the city is mostly provided by Long Beach Transit, the city-owned bus agency.

Long Beach, of all LA area cities, operates the most extensive visitor-oriented bus service. The bright red Passport buses connect downtown Long Beach with the main tourist destinations in the city. The four Passport lines—named A, B, C, and D—run all day, 7 days a week. They're free within the downtown area; outside Downtown, they charge a $1.25 fare. The lines converge at the Transit Mall at the end of the Blue Line light rail.

The aquarium and *Queen Mary* are reached on Passport line C. The main Catalina ferry terminal—Catalina Landing—is reached on lines A and D, which also go east (for a fare) to the Long Beach Art Museum and the attractive Belmont Shores retail district.

Other destinations in the city are served by regular Long Beach Transit lines. Line 46 connects the Transit Mall and downtown with Cambodia Town on Anaheim Street, where numerous Cambodian restaurants are located.

In addition to Metro and Long Beach Transit, Los Angeles's Commuter Express operates line 142 from Long Beach to San Pedro.

A Transit Information Center is at 130 E. First St. on the Transit Mall, at the southeast corner of First and Pine. Phone information is available Monday–Saturday at (562) 591-2301.

Bicycling

Long Beach has made a real effort to make bicycling easier and safer. The largely flat terrain and grid network of streets in the city are ideal for bicycling, and Long Beach has been declared a bike-friendly community. Long Beach Transit buses, including Passport buses, have bike racks. Within Long Beach, you're unlikely to go more than 5 miles, and many trips are far shorter, so the city's scale is quite manageable for cyclists. For a bike map of Long Beach, visit **tinyurl.com/lbbikemap.**

ANAHEIM BIKE SHOP 720 E. Anaheim St.; (562) 436-8823

JONES BICYCLES AND SKATEBOARDS 5332 E. Second St.; **jonesbicycles.com**

LONG BEACH BICYCLE SHOP 507 E. Broadway; (562) 436-7447

Long Beach Bikestation, at 221 E. First St. on the Transit Mall, is first and foremost a place to park your bike while you visit downtown Long Beach or hop on transit. You can also get your bike repaired, rent a bike, and get bike and transit information—it's a state-of-the-art facility.

Seeing Long Beach

QUEEN MARY

The massive *Queen Mary,* which had a passenger capacity of 1,957 with both staterooms and tiny inside cabins, was the regal ship of the Atlantic in the years 1936–1966. Since 1971, the *Queen* has been receiving visitors and generally losing money in Long Beach. The ship is now a hotel, so you can stay overnight if you would like. The ship is docked on a curious peninsula in the harbor—one side of the road has tourist-oriented facilities, while the other side is a very heavy-duty container point.

Located at 1126 Queen's Hwy., the ship offers tours 10 a.m.–6 p.m. (last admission is at 5 p.m.) Basic admission with self-guided tour is $25 for adults and $13 for children ages 5–11. Guided tours are additional. Visit **queenmary.com**.

Transit: Take Long Beach Passport C from Long Beach Transit Mall for free.

AQUARIUM OF THE PACIFIC

The Aquarium of the Pacific is the largest in the Los Angeles region. It has exhibits about the waters of Southern California, Baja, the North Pacific, and the Tropical Pacific with colorful reefs, as well as a Shark Lagoon where you can touch some of the sharks. You can even hand-feed some lorikeet birds here.

The aquarium is located at 100 Aquarium Way and is open daily, 9 a.m.–6 p.m. (closed December 25 and 3 days in mid-April for the Long Beach Grand Prix). Adult admission is $24; for children ages 3–11, it's $12. Visit **aquariumofpacific.org.**

Transit: Walk from the Long Beach Transit Mall. Head south on Pine Avenue (toward the water), turn right at The Paseo, and turn left at Aquarium Way. The entire walk takes less than 10 minutes. Or take Passport C from the Transit Mall for free.

DOWNTOWN LONG BEACH

Downtown Long Beach has a nice collection of buildings from the 1920s, '30s, and '40s, years when it was one of greater Los Angeles's dominant business centers. Some of those treasures were lost in the ravages of urban renewal in the 1960s and '70s, and not all the gaps have been filled in yet.

For visitors, downtown Long Beach is a convention locale, with associated hotels, a transit hub (one of the most important in the region), an eating spot, as well as the site of that somewhat tattered trove of historic architecture. It's not a major retail area, though there is City Place shopping center, which—unusually for a downtown mall—is built around a Walmart, and some boutique shopping in the East Village. These locations are all within walking distance of the Long Beach Transit Mall.

For more information about Downtown Long Beach, see **downtown longbeach.org,** which has good transit information under "Parking."

EAST VILLAGE

Long Beach has deemed the northeast part of its downtown, east of Long Beach Boulevard (the main street for the Blue Line) as the East Village. Official maps show the East Village going north to Tenth Street, but earlier maps that only take it up to Seventh Street give a better picture of where the active area really is. The East Village is the city's art district and hosts an art walk on the second Saturday of each month. Though few galleries are in the area, some artistic businesses are here.

MUSEUM OF LATIN AMERICAN ART

628 Alamitos Ave. between Sixth and Seventh streets; **molaa.com**

▪ Wednesday and Friday–Sunday, 11 a.m.–5 p.m.; Thursday, 11 a.m.–9 p.m.

▪ Adults, $9; children under age 12, free

REMARKABLY, AMONG ALL THE MUSEUMS OF SOUTHERN CALIFORNIA, only this one specializes in the art of Latin America, though the Los Angeles County Museum does have a major collection. Tucked away in the northeast corner of downtown Long Beach, just past the East Village, the museum uses its 30,000 square feet for exhibits of rotating parts of its permanent collection, as well as for changing exhibits. Part of the building was once used as a silent film studio. **Transit:** From the Long Beach Transit Mall take Passport B to Fourth Street and Alamitos Avenue for free, and then walk two blocks north on Alamitos Avenue.

LONG BEACH ART MUSEUM

2300 E. Ocean Blvd. at Junipero St.; **lbma.org**

▪ Tuesday–Sunday, 11 a.m.–5 p.m.

▪ Adults, $7; children under age 12, free; every Friday, free

THIS IS A GREAT LITTLE MUSEUM—a lovely building, a pretty site overlooking the harbor and the ocean, and interesting collections and exhibits focusing

especially on California art and ceramics. A patio restaurant, Claire's, is on-site. It's a sweet spot. **Transit:** Take Passport A or D from the Long Beach Transit Mall (fare required).

VIEWING THE PORT OF LONG BEACH

The Port of Los Angeles/Long Beach (the two are side by side) is hardly your standard tourist attraction. It's the busiest container port in the United States and the fifth-busiest in the world—an enormous industrial operation. You can't just stroll onto the docks. But its gigantic size and activity make it an enthralling destination for some. You can see the port in two ways—from the water on a port tour or from the bridge by bus.

■ *Port Tours*

The Port of Long Beach offers limited seating (110–120 people) on free boat tours of the port May–September. The roughly 2-hour tours are made available online at 8 a.m. on the first of the month for the following month—for example, on March 1 for April. This is a popular trip; they create a standby list as well. The boats leave from Dock 9 at Shoreline Village. **Transit:** Take free Passport C or walk about 0.75 mile from downtown. Visit **polb.com.**

■ *Vincent Thomas Bridge*

To get a glimpse of the port that doesn't require reservations, take the Los Angeles Department of Transportation's Commuter Express bus 142 from Long Beach to San Pedro. This bus goes along the harbor and up over the Vincent Thomas Bridge, which passes high over the harbor. It runs 7 days a week. Visit **tinyurl.com/labus142.**

Where to Eat in Long Beach

DOWNTOWN LONG BEACH RESTAURANTS

Either by chance or design (redevelopment?), a good chunk of downtown Long Beach's restaurants are conveniently grouped on a single block, the 100 block of Pine Avenue between First and Second streets. It's right around the corner from the Transit Mall, where all the bus lines and the Blue Line light rail to Downtown LA converge. A few downtown Long Beach restaurants are on other blocks.

ALEGRIA COCINA LATINA   115 Pine Ave.; **alegriacocinalatina.com** $$$ A Pan-Latino casual but elegant restaurant. It's not connected to the Alegria on Sunset Boulevard in Silver Lake.

CAFÉ SEVILLA   140 Pine Ave.; **cafesevilla.com**   A Spanish tapas bar and restaurant with live music some nights. Part of a small Southern California chain. Zagat rated.

CONGREGATION ALE HOUSE   201 E. Broadway at Locust Ave.; **congregationalehouse.com** $ Presumably named for Belgian brewing abbeys rather than beer worshippers, Congregation has lots and lots of craft beers, sandwiches, sausages, and salads.

555 EAST   555 E. Ocean Blvd. at Linden Ave.; **555east.com** $$$$ A steak house that says, "Yes, we live in California, but that doesn't mean we don't love our beef," 555 East is part of the multistate King's Seafood restaurant group.

GEORGE'S GREEK CAFÉ   135 Pine Ave.; **georgesgreekcafe.com** $$ Well-liked longtime Greek restaurant. Serves from 10 a.m. 7 days a week. Also at 5316 E. Second St. in Belmont Shore and in Lakewood.

MADISON 102 Pine Ave.; **themadisonrestaurant.com** $$$$$ A contemporary American restaurant in a historic bank building. It has a decadent, very pricey Sunday morning brunch buffet.

L'OPERA RISTORANTE 101 Pine Ave.; **lopera.com** $$$ Italian restaurant in a pretty historic building. Has the same chef as Alegria.

LONG BEACH RESTAURANTS BEYOND DOWNTOWN

The **Belmont Shore** commercial district—along Second Street from Livingston Street to Bay Shore Avenue (4600 East–5400 East) is a pleasant strolling area and a good place to look for restaurants. Get there via Passport A or D (fare required for this trip). Naples Island lies beyond.

SOPHY'S 3240 E. Pacific Coast Hwy. $$ Sophy's is a terrific and popular Thai/Cambodian restaurant slightly away from the Anaheim Street Cambodian restaurant strip. Transit: From Long Beach Transit Mall, take Long Beach Transit bus 172 or 173 to Norwalk Boulevard.

STARLING DINER 4114 E. Third St.; **starlingdiner.com** $–$$ A breakfast and lunch place in a pleasant early 20th-century east Long Beach neighborhood. Transit: Take Long Beach Transit bus 111 or 112 to Ximeno Avenue and Third Street.

Grocery Stores and Markets in Long Beach

ALBERTSON'S 450 Long Beach Blvd. near Fifth St. Low-priced grocery store on the northeast edge of downtown Long Beach, across from the Cityplace shopping center.

OLIVES GOURMET GROCER 3510 E. Broadway near Newport Ave., Belmont Heights Long Beach's lower-key answer to Gelson's. Take Long Beach Transit bus 111 or 112 from downtown.

TOP VALUE MARKET 421 Pacific Ave. near Fourth St. Budget, Latino-oriented grocery store on the northwest side of downtown Long Beach, adjacent to The Varden hotel.

Where to Stay in Long Beach

Many visitors see Long Beach on a day trip. It's easy enough to come down on the Blue Line light rail, about a 50-minute ride from Downtown LA. If you stay in Long Beach, stay downtown. It's the single-most interesting neighborhood, and it's where the transit hub is and the largest grouping of hotels are. Long Beach has made a concerted effort to build up its convention and visitors' business, so you can choose from several hotels.

The hotels out along Queensway Drive (such as the Maya or the *Queen Mary*) aren't as good for car-free travelers because you'll need to take the Passport to get anywhere. No stores and restaurants are along the drive, and you're at least a mile from downtown.

AVIA HOTEL   285 Bay St.; **aviahotels.com/hotels/longbeach** $$$$ The Avia is part of a small chain of boutique hotels, bidding to be the next Kimpton or Joie de Vivre, it seems. It's well located near both the harbor front and the core of downtown and has a pool. And I have to give props to a hotel that features the Blue Line light rail on its website.

BEST WESTERN HOTEL AT THE CONVENTION CENTER   517 E. First St.; **bestwestern.com** $$$ Well-run, modest hotel downtown. Not to be confused with the Best Western of Long Beach, which is in a somewhat iffy location not in the downtown area.

RENAISSANCE LONG BEACH HOTEL   111 E. Ocean Blvd.; **marriott.com** $$$ Business-oriented hotel with harbor views; not as fancy as some of the newer Renaissance hotels.

RODEWAY INN   50 Atlantic Ave.; **rodewayinn.com** $–$$ A good bargain motel downtown, near the Convention Center.

THE VARDEN   335 Pacific Ave.; **thevardenhotel.com** $$ This is a great little independent hotel, with small and austere yet attractive rooms, friendly owner-operators, and quiet at night. The Varden is at the northwestern edge of downtown Long Beach, but it's only a few minutes' walk to downtown restaurants and activities. There's no elevator, so ask for a first-floor room if stairs are an issue.

WESTIN LONG BEACH   333 E. Ocean Blvd.; **starwoodhotels.com** $$$ Large, business-oriented hotel; one of the older Westins.

■ 17 Disneyland

SURE, DISNEYLAND IS THE PLACE YOUR KIDS have been pestering you to go, the place where Disney cartoon characters like Mickey Mouse and Goofy spring to life (you can even have breakfast with them). Disneyland was the theme park to begin all theme parks. But architect Charles Moore thought it was even more, as Southern California's signature modern example of community building. Disneyland opened in 1955, highlighting and accelerating Southern California's great lurch outward of that era.

You can visit Disneyland as a day trip from Los Angeles, especially from Downtown LA, where you're close to the train. But if you think you'll be there more than a few hours—say for a whole day—it's easier to stay overnight. Just don't try to use Disneyland as a base for seeing Los Angeles, or you will spend an inordinate amount of unnecessary time in transit.

Disneyland is 27 miles southeast of Downtown Los Angeles in the central Orange County city of Anaheim (and in something of a city within a city known as the Anaheim Resort District).

Getting to Disneyland

Even though it might seem like the most car-oriented place on earth— with 29,000 parking spaces, a ride called Autopia, and a new land based on the movie *Cars*—Disneyland, located in the heart of Orange County,

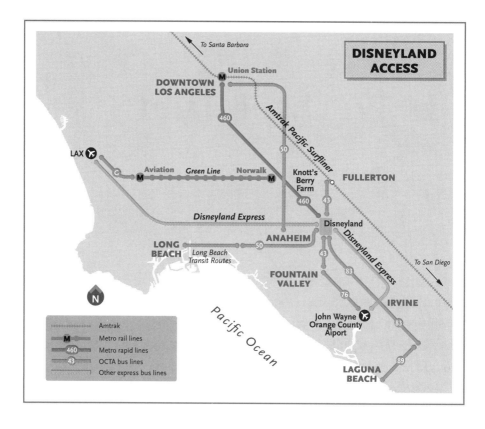

is actually accessible without a car and without too much difficulty. Those parking spaces take up roughly 10,000,000 square feet of space, or almost four times as much built space as in the largest office complex in Downtown LA, the 2.6-million-square-foot City National Plaza.

TRANSIT FROM DOWNTOWN LOS ANGELES

The quickest method is to take the Amtrak Pacific Surfliner south one stop from Los Angeles Union Station to Fullerton. Some Surfliner trains start at Santa Barbara or even as far north as San Luis Obispo. At Fullerton, transfer to Orange County Transit Authority (OCTA) bus 43, which drops you off at a major entrance to the Disneyland Resort.

Trains run roughly every hour, with a few additional Metrolink commuter rail trains mostly during rush hours; the bus runs every 15 minutes. The train ride takes 30–40 minutes, the bus 20–25, for a total trip of about 75 minutes with transfer time. A one-way adult ticket will set you back $9.50 plus $1.50 for the OCTA bus. It's preferable to transfer at Fullerton rather than Anaheim because there's more frequent bus service that gets a little closer to Disneyland itself. Fullerton also has a nicer waiting environment—a station in a town rather than a stadium parking lot.

If you really want to travel on the cheap from Downtown LA, take Metro's semi-express bus 460 from Downtown directly to Disneyland. It's about a 2-hour ride, but it will only cost you $2.90. Catch the bus on Fifth Street heading westbound or on Flower Street south of Fifth. The bus runs roughly every 30 minutes, slightly more often on Saturdays.

TRANSIT TO DISNEYLAND FROM SANTA MONICA AND THE WESTSIDE

There aren't any direct regular transit connections to Disneyland from the other main visitor areas of Los Angeles, but *from the Westside,* you can use the Disneyland Express if you're willing to pay the $20 fare. *From Santa Monica,* take Big Blue Bus 3 or rapid bus 3 to the City Bus Terminal at LAX, and then take the Lot C shuttle to the terminal. From there, take the Disneyland Express. *From Westwood,* take the Flyaway Westwood to LAX, and then take the Disneyland Express.

TRANSIT FROM LAGUNA BEACH

It's a two-bus proposition to travel between these two Orange County destinations. Go to the Laguna Beach Bus Station on Broadway inland of Beach Street. Bus 89 starts there. Ride about 30 minutes northward to the Laguna Hills Transit Center, tucked in the back of a shopping center. Transfer to bus 83, which starts here, and ride it about an hour northward to Katella Avenue and Harbor Boulevard, a few blocks south of the main Disneyland entrance. Bus 89 runs every 40 minutes; bus 83 runs every 30 minutes. Fare is $3 or $4 for the day pass.

FROM ELSEWHERE IN SOUTHERN CALIFORNIA

Connect through Union Station in Downtown Los Angeles and catch the Surfliner or Metrolink train to Fullerton. *From San Diego,* take the Surfliner north to Fullerton.

To get transit routings and times to Disneyland, including OCTA and the Pacific Surfliner, use Metro's Trip Planner at **metro.net.** You can get OCTA schedules at **octa.net.** For the Pacific Surfliner schedules, visit **amtrak.com.**

Seeing Disneyland

Disneyland is *the* Southern California tourist attraction. It is the most important destination in Southern California for the most visitors—the one place just about everyone has to go. Disneyland records an astounding 22 million admissions per year, or an average of almost 61,000 guests per day (exclusive of Downtown Disney). By contrast, Universal Studios logs a mere 5 million admissions per year, and SeaWorld a paltry 3.8 million. Disneyland retains its primacy despite being more than

COURTESY OF MATT PASANT

50 years old, roughly from the early Jurassic period in amusement park and theme park time.

The overall Disneyland site is now known as the Disneyland Resort and is divided into three parts—Disneyland Park, Disney California Adventure, and Downtown Disney. The "happiest place on earth," as the Disney folks call it, does not come cheap. The most basic ticket—a 1-day, one-park ticket—costs $80 for people age 10 and older, $74 for children ages 3–9 (children under age 3 are free). A 1-day Park Hopper ticket, allowing you to visit both Disneyland Park and Disney California Adventure, is $105 for age 10 and older and $99 for ages 3–9. A 2-day Park Hopper ticket will run you $173 for age 10 and older and $161 for ages 3–9. These are the online rates, and Disneyland prices are raised often; you may pay more on-site. Some discounts are available, particularly for Southern California residents (check the Disneyland website), but they're not widespread. More information is available at innumerable fan sites about the park, or visit **disneyland.com.**

DISNEYLAND PARK

The place formerly known as Disneyland, the "flagship" as Disney says. This is where the classic rides are—the Matterhorn Bobsleds, Space Mountain, and the Disneyland Railroad. It's where Disney's "lands" are—such as Frontierland and Tomorrowland. It's where Mickey Mouse and Minnie Mouse and other Disney characters roam the streets. Disneyland can get very crowded, with hour-long waits for rides, especially in summer, so it now has a Fastpass system. The system preassigns times to go on certain rides, so you'll have to spend less time waiting in line.

DISNEY CALIFORNIA ADVENTURE

This is a more recent addition, designed to present an entertaining take on California. You can take a simulated hang glider ride over Yosemite and the Golden Gate Bridge on Soarin' Over California. Grizzly River Run is based on a raft ride in the Sierra foothills. More postmodernist is the Walt Disney Imagineers Blue Sky Cellar, which aims to give parkgoers a glimpse of what Disney is coming up with next.

DOWNTOWN DISNEY

This area is a bit like Universal CityWalk in Universal City, but in Anaheim—a shopping, dining, and entertainment complex. It includes a House of Blues club, an ESPN Zone sports bar and restaurant, and a 12-screen movie theater. Downtown Disney lays outside the gates of the two theme parks, so you don't have to pay admission to get in.

OUTLET MALL: THE BLOCK AT ORANGE

Bargain hunters might want to tear themselves away from the rides and head over to the Block at Orange, an outlet mall that also has regular-price stores, located in the city of Orange. It has outlets from, among others, Guess, Nike, and Neiman Marcus. Visit **simon.com**.

Transit: Take Anaheim Resort Transit bus 15 to the Block at Orange (service runs every hour).

Where to Eat at or near Disneyland

The saying is that people don't go to Disneyland to eat, which is a good thing, because they'd be disappointed. Lots of eateries are in and around Disneyland, but few of them are going to win any culinary awards. You might want to bring some food with you to avoid paying Disneyland's price premium. As of this writing, they're pretty relaxed about people bringing food (but not about glass bottles), which is normally prohibited.

CATAL 1580 Disneyland Dr. in Disneyland; **patinagroup.com/catal** $$$$$ Part of the well-regarded Patina Group (as in Patina at Disney Hall in LA). It serves Mediterranean food.

LITTLE RED WAGON Main Street, U.S.A., Disneyland $ Corn dogs from this now-refurbished truck are possibly the most popular food item in Disneyland.

EL MOCTEZUMA #2 12531 Harbor Blvd., Garden Grove $ Oaxacan food in the heart of Orange County—a find. Take bus 43 south on Harbor to Lampson Avenue.

NAPA ROSE Grand Californian Hotel, 1600 S. Disneyland Dr. $$$$

Well-regarded restaurant inspired by Napa Valley cuisine (sorry about that, Santa Ynez, Paso Robles, and Temecula).

THAI NAKORN   12532 Garden Grove Blvd., Garden Grove; **thainakorn restaurant.com** $$ High-quality, affordable Thai. Take bus 43 south on Harbor to Garden Grove Boulevard, and walk east (left) a short distance.

Grocery Store near Disneyland

VONS   130 W. Lincoln Ave. between Harbor and Anaheim boulevards   Take bus 43 north to Lincoln Boulevard in Anaheim, and then walk 0.33 mile east.

Where to Stay in the Disneyland Area

The easiest thing for car-free travelers visiting Disneyland is to stay a night or two near Disneyland. Dozens of hotels and motels, in every price range, are clustered around Disneyland. In fact there are streets with virtually nothing but hotels, as Disney has fought off proposals for other kinds of buildings, such as apartments, in the area. Disney itself operates three hotels where you can get more of the Disneyland experience, if you feel it's worth the extra cost. Most hotels here are part of a hotel chain; some brands have more than one site near Disneyland. Hotels with a "Good Neighbor" agreement with Disney can sell tickets to Disneyland itself, which is convenient but doesn't usually get you a discount.

If you stay along Harbor Boulevard in the section between Katella Avenue on the south and Ball Road on the north, you'll be within reasonable walking distance of the park. The closest hotels and motels here are in fact closer to the park than the Disney hotels. Except for the Disney hotels, all the hotels listed below are on this section of Harbor Boulevard or immediately off Harbor on Katella Avenue. Be careful about claims from hotels on other streets that they're close to Disneyland; they may in fact be close to the wall of Disneyland but not near actual entrances.

AMERICA'S BEST VALUE INN   425 W. Katella Ave.; **valueinnanaheim.com** $ Part of a lesser-known budget chain, not to be confused with America's Best Inn nearby.

BEST WESTERN PARK PLACE INN 1544 S. Harbor Blvd.; **parkplaceinn andminisuites.com** $$ OK, it's not Boardwalk, but it's Park Place, the next best thing. There are six Best Westerns within 2 miles of Disneyland, but this one is closest to the park entrance. The hotel says it has a "no car discount," but it's not clear when it's actually available—ask about it.

CANDY CANE INN 1747 S. Harbor Blvd.; **candycaneinn.net** $$ Quality independent motel a short walk from the Disneyland main gate.

DISNEYLAND HOTEL 1150 Magic Way; **disneyland.com** $$$$$ The first Disneyland hotel, now modernized. On some days you can enter Disneyland early, ahead of the crowds, if you've paid for park admission. Packages of hotel plus park admission are available.

DISNEY'S GRAND CALIFORNIAN HOTEL 1600 S. Disneyland Dr.; **disneyland.com** $$$$$ Disney bills this hotel as California Mission style. It's the closest to the park of the three Disney hotels. On some days you can enter Disneyland early, ahead of the crowds, if you've paid for park admission. Packages of hotel plus park admission are available.

DISNEY'S PARADISE PIER HOTEL 1717 S. Disneyland Dr.; **disneyland.com** $$$$ Disney tells us that this hotel, complete with a statue of Goofy surfing, recaptures the heyday of California beachfront hotels, some 20 miles inland. It's not cheap, especially by Anaheim standards, but it is the cheapest of the three Disney hotels. It's also farther from the park itself. On some days you can enter Disneyland early, ahead of the crowds, if you've paid for park admission. Packages of hotel plus park admission are available.

FAIRFIELD INN ANAHEIM DISNEYLAND RESORT 1460 S. Harbor Blvd.; **marriott.com** $$ A mid-rise hotel, unusual for a Fairfield Inn. Some rooms, which cost a bit extra, are decorated on the theme of various Disney/Pixar movies (such as *Toy Story, Finding Nemo,* and so on).

HOLIDAY INN EXPRESS MAINGATE 435 W. Katella Ave.; **holiday-anaheim.com** $$ Reliable Holiday Inn for exhausted fun seekers.

HOTEL MENAGE 1221 S. Harbor Blvd.; **hotelmenage.com** $ The place for a modern boutique hotel near Disneyland; it's actually cheaper than many other area choices.

RAMADA MAINGATE 1650 S. Harbor Blvd.; **ramadamaingate.com** $$ Older motor inn very close to the Disneyland entrance, with a large pool your kids can play in.

RESIDENCE INN ANAHEIM MAINGATE 1700 S. Clementine St.; **marriott.com** $$–$$$ A good choice for families with children because many rooms have separate bedrooms.

SHERATON PARK HOTEL 1855 S. Harbor Blvd.; **starwoodhotels.com** $$$–$$$$ One of the fancier non-Disney hotels in the neighborhood.

SUPER 8 ANAHEIM 415 W. Katella Ave.; **super8.com** $ One of the cheapest decent motels in the Disneyland area.

■ 18 Laguna Beach

Fortune's Favored Place

THIS COMMUNITY ON THE ORANGE COUNTY GOLD COAST features beautiful beaches, tasteful hotels fronting the beaches, a lively and walkable downtown filled with good restaurants and bakeries, and even a bit of an art scene. The center of this little downtown gets a rare, perfect Walk Score of 100. (Walk Score rates how many stores and services it is possible to walk to from a given location. Anything over 70 is a good score; anything over 90 is a great score. See **walkscore.com.**)

This city, 50 miles southeast of Los Angeles, is the only one in Orange County to operate its own local bus system. But to get there from Los Angeles or San Diego usually requires a train and two buses.

Among Orange County's beach towns, Laguna Beach is the most walkable, one of the best for chowhounds, and historically the most gay-friendly. For a little place, there's a lot to see. Laguna Beach is now decidedly upscale, though a few vestiges of its earlier, more countercultural days linger. I think it's worth the effort to get there, but you have to be up for some serious transit. Because it takes some effort to get there, Laguna Beach really isn't reasonable for a day trip using transit.

Getting to Laguna Beach

FROM OUTSIDE SOUTHERN CALIFORNIA

You'll probably be reaching Laguna Beach from somewhere else in Southern California. But if you want to fly in directly from outside the region, John Wayne Orange County Airport, 15 miles away, is the airport of choice. LAX is 50 miles distant, while San Diego's airport is 75 miles away.

From John Wayne, take Orange County Transit Authority (OCTA) bus 76 to the Newport Transportation Center, the end of the line. Then take a southbound bus 1 to Laguna Beach. If you hit the transfer right, this could take as little as 45 minutes. The alternative is a SuperShuttle or other airport shared ride shuttle.

FROM SOUTHERN CALIFORNIA

From Downtown Los Angeles, from Union Station, take the Pacific Surfliner or Amtrak to Santa Ana station. Take OCTA bus 83 to Laguna Hills Transit Center at the back of a shopping mall, the end of the line. Take OCTA bus 89 to Laguna Beach bus station, the end of the line. Travel time is approximately 2.5 hours. *From elsewhere in Los Angeles,* connect through Union Station.

From Disneyland, take OCTA bus 83 from the main Disneyland stop to Laguna Hills Transit Center (full length of route). Take OCTA bus 89 to Laguna Hills bus station. Travel time is 1 hour, 50 minutes, or more, depending on wait time at Laguna Hills.

From downtown San Diego, take the Pacific Surfliner to San Juan Capistrano station, close to the Mission. Take OCTA bus 91 to Pacific Coast Highway and Del Obispo. Then take OCTA bus 1 northbound to Laguna Beach (multiple stops are in town, so use the one closest to your hotel).

■ LAGUNA BEACH TRANSIT WEBSITES ■

LAGUNA BEACH CITY BUS tinyurl.com/lagunabus	ORANGE COUNTY TRANSIT AUTHORITY octa.net
PACIFIC SURFLINER amtrak.net	REGIONAL TRIP PLANNER metro.net

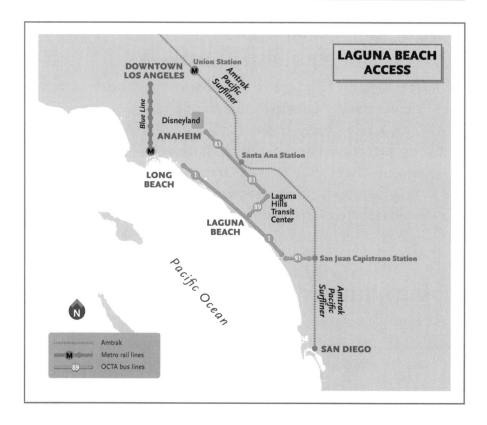

Bicycling

Bring your bike on the OCTA bus and bike in small, linear Laguna Beach. Unfortunately, only one road, busy Coast Highway (CA 1), really runs the length of town. To the north, once you get in Crystal Cove State Park, you will find bicycle and pedestrian trails.

★ BIKE SHOP IN LAGUNA BEACH ★

LAGUNA CYCLERY 240 Thalia St.; **lagunacycleryshop.blogspot.com**

Seeing Laguna Beach

Visit Laguna Beach to see the place itself—the ocean, the beach, and the lovely little town. Those are the main attractions here.

MAIN BEACH

The main draw in Laguna Beach is Main Beach, a sometimes wide, sometimes narrow stretch of sand that you can access from the foot of Broadway in downtown. A very busy playground is right at the entrance to the beach. A boardwalk hugs part of the beach, and you can also walk along the beach to access transportation that will take you to some of the motels south of downtown, where a fairly small cliff overlooks the beach. It's all very lovely.

LAGUNA BEACH ART SCENE

Laguna Beach has a history as an artsy town. The **Laguna Art Museum,** a small but worthwhile place at 307 Cliff Dr. just north of the downtown, has a permanent collection of California artists and changing exhibits. Galleries are across the street and scattered around town.

Laguna Beach also has a unique art activity—the **Pageant of the Masters.** People dress up to be live replicas of major paintings. Each year a theme for artworks to be reproduced is chosen—one year it was "Eat, drink, and be merry." People come through and present the "paintings," one after another, on a stage. A whole arts festival has grown up around this 80-year-old event. Why ask why? The pageant runs through most of July and August. It takes place at 650 Laguna Canyon Rd., a short walk east of the downtown, and tickets are $20–$100, depending on seating. Visit **foapom.com.**

Where to Eat in Laguna Beach

Laguna Beach is a good eating town, especially given its small size. It's not a hearth of authentic ethnic food, but lots of good American/ Californian choices can be found. All restaurants are within walking distance of central Laguna Beach hotels.

THE COTTAGE 308 N. Coast Hwy.; **thecottagerestaurant.com** $$ Longtime landmark across from the art museum; it's open every day of the year.

LAGUNA COFFEE 1050 S. Coast Hwy.; **lagunacoffeeco.com** $–$$ There are coffee places downtown (such as Anastasia Café on Ocean

Avenue, which shares space with a boutique), but Laguna Coffee is a hangout with artisanal coffee.

NIRVANA GRILL 303 Broadway St.; **nirvanagrille.com** $$$ Good California restaurant with lots of veggie choices on downtown's main street.

TACO LOCO 640 S. Coast Hwy.; **tacoloco.net** $ A real honest-to-goodness taqueria—with takeout and outside seating—in Laguna's tony confines.

ZINC CAFE & MARKET 350 Ocean Ave.; **zinccafe.com** $ A great breakfast gathering spot and a ladies-who-lunch location, this elegant but relatively affordable eatery, where you order at the counter, epitomizes Laguna Beach in my opinion. It's immediately next to the bus station.

Grocery Stores and Markets in Laguna Beach

PAVILIONS   600 N. Pacific Coast Hwy. at High Dr. Moderately upscale supermarket.

RALPH'S   700 S. Coast Hwy. at Cleo St.   The basic mid-range supermarket of SoCal.

WHOLE FOODS   283 Broadway   The natural foods behemoth.

ZINC CAFE & MARKET   350 Ocean Ave.   A gourmet market, not a comprehensive grocery. Also has a café.

■ CRYSTAL COVE STATE PARK'S ■ HOTLY SOUGHT-AFTER CABINS

THE TOUGHEST TICKET IN SOUTHERN CALIFORNIA isn't Hollywood's club of the hour or even the Pageant of the Masters—it's the cabins at Crystal Cove. Nestled in the state park near the beach, down the hill from the traffic of Pacific Coast Highway, the cabins could hardly be more idyllic. For years, a tenacious group of inholders clung to the cabins as a private possession, but eventually the state recovered them for visitor use. Cottages for one family range $180–$323. The dorm-style cabins have separate bedrooms with one to two beds, but share a kitchen, dining room, and bathrooms; they range $33–$167.

The Beachcomber Restaurant in Crystal Cove State Park, adjacent to the cabins, is much-loved for its location near the beach.

So here's what you do to have a *chance* of making a reservation. Pretend that you're buying a ticket for a megastar's rock concert. On the first of each month at 8 a.m. sharp, Pacific Time (that would be 11 a.m. on the East Coast and 4 p.m. in London), the cabins are opened for reservations for the seventh month ahead. For example, to reserve a cabin in December, you would reserve on June 1. Visit **reserveamerica.com,** under the Crystal Cove Beach Cottages section, and click furiously.

Get here by taking Orange County Transit Authority bus 1 to the 8471 North Coast Highway/El Morro stop (it can be tricky through here to get the right stop; ask the driver to tell you when you reach the shuttle into Crystal Cove Park). From there—the parking lot on the east side of the road—take the Beachcomber Restaurant's shuttle down into the park; the fare is $1.

Where to Stay in Laguna Beach

The hotels and motels of Laguna Beach are strung out along Coast Highway, mostly south of town, though some are north. They all have bus service from OCTA bus 1 and Laguna Beach's city bus in summer, but once you get very far from the town center, they lose their walkability to restaurants and stores. Laguna Beach is an expensive town in the summertime. Well-located lodgings include the following.

INN AT LAGUNA BEACH   211 N. Coast Hwy.; **innatlagunabeach.com** $$$$ This is the most central of the hotels, right by downtown. Enjoy a little breakfast on the upstairs deck. Be sure of what you're getting because rooms vary a lot in size, amenity, and degree of ocean view.

LAGUNA RIVIERA BEACH RESORT   825 S. Coast Hwy.; **lagunariviera.com** $$$–$$$$ In Laguna terms, a bargain property.

THE SURF AND SAND RESORT   1555 S. Coast Hwy.; **surfandsandresort. com** $$$$$ About a mile south of downtown, this is the most upscale hotel remotely within walking distance of downtown.

THE TIDES   460 N. Coast Hwy.; **tideslaguna.com** $$$ Nicely landscaped motor lodge–style property a bit north of downtown on the inland side of Coast Highway.

v. catalina

■ 19 Santa Catalina Island

Green Island

IN 1958 THE FOUR PREPS (NOW FORGOTTEN BUT VERY POPULAR in their day) sang about Catalina, the "island of romance" 26 miles—or, as they actually also said, 40 kilometers—across the sea (it's actually 22 miles or 35 kilometers, but who's counting).

It might have been Catalina Island's last moment as romantic, just as the Four Preps' barbershop singing style quickly fell from favor. Today's Catalina doesn't have the chic cachet of offshore East Coast islands such as Martha's Vineyard or Nantucket. For some reason, Catalina's reputation has been more down-market, as a day-tripper destination. But Catalina is actually a much greener, more ecological place than island destinations outside California, where one waits for the ferry for hours, often with one's idling car. Santa Catalina is really set up so you take a passenger-only ferry and then walk. Catalina seems to deserve a better reputation than it has.

Getting to Catalina

Almost everybody gets to Catalina by ferry. It is the only California island with a substantial permanent population but no road connection. Unless you own a boat, the only other access option is helicopter, which is both expensive and ecologically debilitating.

You can sail to Catalina from Long Beach, Marina del Rey, San Pedro, Newport Beach, or Dana Point. Long Beach has the two most convenient locations for car-free travelers. The ferries for car-free travelers are operated by Catalina Express (**catalinaexpress.com**), though the Marina del Rey service is operated by Catalina Ferries (**catalinaferries.com**).

The Long Beach dock—Catalina Landing at 370 Golden Shore Dr.—is served by the city's free Passport shuttle buses, a 7-minute ride from the Long Beach Transit Mall. There you can catch the Blue Line light rail to Downtown Los Angeles, as well as other Metro, Torrance Transit, and Long Beach Transit bus routes. The immediate surroundings of the ferry dock are rather odd—a little office park by the waterfront.

At the summer peak, eight trips per day go from Long Beach to Avalon, Catalina Island's only substantial town. The round-trip fare is $70, or $54 for children age 11 and younger. The trip is about an hour.

You could use the Marina del Rey dock if you were starting out on the Westside, rather than trekking into Downtown Los Angeles and then down to Long Beach and over to the dock. But the Marina del Rey site has limited transit—Culver City bus 7 once an hour along Culver Boulevard, Monday–Saturday, and Metro bus 108 across Slauson Avenue in South Los Angeles. You might want to spring for a cab for this, at least from Santa Monica or Venice, which you'd have to add to the $89 (or $64 for children age 11 and younger) round-trip fare to Avalon. Visit **catalinaferries.com.**

If you wanted to go from Laguna Beach to Catalina, the Catalina Express Dana Point site could work, though only one to two round-trips per day are made. Connect via OCTA bus 1, south from Laguna Beach.

TRANSIT ON CATALINA

Within the town of Avalon, the main way you get around is walking. You can walk from one end of town to the other in maybe 20 minutes, so it's not really a big deal. You can rent a golf cart for $40 an hour or so to see if you can pilot the thing, but you really don't need one in town and you're not allowed to take them out of town.

An Avalon trolley (open-air bus) runs every 35 minutes but without a set schedule; it's useful for getting up the hill to the botanical gardens and nature center. Visit **tinyurl.com/avalontrolley.**

Buses connect Avalon to interior points—they're priced like intercity buses, not local transit. One route goes to the hamlet of Two Harbors and to the (private planes only) Airport in the Sky. The Safari Bus to Two Harbors also serves the Black Jack and Little Harbor campgrounds, as well as Airport in the Sky between Avalon and Two Harbors, for back-packers who want to start from those points. The bus runs once a day in winter, twice a day in summer, but you need to make a reservation to assure that the bus will run. Fares from Avalon range from $10 (to the airport) to $33 (to Two Harbors). Use the Santa Catalina Island Company's website, **visitcatalinaisland.com** or call (310) 510-8368.

Seeing Catalina

Among the Channel Islands, the offshore group that stretches north toward Ventura, only Catalina has permanent human residents. Catalina is 75 square miles, but only a small portion of that area is inhabited, mostly in the square-mile incorporated town of Avalon. Avalon's permanent population is around 3,000. Most of the rest of the hilly island is conservation—or, more properly, rehabilitation land—with no towns. The Catalina Island Conservancy, set up by the island's one-time owner William Wrigley (the chewing gum magnate), owns a huge proportion of the island's land. The other main developed area is the tiny village of Two Harbors, with some 300 residents, near the northeastern end of Catalina.

So it's a big island, but a small destination, unless you want to head out into the backcountry (be sure to secure the proper permits). This configuration may seem a bit odd, but it actually makes Avalon very easy to visit.

TOWN OF AVALON

The town of Avalon, which sits next to the ferry dock, is made for strolling. The main stroll is Crescent Avenue, stretching out ahead of the dock. There's nothing really spectacular here, except the (non-gambling) casino at the end of the street. It's a pleasant, sunny, short walk from one end of town to the other. Crescent is lined with shops and restaurants; the streets behind have small street-front hotels and houses. There's no dominant architectural style, but most of the buildings predate World War II. The casino has some nice Art Deco tile work. It's a place to while away some hours.

AVALON CANYON NATURE CENTER

At the uphill end of developed Avalon, the Nature Center (1202 Avalon Canyon Rd.; **catalinaconservancy.org**) gives you a nice sense of what's going on with Catalina, describing the island's natural history and the efforts to restore its natural landscape. A trailhead and the botanic garden are just a little farther on. The trolley stops adjacent, or you can walk. It's a nice visitor-accessible location.

BEACHES

A series of small, sandy beaches is along the harbor front on Crescent Avenue on either side of the Pleasure Pier. This location makes me nervous as a swimming site—a lot of boat activities, including discharges of bilge, are right by there, and there have been problems in the past. Descanso Beach is in a more reassuring location a bit farther on, a short walk past the casino. If you want a cabana and chaise lounge there, it will set you back $50–$125. Catalina has other strengths than as a beach resort.

TOURS ON LAND

Many tours of Catalina are available, and you'll be solicited to take one as soon as you get off the boat. Probably the best-informed tours are the Jeep Eco Tours given by the Catalina Conservancy, which control 88% of the island. They're not cheap—a 2-hour tour is $65, and a 3-hour tour is $98. Visit **catalinaconservancy.org.**

TOURS ON WATER

The cheapest way to get a view of the water is on a glass-bottomed boat—you can see all the colorful and unique fish that hang around Catalina. For a 40-minute tour, adults pay \$18.50. You can also go for a dive or ride in a submersible boat. Many options are listed at **visitcatalinaisland.com.**

WRIGLEY BOTANICAL GARDEN

This 38-acre botanical garden, with many plants unique to Catalina Island, was initiated by Ada Wrigley, William Wrigley's widow. A memorial to William Wrigley is also on-site. It's about a mile up from the

COURTESY OF SANTA CATALINA ISLAND COMPANY

waterfront to the botanical gardens on Avalon Canyon Road just past the golf course and is open daily, 8 a.m.–5 p.m. Admission is $5 for adults, $3 for seniors age 60 and older, and children age 12 and younger are free. Visit **tinyurl.com/3hrbsd7.**

ZIP LINE

Board and alight at Descanso Beach. When I was a kid, I stayed at a place in the country that had a short zip line—we called it a space trolley. This has a series of five rides totaling 3,671 linear feet that take you from the interior of the island to the beach. It's a bit like open ski lifts: They take you out there, you zip line back, and they tell you about island history and nature (I guess that's the "eco" part). The total cost, with fees, is $92.50. People weighing more than 245 pounds— they will weigh you—and pregnant women are not permitted on the ride. It's fairly cool, actually, a fun way to see some of the island. Visit **visitcatalinaisland.com.**

Where to Eat on Catalina

Nobody's going to mistake Catalina for a foodie paradise. Too many places have the tourist trap mentality—we don't have to serve you good food at a good price because you're stuck here. Still, some decent establishments here can keep you fed on a short trip.

AVALON GRILLE   423 Crescent Ave.; **visitcatalinaisland.com** $$$–$$$$ It's almost never a good idea to eat in a place with superfluous Es in its name; they're trying to get cute. As in so many things, Catalina is an exception to this rule. The Avalon Grille is a step up from most of what exists on the island.

BUFFALO NICKEL   57 Pebbly Beach Rd.; **buffalonickelrestaurant.com** $$ Just outside the developed area of Avalon town, Buffalo Nickel runs a shuttle bus from the ferry dock to its soups, salads, burgers, and so on. The name refers to the herd of buffalo that a film crew left on Catalina Island, which are only now, decades later, being removed to their native habitat.

CASINO DOCK CAFÉ   On the dock at the casino; **casinodockcafe.com** $ Serving breakfast and lunch, burgers, dogs, and things. A fun place to watch the harbor and water.

CATALINA COUNTRY CLUB   1 Country Club Dr. off Tremont St.; **visit catalinaisland.com** $$$–$$$$$ American fine dining and cocktails at the top of the hill. Quite walkable, or you can take the Avalon Trolley on Friday or Saturday (when it runs in the evening). The facility was originally built by William Wrigley for the Chicago Cubs baseball team.

CONEY ISLAND WEST   215 Crescent Ave. near Whittley Ave.; **tinyurl.com/ coneywest** $ Avalon's not really like Coney Island, maybe more like Wildwood, New Jersey, but I digress. Coney Island West is a stand with outdoor seating selling burgers, fish-and-chips, fries, and the like.

SALLY'S WAFFLE SHOP   501 Crescent Ave. near Catalina Ave. and the Pleasure Pier $ A good place for waffles and breakfast food, such as chorizo scrambles.

Grocery Stores on Catalina

VONS   123 Metropole Ave.   A superette-size store about a block back from the Crescent Avenue waterfront, in a practical pocket across from a post office. Prices don't seem too bad.

VONS EXPRESS   117 Catalina Ave.   An even smaller store, even closer to the center of town, the size of a large of convenience store.

Where to Stay on Catalina

Most Catalina visitors are day-trippers who come for the day and don't stay overnight. Still, there's enough demand for Catalina's limited supply of hotel rooms to keep rates high in the summer. Many hotels have 2-night minimums on summer weekends. Summer rates are generally much higher than winter rates, so you'd be able to afford fancier hotels in the winter. Catalina hotels are small and independent. The Catalina Canyon Resort is unusually large at 170 rooms. Though it's changing, some of the hotels don't make reservations online, so you'll need to call or e-mail. The Visitors Guide lists 32 hotels and bed-and-breakfasts.

Most of the hotels are clustered on or near the Avalon waterfront and on or just off Crescent Avenue. A few interesting places are up in the hills.

AVALON HOTEL   124 Whitley Ave.; **theavalonhotel.com** $$$$–$$$$$ One of Catalina's more elegant hotels; a heavily reconstructed historic building.

CATALINA CANYON RESORT   888 Country Club Dr.; **catalinacanyon resort.com** $$–$$$ Up on the hill, it bills itself as Catalina's only full-service resort and conference hotel.

VILLA PORTOFINO HOTEL   111 Crescent Ave.; **hotelvillaportofino.com** $$–$$$$ Right in the heart of little Avalon town, facing the water.

ZANE GREY PUEBLO   199 Chimes Tower Rd.; **zanegreypueblohotel.com** $–$$$ This small hotel, decorated with a Southwestern theme, is the former home of famed Western writer Zane Grey. He chose well— the house is high on a hill with a lovely view of the hills and the harbor. The hotel offers free taxi service down the hill at preset times. Though it's not that long of a walk (the hotel says 7 minutes down, 15 minutes up), I wouldn't stay here unless you're a good climber.

vi. san diego

■ **20** Introduction to San Diego

Beaches, Beasts, Beer, and (downtown) Balconies

THE LOS ANGELES AND SAN DIEGO METROPOLITAN AREAS have almost, but not quite, merged. The southern end of metropolitan Los Angeles (San Clemente) almost touches the northern end of metropolitan San Diego (Oceanside). The only open space between them, ironically enough, is on the Camp Pendleton Marine Corps base. But though the two regions are almost one, San Diego is still a quite different place from Los Angeles.

Some would call San Diego a provincial city, in comparison to LA's world city. But San Diegans might say that their city is another thing entirely—a calmer, more relaxed place—a place for sun and swimming and surfing, as well as quaffing local brews. At the same time, San Diego has (re)built a lively, walkable downtown that LA is still working on.

San Diego is laid out quite differently from Los Angeles. In Los Angeles, most of the visitors' city —from Downtown LA to Santa Monica—is essentially one giant area, placed on one giant grid of streets with some interruptions. Not so in San Diego.

Like LA, the city of San Diego is geographically large—324 square miles, compared to Los Angeles's 469—though San Diego's population is only one-third of LA's. San Diego is also long—stretching some 30 miles north to south along the coast, from the poverty of San Ysidro along the Mexican border to the luxury of La Jolla. But no long streets, only the freeways, span this distance. San Diego is a post–World War II city, and 75% of its population growth has occurred since then. By that time American roadway building had moved on from boulevards to freeways. San Diego's neighborhoods are broken up by hills and canyons (and freeways), so the neighborhoods are usually easy to tell apart.

With its great natural harbor, San Diego might have seemed to be the logical place for Southern California's metropolis. But in the 19th century, Los Angeles was able to snag the all-important railroad connections, and then built itself an unnatural harbor with a substantial degree of federal funding. Though paved over today, Los Angeles also had a great salad bowl of farmland next to it, helping to fuel the city's growth. As a result, in 1940, on the eve of World War II, Los Angeles comprised 1.5 million people, while San Diego only had 200,000, not much more than Long Beach. But with the massive expansion of the Navy in the Pacific Ocean during World War II, San Diego would be more than 50% larger in 1950.

San Diego's outer edge is the ocean coast, and its most important internal edge is the harbor, 1 or 2 miles inland from the coast. San Diego's visitors' city is mostly close to the coast and the harbor. Many beachside neighborhoods—La Jolla, Pacific Beach and adjacent Mission Beach, Ocean Beach, and Coronado—are major visitor destinations. SeaWorld and Old Town are close to the water. Downtown runs inland from the harbor. Balboa Park, site of the famed San Diego Zoo, is north

TIP *Visit San Diego during the week. As a car-free traveler, you'll have a much easier time if you visit San Diego during the week. Transit service is much better Monday–Friday than it is on the weekend. Service is more frequent during the week, and some lines run shorter routes on Sunday. If you have weekend time in your trip, use it to visit other places, where there's much less difference between weekday and weekend service. It's not always possible to arrange a trip this way, but if you can do it, you'll be happier for it.*

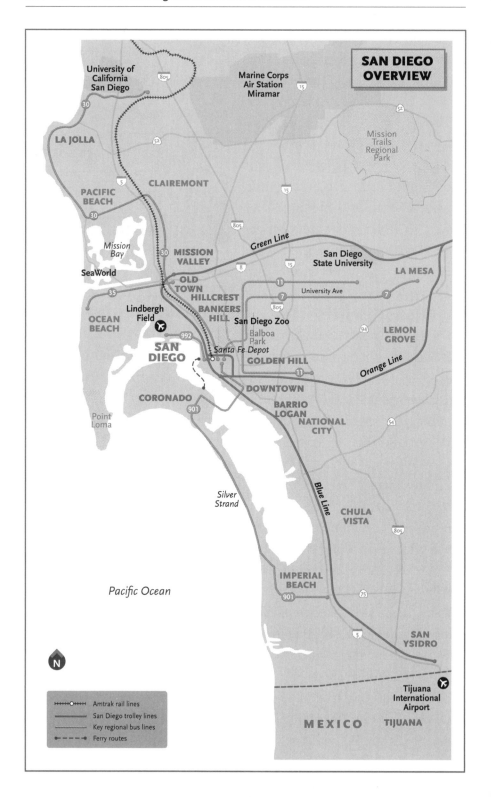

of downtown. Qualcomm Stadium, where the Chargers play football, is an outlier 10 miles inland.

SAN DIEGO FROM DOWNTOWN OUTWARD

In San Diego you can orient yourself from downtown. Downtown has the most hotels, and it is the hub of the transit network, so it is the most convenient place for transit-based visitors to stay. Downtown San Diego is described in Chapter 21, San Diego's beaches are described in Chapter 22, and other places in San Diego are described in Chapter 23. Moving out from downtown San Diego, **Balboa Park** is northeast of downtown. It's roughly 2 square miles and full of cultural and recreational activities such as museums and the zoo (and, alas, full of freeways). The **Bankers Hill** district is due north of downtown and west of Balboa Park, and its streets lead up to **Hillcrest,** center of San Diego's gay community and one of the liveliest areas in the city. Core Chicano community **Barrio Logan** is southeast of downtown, and the reviving **Golden Hill** district is to the east past a light industrial area.

You can go directly south of downtown by ferry, which takes you to **Coronado.** Coronado is a long peninsula with family-oriented beaches and a naval base at its northern end, across the harbor from downtown San Diego. There are no roads or passenger transport going due west across the harbor; going northwest quickly leads you to Lindbergh Field Airport.

This is as far out as you will likely want to go in several directions. North of Hillcrest, transit becomes limited and the roads lead to the auto-oriented hotels of Hotel Circle and shopping centers in the Mission Valley. To the southeast, you will see Navy bases, industrial zones, and residential neighborhoods, along with some budget motels in Chula Vista. Going farther east leads to more inland neighborhoods. However to the northeast, across Balboa Park, is **North Park,** rapidly developing as a restaurant and bar area. You might go farther south along Coronado to beach parks on the Silver Strand, which stretches for miles south from Coronado's main area.

A number of destinations are to the northwest. Beyond the airport is **Old Town,** a major historic attraction, transit hub, and hotel location. Farther in that general direction is the famed **SeaWorld** marine amusement park and the **Mission Beach** and **Pacific Beach** oceanfront neighborhoods. While Mission Beach has few lodgings, numerous hotels and motels are on and near the beachfront in Pacific Beach. Still farther along the coastal route is the elegant ocean-side community of **La Jolla,** at the northern end of the city of San Diego.

Attractive coastal towns and some undeveloped beachfront continue north from La Jolla for almost 30 miles through north San Diego County. **Del Mar** is one of the most exclusive. **Carlsbad** is a major resort community and home to **Legoland,** and **Oceanside** is a beachfront town with a strong connection to adjacent Camp Pendleton, the Marine Corps base.

Eating in San Diego

San Diego is not the culinary giant that Los Angeles is, but your eating options here are getting better, and you'll get a lot less attitude. San

COURTESY OF METROPOLITAN TRANSIT SYSTEM

■ A WORD ABOUT VISITING TIJUANA ■

Unfortunately, that word is, at least for now, *don't*. For the last few years, Tijuana has been one of a handful of Mexican cities that has been engulfed by drug-related violence. Thousands of people have been killed there. For the most part, this endemic murder happens away from tourist-oriented neighborhoods and from tourists, but not always. Until the situation stabilizes, going there is not a good idea.

Diego has an enormous number of Mexican food options and is the American home of the fish taco.

The geography of dining is manageable for the car-free traveler. Downtown San Diego—from Little Italy to the East Village—is definitely the most important area, with the largest number of restaurants and bars. Downtown is particularly prominent among fine-dining restaurants. Hillcrest, roughly 2 miles north of downtown San Diego along several decent bus lines, is another major restaurant area. North Park, some 2 miles east of Hillcrest and 4 miles northeast of downtown—has emerged as a lively eating zone. North Park is served by two of the city's better bus lines. La Jolla village—another prime eating area—is rather far unless you're staying around there.

Your eating options, unfortunately, are somewhat constrained by the time of day and day of week limitations of the transit system. During the day, during the week—for breakfast and lunch Monday–Friday—transit will surely get you there. But bus service is less frequent at night and on the weekends, usually no more often than every 30 minutes. You can get around on this schedule, but it may involve some significant waits.

What to do? Here are some strategies for getting to and from dinner and weekend meals:

1. Eat dinner and weekend meals in the area in which you're staying and walk back to your hotel.

2. Eat dinner and weekend meals along a line that has relatively frequent service. The Blue Line trolley runs every 15 minutes, 7 days a week; the other trolleys run every 15 minutes Monday–Saturday. Bus 7, via Park Boulevard and University Avenue through North Park, runs every 15 minutes on Saturday and every 20 minutes on Sunday.

3. Be very aware of when your bus comes. Perhaps even let the restaurant know when you need to leave to catch it.

4. In the evening, take the bus there and take a cab back.

■ 21 Transit and Getting around in San Diego

San Diego's Transit System

SAN DIEGO'S TRANSIT SYSTEM IS SIMPLE AND BASIC. It will get you where you want to go. The people who say that you can't visit San Diego without a car are, once again, incorrect. It's actually quite a pleasant (if not necessarily rapid) experience, riding the plush buses of San Diego with their polite, helpful drivers through the landscaped streets. In San Diego, walking will probably be as important to your visit here as riding transit, especially if you stay downtown. But as in Los Angeles, most visitors won't want to walk the miles between neighborhoods. You can in effect walk to Coronado from downtown by walking to the Broadway pier at the west end of downtown, taking a short ferry ride, and then walking the mile or so to the main area of Coronado.

The good news about the San Diego transit system's simplicity is that it's not confusing; it's easy to figure out which line you're supposed to take. But there's also little choice of routes or the types of service that you'd find in Los Angeles. For the most part, San Diego runs the trolley and local buses only; a few rush-hour express buses are designed for commuters. The network of lines is also thinner in San Diego.

San Diego's transit has been seriously eroded by recent cuts. The result is a system that is pretty good during the week during the day, adequate on weeknights and on Saturday, and skeletal on Sunday. The system shuts down completely midnight–5 a.m. A few routes end a bit later or start a bit earlier, but you will have to hail a cab or take a hike at 2 a.m.

Transit in San Diego County is operated as a single system, with essentially a single-fare structure, throughout the county. There are two main bus operators—the Metropolitan Transit System (MTS) and the North County Transit District.

THE STRUCTURE OF TRANSIT

San Diego's transit system—at least the part of the system important to visitors—is based on the main routes radiating out from downtown. These are the trolley lines and about two dozen bus routes. Most of the bus routes are regular on street routes serving the central neighborhoods of the city.

Downtown bus routes cover most of the areas within about 10 miles. The Point Loma peninsula is an unfortunate exception. Other bus routes extend farther out, starting at the main transit centers along the trolley lines. Some of the key transit centers are Old Town Transit Center, 12th and Imperial Transit Center (at the southeast edge of downtown), and the Euclid Avenue Trolley Station in southeast San Diego. A few crosstown routes outside of downtown make a sort of grid of routes, but for the most part they're not in visitor-oriented areas.

Unlike Los Angeles, most San Diego bus routes don't follow a single street for miles and miles. This is mostly because San Diego doesn't have that many streets that run for miles and miles—streets get interrupted by hills, canyons, and other features. Bus routes instead go in a general direction—bus 30 goes northwest of downtown, bus 11 goes northeast of downtown, and bus 923 runs essentially west of downtown as much as possible. University Avenue and El Cajon Boulevard, running east-west a couple of miles north of downtown, are exceptions; long bus routes serve those two streets.

THE SAN DIEGO TROLLEY: WHERE IT GOES AND WHERE IT DOESN'T

San Diego is famed for its trolley, which was the first light rail system built in the U.S. after World War II. The three-line, 54-station trolley has a north-south route (the Blue Line), a route east from downtown (the Orange Line), and a route east from Old Town through Mission Valley (the Green Line), which eventually meets the Orange Line.

The San Diego Trolley serves some useful destinations for visitors—notably in downtown, at Old Town, Qualcomm Stadium, and the San Diego Mission. It's moderately comfortable, pleasant enough, and pretty quick, once it clears downtown San Diego. But the trolley does not serve any of the beach communities, Balboa Park or the zoo, or SeaWorld. For any of those destinations and others, you must take the bus.

BUS ROUTES

The Regional Transit Map (available online at **511sd.org**) lists about 120 bus lines over the length of San Diego County, from Oceanside to San Ysidro. But most visitors will use no more than 10% of the routes.

Helpfully, most of the system's most important bus lines have the lowest route numbers, 1–15. Many of these lines start in downtown San Diego or pass through downtown. Most of the lines operate on Broadway downtown, in at least part of the segment of Broadway from Pacific Highway to 11th Avenue, the city's transit spine.

SAN DIEGO SERVICE BY DAY AND TIME

San Diego's transit service varies even more than usual by time of day and day of week.

■ *San Diego Service on Weekday Evenings*

Lines that run every 15 minutes during the day are generally cut back to every 30 or 60 minutes at night. The Blue Line Trolley has 15-minute service in the early evening. Routes typically run until roughly midnight, though each route has a somewhat different schedule. Service resumes around 5 a.m. Line 30 to La Jolla has its route cut back in the evening—instead

■ DOWNTOWN BUSES ■

San Diego has about two dozen bus routes that run relatively frequently—every 15 minutes or more often—during the day on weekdays. Most, though not at all, of these routes radiate out from downtown San Diego. To reach major visitor-oriented destinations, use the following lines from downtown. You can board all of these lines, except bus 11, on Broadway; bus 11 crosses Broadway at First Avenue. Each route runs on a slightly different segment of Broadway, but most are on the street between Front Street (just west of First Avenue) and Ninth Avenue.

To Balboa Park and the San Diego Zoo: Bus 7 via Park Blvd.

To Hillcrest: Bus 3 via Fourth and Fifth Ave., or bus 11 via First Ave.

To North Park: Bus 2 via 30th St. or Bus 7 via University Ave.

To Pacific Beach: Bus 30 via Old Town (starts at Old Town nights and weekends)

To La Jolla: Bus 30 via Old Town and Pacific Beach and La Jolla Blvd.

To Ocean Beach: Bus 923 (does not operate on Sunday)

To Coronado: Bus 901 via the 12th and Imperial Transit Center

To the Airport: Bus 992 via Harbor Dr.

To Old Town: Blue Line Trolley

of starting in downtown San Diego, it starts at Old Town Transit Center (take the Blue Line Trolley from downtown to connect).

■ *San Diego Service on Saturdays*

On Saturdays, buses generally run the same routes as during the week, just less frequently. The major routes run approximately 5 a.m.–midnight, typically every 30 minutes, on their full routes. A few routes, notably bus 30, have their routes cut back on Saturday. Bus 923 doesn't go all the way from Ocean Beach to downtown but instead ends at the airport, where you can connect to bus 992 to downtown. The trolley lines operate every 15 minutes on Saturday, as does bus 7; bus 2 operates every 20 minutes.

■ *San Diego Service on Sundays*

Service is significantly shortened on Sunday. It's very possible that you'll have to transfer more and walk farther. Most lines run every 30 minutes on Sunday, including the Green Line and Orange Line trolleys. The only lines with more frequent Sunday service are the Blue Line Trolley and bus 7.

To Ocean Beach: Bus 923 from downtown to Ocean Beach does not operate on Sunday. Bus 35 from Old Town to Ocean Beach is cut back to Newport Avenue, and there's no bus service on any line south of there.

To Hillcrest: There's no service on bus 11 from downtown to Hillcrest and Normal Heights via First Avenue and Adams Avenue. Bus 3 to Hillcrest also doesn't run on Sunday; the only service is provided by bus 120, which is an express other days but makes local stops on Sundays.

To Pacific Beach and La Jolla: Bus 30 is truncated to Old Town Transit Center, as it is on nights and Saturdays.

To Coronado: Bus 901 to Coronado starts at the 12th and Imperial Transit Center, instead of starting in downtown San Diego. It runs once every 60 minutes.

FARES AND PASSES

If you plan to travel out of your hotel's neighborhood, you will probably want to buy a day pass or a pass for multiple days. The basic trolley fare is $2.50; the basic bus fare is $2.25. You pay each time you board a vehicle, and there are no transfers, except from one trolley to another.

But day passes cost only $5, so you break even on a round-trip. The 2-day passes are $9, 3-day passes are $12, and 4-day passes are $15, which are even cheaper on a daily basis. These are good for 2, 3, or 4 consecutive days of service, including the day you buy it. You can buy all of these passes on the bus, though you'll need the exact amount, or, perhaps more conveniently, you can buy them at a ticket machine at a trolley station. The passes are also good on the North County system, should you venture up there. There are no weekly passes.

TRANSIT INFORMATION

Online information about transit in San Diego is a bit tricky to obtain because there are three main websites. Transit 511 (**transit.511sd.com**) covers the whole regional system. The Metropolitan Transit System (**sdmts. com**) seems easier to use. The MTS site has the Trip Planner, which gives you transit directions from your starting point to your destination. The MTS Trip Planner, unlike Metro's, can give you walk directions and distances to the first transit stop and from the last one. It has some good search features, such as a "Popular Places" tab that provides live links to the bus routes serving key destinations, such as the zoo. The website also has an updated regional transit map.

Finally, there's a separate website for the North County Transit District, which most car-free visitors won't need because it's so hard to get to North County in the first place.

The best place to get printed maps and timetables for San Diego transit is MTS's Transit Store at 102 Broadway at First Avenue in downtown San Diego, open 9 a.m.–5 p.m., Monday–Friday. You can also buy passes and transit souvenirs there. Santa Fe Station, the Amtrak station, also has timetables available, and they are often, though not always, available on the bus itself. The Google Transit Trip Planner is also available for San Diego at **google.com/transit**.

San Diego MTS doesn't offer its own applications for mobile devices, but a commercial app called TransitGuru provides the information for iPhone and iPad users. MTS is making its information available to application developers, so more apps may appear in the future.

English- and Spanish-speaking transit information specialists are available daily at (619) 233-3004 from 5:30 a.m.–8:30 p.m. on weekdays and 7 a.m.–7 p.m. on weekends and most holidays. Dial 511 for 24-hour information.

The level of information at transit stops varies significantly. On Broadway in downtown, big signs spell out which routes to which destinations stop there at which times. Some of the trolley stations, notably the key transfer point of Old Town, have pretty good signs too. Some bus stops have a board posted that lists the time each bus stopping there will arrive. Other stops have nothing. In general, the more central stops seem better equipped with information.

Bicycling

Coastal San Diego's mild, dry weather is good for biking; it can get extremely hot in the summer farther inland. San Diego traffic volumes are generally lower than Los Angeles's, making it safer for cyclists. The scale of San Diego is much more manageable for cyclists—a 5-mile ride from downtown will get you to most destinations, though Pacific Beach and especially La Jolla are farther.

The city has developed a substantial network of bikeways, but much of it serves more suburban sections less useful to visitors. A well-developed set of paths and bike lanes go from downtown to Ocean Beach and North Park. To Old Town and Hillcrest, it's mostly just bike routes with signs. San Diego bicyclists must also get over freeways and canyons and around (or over) hills to reach their destination. Cycling doesn't seem as death-defying here as in LA, but it has its challenges. This guidebook has no religious test, but I can't help mentioning one unusual San Diego bicycle club—the Christian bicycle group Outspokin' for Jesus (**outspokin4jesus.com**). Visit **www.icommutesd.com/ Bike/BikeMap.aspx** for a bikeway map for most of San Diego.

BICYCLES ON TRANSIT

Bikes are permitted on all transit vehicles at all times. Buses have front racks that hold two bicycles. Trolleys allow one bike per car during rush hours—enter the car through the last door. Two bikes per car are allowed other times. Simply stand with your bike on the trolley. Bikes plus transit can be a powerful combination in San Diego. The train or bus can get you past hills, canyons, waterways, freeways, railways, military bases, and other barriers. The bike gets you the last mile from a somewhat thin transit network to your actual destination. Using a bike on San Diego transit is routine, not difficult.

Taxis

Taxis are not a major transport mode in San Diego, but you may find them useful, especially at night. Within the downtown area, distances are short and conducive to taxi use. Even between some areas, distances produce reasonable fares, given San Diego's lower-than-average rates. The cost is $4.50 for the first mile, plus $2.20 for each additional mile (plus tips). So if you want to take a cab back downtown after pigging out at The Linkery in North Park, about a 4-mile trip, it would cost roughly $11 plus tip. Three miles in from Hillcrest to downtown would be about $9, plus tip. In general, cabs aren't hailed in San Diego but are called or picked up at taxi stands, but it is legal for a cab to stop in a no-stopping zone. Just don't try to use a cab for the 33-mile jaunt from downtown San Diego to the Safari Park, or you'll be out about $100 and howling yourself!

■ 22 Downtown San Diego

IF YOU COME IN FROM SUBURBAN SAN DIEGO, downtown can come as a surprise. In a city that treasures, indeed demands, open vistas and low buildings, downtown San Diego is a high-rise and high-density island, compact and walkable. It is a place scaled for pedestrians in a city dominated by wide, fast roads. Of course, San Diego's promoters trumpet the 55,000 parking spaces in downtown, so it's not exactly a car-free zone. That's easily enough space to house 55,000 people instead of 55,000 cars.

Still, with the support of redevelopment funds (after they stopped using them to demolish the old downtown), downtown has retained and reinforced its role as a true center in a sprawling, low-density city. The historic buildings of the Gaslamp Quarter, a section of downtown, were retained, even as their former residents (or denizens, some would say) were forced to move elsewhere.

Not so long ago, much of downtown was given over to sailors looking for a good time, but, for better or worse, redevelopment has made the tattoo shops, billiard parlors, and dive bars pretty much disappear (where do today's sailors go for a good time?). Now downtown San Diego is an office core, an urban residential neighborhood (or a series of them), and a decidedly more upscale urban playland.

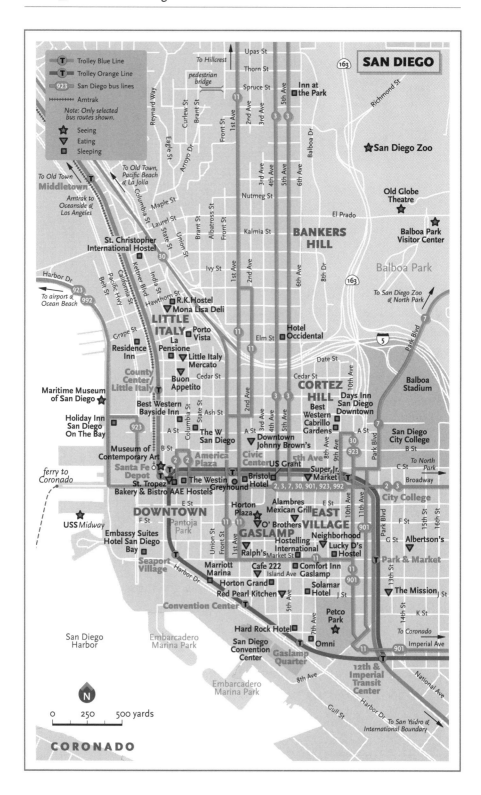

Map legend:

- T Trolley Blue Line
- T Trolley Orange Line
- 923 San Diego bus lines
- Amtrak

Note: Only selected
bus routes shown.

- ☆ Seeing
- ▽ Eating
- ◻ Sleeping

SAN DIEGO

To Hillcrest

Upas St
Thorn St
Spruce St
pedestrian bridge

Inn at
the Park

163

Richmond St

Reynard Way
Eagle St
Curfew St
Brant St
Front St
1st Ave
2nd Ave
3rd Ave
5th Ave
Balboa Dr

☆San Diego Zoo

To Old Town,
Pacific Beach
& La Jolla

To Old Town
Middletown

Amtrak to
Oceanside &
Los Angeles

Arroyo Dr
Columbia St
Maple St
Laurel St
State St
Union St
Brant St
Albatross St
Front St

Nutmeg St

3rd Ave
4th Ave
5th Ave
6th Ave

Kalmia St

**BANKERS
HILL**

Old Globe
Theatre
☆

El Prado

☆
Balboa Park
Visitor Center

St. Christopher
International Hostel

Ivy St

1st Ave
2nd Ave

6th Ave
8th Dr

Balboa Park

Harbor Dr
Pacific Hwy
Belt St
California St
Ketner Blvd
India St
Hawthorn St

163

To San Diego Zoo
& North Park

To airport &
Ocean Beach

923
992

R.K.Hostel
▽Mona Lisa Deli

**LITTLE
ITALY** ▽Porto
Vista

La
Pensione

Hotel
Elm St ◻ Occidental

Park Blvd

7

5

Grape St

Residence
Inn

▽Little Italy
Mercato

Date St

Cedar St
10th Ave

Balboa
Stadium

County
Center/
Little Italy

Buon
Appetito

Cedar St

**CORTEZ
HILL**

Maritime Museum
of San Diego ☆

Best Western
Bayside Inn

Ash St

Days Inn
San Diego

Best
Western
Cabrillo
Gardens

7

Holiday Inn
San Diego
On The Bay

923

The W
San Diego

Downtown
Johnny Brown's

San Diego
City College

B St

Museum of
Contemporary Art

B St

2nd Ave
3rd Ave
4th Ave
5th Ave
8th Ave
9th Ave

30
923

Park Blvd

To North
Park

ferry to
Coronado

Santa Fe
Depot

America
Plaza

Civic
Center

US Grant

Super Jr.
Market

C St

St. Tropez
Bakery & Bistro AAE Hostels

The Westin
Greyhound

Bristol
Hotel

2, 3, 7, 30, 901, 923, 992

Broadway

E St

Alambres
E St

City College

☆
USS Midway

DOWNTOWN

F St
Pantoja
Park

Horton
Plaza ☆

Mexican Grill

**EAST
VILLAGE**

10th Ave
11th Ave

Park Blvd

13th St
15th St
16th St

F St

901

Embassy Suites
Hotel San Diego
Bay

Union St
Front St
1st Ave

O' Brothers
GASLAMP

Ralph's Market St

Hostelling
International
Lucky D's

Neighborhood
◻ Hostel

G St Albertson's
▽

Seaport
Village

Harbor Dr

Marriott
Marina

Cafe 222
Island Ave

Comfort Inn
Gaslamp

T Park & Market

901

Horton Grand

13th St

Red Pearl Kitchen ▽

Solamar
Hotel J St

▽ The Mission J St

Convention Center T

5th Ave

Petco
Park
☆

14th St
K St

San Diego
Harbor

Embarcadero
Marina Park

Hard Rock Hotel

San Diego
Convention
Center

Gaslamp
Quarter

7th Ave
8th Ave

T Omni

To Coronado

Imperial Ave

901

12th &
Imperial
Transit
Center

National Ave

Embarcadero
Marina Park

Gull St

Harbor Dr

To San Ysidro &
International Boundary

N

0   250   500 yards

CORONADO

In LA, few visitors focus just on the downtown. But it's common enough for a couple days in San Diego, where downtown has museums, the baseball stadium, a major shopping center, and the largest cluster of fine-dining restaurants in the city. The San Diego Zoo is nearby. What downtown doesn't have are beaches; it has a harbor-based waterfront. Aquariums and theme parks are widely scattered around the region, and moderate-priced and ethnic restaurants are largely found outside of downtown.

Downtown is mostly a good walking environment, so while you're there, you don't have worry so much about the city's limited transit service. From the northwestern side of downtown in Little Italy to the southeastern side near Petco Park is about a 2-mile, or 40-minute, walk. The Orange Line and Blue Line trolleys also have 11 stations in the downtown, providing frequent service (except on Sundays) for local trips. I provide transit directions, but remember that within downtown you can easily walk to most destinations.

One of the pleasures of downtown San Diego is its diverse sections. You can walk along the waterfront and see boats—big boats and little boats, old boats and new ones. The west end of Broadway features glass box office towers. The Gaslamp Quarter is a moderate-scale Victorian district, physically a bit like what LA destroyed on Bunker Hill. The harbor down here is lined with mega-hotels and mega–convention center buildings. You can head east into the East Village (apparently every city needs an East Village nowadays) and look at the new condos competing for buyers. Up toward City College you'll find remnants of the old downtown San Diego, low-cost residential hotels, and liquor stores. The grand restored pile of the El Cortez Apartments (once a hotel) beckons from the top of Cortez Hill, even if there isn't much right around it (yet). The attractions are great, but visiting downtown San Diego is also about seeing the place itself.

It's easy to find your way around downtown San Diego. It's pretty much a perfect grid of streets. The east-west streets in the main part of downtown are lettered from A to L, north to south, with Broadway taking the place of D Street, Market Street taking the place of H, and Island

---

★ BIKE SHOPS IN DOWNTOWN SAN DIEGO ★

THE BIKE REVOLUTION 522 Sixth Ave., Gaslamp Quarter; **sandiegobiketoursinc.com**
Also has bike tours.

PENNYFARTHING'S BICYCLES 630 C St.; **pennyfarthingsbicycles.sdcausa.com**

SAN DIEGO BIKE SHOP 619 C St.; **sdbikeshop.com**

Avenue taking the place of I Street. The east-west streets in the northern part of downtown are alphabetically named after trees (Ash, Beech, Cedar, and so on) going south to north. One quirk of addresses: from First Avenue east, addresses have no direction designation (that is, it's simply 300 Broadway). But addresses west of First Avenue are designated west—so there is a 300 West Broadway but no 300 East Broadway.

The north-south streets covering most of the downtown are numbered from First Avenue to 11th Avenue, with Park Boulevard taking the place of 12th. On the west side of downtown, the north-south streets are named with no discernible pattern. Most downtown San Diego streets don't extend much past the downtown, unlike Los Angeles, where many downtown streets radiate out into the city for miles.

Seeing Downtown San Diego

GASLAMP QUARTER

Fourth Ave. to Sixth Ave. and Broadway to Harbor Dr.; **gaslamp.org**

THE GASLAMP IS SAN DIEGO'S SURVIVING VICTORIAN-ERA DISTRICT. Once an eating, drinking, and, uh, personal recreation quarter for dissolute sailors, the Gaslamp is now an eating and drinking quarter for middle-class San Diegans.

The Gaslamp is also noteworthy for copious architectural documentation—nearly every building has a plaque carefully relating the building's history. Some of the plaques have been around so long that they're getting historic and worn themselves. In the Gaslamp, traffic speeds and volumes are carefully controlled; the quarter is planned to be a pedestrian-friendly place.

The Gaslamp is officially mapped as going all the way to the southern edge of downtown at Harbor Drive. But the southernmost blocks mostly have new buildings, albeit with Gaslamp-style uses such as the Hard Rock Hotel.

Transit: *From Old Town,* take the Blue Line Trolley to Fifth Avenue Station, and then walk south one block on Fifth Avenue to Broadway, the beginning of the Gaslamp Quarter.

HORTON PLAZA

Bounded by E St., G St., First Ave., and Fourth Ave.; **westfield.com/hortonplaza**

SOME SAY THAT THIS POSTMODERN 1985 shopping center designed by John Jerde was the first to be built explicitly as an entertainment site (the Rouse folks at Baltimore Inner Harbor might contest that). In any event, the Horton Plaza is a five-level confection of diagonal escalators, Day-Glo colors, uneven heights, and whimsical ornamentation. It doesn't look anything like the Victorian-era Gaslamp Quarter next to it, and yet there's a shared attitude, an exuberance of architectural play. The mall itself becomes a major attraction, while most malls want your eyes only on the merchandise. Not so exuberant were the poor down-towners displaced by the mall's construction, pushed farther east and away from the center of downtown. Some also argue that the mall is too walled off from commercial streets outside and that it helps stores there less than it should.

If you want to shop here, you'll find Macy's, Nordstrom, and a raft of national brand stores such as Banana Republic, Coach, and Levi's.

Transit: *From Old Town,* take the Blue Line Trolley to Civic Center, and then walk two blocks south to Horton Plaza. *From Fifth Avenue station,* walk two blocks south to E Street and then one block west to Fourth Avenue.

MARITIME MUSEUM OF SAN DIEGO

1492 N. Harbor Dr. at Ash St.; **sdmaritime.org**

■ Daily, 9 a.m.–8 p.m.

■ Adults, $14; seniors and active military, $11; children ages 6–17, $8. Packages with San Diego Bay cruises also available.

THE MARITIME MUSEUM IS GENUINELY SPECIAL. It has a collection of a half dozen historic ships and two historically accurate replicas of sailing ships (they're building a third now). The *Star of India,* built in 1860, is the world's oldest active sailing ship. The museum also has a San Francisco Bay ferry (the *Berkeley*), harbor boats, and submarines. And sometimes guest ships come to call. You can board and explore all these boats or browse exhibits on topics such as the Navy in San Diego and the technology of charting the sea. There is no museum like this anywhere else in California.

Transit: *From Old Town,* take the Blue Line Trolley to County Center/Little Italy, and then walk one block west on Beech Street and one block west on the pedestrian path, which continues Beech Street to Harbor Drive, and then walk one block south. *From Fifth Avenue station,* take the Blue Line Trolley four stations (toward Old Town) to County Center/Little Italy station, and then follow the directions from Old Town.

MUSEUM OF CONTEMPORARY ART SAN DIEGO (DOWNTOWN)

1100 and 1001 Kettner Blvd. between Broadway and B St.; **mcasd.org**

■ Thursday–Tuesday, 11 a.m.–5 p.m.

■ Adults, $10; students age 26 and older and seniors, $5; students age 25 and younger and military, free. Admission is valid at both the downtown and the La Jolla locations for 7 days.

YOU MAY NOT THINK OF SAN DIEGO as an art capital, but the Museum of Contemporary Art San Diego (MCASD) has long been a sophisticated exhibitor of art made since 1950. MCASD is particularly noteworthy for its interest in contemporary art from Tijuana and Mexico, often neglected in the American art world. The museum is adjacent to Santa Fe Depot (Amtrak); one museum building was the former Santa Fe baggage depot. And kudos for a good transit page on the website.

Transit: *From Old Town,* take the Blue Line Trolley to Santa Fe Depot, and walk through the depot to Kettner Boulevard. *From Fifth Avenue station,* walk south to Broadway, west to Kettner Boulevard, and one block north to the museum (0.7 mile total), or take the Blue Line Trolley two stops to Americas Plaza station and cross Kettner Boulevard.

PETCO PARK

100 Park Blvd.; **mlb.com/sd/ballpark**

PETCO PARK IS THE HOME FIELD of the San Diego Padres Major League Baseball (MLB) team. MLB teams have been moving downtown—in Baltimore, San Francisco, and even Houston. Some stadiums have attracted not only bars and restaurants but also hotels and even new condos around them, despite their noise and traffic. San Diego's Petco Park has been one of the most successful at both fitting into and building up its neighborhood, even if the Padres have rarely excelled on the field.

Transit: *From Old Town,* take the Blue Line Trolley to 12th and Imperial station, and walk two blocks west on Imperial Avenue to the ballpark. *From Fifth Avenue station,* walk south on Fifth Avenue to K Street, and then walk two blocks east on K Street (total walk 0.7 mile), or take the Blue Line Trolley (toward San Ysidro) or Orange Line Trolley three stations (toward Gillespie) to 12th and Imperial station, and walk two blocks west.

USS *MIDWAY*

910 N. Harbor Dr. at E St.; **midway.org**

▨ Daily, 10 a.m.–5 p.m.; last admission at 4 p.m.

▨ Adults, $18; seniors and students, $15; retired military and children ages 6–17, $10

DOWN HARBOR DRIVE ABOUT 0.5 MILE from the Maritime Museum is the USS *Midway,* the longest-serving American aircraft carrier of the 20th century. The massive ship is almost 1,000 feet long, longer than any skyscraper in California. Launched in 1945, it was used during various Cold War crises, the Vietnam War, and Operation Desert Storm (the first Iraq War). You can go see many parts of the ship, such as the engine room, and 25 planes from various eras, planes like those once flown from the ship. Whatever you may think of the history of American wars, it's undeniable that the Navy has been a central institution in the life of San Diego.

Transit: *From Old Town,* take Blue Line Trolley to Santa Fe Depot, and then walk two blocks west on Broadway and one block south on Harbor Drive. *From Fifth Avenue station,* walk west on Broadway and south one block on Harbor Drive (total walk 0.9 mile), or take Blue Line Trolley (toward Old Town) or

COURTESY OF DENIS DESMOND/METROPOLITAN TRANSIT SYSTEM

Orange Line Trolley (toward 12th and Imperial) to Americas Plaza station, and then walk two blocks west on Broadway and one block south on Harbor Drive.

BALBOA PARK

Balboa Park (**balboapark.org**) is a 1,200-acre (almost 2 square miles) "urban cultural park," as its promoters describe it, on the northeastern edge of downtown San Diego. The park is bounded by Sixth Avenue on the west, 28th Street on the east, Russ Boulevard on the south, and Upas Street on the north. It was originally 1,400 acres, but numerous military, educational, and roadway facilities have reduced its size. It feels to me more like a series of spaces than a single unified park both because of its hills and canyons and because a freeway runs right up the middle of it.

The park was developed for the 1915–16 Panama-California Exposition, though it had existed before. It is known less as a place for outdoor recreation than as a place for cultured recreation. Balboa Park is a product of the City Beautiful–era notion that cultured outdoor recreation is uplifting. It's the home of 15 museums, the Old Globe Theatre, and the San Diego Zoo. A Japanese garden and a network of trails cover areas of the park. The park is also a venue for summer festivals. The Balboa Park Visitors Center is along El Prado in the 1915 House of Hospitality.

■ *Museums*

Along El Prado, a street that's mostly pedestrian, you can visit more than a dozen mostly small museums, with subjects ranging from European old master paintings to San Diego sports champions. The museums are separate with separate admissions. But if you're a real culture vulture, you can buy a Stay for the Day pass, which will admit you to five of the museums on the same day for $35. There are rotating free admissions on Tuesdays for San Diego city and county residents, as well as for active duty military and their families. Transit: To find your way to and through the central part of the park, visit **balboapark. org** and click on "Maps." *From Old Town,* take bus number 10 to University Avenue and Park Boulevard, and then take bus number 7 to

Park Boulevard and Village Place. Walk west a short distance on Village Place to El Prado. *From Fifth Avenue Trolley station,* walk one block south to Fifth Avenue and Broadway, and take bus number 7 to Park Boulevard and Village Place.

■ San Diego Zoo

The zoo of zoos, with pandas, polar bears, elephants, and lots of endangered species. It's one of San Diego's top attractions with more than 4,000 animals of 800 species, as well as a botanical garden within the zoo. Admission for adults is $37; for children under age 12, it's $27. Two-day tickets are also available. Visit **sandiegozoo.org.** Transit: *From Old Town,* take bus 10 to University Avenue and Park Boulevard, and then take bus number 7 to Park Boulevard and Zoo Place, and walk west on Zoo Place past zoo parking lots. *From Fifth Avenue Trolley station,* walk one block south to Fifth Avenue and Broadway, and take bus number 7 to Park Boulevard and Zoo Place.

■ Old Globe Theatre

The Old Globe is a three-stage regional theater, especially known for a theater modeled after Shakespeare's Old Globe and for its productions of Shakespeare. For the schedule, see **theoldglobe.org.** Transit: See directions on the previous page for museums.

SAN DIEGO MUSIC AND THEATER

San Diego's scene doesn't rival LA's, but check the *San Diego Reader,* free in news boxes or at **sandiegoreader.com.**

Where to Eat in Downtown San Diego

ALAMBRES MEXICAN GRILL   756 Fifth Ave. near F St., Gaslamp Quarter $ Mexico City–style sit-down Mexican restaurant, not a taco shop. Transit: *From Old Town,* take the Blue Line Trolley to Fifth Avenue station, and then walk three blocks south.

BUON APPETITO   1609 India St. near Cedar St.; **buonappetito.signon sandiego.com** $$$ Trattoria in the Little Italy section of downtown. Though the neighborhood is pretty yuppie now, the food is good in this sister restaurant to Hillcrest's Arrivederci. Transit: *From Old Town*, take the Blue Line Trolley to County Center/Little Italy Station, and then walk two blocks east on Cedar Street. *From Fifth Avenue station*, take the Blue Line Trolley (toward Old Town) to County Center/Little Italy.

CAFE 222 222 Island Ave. near Third Ave.; **cafe222.com** $ A popular, pleasant breakfast and lunch spot in a modern long-term stay hotel south of Horton Plaza. Expect waits on the weekend. Transit: *From Old Town*, take the Blue Line Trolley to Civic Center station, and then walk one block east to Fourth Avenue, then south to Island Avenue, and then two blocks west (total walk 0.6 mile or slightly more than 10 minutes). *From Fifth Avenue station*, walk south to Island Avenue, and then three blocks west (total walk 0.6 mile or slightly more than 10 minutes).

DOWNTOWN JOHNNY BROWN'S 1220 Third Ave. in the Civic Center Concourse; **downtownjohnnybrowns.com** $ Cavelike spot notable for a good selection of local San Diego brews. Transit: *From Old Town*, take Blue Line Trolley to Civic Center station, and then walk just north to Third Avenue. *From Fifth Avenue station*, walk two blocks west to Third Avenue and then just north.

MARYJANE'S COFFEESHOP 207 Fifth Ave. at L St. in the Hard Rock Hotel; **hardrockhotelsd.com** $$ You expect a decadent, expensive diner from the hotel spin-off of the Hard Rock Cafes, and you get it. Transit: *From Old Town*, take Blue Line Trolley to Americas Plaza. Then cross the track and transfer to Orange Line Trolley (toward 12th and Imperial) to Gaslamp Quarter; the hotel is immediately north. *From Fifth Avenue station*, walk south to L Street (walk is 0.7 mile, less than 15 minutes) or take Orange Line Trolley (toward 12th and Imperial) to Gaslamp Quarter station; the hotel is immediately north.

THE MISSION 1250 J St. near 13th St., East Village; **themissionsd.com** $ It's hard to know if *mission* here refers to outpost or cause. The Mission serves "simple, healthy, tasty" food crossed with "Chino-Latino" cuisine for breakfast and lunch in an old house. It's good. Also in North Park and Mission Beach. Transit: *From Old Town*, take the Blue Line Trolley to Park and Market station, and then walk two blocks south on Park

22. Downtown San Diego

Boulevard and walk one block east on J Street. *From Fifth Avenue station,* walk south on Fifth Avenue to J Street, and then east to 13th Street (0.9-mile walk or approximately 20 minutes). Or take the Blue Line Trolley (toward San Ysidro) or Orange Line Trolley (toward Gillespie) to Park and Market station, and then walk two blocks south on Park and one block east on J Street.

NEIGHBORHOOD   777 G St. at Eighth Ave.; **neighborhoodsd.com** $$ Trendy but friendly dining spot in a new building in the East Village; it's also noted for numerous local brews. Transit: *From Old Town,* take the Blue Line Trolley to Fifth Avenue station, and walk four blocks south on Sixth Avenue, and then two blocks east on G Street.

O'BROTHERS   188 Horton Plaza; **obrothersburgers.com** $ O for *organic,* presumably, this rare non-chain Horton Plaza eatery serves organic burgers, organic beers, and other organic foods. Transit: *From Old Town,* take the Blue Line Trolley to Civic Center station, and walk two blocks south on Third Avenue. *From Fifth Avenue station,* walk two blocks south on Fifth Avenue and then one block west on E Street.

RED PEARL KITCHEN   440 J St. at Fifth Ave.; **redpearlkitchen.com** $$$ High-style pan-Asian restaurant in what was once the Chinatown section of the Gaslamp Quarter. Also in Hollywood and Huntington Beach. Transit: *From Old Town,* take the Blue Line Trolley to Fifth Avenue station, and walk south on Fifth Avenue to J Street (0.6-mile walk, slightly more than 10 minutes), or take the Blue Line Trolley to Americas Plaza, and transfer to the Orange Line Trolley to Convention Center, and then walk three blocks east on J Street.

ST. TROPEZ BAKERY & BISTRO   926 Broadway Cir., Horton Plaza, and 600 W. Broadway, Ste. 130, Little Italy; **sttropezbistro.com** $$ Small local chain serving high-quality French-inspired salads, sandwiches, and pastries for breakfast, lunch, and dinner, usable as a coffee house. The Little Italy location is conveniently across the street from Santa Fe Depot and the Museum of Contemporary Art. Also in Hillcrest. Transit: For Horton Plaza, see directions for O'Brothers above. For Little Italy, *from Old Town,* take the Blue Line Trolley to Americas Plaza; St. Tropez is adjacent to the station. *From Fifth Avenue station,* walk one block south to Broadway and then west to Kettner Boulevard (total walk 0.6 mile, or a little more than 10 minutes).

Grocery Stores and Markets in Downtown San Diego

ALBERTSON'S   655 14th St. at G St.   Lower-priced supermarket at the eastern end of downtown. Transit: *From Old Town,* take the Blue Line Trolley to Park and Market station, and then walk one block north on Park to G Street and two blocks east. *From Fifth Avenue station,* take the Blue Line Trolley (toward San Ysidro) or Orange Line Trolley (toward Gillespie) to Park and Market station.

LITTLE ITALY MERCATO (FARMERS MARKET)   India and Date streets Saturday mornings, year-round. Transit: *From Old Town,* take the Blue Line Trolley to County Center/Little Italy station, walk two blocks east on Cedar Street to India Street, and then one block north on India to Date. *From Fifth Avenue station,* take the Blue Line Trolley (toward Old Town) to County Center/Little Italy station (walking distance is approximately 1 mile).

MONA LISA DELI AND ITALIAN RESTAURANT   2061 India St. near Hawthorne St., Little Italy   The real deal for Italian cheese, sandwiches, desserts, and wine. Transit: *From Old Town,* take the Blue Line Trolley to County Center/Little Italy, and then walk two blocks east on Cedar Street to India Street, and then four blocks north to Hawthorne Street. *From Fifth Avenue station,* take the Blue Line Trolley (toward Old Town) to County Center/Little Italy station.

RALPH'S   101 G. St. at First Ave.   This is pretty much a normal supermarket, complete with large underground parking area, but it's notable as one of the first modern downtown supermarkets in California. It's essentially behind Horton Plaza. Transit: *From Old Town,* take the Blue Line Trolley to Civic Center, and then walk one block south on Second Avenue, one block west on Broadway, and three blocks south on First Avenue. *From Fifth Avenue station,* walk four blocks south on Fifth

Avenue to G Street, and then four blocks west on G Street (total walk 0.5 mile or about 10 minutes).

SPECIALTY PRODUCE   1929 Hancock St.   These wholesale distributors of organic and other produce are open to the public 8 a.m.–4 p.m. daily. They're not downtown but in a light industrial district just a few blocks north of the Washington Street Trolley Station, therefore easily accessible to both downtown and Old Town. Transit: *From Old Town*, take the Blue Line Trolley one stop to Washington Street. Walk east across tracks one block to Hancock Street, and walk north two blocks. The public entrance to the store is on the northwest side of the building. Walk down the driveway all the way to the fence by the train tracks, and then go up the steps to the left at the back of the building. *From Fifth Avenue station*, take the Blue Line Trolley (toward Old Town) to Washington Street station.

SUPER JR. MARKET   1036 Seventh Ave. near C St.   It's barely the size of a superette, but it has an incredible selection of beers; it's the place to go to buy San Diego–produced beer. Transit: *From Old Town*, take the Blue Line Trolley to Fifth Avenue, and then walk two blocks east on C Street to Seventh Avenue.

Where to Stay in Downtown San Diego

Much more than in LA, San Diego's best and most interesting hotels cluster strongly in downtown, though plenty of others are throughout the city. Downtown hotels are not on the beach, however. For beachside hotels, look in the next chapter under Coronado, Pacific Beach, La Jolla, or Oceanside. There are some budget hotels in downtown San Diego, and Old Town is a transit-accessible area with cheaper hotels and motels. Avoid Hotel Circle—though it has lots of cheap hotels and motels, transit access is very poor.

Hotels are listed by the subareas of downtown. Several chains have multiple locations in San Diego, so make sure that you've picked out the right one, or your transit access could suffer greatly.

For transit access to hotels, the primary points of arrival are listed— the airport, Santa Fe Station (Amtrak), and Greyhound as the transit start points. Santa Fe Station and Greyhound are also potential start points from locations within downtown. Amtrak is located in the Santa Fe Depot at 1250 Kettner Blvd. at Broadway, at the western end of downtown San Diego. Greyhound is located at 400 W. Broadway at Front Street, in the heart of downtown San Diego.

HOTELS IN LITTLE ITALY AND NEARBY

BEST WESTERN BAYSIDE INN   555 W. Ash St. at Columbia St.; **baysideinn. com** $$–$$$ Decent mid-rise hotel at the edge of Little Italy and the downtown core. Transit: *From the airport,* take bus 992 to Broadway and Columbia Street, and then walk four blocks north to Ash Street. *From Amtrak,* walk three blocks north on Kettner Boulevard and then two blocks east on Ash Street. *From Greyhound,* walk four blocks west on Broadway to Columbia Street, and then four blocks north to Ash Street (total walk is 0.5 mile or about 10 minutes).

LA PENSIONE   606 W. Date St.; **lapensionehotel.com** $ This is, in my honest opinion, a great budget hotel. It's ideally situated on the Little Italy India Street commercial strip, close to the trolley and downtown. A café and a restaurant are downstairs. Rooms are clean and functional but small, fitting two people at most. There's no air-conditioning—just cool breezes off the harbor. And you might hear a freight rail line sometimes. Transit: *From the airport,* take bus 992 to Broadway and Kettner Boulevard, and then walk one block east on Broadway to India Street and seven blocks north (total walk 0.6 mile or slightly more than 10 minutes). This walk is also the walk from Amtrak. *From Greyhound,* walk five blocks west on Broadway, and then walk seven blocks north on India Street (total walk 0.7 mile or about 15 minutes).

PORTO VISTA   1835 Columbia St. at Fir St.; **portovistasd.com** $$–$$$ A recently renovated and upgraded motel with outdoor corridors at the growing edge of Little Italy. Their courtesy shuttle could be really useful. There's potential for train and trolley noise. Glass Door restaurant is on the fourth floor. Transit: *From the airport,* take bus 992 to Harbor Drive and Hawthorn Street, walk six blocks east on Hawthorn Street, and then walk three blocks south on Columbia Street (total walk 0.5

mile or approximately 10 minutes). *From Amtrak,* walk north three blocks on Kettner Boulevard, then walk east two blocks on Ash Street, and then walk north five blocks on Columbia Street (total walk 0.7 mile or approximately 15 minutes). There's no good transit alternative available. *From Greyhound,* walk four blocks west on Broadway and then nine blocks north on Columbia Street (total walk 0.8 mile, slightly more than 15 minutes).

HOTELS NEAR THE HARBORFRONT

EMBASSY SUITES HOTEL SAN DIEGO BAY   601 Pacific Hwy. at Harbor Dr.; **embassysuites.com** $$$$ Large convention-area hotel with family-oriented suites. Transit: *From the airport,* take bus 992 to Broadway and Pacific Highway, and then walk south three blocks. *From Amtrak,* walk one block west on Broadway, and then three blocks south on Pacific Highway. *From Greyhound,* walk west six blocks to Kettner Boulevard and then south four blocks to Harbor Drive. Then walk west one block (total walk is 0.7 mile or approximately 15 minutes).

HOLIDAY INN SAN DIEGO ON THE BAY   1355 N. Harbor Dr. south of Ash St.; **hisandiegoonthebay.com** $$ This well-situated high-rise Holiday Inn across Harbor Drive from the Bayfront operates a courtesy shuttle. Transit: *From the airport,* take bus 992 to Broadway and Pacific Drive, and then walk one block north. This is the same walk as from Amtrak. *From Greyhound,* walk west to Harbor Drive and then one block north (total walk 0.7 mile, approximately 15 minutes).

MARRIOTT MARINA SAN DIEGO   333 W. Harbor Dr. at Front St.; **marriott.com** $$$$ Massive high-rise adjacent to the Convention Center. Transit: *From the airport,* take bus 992 to Broadway and First Avenue, and then walk six blocks south (0.5-mile walk, approximately 10 minutes). *From Amtrak,* walk four blocks south on Kettner Boulevard, and then 0.3 mile southeast on Harbor Drive (0.6 mile total or slightly more than 10 minutes). Or take the Orange Line Trolley (toward Gillespie) from Americas Plaza to Convention Center station and cross Harbor Drive. *From Greyhound,* walk six blocks south on Front Street (0.5 mile, approximately 10-minute walk).

RESIDENCE INN SAN DIEGO DOWNTOWN   1747 Pacific Hwy. north of Cedar St.; **marriott.com** $$$–$$$$ The Residence Inn is a suites hotel a few blocks north of the downtown core, a few blocks west of Little Italy. Transit: *From the airport,* take bus 992 to Harbor Drive and Hawthorn Street; walk two blocks east to Pacific Highway and then two blocks south. *From Amtrak,* walk three blocks north on Kettner Boulevard, two blocks west on Ash Street, and then three blocks north on Pacific Highway (0.6 mile, slightly more than 10 minutes). *From Greyhound,* walk one block east on Broadway and one block north on Second Avenue to the Civic Center Trolley Station. Take the Blue Line Trolley to County Center/Little Italy Station. Walk one block west on Cedar Street and one block north on Pacific Highway.

HOTELS IN THE DOWNTOWN CORE

The Downtown Core hotels are all within easy walking distance of Greyhound and Amtrak, which are 0.5 mile or less distance from the hotels.

BRISTOL HOTEL   1055 First Ave. at C St.; **greystonehotels.com/bristol** $$ It is relatively cheap, central, and reasonably attractive, and it has free Internet in the lobby. It doesn't have much of a view, though, because neighboring buildings are taller. Transit: *From the airport,* take bus 992 to Broadway and First Avenue, and then walk one block north to the hotel.

US GRANT   326 Broadway at Fourth Ave.; **usgrant.net** $$$$ This 270-room hotel must be San Diego's grandest, with a chandelier-bedecked lobby. It's extremely central to downtown San Diego—Horton Plaza is essentially across the street. The hotel dates back to 1910 when it was undoubtedly far less grand. A grill, a lounge, and lobby bar service provide food and drink. Transit: *From the airport,* take bus 992 to Broadway and Fifth Avenue, and walk one block west.

W SAN DIEGO   421 W. B St. at State St.; **starwoodhotels.com** $$$–$$$$ The San Diego outpost of the trendy chain, with cheaper rates than in other cities. Transit: *From the airport,* take bus 992 to Broadway and State Street, and walk two blocks north.

WESTIN SAN DIEGO 400 W. Broadway at Columbia St.; **starwood hotels.com** $$$ Business-oriented high-rise hotel in the very core of downtown. Transit: *From the airport,* take bus 992 to Broadway and State Street, and walk one block west.

HOTELS IN THE GASLAMP QUARTER AND NEARBY

COMFORT INN GASLAMP 660 G St. at Seventh Ave.; **comfortinn gaslamp.com** $$ Relatively affordable choice close to attractions but slightly away from the pricey precincts of the Gaslamp. Transit: *From the airport,* take bus 992 to Broadway and Seventh Avenue, and then walk three blocks south. *From Amtrak,* walk south three blocks on Kettner Boulevard, and then east to Seventh Avenue (total walk 0.9 mile, approximately 20 minutes). Alternatively, take bus 2 from Broadway and Kettner (across Broadway from Amtrak station) to Broadway and Seventh Avenue, and then walk three blocks south. *From Greyhound,* walk three blocks south on First Avenue, and then walk six blocks east on G Street (total walk 0.5 mile, approximately 10 minutes).

HARD ROCK HOTEL 207 Fifth Ave. at L St.; **hardrockhotelsd.com** $$$–$$$$ Aren't hotels mostly for sleep? Maybe not for hard rockers. This brand-new high-style property at the growing southern edge of the Gaslamp near the Convention Center is trying to out-W the W. And it has a restaurant, a diner, a bar, and poolside cocktails. Transit: *From the airport,* take bus 992 to Broadway and Fifth Avenue, and then walk 0.6 mile south to the hotel. *From Amtrak,* take the Orange Line Trolley southbound to Gaslamp Quarter station; the hotel is adjacent to the station. *From Greyhound,* walk six blocks south to Harbor Drive, and then two blocks southeast to hotel, or walk one block north to C Street and one block east to Civic Center trolley station, and take the Orange Line Trolley southbound to Gaslamp Quarter trolley station.

HORTON GRAND 311 Island Ave.; **hortongrand.com** $$–$$$ Several buildings were assembled together to create this 132-room Victorian-style hotel. Great for history buffs—maybe not so great for little kids who might break things. Transit: *From the airport,* take bus 992 to Broadway and

Fourth Avenue, walk five blocks south on Fourth Avenue, and then walk one block west on Island Avenue. *From Amtrak,* walk three blocks south of Kettner Boulevard, one block southeast on the path next to the trolley tracks, seven blocks east on Market Street, and then one block south to hotel on Third Avenue (total walk 0.8 mile, slightly more than 15 minutes). Or take the Orange Line Trolley southbound from Americas Plaza Trolley station—across Kettner Boulevard from depot—to Convention Center station, and then walk one block north on First Avenue and two blocks east on Island Avenue. *From Greyhound,* walk five blocks south on First Avenue, and then two blocks east on Island Avenue (total walk 0.5 mile).

OMNI   675 L St. at Seventh Ave.; **omnihotels.com** $$$$ The Omni has an upper-level walkway into Petco Park. How cool is that? The Omni delivers good customer service, attractive if unexciting rooms, and a location close to the Convention Center and East Village restaurants. Seafood chain McCormick & Schmick is the hotel restaurant. Transit: *From the airport,* take bus 992 to Broadway and Kettner Boulevard. Transfer to the Orange Line Trolley southbound at Americas Plaza station, ride three stops southbound to Gaslamp Quarter station, and walk one block east on L Street to the hotel. *From Amtrak,* take the Orange Line Trolley southbound at Americas Plaza station; see directions above. *From Greyhound,* walk six blocks south to Harbor Drive, then two blocks southeast to L Street, and then two blocks east to the hotel (total walk 0.9 mile, approximately 20 minutes walk), or walk one block north to C Street and one block east to Civic Center Trolley station, and take the Orange Line Trolley southbound to Gaslamp Quarter trolley station.

SOLAMAR HOTEL (KIMPTON)   435 Sixth Ave. at J St.; **hotelsolamar.com** $$$–$$$$ Another brand-new south Gaslamp property, this one from Kimpton, the national mass marketers of urban trendiness. Rooms are pleasant, new, and clean. Ask if your room faces the giant projection screen in the bar area if you don't want to watch it all evening. Dining options include Jsix restaurant and a poolside bar. The land is owned by the Sycuan band of the Kumeyaay (Native American) nation. Transit: *From the airport,* take bus 992 to Broadway and Fifth Avenue, and walk seven blocks to J Street, then one block east (walk is 0.5 mile or approximately 10 minutes). *From Amtrak,* take the Orange Line Trolley (toward 12th and Imperial) to Convention Center station, and then walk two blocks east on J Street. *From Greyhound,* walk south four blocks to Market Street, walk east one block to Second Avenue, walk south three blocks to J Street, and then walk east two blocks (total walk 0.7 mile or approximately 15 minutes). Alternatively, walk one block west to Front Street, take bus 11 south to Market Street and Third Avenue, walk one block south on Third Avenue, and then walk two blocks east on J Street.

HOTELS IN CORTEZ HILL

These two motor inns are one block from each other, so the same transit directions apply for both. *From the airport,* take MTS bus 992 to Broadway and Eighth Avenue, and walk three blocks north to A Street or four blocks north to Ash Street and turn right—the hotels will be on those blocks. *From Amtrak,* the walk is 0.9 mile. Walk east on Broadway to Ninth Avenue, and then north on Ninth Avenue three blocks to A Street or four blocks to Ash Street. Or take the trolley from Americas Plaza station (across Kettner Boulevard from Amtrak) two stops to Fifth Avenue—take the Blue Line toward San Ysidro or the Orange Line toward Gillespie. Then walk three blocks east on C Street to Eighth Avenue, and then north on Eighth Avenue two blocks to A Street or three blocks to Ash Street and turn right. *From Greyhound,* walk 0.6 mile— east on Broadway, north on Eighth Avenue, and then right on A Street or Ash Street. There is no convenient transit alternative for this trip.

BEST WESTERN CABRILLO GARDENS 840 A St. at Ninth Ave.; **best western.com** $$ Best Western has two properties in downtown San Diego and many around the city. This one is the cheaper, low-rise motor inn on Cortez Hill, in the northeast section of downtown San Diego. There's not a lot right there, but a short walk will get you anywhere in downtown.

DAYS INN SAN DIEGO DOWNTOWN 833 Ash St. at Ninth Ave.; **daysinn.com** $$ Also a Cortez Hill motor inn; a block farther north from Broadway than the Comfort Inn.

HOTELS IN BANKERS HILL

HOTEL OCCIDENTAL 410 Elm St.; **hoteloccidental-sandiego.com** $
At the downtown end of Bankers Hill. The "European"-style Occidental
is going for the young, hip, but not moneyed crowd, with some rooms
(not all) sharing bathrooms. The Occidental has free beach cruiser bicycles, which many car-free travelers might like for Balboa Park and downtown. Transit: *From the airport,* take bus 992 and either ride to Broadway
and Fourth Avenue and then walk 0.6 mile north to Elm Street, or ride
to Broadway and Fifth Avenue and transfer to bus 3, which you will
ride to Elm Street, and walk one block west. *From Amtrak,* walk 1 mile
total—east on Broadway, then north on Fourth Avenue to the hotel at
Elm. Alternatively, at Americas Plaza station, across Kettner Boulevard,
take the Orange Line Trolley northbound or the Blue Line Trolley southbound (they're on the same platform) two stops to Fifth Avenue station,
and then take bus 3 to Elm Street and walk one block west. *From Greyhound,* walk 0.8 mile total, north on First Avenue to Elm Street, and
then east on Elm to Fourth Avenue, or take bus 11 on First Avenue north
to Elm Street, and then walk three blocks east.

INN AT THE PARK (formerly known as the Park Manor Hotel) 525 Spruce
St. at Fifth Ave.; **shellhospitality.com/hotels/inn_at_the_park** $$ The
Inn at the Park is an older, restored hotel with large rooms. It's located
a bit north of downtown in the Bankers Hill district, partway to Hill-
crest. The rooms are large and not air-conditioned. Rooftop gay happy
hours are held on Friday afternoon. If you want a hotel that gives you
the feeling of a staying in a city neighborhood, this is one of San Diego's
best choices. Transit: *From the airport,* take bus 992 to Broadway and
Fifth Avenue, and then take bus 3 north to Fifth Avenue and Redwood
Street. Walk one block north. *From Amtrak,* take the Blue Line Trolley
(toward San Ysidro) to Fifth Avenue station, and then take bus 3 north
to Fifth Avenue and Redwood Street, and walk one block north. *From
Greyhound,* walk east to Fifth Avenue and Broadway, and take bus 3 to
Fifth Avenue and Redwood Street.

HOSTELS

AAE HOSTELS 500 W. Broadway, downtown; **aaehotels.com** Rooms are $22.50–$29; private rooms are available.

HOSTELLING INTERNATIONAL DOWNTOWN SAN DIEGO 521 Market St., Gaslamp Quarter; **sandiegohostels.org** Rooms are $25–$31; private rooms are available. Very centrally located and can get noisy. Hostelling International is an international nonprofit.

LUCKY D'S HOSTEL 615 Eighth Ave. at Market St., East Village; **luckyds hostel.com** Rooms are $20–$25; private rooms are available. Hosts a pub crawl.

R.K. HOSTEL 642 W. Hawthorn St. at Columbia St., Little Italy; **rkhostel.com** Rooms are $23–$28; private rooms are available. At the north end of Little Italy. It's close to the freeway, so noise could be an issue.

ST. CHRISTOPHER INTERNATIONAL HOSTEL 2420 India St. at Kalmia St., Little Italy; **hostelworld.com** Rooms are $25–$28. On the edge of Little Italy.

■ **23** San Diego Beaches

MANY PEOPLE COME TO SAN DIEGO not for the downtown life, not for the animal parks, and not even for the beer (imagine). They come for the beaches. San Diego County boasts miles of Pacific Ocean beaches, most of them (at least after some "management") wide, sandy, and tranquil. All beaches in California are public below the mean high-tide line, but sometimes there are problems getting access to the beach. Most of San Diego's beaches are part of state or local parks, so pedestrian access to the beach is rarely a problem.

Transit access to San Diego beaches is another story. The San Diego Trolley doesn't go to the beach, nor are there any plans to extend it there. Bus service to the beach is spotty. Pacific Beach and La Jolla get a bus from downtown every 15 minutes during the day on weekdays, but at night and on weekends, the two have no direct service to downtown San Diego. Parts of Mission Beach are beyond easy walking distance to a bus stop. Ocean Beach has no direct service to downtown on Sundays, though there is a bus to Old Town Transit Center. Coronado also loses its direct bus service on Sunday. Night service is limited or stops altogether.

But of course you should still go to the beach—it's one of the main things that make San Diego San Diego. Just plan accordingly in terms of getting around.

Pacific Beach

Pacific Beach is San Diego's most urban beach with the largest selection of hotels. Small apartment buildings lie among and behind the hotels, a classic Southern California beach town pattern. The hotels and motels dot the oceanfront for almost a mile between Pacific Beach Drive on the south and Law Street on the north. Pacific Beach is thought of as a hangout for the young and the surfers. Plenty of bars and tattoo shops are on the Garnet Avenue commercial strip. But the neighborhood has other folks staying as well, such as older people and families with children (it's close to SeaWorld after all). With the pedestrian and bicycle Ocean Front Walk, Pacific Beach is a great place to cycle and has numerous bike shops. Don't come if you don't want youngsters, but don't stay away just because you're not one.

★ BIKE SHOPS IN PACIFIC BEACH ★

BICYCLE DISCOVERY 742 Felspar St.; **bicycle-discovery.com**

BIKE SHOP CHRIS 1484 Garnet Ave.; **bikeshopchris.com**

THE BIKESMITH 1936 Garnet Ave.; (858) 274-4220

PACIFIC BEACH CRUISERS 1400 Garnet Ave.; **pacificbeachcruisers.com**

PACIFIC COAST BICYCLE 1637 Garnet Ave.; **pacificcoastbicycle.com**

RUSTY SPOKES BIKE SHOP 1344 Garnet Ave.; **rustyspokes.com**

TRANSIT

Bus 30 from downtown (stops along First Avenue downtown) makes the trip in about 30 minutes and runs every 15 minutes. It also heads up to La Jolla. (Pacific Beach would be a good base for seeing La Jolla.) At night and on weekends, bus 30 starts at Old Town Transit Center, so use the trolley to connect to downtown. Bus 9 from Old Town Transit Center provides a quick ride to SeaWorld.

WHERE TO STAY IN PACIFIC BEACH

Pacific Beach has many hotel choices. Mission Beach, adjacent to the south, has some bed-and-breakfasts, but no real hotels in easily transit-accessible areas.

CRYSTAL PIER HOTEL 4500 Ocean Blvd.; **crystalpier.com** $$$$–$$$$$ The most unique Pacific Beach hotel, it is built on a pier over the water, but you'll have to reserve months in advance. No online reservations.

THE SURFER BEACH HOTEL 711 Pacific Beach Dr.; **surferbeachhotel.com** $$$ It has more affordable lodging.

TOWER 23 4551 Ocean Blvd.; **tower23hotel.com** $$$$$ A four-story mountain with a modern entry right on the beach.

■ *Hostel*

BANANA BUNGALOW SAN DIEGO HOSTEL 707 Reed Ave. at the beach; **bananabungalowsandiego.com** Rooms are $20–$22 per night; private rooms are available.

Coronado

With an oceanfront walk and a charming retail district, Coronado is a lovely beach neighborhood that attracts many families with children. A separately incorporated city, Coronado is geographically the closest beach to downtown San Diego, though transit to Pacific Beach is better. Coronado has been a beach resort since the construction of the Hotel del Coronado in 1888. The town has the wide, sandy beach on which beachgoers like to set up their blankets (and volleyball nets). Coronado is notable for combining a beach town with a Navy town; a major naval air station sits (and launches noisy planes) at the northern end of the peninsula.

TRANSIT

The main transit to Coronado is bus 901, which runs every 30 minutes from downtown San Diego on weekdays and Saturdays. Downtown, the bus stops along Broadway. On Sundays, the bus runs only once an hour

★ BIKE SHOP IN CORONADO ★

HOLLAND'S BICYCLES 977 Orange Ave.; **hollandsbicycles.com** Holland's also has Bikes & Beyond, a bike-rental unit at the Coronado ferry landing.

and starts at the 12th and Imperial Transit Center; connect to the bus using the Blue Line or Orange Line Trolley. An hourly ferry from the foot of Broadway goes to the east side of Coronado, about a mile from the beach, commercial area, and Hotel del Coronado.

WHERE TO STAY IN CORONADO

If you want to stay on Coronado, you'd do best to stay at either the pricey Hotel del Coronado or at one of the nearby hotels or motels. Hotels elsewhere on the peninsula are less convenient to both transit and restaurants.

EL CORDOVA HOTEL   1351 Orange Ave.; **elcordovahotel.com** $$–$$$$$

CORONADO BEACH RESORT   1415 Orange Ave.; **coronadobeachresort.com** $$$–$$$$$

GLORIETTA BAY INN   1630 Glorietta Blvd.; **gloriettabayinn.com** $$$–$$$$

HOTEL DEL CORONADO   1500 Orange Ave.; **hoteldel.com** $$$$$

Ocean Beach

Ocean Beach is known as the hippie beach, a bit of San Francisco's Haight Street by the sea. The neighborhood has only a couple of hotels and motels, so you'll almost certainly be seeing it as a day trip. Newport Avenue, the area's busiest commercial street, is lined with cheap cafés and antiques shops, but chain stores have been kept at bay. Ocean Beach has not experienced the level of change seen in Venice, LA's beachside bohemia. Visit the longest concrete pier on the West Coast for ocean viewing (or fishing). The beach is rather wilder in appearance (and occasionally people) than other San Diego area beaches, and it's fun to walk on.

★ BIKE SHOP IN OCEAN BEACH ★

BERNIE'S BICYCLE SHOP 1911 Cable St.; (619) 224-7084

TRANSIT

Transit to Ocean Beach has been cut back. Bus 35 from Old Town Transit Center runs every 30 minutes every day, but it ends sooner in Ocean Beach on Sunday. Bus 923 from downtown only runs every 30 minutes on weekdays; on Saturday it starts at the airport, and on Sunday it doesn't run at all. Both lines stop along Sunset Cliffs Boulevard, a couple of blocks inland from the beach.

WHERE TO STAY IN OCEAN BEACH

Minimal and beset by transit difficulties.

INN AT SUNSET CLIFFS 1370 Sunset Cliffs Blvd., Point Loma; **innat sunsetcliffs.com** **$$$$** If you're determined to stay nearby, try this attractively sited inn. Buses are 0.8 mile away on Sunday, so stay on a different day.

COURTESY OF BRETT SHOAF/METROPOLITAN TRANSIT SYSTEM

■ *Hostel*

OCEAN BEACH INTERNATIONAL HOSTEL 4961 Newport Ave. near Bacon St.; **californiahostel.com** It's on Ocean Beach's main drag. Hard to get to (use bus 923 or 35), but Ocean Beach is exactly the kind of neighborhood many hostelers would like. Rooms are $20–$25.

La Jolla

La Jolla has long been a redoubt of San Diego's wealthy. Famed mystery writer Raymond Chandler, who lived in La Jolla, satirized their hidebound ways. La Jolla mixes rocky coastlines with sandy beaches. The Children's Pool (a spot on the coast) is a birthing place for seals, leading to ongoing tussles over the allocation of time and space for seal versus human young. La Jolla has numerous notable examples, both houses and larger buildings, of works by leading early 20th-century San Diego architects, such as Irving Gill. In the rather new city of San Diego, La Jolla gives you the feeling of old money.

★ BIKE SHOP IN LA JOLLA ★

CALIFORNIA BICYCLE INC. 7462 La Jolla Blvd.; **calbike.com**

TRANSIT

Metropolitan Transit System (MTS) bus 30 runs from downtown, Old Town, and Pacific Beach to La Jolla, stopping along Broadway downtown. It's one of MTS's more scenic routes. From downtown, the bus takes about 50 minutes. The bus runs every 15 minutes during the day on weekdays. At night and on weekends, the route is cut back to Old Town Transit Center; you'll have to take the Blue Line Trolley there and connect for downtown. Bus 30 runs every 30 minutes on Saturday, Sunday, and evenings, except hourly on Sunday evenings. It's not quite extreme transit to reach La Jolla, but it takes commitment, especially on nights and weekends.

SEEING LA JOLLA

BIRCH AQUARIUM (**aquarium.ucsd.edu**), a couple of miles north of La Jolla Village, is everything the water shows are not—a low-key, research-based display of marine life. *Transit: From downtown San Diego (stops on Broadway), Old Town, Pacific Beach, or La Jolla Village,* take bus 30 north to Downwind Way on the Scripps Institute campus. It's a bit tricky, so ask the driver to tell you when you're there. Then take about a 10-minute walk uphill on Downwind to Expedition Way and the aquarium (2300 Expedition Way). Admission for adults is $12, and for children age 17 and younger, it's $8.50.

LA JOLLA PLAYHOUSE (**lajollaplayhouse.org**) is one of San Diego's leading theater companies. It is located at 2910 La Jolla Village Dr. on the University of California San Diego campus, near Expedition Way, about a mile or so past the aquarium. *Transit: From downtown San Diego (stops on Broadway), Old Town, Pacific Beach, or La Jolla Village,* take bus 30 to La Jolla Village Drive at North Torrey Pines Road, and then walk one block east on La Jolla Village Drive to the theater.

LA JOLLA VILLAGE (**lajollabythesea.com**), centered along Girard Avenue around Silverado Street, is an attractive, upscale street of shops and restaurants. Among other things, it is home to one of San Diego's few high-quality independent bookstores, Warwick's. Girard ends at Prospect Street, on a cliff overlooking the water. Prospect has several hotels and visitor-oriented shopping.

WHERE TO STAY IN LA JOLLA

If you like the ambience of La Jolla, it might be worth spending at least 1 night. La Jolla has many places to stay, but they tend to be costly.

EMPRESS HOTEL   7766 Fay Ave.; **empress-hotel.com** $$$–$$$$

HOTEL PARISI   1111 Prospect St.; **hotelparisi.com** $$$$

LA JOLLA TRAVELODGE   6750 La Jolla Blvd.; **lajollatravelodge.com** $$
It is more than 0.5 mile south of La Jolla, but it's much cheaper than La Jolla hotels and near the beach.

LA JOLLA VILLAGE LODGE   1141 Silverado St. at Herschel Ave.; **lajolla villagelodge.com** $$ A less costly option. No online reservations.

Oceanside

Oceanside is the grittiest, and the cheapest, Southern California beach town. Here you might actually be able to get an adequate motel room for under $100 per night in summer. It's pretty much the other end of the scale from La Jolla. Oceanside is shaped by the adjacent giant Marine Corps base, Camp Pendleton (a base which is all that stands between metro Los Angeles and metro San Diego). So where other towns have tea shops, Oceanside has barber shops, so that Marines are properly shorn. Still, Oceanside has a wide, well-used beach, train service from San Diego and Los Angeles (it's actually the biggest transit hub between San Diego and Orange County), a walkable if inelegant downtown, and some sporadic attempts to get fancier.

Oceanside is fairly close to Legoland in Carlsbad. You can get to Carlsbad Village train station, the connection point, via North County Transit District's bus 101 (see page 359 under Legoland for more details). I recommend the bus from Oceanside to Carlsbad because it is much more frequent than the Coaster train. Amtrak does not stop in Carlsbad.

TRANSIT

Amtrak's Pacific Coast Surfliner and the less frequent commuter train Coaster serve Oceanside station in the small downtown. Greyhound also stops there as well. You can even catch a bus from here to Riverside County.

★ BIKE SHOPS IN OCEANSIDE ★

ALAN'S BIKE SHOP 805 S. Coast Hwy.; **alansbikeshop.com**

BIKE & PARTS 2027 Mission Ave., Unit C; (760) 757-9642

PACIFIC COAST CYCLES 2003 S. Coast Hwy.; (760) 967-4900

WHERE TO STAY IN OCEANSIDE

The hotels here are more basic than boutique. Get a place within walking distance of the station. The first four listings are away from the water but still close in.

AMERICA'S BEST VALUE PACIFIC INN   901 N. Coast Hwy.; **americasbest valueinn.com/bestv.cfm?idp=893** $

COMFORT SUITES MARINA   888 N. Coast Hwy.; **tinyurl.com/comfort oceanside** $$–$$$

LA QUINTA SAN DIEGO—OCEANSIDE   937 N. Coast Hwy.; **laquintaocean side.com** $–$$$

MOTEL 6 OCEANSIDE DOWNTOWN   909 N. Coast Hwy.; **motel6.com** $

THE SOUTHERN CALIFORNIA BEACH CLUB   121 S. Pacific St.; **southern califbeachclub.com** $$$$$

WYNDHAM OCEANSIDE PIER RESORT   333 N. Myers St.; **wyndhamocean sidepier.com** $$$

■ 24 Other San Diego Places

DOWNTOWN, BALBOA PARK, AND THE BEACHES, as well as near-beach attractions such as SeaWorld, make up much of visitors' San Diego. But there are some other places to go. Moving out from downtown, Hillcrest is San Diego's great city neighborhood, a place to browse and to eat. The Washington Street Trolley Station feels like a secret portal to some of San Diego's best food. North Park has emerged recently as a major restaurant and bar locale. Old Town is the birthplace of San Diego as a city, as well as a possible place to stay. If you're born to shop the malls, you can head for Mission Valley, while outlet shoppers can go down to San Ysidro. Finally, Legoland and the zoo's safari park are two major, hard-to-reach destinations in San Diego's North County.

Hillcrest

This neighborhood is notable for the food, a few hotels, and the neighborhood itself. It has been officially designated a great neighborhood by the American Planning Association (APA), joining such storied locales as North Beach in San Francisco and Park Slope in Brooklyn, as well as Echo Park in Los Angeles. APA correctly calls Hillcrest "San Diego's most diverse, vibrant, and urbane neighborhood" and notes the central role that gays and lesbians have played in its revitalization.

For your great time in Hillcrest, you can wander around, particularly on the shopping streets of Fifth Avenue north of Robinson Street and especially on University Avenue in the mile between First Avenue and Park Boulevard. Washington Street is a through street but much less of a shopping street. You won't see a ton of historic buildings, but there's a nice neighborhood feel and fabric anyway.

TRANSIT

Bus 3 comes up Fifth Avenue from downtown, bus 11 comes up First Avenue, and bus 7 comes up Park Boulevard. Bus 10 crosses the neighborhood along University Avenue, starting in Old Town, passing Washington Street Trolley Station, and serving Mission Hills, Hillcrest, North Park, and City Heights.

WHERE TO EAT IN HILLCREST

An urban neighborhood like Hillcrest can offer a visitor great food.

ARRIVEDERCI RISTORANTE   3845 Fourth Ave.; **arrivederciristorante.com** $$ For some of San Diego's best Italian.

BREAD & CIE   350 University Ave. near Fourth Ave.; **breadandcie catering.com** $ It has wonderful breads and pastries, as well as sandwiches and good café food in a lovely environment for hanging out.

CREST CAFE   425 Robinson Ave. (one block south of University Ave. near Fifth Ave.); **crestcafe.net** $$ It does the diner thing 7 a.m.–midnight.

MAMA TESTA TAQUERIA   1417 University Ave.; **mamatestataqueria.com** $$ It's a good walk east near Richmond Street for more traditional, less Americanized Mexican food.

WHERE TO STAY IN HILLCREST

In addition to the two listed below, **Inn at the Park** listed on page 340, is a little under a mile from Hillcrest.

BALBOA PARK INN   3402 Park Blvd.; **balboaparkinn.com** $$–$$$ At the eastern edge of the neighborhood, the highly eccentric inn has decorated each of the 26 suites in a different theme, such as Bon Vivant or Jungle Nook. It's right next to Balboa Park and close to the zoo.

MISSION HILLS BICYCLE SHOP 141 W. Washington St.; (619) 296-0618

SOMMERSET SUITES 606 Washington St.; **sommersetsuites.com**
$$$–$$$$ If you really want to stay in Hillcrest, it's a good hotel, though be forewarned that the hotel does overlook a freeway ramp.

Washington Street Trolley Station

Washington Street on the Blue Line seems to be one of the quietest of San Diego's 54 trolley stations. Tucked into a light industrial area near the airport, near the freeway, nothing seems to be happening. But if you walk up Washington Street under the freeway and two more blocks to India Street, you will find all sorts of good eats. Sometimes this neighborhood is called Mission Hills, but that confuses it with the completely different ambience up the hill on Washington Street, the core area of Mission Hills. If you're coming from the Old Town Transit Center, you can take bus 10 to Washington and India streets.

WHERE TO EAT NEAR WASHINGTON STREET TROLLEY STATION

BLUE WATER SEAFOOD MARKET & GRILL 3667 India St.; **bluewater. sandiegan.com** $$ It's about a block down from the corner of Washington and India streets. It's a combination seafood market and fish restaurant and produces fresh grilled fish platters at very reasonable prices. Don't expect fast service, though. On a busy day, it can take 30 minutes just to get through the ordering line.

EL INDIO 3695 India St.; **el-indio.com** $ This place delivers the Mexican food of nostalgia, which you can consume in an outdoor seating area across the street.

LUCHA LIBRE 1810 W. Washington St.; **tacosmackdown.com** $ Named for a type of Mexican wrestling known as "free fighting" (no rules), this is a fun taco shop.

THE REGAL BEAGLE ALE HOUSE & SAUSAGE GRILL   3659 India St., Ste. 101; **regalbeaglesd.com** $$ A new brewpub in what looks to be a converted motel. And in case you were wondering, this is the same India Street as in Little Italy, about 2 miles farther north.

SAFFRON   3731B India St.; **saffronsandiego.com** $ One of San Diego's best Thai restaurants, with the more budget-oriented Saffron Noodles and Saté next door.

SHAKESPEARE PUB & GRILLE   3701 India St.; **shakespearepub.com** $$ It has craft beer pints and pub grub.

North Park

North Park was a quiet city neighborhood that has somehow transformed into an eating and drinking Mecca. The neighborhood is in fact north of Balboa Park. The northeast corner of Balboa Park is at 30th and Upas streets, at the southern edge of the neighborhood. North Park is not exactly on the tourist circuit, at least not yet (though it has been written up in *The New York Times*), but it's easy to find and reach around the intersection of University Avenue and 30th Street.

★ BIKE SHOPS NEAR NORTH PARK ★

ADAMS AVENUE BICYCLE SHOP 2606 Adams Ave., Normal Heights; **aabikes.net**

CAL COAST BICYCLES 3020 Adams Ave., Normal Heights; **calcoastbicycles.com**

TRANSIT

The neighborhood is served by bus number 2 from downtown via 30th Street (slow but scenic), bus number 7 from downtown and the zoo via Park Boulevard and University Avenue, and bus 10 from Old Town and Hillcrest (bus number 6 goes to Mission Valley).

WHERE TO EAT IN NORTH PARK

If you need reading matter with your meal, the **Paras Newsstand** at 3911 30th St., just north of University Ave., is probably the best in the city, with everything from the daily paper to literary journals to fashion magazines. I've found magazines here that I have never seen anywhere else.

CAFFÉ CALABRIA 3833 30th St.; **caffecalabria.com** $ Calabria roasts as well as serves coffee and does it in a lovely big, airy space for hanging out.

EL COMAL 3946 Illinois St. (three blocks east of 30th St.); **elcomal sd.com** $$ This is the kind of Mexican restaurant that many urban eaters yearn for—family-owned place that uses high-quality cooking and ingredients but is also vegetarian friendly. Also in Chula Vista.

THE LINKERY 3794 30th St. at North Park Way (one block south of University Ave.); **thelinkery.com** $$–$$$ The Linkery is a restaurant that strives to be more than a restaurant. It serves farm-to-table California cuisine, identifying exactly who provides each ingredient. It has a huge list of local beers, and it makes its own sausages and other meats. The Linkery doesn't accept tips but adds an 18% service charge, as is standard in Europe. The food is terrific and moderately priced, though the Lardo ice cream is a bit much. But perhaps the rarest touch is that it has transit directions on its website!

THE MISSION 2801 University Ave. at 28th St.; **themissionnp. signonsandiego.com** $ As at the East Village branch downtown, The Mission is a cheerful, reasonably priced breakfast-lunch place that serves cuisine along the lines of Chino-Latino and American.

URBAN SOLACE 3823 30th St. (just south of University Ave.); **urban solace.net** $$$ "New American comfort food," they say, so expect to be served something like a cinnamon-brined pork chop or Not Your Momma's Meatloaf, along with cocktails or local beers.

The Food and Drink Bus: Line 2

In recent years San Diego has been flexing its culinary muscles, asserting that it too can be a fine-dining town. Even more strikingly, San Diego has emerged as a center of craft beer brewing that rivals (some would say surpasses) Portland. Seemingly all of a sudden, San Diego is a great beer town.

There's actually a semiofficial bus route of San Diego Beertown: bus line 2. The route heads east of downtown San Diego and then goes up 30th Street. You can visit a half-dozen beer-oriented restaurants and bars on or near 30th Street. On the 30th of each month, many of the 30th Street restaurants sponsor 30th on 30th (**30thstreet.org**), where $2 food or drink—pints of beer, small plates, and glasses of wine—are on offer, in honor of bus 2.

DRINKABOUT

If you want the more social version of drinking in San Diego's cool neighborhood bars, find out when the Drinkabout (**sddrinkabout.blogspot. com**) is. For Drinkabout, eight bars, known for interesting brews and located along 30th Street and connecting streets, run a free bus connecting them. The Drinkabout runs a one-way loop every 30 minutes. The event is held 1 weekday evening a month. Then when you've drunk your fill, take bus number 2 (or perhaps bus number 7) back to your downtown hotel.

Old Town: History and Hotels

Now one of San Diego's most intensely touristy zones, Old Town is where San Diego began as a city. As such, it's still worth a visit if you focus on the good stuff that's there. The good stuff is mostly in the Old Town State Historic Park (**parks.ca.gov/?page_id=663**), which seeks to re-create Mexican and early American life in San Diego 1821–1872. A number of restored and reconstructed buildings are open for free. The park is in the center of the neighborhood, along San Diego Avenue between Taylor and Twiggs streets. You can follow the way-finding signs from the transit center, which is essentially next to the historic park. Pick up a walking guide leaflet at the visitor center near the trolley station. If you're at all interested in early California, spend a little time here.

★ **BIKE SHOP IN OLD TOWN** ★

PERFORMANCE BICYCLE SHOP 3619 Midway Dr.; **performancebike.com**

TRANSIT

Old Town Transit Center is the end of the Blue Line Trolley from downtown and the end of the Green Line Trolley to Mission Valley. It has bus connections to Pacific Beach (bus 8, 9, and 30), La Jolla (bus 30), Ocean Beach (bus 35), Hillcrest and North Park (bus 10), and other locations.

SEEING OLD TOWN

SEAWORLD

500 SeaWorld Dr. in Mission Bay Park, between Old Town and Pacific Beach; **seaworld.com/sandiego**

■ Daily, 10 a.m.—6 p.m.; open longer on weekends and during summer

■ Adults, $70; children ages 3–9, $62. Check the website for the Fun Card offer, which admits you for the rest of the year for the price of a single-day admission. Bayside Skyride and Skytower have additional charges.

SEAWORLD IS THE FAMED AQUATIC THEME PARK, the home of Shamu the dancing orca (killer whale). SeaWorld draws millions of visitors each year (thousands every day), so go early to beat the crowds; crowds are comparable to the San Diego Zoo. It's like a Disneyland of the sea, with prices similar to Disneyland. Like Disneyland, it has spawned newer versions in the inland cities of Orlando, Florida, and San Antonio, Texas.

SeaWorld San Diego has aquariums and exhibits of marine life, but the emphasis is on shows and water-related rides. (The much smaller Birch Aquarium north of La Jolla offers an aquarium-focused experience.) At SeaWorld, orcas, dolphins, and sea lions do tricks, perform, and splash the folks sitting in the front row. Some of the rides are water related, such as Journey to Atlantis, a water-connected roller coaster. Others are just around the water, such as the Bayside Skyride, a gondola over the bay, and the Skytower, a trip up a glass tower to a major view. Most of the rides have minimum height requirements, so check the website if you're traveling with a young child. Some people feel that SeaWorld's shows exploit the marine mammals that perform in them.

Transit: *From Old Town Transit Center,* take MTS bus 9 northbound, a 15-minute or less ride (bus runs every 20 minutes every day). *From downtown San Diego,* take the Blue Line Trolley to Old Town Transit Center, and then take bus 9. *From Pacific Beach,* take bus 9 southbound; it originates at Garnet Avenue and Mission Boulevard. *From La Jolla,* take bus 30 southbound to Mission Boulevard and Garnet Avenue, and transfer to bus 9. Some bus 9 trips early and late in the day do not stop at SeaWorld, so ask the driver.

WHERE TO EAT IN OLD TOWN

Unfortunately, many of the eateries in the area are basically tourist traps.

EL AGAVE TEQUILERIA & RESTAURANT   2304 San Diego Ave.; **elagave. com** $$–$$$ A little south of the neighborhood core, it credibly describes itself as a nouvelle cuisine Mexican restaurant.

WHERE TO STAY IN OLD TOWN

Old Town is also a possible place to stay if you want to save a few bucks because it has the trolley to downtown as well as numerous bus lines.

BEST WESTERN HACIENDA HOTEL   4041 Harney St.; **hacienda hotel-oldtown.com** $$$$ The most central to the area.

COURTYARD BY MARRIOTT SAN DIEGO   595 Hotel Cir. South; **courtyard sd.com** $$$$

LA QUINTA INN OLD TOWN   2380 Moore St.; **laquintaoldtown.com** $$

OLD TOWN INN   4444 Pacific Hwy.; **oldtown-inn.com** $–$$ Cheap and comfortable, just on the other side of the freeway, but an easy walk.

WESTERN INN   3889 Arista St.; **westerninn.com** $

COURTESY OF METROPOLITAN TRANSIT SYSTEM

North County Destinations

Some of the leading visitor destinations in northern San Diego County are extremely difficult to visit without a car. Notably there's Legoland, an amusement park built around the construction toy, and the San Diego Zoo's Safari Park. In recent years, transit service in North County has been cut and cut again.

LEGOLAND

One Legoland Dr., Carlsbad; **california.legoland.com**

■ Daily, 10 a.m.–5 p.m.; open longer on weekends and during the summer

■ Adults (age 13 and older), $69; children ages 3–12 and seniors age 60 and older, $59

LEGOLAND IS A FUN PLACE, especially for young kids. Some people think that it's better than Disneyland for the youngest children. Legoland has added a water park and an aquarium, each of which cost extra.

Transit: The only transit service to Legoland is the Flex Southwest Carlsbad, available at the Carlsbad Village Coaster station. Call (855) 844-1454 at least 30 minutes in advance, and they will pick you up. The one-way fare is $5. It's pricey quasi-transit, though cheaper than a cab.

From downtown San Diego, take the infrequent Coaster commuter train from Santa Fe Station or Old Town to Carlsbad Village. From Carlsbad Village, you could take a cab from the Carlsbad coaster station to Legoland, about a 5-mile trip. Alternatively, it's possible to walk from Legoland to a stop along Carlsbad Boulevard on the coastal bus 101 route. Bus 101 runs every 30 minutes between Oceanside (an Amtrak station) and La Jolla.

Another approach is to take a bus tour from San Diego with a company such as StarLine Tours (**starlinetours.com**). The cost for adults is $92, including admission. Compare that to the adult admission for Legoland of $69. If Legoland is a priority, spend a night in either Oceanside or Carlsbad and go from there.

SAN DIEGO SAFARI PARK

15500 San Pasqual Valley Rd., Escondido; **sdzsafaripark.org**

■ Daily, 9 a.m.–6 p.m. Hours vary by season. Call or check the website before leaving.

■ Adults (age 12 and older), $40; children ages 3–11, $30. Other admission options are available.

THE RECENTLY REBRANDED (THEIR TERM) San Diego Safari Park—formerly known as the Wild Animal Park—is pretty special. It's a place where the animals genuinely roam free in a landscape, not a cage, and the people are confined to particular pathways and a train that goes through. The Safari Park, because of its inland location, can get very hot, with temperatures sometimes exceeding 100°F, so take plenty of water if you go.

Transit: Getting there on transit, alas, is a safari in itself. There are only three bus trips a day to the Safari Park at times when it is open, rendering it basically inaccessible. To reach the park from downtown San Diego would require a train and two buses. Your options for the Safari Park are similar to Legoland, except that the Safari Park is, by design, more remote. You can take a bus tour to the park, which costs some $67—standard park admission is $40. *From downtown San Diego,* you could take the Coaster or Amtrak to Oceanside and then the Sprinter light rail to Escondido. The Coaster is infrequent and doesn't run on Sundays, but the Sprinter runs every 30 minutes. *From Escondido,* take a bus on weekdays or a cab for the 7-mile trip.

Shopping

■ *Mission Valley: Shopping Malls*

Fountains of Wayne's song "Valley of the Malls" could have been written for Mission Valley (it was actually about New Jersey). Mission Valley is a few miles north of downtown, along the San Diego River Valley. (Though the area has some bike paths and natural areas, some San Diego old-timers lament the lost opportunity to plan the river valley more naturally. Recent flooding in Mission Valley gives more credence to this perspective.) Three major shopping centers—**Fashion Valley (simon.com/mall/?id=765)**, **Mission Valley (westfield.com/missionvalley)**, and **Hazard (hazardcenter.com)**—are all adjacent to Green Line Trolley stations.

■ *San Ysidro: Outlet Shopping*

The Las Americas Premium Outlets mall (**premiumoutlets.com/outlets/outlet.asp?id=76**) with 125 outlet stores is almost at the U.S.–Mexico border and draws shoppers from throughout San Diego and Tijuana. The Plaza Mayor Shopping Center is adjacent.

Transit: Take the Blue Line Trolley from Old Town or from downtown stations to San Ysidro on the other side of the I-5 freeway.

vii. santa barbara

■ 25 Santa Barbara

Almost Paradise

MANY PEOPLE WOULD SAY THAT SANTA BARBARA is something approximating paradise. Lying on a south-facing stretch of coastline, Santa Barbara is always warm but rarely hot. Beautiful landscaping, often with brilliant orange spiky bird-of-paradise flowers, is the norm, even on rather modest properties.

But there are reasons beyond great weather to come here. Santa Barbara has always sought to be more than a resort. It possesses a respectable art museum and a quite fascinating small Natural History Museum, both accredited by the American Association of Museums. In fact, little Santa Barbara—the 81st-largest city in California—has the fourth-largest number of accredited museums in the state, behind only Los Angeles, San Diego, and San Francisco.

Downtown Santa Barbara possesses architectural coherence and urban vitality, a major reason that Santa Barbara was named a distinctive destination for history-minded visitors by the National Trust for Historic Preservation. And Santa Barbara is actively seeking car-free travelers, thus far the only city in Southern California to do so.

Santa Barbara has the problem of desirable places—it's expensive. Santa Barbara attracts many rich people and has prevented mass scale development, additional factors that drive up costs. If you can swing it,

I think it's worth it, at least for 1 or 2 nights. Santa Barbara is a great destination from elsewhere in Southern California for an overnight or a weekend.

Santa Barbara Car Free: The Project

Santa Barbara Car Free describes itself as a sustainable tourism guide. Through its website, **santabarbaracarfree.org,** you can register and get a 20% discount on your Amtrak train ticket to Santa Barbara. The website also offers a Carbon Footprint Certificate that you can present for discounts at many area hotels and motels. The overall mission is clear: "to promote cleaner air and a healthier planet."

The site and a widely available (at motels, museums, and so on) Santa Barbara Car Free printed map have a ton of information about getting around the city without a car. It even includes information on getting out to the county's wineries, some of them featured in the movie *Sideways*. Santa Barbara Car Free is an inspiration to me—they were some of the first to spread the word that you could visit a Southern California city car-free. Check them out.

Getting around Santa Barbara

Unlike some places that promote themselves as car-free destinations, Santa Barbara actually is easy to get around without a car. The city's two open-air electrically powered shuttles (short bus routes) along State Street and the waterfront reach many of the places visitors want to go. An easily understood, user-friendly bus system gets to the rest of them.

Santa Barbara is good biking territory as well and has been officially declared a bicycle-friendly community by the League of American Bicyclists. Finally, you can walk to many places in this city, where walking is almost always a pleasure.

TRANSIT

The Santa Barbara Metropolitan Transit District (MTD), the transit operator, runs a thorough network of more than two dozen routes in Santa Barbara and the adjacent communities of Goleta, Montecito, and Carpinteria.

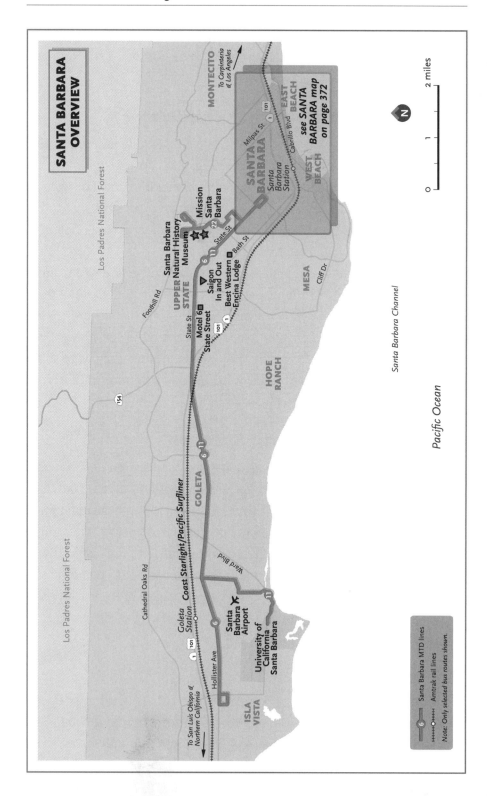

SANTA BARBARA OVERVIEW

MONTECITO
To Carpinteria & Los Angeles

Los Padres National Forest

SANTA BARBARA
Milpas St
EAST BEACH
Cabrillo Blvd
Santa Barbara Station
see SANTA BARBARA map on page 372
WEST BEACH

Mission Santa Barbara

Santa Barbara Natural History Museum

UPPER STATE
State St
Saigon In and Out
Best Western Encina Lodge
Bath St

State St
Motel 6
State Street

Foothill Rd

MESA
Cliff Dr

HOPE RANCH

Coast Starlight/Pacific Surfliner

GOLETA

Ward Blvd

Cathedral Oaks Rd

Santa Barbara Channel

Pacific Ocean

Los Padres National Forest

Coleta Station

Santa Barbara Airport

University of California Santa Barbara

Hollister Ave

To San Luis Obispo & Northern California

ISLA VISTA

N

0   1   2 miles

Santa Barbara MTD lines
Amtrak rail lines
Note: Only selected bus routes shown.

Most visitors will use only a few of those routes, namely the downtown electric shuttle, waterfront electric shuttle, State Street buses (lines 6 and 11), and bus 22 Old Mission/Botanic Garden. You might also take bus 1–2 Eastside/Westside to get over to Milpas Street, the main commercial street of the largely Latino Eastside, especially for food.

■ Hours of Service

MTD service operates during the day with some routes going into the evening. You may have some difficulty using the system in the evening. The downtown shuttle only runs until 6 p.m., except on Friday and Saturday evenings in the summer, when it runs until 10 p.m. The waterfront shuttle has a similar schedule, though its extended hours only covers the portion of the route from Stearns Wharf to the zoo, meaning that it doesn't run the western end of the route to the marina. What this schedule means is that if you're staying in East or West Beach and want to go to dinner downtown, you'll need to walk back (not too onerous, really) or take a cab. Service from downtown up State Street to upper State and out to the University of California Santa Barbara runs until 11:30 p.m. on weekdays, somewhat earlier on weekends.

■ Fares

The State Street and waterfront shuttles cost only 25 cents each. You can get a free transfer from one shuttle to the other, good only on the shuttles. Other buses cost $1.75, with free transfers. MTD sells a day pass for $6, but unless you plan to do a whole lot of riding around on regular buses, you won't need it.

All buses have bike racks in front, except for the State Street and waterfront electric shuttles, which go distances that are short enough to easily bike anyway.

■ Transit Information Sources

Santa Barbara MTD puts all its information—schedules, maps, stop lists, and so on—in a free **Schedule Guide** booklet, available on the buses and at the Downtown Transit Center. It's very useful, so pick one up.

Schedule, frequency, route map, diagram-style system maps, and fare information are available at **sbmtd.gov.** The site also has links to other Santa Barbara County transit providers and transportation-related organizations.

Many but not all bus stops have schedules posted. Real-time information is not available. To get transit information by phone, call (805) 963-3366, Monday–Friday, 8 a.m.–5 p.m.

BICYCLING

Santa Barbara is rated a bicycle-friendly community by the League of American Bicyclists. It deserves it for the oceanfront biking and walking path apart from anything else. Terrific maps show the county's bikeways—the southern one covers the main visitor area around the city of Santa Barbara. Visit **trafficsolutions.info/bikemap-south.htm** or get a print map at the Traffic Solutions office, which is transit-accessible but a bit out of town. This is a fine page of information on bike rentals, bike tours, bike books, and so on. Bicycling information can also be found on Santa Barbara Car Free's website, **santabarbaracarfree.org.** The very useful website of the Santa Barbara County Bicycle Coalition, **sbbike.org/region/region,** not only has bike maps but also information about bike shops, bike rentals, books about Santa Barbara biking, and more.

Seeing Santa Barbara

Unlike Los Angeles or San Diego, Santa Barbara—especially visitors' Santa Barbara—is a relatively small place. If you had to see it on foot, you could, but with the aid of some short bus or bike rides, it becomes very manageable.

Santa Barbara's urban area sits on a long, thin strip between the ocean and the mountains. It's about 20 miles from Goleta to Summerland in the long direction along US 101, but only about 4 miles across from ocean to hills. The land tilts up to the hills, then sharply up into the higher hills and mountains, a beautiful, sharply defined landscape whose contours are visible from many places. Most California coastlines

★ BIKE SHOPS IN DOWNTOWN SANTA BARBARA ★

BICYCLE BOB'S 15 Hitchcock Way; **bicyclebobs-sb.com**

CRANKY'S BIKES 1014 State St.; **crankysbikes.com**

FASTRACK BICYCLES 118 W. Canon Perdido St.; **fastrackbicycles.com**

OPEN AIR BICYCLES 1303 State St.; **openairbicycles.com**

TRUE FLIGHT CYCLE WORKS 428 Anacapa St., Unit C; **trueflightcycleworks.com**

WHEELHOUSE 528 Anacapa St.; **wheelhousebikes.com**

run north-south and face west. But Santa Barbara's coastline runs east-west and faces south, producing an almost perpetually balmy climate.

Santa Barbara has long had a reputation for wealth and was ranked 16th wealthiest among the nation's 250-plus urban areas. The wealthiest areas are along the coast and in the hills; the poorest are in the flatlands near the city center. Despite the wealth, there are also many lower income areas, mostly Latino service workers who staff the tourism industry.

The Santa Barbara area has a population of about 200,000. The population probably could have been more, but Santa Barbara has constrained growth quite tightly. For many years, it refused to join the State Water Project because additional water could facilitate additional growth. The upper hills are part of the Los Padres National Forest, preventing development there.

The main center for business, government, and tourism is central Santa Barbara, encompassing both downtown and the waterfront. This central area is roughly L-shaped, running along State Street south of Sola Street down to the freeway. South of US 101, most of the area between the freeway and the beach, from Castillo Street east to about Milpas Street, is occupied by hotels and other visitor-related activities. The waterfront area west of State Street is known as West Beach, and the area east of State Street is East Beach.

For most visitors, especially car-free ones, the downtown and waterfront areas contain most destinations. This concentration makes getting around Santa Barbara far less onerous than negotiating Los Angeles or

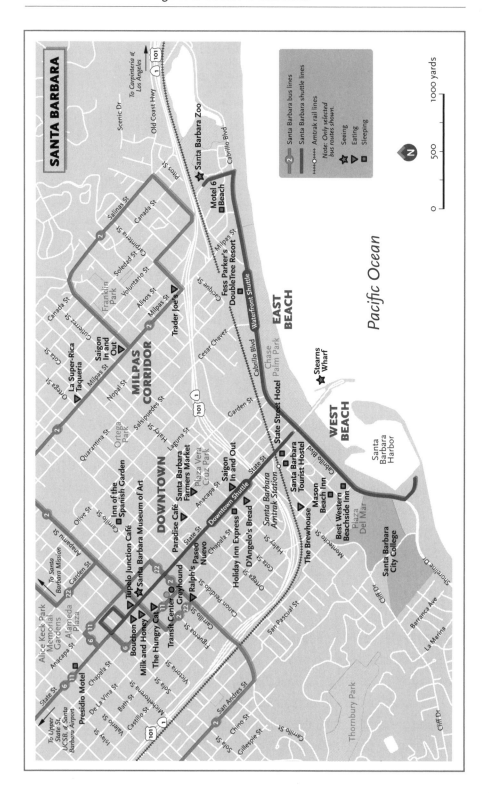

San Diego. The Mission and the Natural History Museum are among the few major attractions outside the central area; the zoo is at the edge of this area. The University of California Santa Barbara, near the ocean in Isla Vista, is Santa Barbara's other large activity center, but it is not a major destination for visitors unless they have business there.

DOWNTOWN SANTA BARBARA

The Santa Barbara Downtown Organization defines the downtown as extending from Gutierrez Street, one block north of the freeway, to Micheltorena Street, 11 blocks north of Guiterrez, between Anacapa and Chapala Streets (one block on either side of State Street).

The Downtown Organization makes the immodest claim that it is "the most beautiful downtown in America." Less grandly, some SoCal planners rated it the second-best downtown among medium-size California cities (after Pasadena). It is hard to think of a prettier downtown. However, some find that downtown Santa Barbara is too artificially beautified, too carefully controlled, to have the chaotic life that downtowns need. Even the street people seem calmer in Santa Barbara.

Downtown Santa Barbara has been shaped as a work of civic art since the 1920s. A powerful earthquake in 1926 destroyed many buildings and gave designers the chance to start shaping a Spanish-influenced city in their place. Though purists would no doubt identify examples of apostasy, this design idea has been maintained through the decades. The result is a downtown of generally modest-size buildings, brown and white walls, and red tile roofs. Like it or not, it makes downtown Santa Barbara a distinct and memorable place.

Most of Santa Barbara's historic sites, shopping, and restaurants, as well as many of its cultural and entertainment venues, are concentrated in downtown. This makes life much easier for a car-free traveler.

Downtown is very concentrated along, and just off, State Street. Once you're about a block east or west of State Street, the downtown really trails off. State is one of the best walking streets you'll find anywhere—with sidewalks lined with stores, benches, fountains, and even (gasp) public restrooms. No driveways cut into State Street in the downtown, so you have fewer cars to worry about. Many locally owned boutiques, bakeries, and restaurants are found on the blocks just off State to the east or west, though the street itself has an increasing number of chain stores.

If there's a center to the downtown shopping zone, it's Paseo Nuevo, a carefully disguised shopping mall along State Street at De La Guerra Street, in the middle of downtown. Paseo Nuevo strives to look like the rest of Santa Barbara while still functioning as a shopping mall—you decide if it succeeds. It's where you can find Macy's, Nordstrom, and other national retailers in Santa Barbara.

Transit: The State Street electric shuttle runs from the beach and Stearns Wharf. Metropolitan Transit District buses 6 and 11 come downtown from Upper State Street. Additional bus routes converge at the Santa Barbara Transit Center at 1020 Chapala St. MTD notes that more than 10,000 passengers per day use the Santa Barbara Transit Center.

SANTA BARBARA MUSEUM OF ART

1130 State St. at Anapamu St.; **sbmuseart.org**

∎ Tuesday–Sunday, 11 a.m.–5 p.m.

∎ Adults, $9; children ages 6–17, students with ID, and seniors age 65 and older, $6

THIS IS ONE OF SANTA BARBARA'S accredited museums, a small but high-quality facility.

RED TILE WALKING TOUR

THE RED TILE WALKING TOUR is a self-guided tour around the core of historic Santa Barbara, which focuses on pedestrian-only (car-free) paseos (boulevards). You can download the tour from **tinyurl.com/redtiletour.** The tour includes a clutch of historic structures, including El Paseo, the Hill-Carrillo Adobe, the Presidio, and, perhaps the premier building of all, the Santa Barbara County Courthouse.

Santa Barbara has a long, wide beach, good for sitting, strolling, biking, or the occasional political protest. Most of the oceanfront is beach, except for the marina, located between Bath Street and Harbor Way, and the area around Stearns Wharf, at the foot of State Street. Being at the foot of the city's main street, Stearns Wharf acts as a kind of extension of it. Still, with the freeway (and the railroad tracks) between the beach and downtown, the two areas do feel somewhat separate. If you don't want to be on the beach itself, you can walk along the wide sidewalks on Cabrillo Boulevard, the oceanfront street.

Transit: Catch the State Street shuttle from downtown or the Waterfront shuttle from East Beach. You can walk from downtown to Stearns Wharf—just walk through the world's (possibly) most beautiful freeway underpass.

MISSION SANTA BARBARA

2201 Laguna St. at Los Olivos St. in the Riviera section; **santabarbaramission.org**

■ Daily, 9 a.m.–5 p.m. Closed Good Friday afternoon, Easter, Thanksgiving, and Christmas.

■ Adults, $5; seniors, $4; children ages 5–15, $1

MISSION SANTA BARBARA IS THE MOST TRANSIT-ACCESSIBLE of the five missions in Southern California communities covered by this book. (The other missions are Mission San Fernando in the city of San Fernando [Los Angeles], Mission San Gabriel in the city of San Gabriel [Los Angeles], Mission San Juan Capistrano, and Mission San Diego.) It's been called the queen of the 21 California missions, and it certainly has been lovingly, if not necessarily accurately, restored. The mission is still in use as a church, so parts of it are closed off to non-worshippers when Mass is being held.

Mission Santa Barbara received a lot of attention as part of Santa Barbara's love of things Spanish. Restoration efforts started in the 19th century, much earlier than many other missions. Because the city of Santa Barbara stayed small, the mission site didn't become marginal to the city, as happened in Los Angeles and San Diego. The mission today functions as a church, with a side chapel, but also a retreat (meeting) center for Catholics, a fitting role for resort city Santa Barbara.

If you're looking for food before or after your visit to the mission, the section of State Street nearest the mission is not commercial, but downtown starts a few blocks to the south along State, so you can just head back there.

Transit: Take bus 22 from the Transit Center or from stops at Anapamu and State streets or Anapamu and Santa Barbara streets right to the mission, but much more frequent service to downtown (every 15 minutes) is available on State Street at Pueblo Street, about a 10-minute walk away. The mission is uphill from State Street.

SANTA BARBARA NATURAL HISTORY MUSEUM

2559 Puesta del Sol at Sycamore in the Riviera section, uphill from the mission; **sbnature.org**

■ Daily, 10 a.m.–5 p.m. Closed Thanksgiving, Christmas Eve (at 3 p.m.), Christmas Day, New Year's Day, and last Saturday in June for the Santa Barbara Wine Festival.

■ Adults, $10; seniors age 65 and older, $7; children ages 13–17, $7; and children ages 3–13, $6

Not every little burg has a natural history museum, but Santa Barbara has one that can trace its origins back to 1876. It's on the onetime homesite of early Santa Barbara naturalist William Leon Dawson. The museum doesn't have lions, tigers, or bears, but it does have a reconstructed dinosaur, whale skeletons, collections of birds and insects, and a lot about the Chumash tribe, who were the earliest inhabitants of the Santa Barbara region. It's a lovely and informative little museum.

Transit: On the weekend, bus 22 runs hourly from the transit center downtown right to the museum. During the week, bus 22 runs primarily in morning and afternoon commute hours, with only one midday trip. The museum is a mile uphill from State Street transit, which works for the way down.

SANTA BARBARA ZOO

550 Ninos Dr. near Por La Mar Dr., East Beach; **sbzoo.org**

■ Daily, 10 a.m.–5 p.m.; only open 10 a.m.–3 p.m. on Thanksgiving and Christmas.

■ Adults, $12; children ages 2–12, $10

The Santa Barbara Zoo is small and pleasant, and though educational, it is not big and comprehensive. Prior to opening as a zoo in 1963, the site was an estate whose owner had allowed what she called "knights of the road" (homeless men) to live in shanties on the property since the 1930s. The zoo has 500 animals from 160 species. They include five California condors, remarkably grim-looking black birds that conservationists are bringing back from the very edge of extinction.

Transit: Take the Waterfront shuttle from Stearns Wharf to the end of the line, and you'll be right at the zoo entrance.

SANTA BARBARA COUNTY WINE COUNTRY

The Santa Ynez Valley in central Santa Barbara County has emerged as Southern California's most important wine-growing region. The area was developing even before the movie *Sideways,* but the film definitely jump-started its popularity.

No transit reaches the largely rural wineries, but numerous companies run tours to the area. See **sbcountywines.com** (you have to go in a couple of pages to find tours). Santa Barbara Car Free also lists some wine tour companies on its website at **santabarbaracarfree.org.**

If you want to get a taste of Santa Barbara County wine without venturing out to the hinterlands, pick up the leaflet for the wine walk in the city of Santa Barbara. You can get a nice sample of wineries and tasting rooms. See **urbanwinetrailsb.com.**

Where to Eat in and near Downtown Santa Barbara

Given its modest size, Santa Barbara provides a good range of culinary options, feeding visitors, students, and the swells. Some people spend a lot of time hanging out here, so they want the food to be good. All restaurants are located downtown unless otherwise noted.

BOUCHON 9 W. Victoria St. off State St.; **bouchonsantabarbara. com** $$$$$ Bouchon is a top California cuisine dinner house in Santa Barbara and bills itself as "Wine Country cuisine." One of a number of restaurants on and around the 1100–1300 blocks of State Street (see the Hungry Cat and Tupelo Junction below).

THE BREWHOUSE 229 W. Montecito St. at Bath St., West Beach; **brewhousesb.com** $$ In a neighborhood of cheap (for Santa Barbara) apartment buildings, this place looks like a student dive. There are plenty of students, but the beer it brews on-site is first-rate, and the sandwiches and entrées are very good too. This restaurant will sneak up on you. It's also two blocks west of the Amtrak station, so it's a good pre- or post-train stop.

D'ANGELO'S BREAD   25 W. Guiterrez St. $$ A bakery just off lower State Street with lovely pastries, sandwiches, brunch, and breads to go. It's been on Food Network but hasn't lost its touch. From the Amtrak station, it's a 5-minute walk.

THE HUNGRY CAT   1134 Chapala St.; **thehungrycat.com** $$$ One block west of State Street at Anapamu Street. The Hungry Cat prowls in two hot spots—Santa Barbara and Hollywood. It's the place to go in Santa Barbara for shrimp, crab claws, grilled fish, and even caviar.

MILK AND HONEY   30 W. Anapamu St. between State and Chapala streets; **milknhoneytapas.com**   If there ever was a land of milk and honey, it has to be Santa Barbara. The restaurant is a faux-brick tapas place, with lots of cocktails, as tapas places should have, and tapas sorted by vegetarian, fish, meat, and so on.

PARADISE CAFÉ   702 Anacapa St.; **paradisecafe.com** $$$ One block east of State Street at Ortega Street. You don't really go to the Paradise Café for the burgers or the chops. You go because you can sit on the patio and really feel as if you're sitting in paradise. Or sit in the little Art Deco bar inside and feel as if you're in the side room of paradise.

SAIGON IN AND OUT   1230 State St., Unit A, at Victoria St., Downtown $–$$ Good, reasonably priced Vietnamese food and pho. Also at 3987 A State St., Upper State, and 318 N. Milpas St. in Eastside.

LA SUPER-RICA TAQUERIA   622 N. Milpas St. near Cota St., Eastside $ Take bus 1 or 2 or Crosstown Shuttle bus 37 to Milpas Street. La Super-Rica has gotten incredibly famous for a taqueria—some would say too much so. It was even written up in the *New York Times*. The food is very good and cheap. You'll probably wait in line and dine under tent-style seating. You'll have to decide if you like this Santa Barbara scene. If not, several other taquerias are along Milpas Street.

TUPELO JUNCTION CAFÉ   1218 State St. at Anapamu St.; **tupelo junction.com** $$$ Southern-style cooking in historic Santa Barbara. Curiously, dinner isn't that much more expensive than brunch.

RESTAURANTS NEAR SANTA BARBARA BEACH

It's a truism in California that you shouldn't eat on a pier, unless you're a sea lion. With that in mind, I would urge a retreat to downtown Santa Barbara, where you have dozens of choices (see page 373). On the wharf, you have about a half-dozen choices, plus some scattered possibilities in beachfront hotels.

Grocery Stores and Markets in Santa Barbara

RALPH'S   100 W. Carrillo St. at Chapala St.   The only full-scale super-market in downtown Santa Barbara. One block west of State Street, across from the Santa Barbara Transit Center.

SANTA BARBARA FARMERS MARKET   A substantial farmers market, drawing on the Central Coast growing area. On Saturday mornings at Santa Barbara and Cota streets downtown and on Tuesday afternoons in the 500–600 block of State Street (Haley to Cota streets).

TRADER JOE'S   29 S. Milpas St. at Quinientos St., Milpas Corridor The famed chain, almost a full-line grocery, though stronger on snack foods than fresh produce.

Where to Stay in Santa Barbara

Santa Barbara's transit-accessible hotels are found in four main clusters—West Beach, East Beach, Downtown, and Upper State. The largest and densest cluster is in **West Beach,** the neighborhood from State Street west to Castillo Street, between US 101 and the waterfront. The area is immediately adjacent to the Amtrak station and a few blocks south of the downtown core. These blocks contain some 20 hotels, motels, and bed-and-breakfasts, with prices ranging from almost budget to quite high. On the east side of State Street, also between the freeway and the waterfront, is **East Beach.** Eight hotels and motels are spread out over a mile between Chase Palm Park and the Santa Barbara Zoo. The hotels on this side tend to be fancier, with some of them quite elaborate indeed, such as Fess Parker's DoubleTree Resort, but there's also the bare-bones Motel 6 too. **Downtown Santa Barbara** itself has some hotels and a bunch of bed-and-breakfasts. The bed-and-breakfasts are grouped at the north end of the downtown.

Upper State Street is the fourth locale, along State Street from Alamar Avenue to La Cumbre Road (roughly street numbers 2800–3800). The only reason to stay on Upper State Street is to save money, as Santa Barbara room rates tend to be high. It's basically a kinder and gentler version of your typical suburban highway strip where you won't get much Santa Barbara flavor. Also you won't be able to easily walk to the city's sights, one of Santa Barbara's great pleasures. Fairly frequent bus service (every 15 minutes much of the time) on MTD bus 6 and bus 11 runs along State Street.

A few high-priced hotels are up in the hills—these have no transit service. Montecito, the famed oceanfront mega-millionaire's neighborhood, has a few hotels and a little bit of bus service, but it would not be very convenient for a car-free traveler.

Before you book in Santa Barbara, check **santabarbaracarfree.org** to see if any hotels have deals for car-free travelers.

BEST WESTERN BEACHSIDE INN   336 W. Cabrillo Blvd.; **beachsideinn santabarbara.com** $$–$$$ Best Western's property in the West Beach hotel area. It's a more basic than the Best Western Encina.

BEST WESTERN ENCINA LODGE   2220 Bath St.; **encinalodge.com** $$$ Attractive motor inn located in an unusual but pleasant neighborhood location about a mile north of the downtown core. The main bus line is on State Street, three blocks east of the motel; there is also the less frequent MTD bus 3 on Bath Street. It's a 5-minute walk to McConnell's ice cream—kids will love it!

FESS PARKER'S DOUBLETREE RESORT   633 E. Cabrillo Blvd., East Beach; **fessparkersantabarbarahotel.com** $$$$–$$$$$ Lavish beachfront hotel with tennis courts, a swimming pool, and an airport shuttle.

HOLIDAY INN EXPRESS (VIRGINIA HOTEL)   17 W. Haley St., Downtown; **hiexpress.com** $$$ An unusual case where a historic downtown hotel has become a Holiday Inn property.

INN OF THE SPANISH GARDEN   915 Garden St.; **spanishgardeninn.com** $$$$–$$$$$ Lovely, lushly landscaped, small boutique hotel at the northern edge of downtown Santa Barbara.

MASON BEACH INN   324 W. Mason St., West Beach; **masonbeachinn.com** $$$ Good basic motel a block back from the beach and close to lower State Street and Amtrak.

MOTEL 6 BEACH   433 Corona del Mar, East Beach; **motel6.com** $–$$ Two blocks from the beach. The very byword for cheap motels, and the very first property of the Motel 6 chain.

MOTEL 6 STATE STREET   3505 State St. at Toyon Dr.; **motel6.com** $–$$ Basic motel on the Upper State strip. You might choose it if the beach area Motel 6 is full.

PRESIDIO MOTEL   1620 State St., Downtown; **thepresidiomotel.com** $$ At the upper end of downtown, a stylishly remodeled motel that gives you the use of a bicycle for your stay.

STATE STREET HOTEL   121 State St., West Beach; **hotelstatestreet.net** $ No online reservations. The cheapest place in town, with some rooms having shared bathrooms.

HOSTEL

SANTA BARBARA TOURIST HOSTEL   134 Chapala St. at Yanonali St. Santa Barbara's only hostel, immediately adjacent to the Amtrak station and two blocks from the beach (location, location, location). Rates are generally $22–$39 per night, depending on season and day of week; private rooms are available. No promises here with hostels.

viii. the big picture of socal

■ 26 Deeper into SoCal

Southern California's History

AMERICANS IN GENERAL, AND SOUTHERN CALIFORNIANS in particular, are famous for being unconcerned with history. We do not look back—we look forward, to the future. Despite this attitude, Southern California has more than three centuries of Euro-American history, not to mention its Native American history and prehistory. The Southern California that you see today reflects those surprisingly deep roots.

Coastal Southern California was a good place both to fish for and grow food. As a result, numerous Native American villages populated the areas near the shoreline. None of their settlements remain today. The Chumash culture is displayed at Santa Barbara's charming Museum of Natural History. In San Diego, the culture of the local Kumeyaay nation is exhibited at Balboa Park's Museum of Man.

In the 1770s, Spain's colonial government in Mexico decided that its remote northern frontier—California—should be better secured against (imagined) English and Russian incursions. So it created a string of missions and presidios (forts) along the California coast, stretching some 500 miles north from San Diego to the town of Sonoma, north of San Francisco. The Spanish typically settled near either existing Native American villages, freshwater supplies, or both. The settlements that the Spanish established became many of the key cities of Southern

California—including San Diego, Los Angeles, Ventura, and Santa Barbara. The road that connected them, El Camino Real (the king's road), became the main transportation spine of coastal California. The Southern Pacific Railroad largely followed its route, as did US 101.

Southern California's 19th-century American growth had unusual demographics. In most places, the men—and they were mostly men initially—who would go out to a frontier place were roughnecks, unattached single men ready to seek their fortune in a raw, new place. Los Angeles was different. Many of the earliest Americans who moved there were the gentry—lured by visions of a leisured and refined life among the orange trees. The railroads enticed relatively affluent Midwesterners to settle in Los Angeles, Pasadena, and to a lesser extent San Diego. Los Angeles would in time develop as an industrial powerhouse, build itself a world-class port, and gain primacy in cultural industries. But though many in the 20th century came for jobs or to join families, many continued to come because they wanted to—because they wanted to live here.

Tourism was at the very center of Southern California's early development. Coronado was a remote sandbar when the Hotel del Coronado sparked tourism and consequently permanent settlement in 1888. The Hotel Green in downtown Pasadena was so successful at attracting residents that it had to be expanded three times. More than a decade later, the Beverly Hills Hotel was built to attract home buyers to the city of the swells. Today—if you're sufficiently flush—you can still stay at the Beverly Hills Hotel or the Hotel del Coronado, but the Hotel Green is now senior citizens' housing. Other similar hotels have been demolished.

The mild Southern California climate beckoned powerfully to freezing Midwesterners. From a national standpoint, outposts on the Pacific had an obvious value to a nation reaching outward both militarily and economically.

A TALE OF THREE CITIES

Los Angeles, San Diego, and Santa Barbara share the Pacific Coast, but their fates diverged sharply. Los Angeles had a deep agricultural hinterland, leading to the construction of the largest wholesale produce market outside New York. Starting in the 1950s, these farmlands would become suburbanized, home to massive suburban sprawl. San Diego, hemmed in more closely by mountains and desert, never had such an area, though the Imperial Valley in far southeastern California would partially substitute.

Los Angeles, powered in part by the construction of a federally funded port, would simply grow far faster than San Diego. By 1890 metropolitan Los Angeles had four times the population of San Diego. By 1910 booming LA's population was 10 times that of stagnating San Diego. But as a Navy and military town, San Diego, with its unparalleled natural harbor, would far outstrip Los Angeles.

Los Angeles's growth in this era is felt by car-free travelers today. By 1920, when automobiles began to overtake streetcars, the city of Los Angeles had 576,000 people. Though they would later be deeply changed by the petroleum era, whole districts that we would today call mixed-use and transit-oriented had been created. To a large extent they are the neighborhoods that are still most transit-friendly—Downtown Los Angeles and the nearby neighborhoods to the west, central Pasadena, and bay-side Santa Monica. What Los Angeles did not do until the 1970s was build a rail rapid transit system to support these neighborhoods. San Diego had a much less extensive streetcar system serving such close-in neighborhoods as Hillcrest, Normal Heights, and Coronado.

Santa Barbara opted out of metropolitan competition. Important aerospace and movie companies were founded and prospered there. But by 1930 these businesses had moved to Los Angeles, recognizing that Santa Barbara was inadequate for their needs. Meanwhile, City Beautiful–style reformers in Santa Barbara moved to require historic building styles in downtown after the 1925 earthquake destroyed much of the city's downtown. The result, visible today, was an unusually cohesive and attractive district, but one that tightly constraints growth. Meanwhile, San Diego pulled off its own feat of romantic city planning. That was the 1915 Panama-California Exposition whose buildings along El Prado in Balboa Park are the home of numerous museums today.

BOOM AND BOOM

Growth in Southern California surged in the 1920s, an era of real estate scandals and creative financing not unlike the early 2000s. Growth slowed but did not stop during the Great Depression of the 1930s, only to surge again with World War II. During World War II, thousands upon thousands of migrants, especially African Americans from Louisiana and Texas, were recruited to come and work in Los Angeles's aircraft plants and shipyards. The migration stressed the segregated housing supply, and tensions rose as the migrants pressed for more fairness in housing and employment.

Even more people flooded in to the burgeoning tract homes in the decade after World War II, an era that did little for positive urban development. But the groundwork for today's multicultural Southern California was laid. With the Chinese as U.S. allies in World War II, Chinese exclusion was no longer a viable policy and was eased. After 1965, a new immigration law championed by Senator Ted Kennedy ended discrimination against non-Europeans, ultimately allowing influxes from China, India, Vietnam, Korea, Mexico, and elsewhere.

REDISCOVERING THE CITY

By the 1970s, there were positive urban signs again. Though later than elsewhere, Angelenos rebelled against the destructive effects of some freeways. The small, affluent, history-minded city of South Pasadena has managed to stall a major freeway link for decades. (What to do on the segment is still being debated.) In San Diego, activists in the Barrio Logan neighborhood were able to force the dedication of land under the new Coronado bridge for Chicano Park. Los Angeles Mayor Tom Bradley—the city's only African American mayor to date—convinced voters to tax themselves to fund rail rapid transit. The Red Line subway and the Blue Line light rail to Long Beach ultimately emerged from this funding. San Diego built the trolley, the first new light rail system in the United States in decades.

Hundreds of thousands of apartments had been built in LA and San Diego in the 1960s and '70s, providing the population base for a walkable, store-filled city for those who wanted to walk. Fear of crime was high in the 1970s, and much of the architecture was atrociously defensive and fearful of the city. But few realized that, aesthetically challenged as they were, these were the building blocks of a new, denser, and more vibrant city.

The urban promise of Los Angeles and San Diego was gradually rediscovered in the following decades. A key moment for San Diego was the 1981 opening of the first segment of the trolley, which was repeatedly expanded in later years. Aided by a focused redevelopment effort, downtown San Diego would gain thousands of new apartments and condominiums, though not without displacing low-income residential hotel dwellers. Downtown San Diego has thrived as an intense urban place, even as much of the city around it remains low-density suburban, even when located within the central city's boundaries. San Diego has planned for transit-based communities around the city, but many have yet to be built.

Today's Los Angeles has embraced its future, if sometimes reluctantly, as a great urban center. The city is no longer (if it ever really was) merely a collection of suburbs. Los Angeles has built the subway and light rail lines and is building more even as this is written. The 1999 Adaptive Reuse Ordinance, relaxing building code requirements for the renovation of historic buildings, unleashed a torrent of building

conversions downtown and was later extended to the whole city. Thousands of lofts and apartments in historic buildings downtown are a direct result of that law. On main streets across the city, apartment buildings with stores on the ground floor are being built. The city is grappling with how it can be a more bike-friendly and walk-friendly city, even as auto drivers sometimes lash out at cyclists with whom they must share the road. As a car-free traveler, you are both a beneficiary of and a participant in Southern California's ongoing transformation.

■ 27 Looking Forward

The Future of Car-Free Travel in Southern California

LOS ANGELES COUNTY IS BUILDING ITS TRANSIT NETWORK for its 11 million (and counting) residents more than for its visitors. Los Angeles must do so to reduce the amount of motor vehicle travel and fight against catastrophic global warming. (Suddenly, public access to Malibu beach won't seem like an issue any more.) But visitors will benefit greatly as the rail network reaches Santa Monica, as the subway is extended down Wilshire Boulevard, and as new connections are forged between existing lines.

No region in the country is working harder than Los Angeles to improve its transit network. And while many places dream big dreams and hope the feds will fund them, car-crazed Angelenos have taxed themselves to pay for their system. Los Angeles is now working to speed up the construction of those lines by getting federal help to build 30 years' worth of transit in 10 years. Future visitors should find it easier and faster to get around the city.

A new light rail line (the Expo Line) to culturally vibrant Culver City, as of press time, is scheduled to open in early 2012. Within a few years that line will be extended to Santa Monica, bringing rail transit back to the traffic-choked Westside after decades without it. The highly successful Orange Line Bus Rapid Transit in the San Fernando Valley is being extended to the Chatsworth Amtrak/Metrolink station. This will, among other things, make it easier to connect from Santa Barbara to destinations in the San Fernando Valley. Metro has also begun planning on how to make it easier to go from the Westside to the Valley through the Sepulveda Pass, a rather weak link in the current system.

More ambitious rail extensions are in the works in Los Angeles. The short Wilshire Boulevard Purple Line will be extended as far as the Westwood/UCLA area, and possibly all the way to Santa Monica—a project some call "the subway to the sea." A spur of the Green Line light rail will go into LAX, instead of stopping at its periphery, or perhaps a people mover will make the connection. There will be a new light rail line in the Crenshaw district in South Los Angeles. The Gold Line light rail will

be extended east from Pasadena, with some arguing that it should go all the way to LA/Ontario International Airport. In Downtown Los Angeles, the Blue Line, which now ends at Seventh Street, will be extended to Union Station, so that it connects with the Gold Line and other services.

These projects will be major improvements for visitors and residents. Within about 5 years, visitors will be able to get to Santa Monica by rail and avoid paralyzing Westside traffic jams. When the Purple Line is completed, visitors will be able to go to Beverly Hills and Westwood—two major destinations with no rail service now—by fast subway.

San Diego is planning to extend its trolley north to UC San Diego and University Town Center, a major transit hub. The line will not directly serve the visitor-oriented La Jolla village, but will make it easier

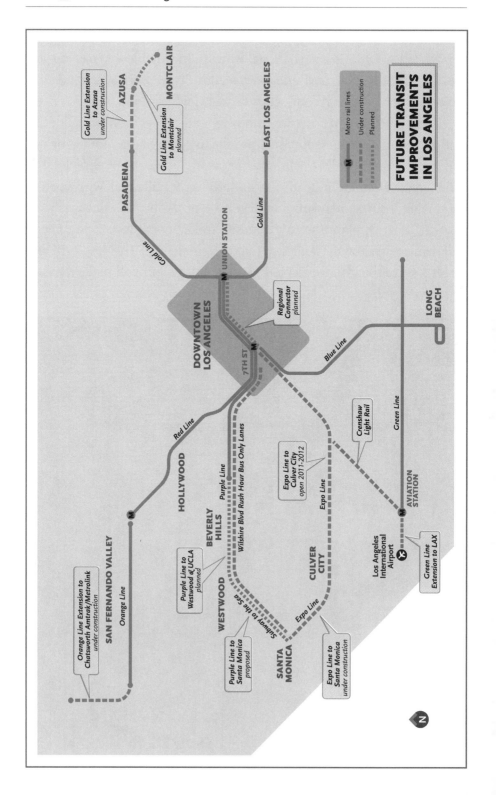

to get there with a short bus connection. San Diego is also planning a rapid bus on the route of line 7, from downtown San Diego through Balboa Park to North Park and beyond. If San Diego's Villages concept takes hold, compact, walkable communities will flower around the city, not just in downtown. Then the transit system, whether trolley, express bus (using the city's many freeways), or other bus, can connect them.

Statewide high-speed rail is the most ambitious project of all. Currently being planned, the line will link San Diego, Los Angeles, San Jose, and San Francisco (and ultimately Sacramento). The trains are designed to operate at speeds of up to 220 miles per hour and cut the San Francisco–Los Angeles travel time to less than 3 hours. Union Station will be Los Angeles's high-speed rail hub, further reinforcing its importance and recapturing its historic role. It will of course take years—the years really needed to build the line, and additional years for unnecessary and "not in my backyard" political infighting. Airline interests are in an all-out fight to prevent high-speed rail. Presumably California can follow where countries such as Spain, Korea, and Taiwan have led on high-speed rail.

Building rail lines and bus lanes is vital and necessary, but changing hearts and minds is equally important. All parts of Southern California society need to celebrate, embrace, and use their transit system. Transit needs to be understood as a normal way to get around, not a last resort. Websites for stores, restaurants, and destinations of all types should include transit information as routinely as they include parking information. Hotel staff should be as adept at directing visitors to transit routes as to freeways. This cultural change is starting to happen, especially among the young, though many people still believe that everybody must always drive everywhere.

If new attitudes take hold, choosing to visit car-free would be seen as a neutral or positive choice and the information in this guidebook would, as a matter of course, be in every guidebook. When I've worked myself out of a job, we'll know that the world has really changed. It's easy to be cynical about this, but Southern Californians have embraced great change before. That is what is needed now.

AGAIN, FEEDBACK WANTED

But the very last word comes, I hope, from you. How did your car-free trip in Southern California go? Would you do it again? What would you do differently? Did this book serve you well or not (why or why not)? You can help car-free travelers from around the world. Write to me at **landorf1@gmail.com.** Thanks.

appendixes and index

■ Appendix A
Books

THERE WAS A TIME, NOT SO VERY LONG AGO, that neither scholars nor novelists of Los Angeles could get taken seriously nationally (that is, on the East Coast). Scholars were surely wasting their time; novelists were undoubtedly writing about Hollywood superficiality. Happily, this situation has thoroughly changed. Now there's a flood of LA literature of all kinds. Here are some of the better titles.

Banham, Reyner. *Los Angeles: The Architecture of Four Ecologies.* Berkeley, CA: University of California Press, 2009. Banham, a British architect, made a pioneering effort to understand Los Angeles as a city on its own terms and not as an inferior copy of something else. Because he wrote this book in 1971, Banham got certain things wrong—such as the impending death of Downtown LA—but the book remains humorous and insightful today.

Davis, Mike. *City of Quartz: Excavating the Future in Los Angeles.* New York: Vintage Books, 1992. Davis is an apocalyptic leftist sometimes prone to exaggeration, but he does know where some of the bodies are buried. This book and Davis's subsequent *Ecology of Fear: Los Angeles and the Imagination of Disaster* were widely read and much debated in Los Angeles.

Didion, Joan. *Play It as It Lays.* New York: Farrar, Straus and Giroux, 2005. This is probably the classic novel of ennui among LA's moneyed movie class. It comes with a strong antiabortion subtext from Catholic Didion. First published in 1970, it was made into a 1972 movie starring Tuesday Weld. Didion is an essayist and a screenwriter as well; she has retained a lifelong connection to Los Angeles although she and her husband, John Gregory Dunne, mostly lived in Manhattan.

Ford, Larry R. *Metropolitan San Diego: How Geography and Lifestyle Shape a New Urban Environment*. Philadelphia: University of Pennsylvania Press, 2005. Books about San Diego are few and far between; good ones are even rarer. Ford, who was a geography professor at San Diego State University, paints a clear, brief picture of the urban landscape of metropolitan San Diego and how it got to be this way. The book is one of a series of Metropolitan Portraits published by the University of Pennsylvania Press. It is an essential companion to this guidebook for San Diego.

Gebhard, David, and Robert Winter. *An Architectural Guidebook to Los Angeles, Revised Edition*. Layton, Utah: Gibbs Smith, 2003. The single best book to learn about Los Angeles on a structure-by-structure level.

Gruber, Frank J. *Urban Worrier: Making Politics Personal*. Santa Monica, CA: City Image Press, 2009. Journalist and activist Gruber, a friend of mine, has been present at the creation of Santa Monica's efforts to build a more humane, pedestrian-oriented city. This is a collection of some his print and online columns on various topics.

Hansen, Joseph. *Fadeout*. Madison, WI: The University of Wisconsin Press, 2004. and *The Little Dog Laughed*. London: No Exit Press, 2002. Hansen began his career at a time when gay (a term he disliked) men needed to write under pseudonyms. From 1970–1991, he wrote a series of 12 taut mysteries with a classic (gay) no-nonsense protagonist known as Dave Brandstetter.

McWilliams, Carey. *Southern California Country: An Island on the Land*. Layton, Utah: Gibbs Smith, 2009. Originally published in 1946, this book is still regarded as a classic of description and social analysis of Southern California. McWilliams, one of the first SoCal intellectuals to gain national recognition, would ultimately become editor of *The Nation* magazine.

Mosley, Walter. The Easy Rawlins mysteries. 11 vols. New York: Washington Square Press and Grand Central Publishing and Boston: Little, Brown, and Co., 2002–2009. These 11 books are good stories and also paint a portrait of black life in South Los Angeles from World War II through the Watts riot of 1965. *Devil in a Blue Dress* and *Little Scarlet* are two examples. *Devil in a Blue Dress* was made into a pretty good 1995 movie starring Denzel Washington.

Ulin, David L., ed. *Writing Los Angeles: A Literary Anthology.* New York: Library of America, 2002. Published by the prestigious Library of America, this anthology of dozens of fiction writers, poets, and essayists made it abundantly clear that LA had arrived on the literary scene.

Waldie, D. J. *Holy Land.* New York: W. W. Norton & Company, 2005. Waldie's memoir, a lyrically written song of praise to his middle-class suburban hometown, 1950s instant city Lakewood, has unusual credibility because Waldie has lived there his entire life and worked for decades as the city's public information officer.

◼ Appendix B
Where to Find Books

Pasadena

VROMAN'S 695 E. Colorado Blvd. at El Molino Ave.; **vromans bookstore.com** Probably the biggest independent bookstore in Southern California, it's a little complex with a stationery store, a newsstand, and a café, right in downtown Pasadena. Transit: *From Downtown Los Angeles,* take the Gold Line light rail to Lake station, and walk south on Lake Avenue and west on Colorado Boulevard (total walk 0.6 mile, 12 minutes). *From Hollywood,* take the Red Line subway to Union Station, then transfer to the Gold Line light rail, and see transit directions above. *From Hollywood,* take rapid bus 780 to Colorado and Lake avenues, and walk three blocks west. *From Santa Monica,* take Big Blue Bus express 10 to Union Station, transfer to the Gold Line light rail, and see transit directions above.

Between Downtown LA and Hollywood

ESO WON BOOKSTORE 4331 Degnan Blvd., Leimert Park; **esowon bookstore.com** The leading bookstore of black LA and host to many author readings. Transit: *From Downtown Los Angeles,* take Metro bus 40 to Crenshaw Boulevard and Homeland Drive near 43rd Street, and walk east on 43rd Street to Degnan Boulevard, and then walk south. Or take rapid bus 740 from Broadway to Crenshaw Avenue and Vernon Boulevard, and then cross a small park to Degnan Boulevard and walk north. *From Hollywood,* take Metro bus 210 from Hollywood Boulevard and Vine Street to Crenshaw Boulevard and Homeland Drive near 43rd Street, and walk east on 43rd Street to Degnan Boulevard, and then south. *From Santa Monica,* take Metro bus 534 at Colorado and Ocean avenues to Venice Boulevard and Cadillac Avenue, and then take bus 105 to Crenshaw Boulevard and Stocker Street. Walk south on Crenshaw to 43rd, and then walk east on 43rd to Degnan and south on Degnan (total walk 0.4 mile or less than 10 minutes). Check Metro's Trip Planner for potential alternative routings at your specific trip time.

SKYLIGHT BOOKS 1818 N. Vermont Ave. near Russell Ave., Los Feliz; **skylightbooks.com** A top-notch general bookstore that caters to its hip, artsy neighborhood, with the best selection of books about LA. Transit: *From Downtown Los Angeles or Hollywood,* take the Red Line subway to the Vermont Avenue/Sunset Boulevard station, and then walk 0.4 mile north (less than 15 minutes) on Vermont Avenue to store. *From Santa Monica,* take Big Blue Bus express 10 to Figueroa and Seventh streets, and then take the Red Line subway to Vermont Avenue/Sunset Boulevard station, and walk north 0.4 mile to store.

SOAP PLANT 4633 Hollywood Blvd. near Vermont Ave., Sunset Junction; **soapplant.com** A highly idiosyncratic collection of books (many about unusual sexual and/or artistic activities) and other pop culture items, but many years ago I bought a pamphlet there that transformed my understanding of Los Angeles. Transit: *From Downtown LA,* take the Red Line subway to Vermont Avenue/Sunset Boulevard station, and then walk north two blocks on Vermont Avenue and southeast one block on Hollywood Boulevard (total walk 0.3 mile). *From Hollywood,* take the Red Line subway to Vermont Avenue/Sunset Boulevard and walk as above. *From Santa Monica,* take Big Blue Bus express 10 to Figueroa and Seventh streets, and then take Red Line subway to Vermont Avenue/Sunset Boulevard station and walk as above.

West Hollywood

BOOK SOUP   8818 Sunset Blvd., West Hollywood; **booksoup.com**
A bookstore that has the energy and show-business creativity of its
Sunset Strip locale. Transit: *From Downtown LA or from Hollywood,* take
Metro bus 2—catch it at stops along Broadway in Downtown or along
Sunset Boulevard in Hollywood to Sunset and Horn Avenue, the corner
where the bookstore is. The ride is more than an hour from Downtown
LA. *From Santa Monica,* take Big Blue Bus 1 from stops on Santa Monica
Boulevard to Hilgard and Le Conte avenues in Westwood Village. Take
Metro bus 2 Sunset Boulevard from there to Sunset Boulevard and
Holloway Drive, adjacent to the store. This ride is approximately 1 hour.

Santa Monica

HENNESSEY + INGALLS   214 Wilshire Blvd.; **hennesseyingalls.com**
One of the leading art and architecture bookstores in the country. It's
also a publisher of architectural books. Transit: The store is located in
downtown Santa Monica. *From Downtown LA,* take Big Blue Bus express
10 to Second Street and Colorado Avenue, and then walk three blocks
north to Wilshire Boulevard. *From Hollywood,* visit the Hollywood
store or take bus 217 or rapid bus 780 to Fairfax Avenue and Wilshire
Boulevard, and then take rapid bus 720 westbound to Wilshire Boulevard
and Fourth Street and then walk two blocks west. A pint-size offshoot is
in the trendy Space 15 Twenty complex in Hollywood—1520 Cahuenga
Blvd. Take the Red Line subway to Hollywood Boulevard/Vine Street,
and then walk west three blocks on Hollywood Boulevard and south two
blocks on Cahuenga Boulevard (total walk 0.3 mile).

Near Santa Monica

DIESEL   225 26th St., Ste. 33, Brentwood; **dieselbookstore.com**
Diesel had the unusual strategy of branching from Oakland to SoCal. This
mini-store is in the Brentwood Country Mart. Also in Malibu. Transit:

From downtown Santa Monica, take Big Blue Bus 4 from stops on Fourth Street to San Vicente Boulevard and 26th Street, adjacent to the Mart. *From Downtown LA,* take Big Blue Bus express 10 to Broadway/Fourth Street in downtown Santa Monica, and then take Big Blue Bus 4 to San Vicente Boulevard and 26th Street. *From Hollywood,* take Metro bus 2 from stops along Sunset Boulevard to Sunset Boulevard and Burlingame Avenue in Brentwood. From there, walk left on Burlingame, right on Marlboro Street, left on Rockingham Avenue, and left on 26th Street (total walk 0.7 mile or about 15 minutes).

Venice

SMALL WORLD BOOKS   1407 Ocean Front Walk; **smallworldbooks.com** The Beats go on at the literary bookstore on the freewheeling Venice walk. Transit: *From Santa Monica,* take Big Blue Bus 1 to Windward Avenue and Main Street, and then walk five blocks west to Ocean Front Walk and one block north on Ocean Front Walk (total walk 0.2 mile). *Note:* Metro's Trip Planner does not recognize Ocean Front Walk as an address, so use Speedway and Horizon Avenue—the nearest road intersection—instead. *From Downtown LA,* take Metro bus 33 or rapid bus 733 to Main Street and Windward Avenue, and then walk five blocks west to Ocean Front Walk and one block north on Ocean Front Walk (total walk 0.2 mile). *From Hollywood,* two buses will be required; use Metro's Trip Planner to determine the best combination at the time you plan to travel.

San Diego

BAY BOOKS   1029 Orange Ave., Coronado; **baybookscoronado.indie bound.com**   A small independent bookstore with a strongly conservative bent. Transit: *From downtown San Diego,* take MTS bus 901 from stops on Broadway between Union Street and Tenth Avenue to Orange Avenue at Park Place, and then walk two blocks east on Orange Avenue.

WARWICK'S 7812 Girard Ave., La Jolla; **warwicks.com** Possibly the only full-scale (non-college) independent new books bookstore in San Diego. Transit: Take MTS bus 30 from stops on Broadway between Tenth Avenue and Front Street, or from Old Town Transit Center to Herschel Avenue and Silverado Street, and then walk one block west to Girard Avenue.

Santa Barbara

CHAUCER'S BOOKSTORE 3321 State St.; **chaucersbooks.com** Santa Barbara's only major remaining independent bookstore, in Loreto Plaza on the Upper State strip north of downtown. Transit: *From downtown Santa Barbara,* take Metropolitan Transit District bus 6 or 11 from the Transit Center or Chapala and Anapamu streets to State Street and San Roque Road, adjacent to Loreto Plaza.

■ Appendix C
Movies about Los Angeles

NOT SURPRISINGLY, LA IS A MUCH-FILMED CITY. But often movies filmed in LA pretend that they're taking place somewhere else, whether it's New York, San Francisco, or Italy. Still, LA does actually "play itself" sometimes. And while dozens, if not hundreds, of forgettable flicks are set in LA, there are some that give you insight into the city's soul.

Ask the Dust (2006)   John Fante was the struggling, hustling bard of the struggling, hustling, working folks of Bunker Hill, until it was swept away by urban renewal. *Ask the Dust* was published in 1939 but not filmed until 2006.

Blade Runner (1982)   Author Mike Davis has pointed out that *Blade Runner*'s filmmakers actually intended to film it in New York and only shifted to Los Angeles at the last minute. Still, the movie's vision of LA as an urban dystopia has been a lasting image.

Boys 'n the Hood (1991)   A fine performance by Denzel Washington (and beautiful filming) is the highlight of this early 1990s gang movie, in which South Central's gang culture swallows up almost everyone.

Chinatown (1974)   *Chinatown* was actually created to make a point, a point wrapped around a sometimes creepy mystery story. The point was that building Los Angeles's water system was steeped in original environmental (and personal) sin.

Crash (2004) *Crash* was not universally loved by any means. Many felt that its vision of a racially polarized LA was anachronistic in the multicultural 21st-century city. It won the Oscar for Best Picture. I thought the movie was a bit heavy-handed but showed lives and issues not often filmed, and in particular has some great bus ride scenes.

The Day of the Locust (1975) Based on an apocalyptic Depression-era novella by Nathaniel West.

Echo Park (1986) If LA is the most-filmed city in America, downtown-adjacent Echo Park might be the most-filmed neighborhood. This long-forgotten film presents a sweet, sunny vision of the bohemian life there.

Falling Down (1993) A crazed Michael Douglas must make his way across Los Angeles on foot when he gets tied up in a monumental traffic jam (I guess Metro just stopped running). Along his journey he encounters uncooperative storekeepers and predatory gang members of various non-white ethnicities. Many consider this an appallingly racist film. I list it because it captures the pessimism of LA's early 1990s.

Five Hundred Days of Summer (2009) The indie breakout movie of the year, even if it wasn't nominated for any Oscars. *Five Hundred Days of Summer* is a pretty cute story of doomed love, but it's also a cinematic love letter to Downtown Los Angeles. It feels like some kind of breakthrough for Downtown that this works—it's about time that district got some cinematic love.

The Grifters (1990) Based on a very hard-boiled Jim Thompson novel, this story of love and betrayal among petty criminals is really more a story taking place in LA than a story about LA. But I've never forgotten some of the beautiful cinematography of older LA neighborhoods.

Killer of Sheep (1977) One of the few movies about life in black LA that isn't about gangs or rappers. Stan is a killer of sheep, working in a slaughterhouse at a job that doesn't help his spirit (by now the place has probably been shut down).

LA Confidential (1997) *LA Confidential* succeeds in showing the corrupt, brutal underside of LA in its supposed golden age, the 1950s. From James Ellroy's novel.

The Late Show (1977)   A rare vision of LA as an urban place, for people leading small, ordinary lives and doing things like riding the bus. It stars Lily Tomlin.

Los Angeles Plays Itself (2004)   If you only see one movie about Los Angeles, see this one because it explains all the others. It's an almost 3-hour epic work, drawing on some 200 movies to show how LA has been portrayed. Among the movie's many nuggets is the fact that in movies, people who live in modernist houses are almost always villains.

Mi Vida Loca (1993)   The hard side of Echo Park, as gang life for girls is portrayed.

Quinceañera (2006)   Echo Park yet again, this time with Latino families and a gentrifying gay male couple who moves in, resulting in entangling alliances.

Real Women Have Curves (2002)   An energetic movie told from the rare viewpoint of a Latina teenager trying to get ahead academically. She has a three-bus commute from East LA home to Beverly Hills High School.

Repo Man (1984)   Long before *X Files*, there was *Repo Man*, street-level surrealism and conspiracy as a slice of life. *Repo Man* was constantly inventive, as when a character opens a can labeled only "Food."

Save the Tiger (1973)   This elegiac film won Jack Lemmon his only Best Actor Oscar as a businessman whose clothing business is falling apart, with increasingly strange consequences. The film's melancholy tone is quite different from most LA films.

The Slums of Beverly Hills (1998)   The semiautobiographical, semi-comic travails of a seriously underfinanced family that manages to stay in Beverly Hills for the schools.

Sunset Boulevard (1950)   One of the earliest movies on the perils of Hollywood stardom, complete with a dead narrator.

■ Index

■ About the Author

NATHAN LANDAU IS A TRANSPORTATION/CITY PLANNER who works for a bus transit agency in Oakland, California. He grew up in New York, Chicago, suburban Philadelphia, and Atlantic City in what then seemed to be America's only non-driving family. As an adult, he has lived in California car-free or car-light for 30 years. He has usually lived in homes a short walk from rail stations—"transit-oriented development" before the term was coined. As a child, rather than collecting stamps or coins, he collected maps and schedules (his wife has occasionally hidden his map boxes, hoping that he'd get discouraged). In the Los Angeles area alone, Landau has taken more than 80 bus and train lines, operated by 11 different transit agencies. In New York, he took a transit trip touching all five boroughs in pouring rain. Landau organized his workplace's first "learning from Los Angeles transit" trip. At home and elsewhere, he likes to ride trains and buses to art museums, live theater, independent bookstores, Chowhound-ish restaurants, craft beer bars, and walkable retail streets. He has previously worked for the cities of Berkeley and New York and lives with his wife, daughter, and two cats who hate to travel by any mode.

PHOTOGRAPHED BY CAROL DORF